GLOBAL PERSPECTIVES ON AMATEUR FILM HISTORIES AND CULTURES

GLOBAL PERSPECTIVES ON AMATEUR FILM HISTORIES AND CULTURES

Edited by Masha Salazkina and
Enrique Fibla-Gutiérrez

INDIANA UNIVERSITY PRESS

This book is a publication of

Indiana University Press
Office of Scholarly Publishing
Herman B Wells Library 350
1320 East 10th Street
Bloomington, Indiana 47405 USA

iupress.org

© 2020 by Indiana University Press

Manufactured in the United States of America
First printing 2020
Library of Congress Cataloging-in-Publication Data

Names: Salazkina, Masha, editor. | Fibla-Gutiérrez, Enrique, editor.
Title: Global perspectives on amateur film histories and cultures / edited
  by Masha Salazkina and Enrique Fibla-Gutiérrez.
Description: Bloomington : Indiana University Press, 2020. | Includes
  bibliographical references and index.
Identifiers: LCCN 2020021769 (print) | LCCN 2020021770 (ebook) | ISBN
  9780253052025 (hardback) | ISBN 9780253052032 (paperback) | ISBN
  9780253052049 (ebook)
Subjects: LCSH: Amateur films—History and criticism.
Classification: LCC PN1995.8 G56 2020 (print) | LCC PN1995.8 (ebook) |
  DDC 791.43/3—dc23
LC record available at https://lccn.loc.gov/2020021769
LC ebook record available at https://lccn.loc.gov/2020021770

CONTENTS

ACKNOWLEDGMENTS

THIS BOOK STARTED FOUR YEARS AGO AT CONCORDIA University with the organization of a small international workshop titled "The Amateur and the Institution." Since then we have had countless conversations with friends and colleagues who have been instrumental to the shape and content of this project. We would like to thank the students and faculty at the Mel Hoppenheim School of Cinema for participating in the events and discussions that have inspired many of our ideas. Haidee Wasson, Lee Grieveson, and Vinzenz Hediger read our first manuscript proposal and gave us precious feedback and advice about choosing the best possible publisher. Luca Caminati read parts of the manuscript and provided insightful suggestions.

Working with seventeen contributors from around the world has been a rare intellectual privilege but also somewhat of an editorial challenge, and we greatly benefited from expert assistance provided by Kaia Scott, Patrick Brian Smith, and Tess McClernon. Their contributions to the book were made possible by the support of the Concordia University Aid to Research Related Events, Exhibition, Publication, and Dissemination Activities Program. During these years we have asked contributors to revise their chapter drafts countless times, in great part thanks to the astute comments of the external readers and the insistence of the editorial staff at Indiana University Press on achieving the best possible result. We are grateful for their efforts and support.

We want to especially thank each and every one of the authors who have endured endless rounds of revisions, copy editing, and email exchanges. This book belongs to them as much as anyone else. We want to take this opportunity to assert the value of collective projects and collaborative work to further internationalize the conversations within our discipline and beyond.

Finally, we thank our friends and families who have sheltered us throughout this demanding process.

GLOBAL PERSPECTIVES ON
AMATEUR FILM HISTORIES
AND CULTURES

INTRODUCTION

Global Perspectives on Amateur Film Histories and Cultures

Masha Salazkina and Enrique Fibla-Gutiérrez

W HEN CHINESE FILMMAKER JIA ZHANGKE WAS ASKED IN the early 2000s what he thought the driving force behind the development of films in the future would be, he tellingly replied, "The age of amateur cinema will return" (MacKenzie 2014, 622–23). Although his response is situated specifically within the popularization of mini DV filmmaking in China, this prediction is certainly not new. In a decidedly more misogynist and US-centered version of this same sentiment, expressed at the end of the 1991 documentary about the making of *Apocalypse Now* (Bahr, Hickenlooper, and Coppola 1991), Francis Ford Coppola (in)famously claims:

> To me, the great hope is that now these little 8 mm video recorders and stuff have come out, and some . . . just people who normally wouldn't make movies are going to be making them. And you know, suddenly, one day some little fat girl in Ohio is going to be the new Mozart, you know, and make a beautiful film with her little father's camera recorder. And for once, the so-called professionalism about movies will be destroyed, forever. And it will really become an art form. That's my opinion.

Much has already been said about the way these predictions reflect on a series of practical and theoretical developments across the world within contemporary media environments. The global reach of YouTube and other social media platforms, the popularization of mini DV and consumer-level cameras as filmmaking devices around the world, the role of citizen media in the cycle of protests triggered by the 2008 financial crisis, the use of informal recordings during the Arab Spring, and the growing importance of institutional back channels and user-generated content all decidedly signal a critical moment in the relationship between professional and nonprofessional media and the need for its scholarly reconsideration. Indeed, much work within media studies has recently been centered on different articulations and theorizations of so-called participatory culture, governed by a theoretical and ethnographically based understanding of media users and producers that suggests active engagement rather than passive spectatorship.

To fully understand how these media practices reached the center stage they currently occupy—which is inseparable from the larger project of assessing their political and ideological effects—they need to be seen as part of a much longer tradition of vernacular media, one which has existed since the very early days of cinema. Once we begin to look further back in time, we discover that the relationship between what could be considered "formal" versus "informal" or "professional" versus "amateur" cinematic practice has varied a great deal at different moments of the twentieth century. We can also trace the deep history of the dream of a radical democratization of culture through media production, which comes across as vividly through many of the historical writings on amateur cinema as it does through some of the contemporary discourses on "prosumer" culture. Thus, instead of reproducing an artificial—and historically unjustifiable—break in media history by assuming that participatory culture is exclusive to the new media, this volume offers a reconsideration of film and media history of the twentieth century that places amateur production at its conceptual center. At the same time, this reconsideration shifts the familiar geographic contours of traditional narratives about the development of film and media apparatus away from European and North American points of origin.

What we learn once such an inclusive history is slowly unearthed is that amateur filmmaking—like all vernacular media—has played an important role within the more familiar developments (technological, institutional, economic, political, and cultural) of the cinematic apparatus around the world. Thus, shifting the focus onto amateur cinema allows us to consider the more traditional aspects of film history in a different light. But it also reveals unexpected conjunctures that resonate powerfully with our present moment in global media culture, making amateur media production look less like quaint self-indulgence and more like a harbinger of things to come.

This is particularly relevant when thinking about the degree to which the contemporary economy of precarity, both inside and outside of film and media industries, relies heavily on practices and concepts that have traditionally been associated with amateurism—such as unpaid labor performed "out of love" (from internships to fan-generated content) and shifting the funding of projects on to communities or individual supporters (crowdsourcing). These practices and their justifications do, indeed, hold a distorted mirror to the aspirations of generations of amateur cultural producers seeking to break away from the constraints and gatekeeping of film industries, institutions, and/or repressive state structures in their search for freedom to follow the love of cinema. Sociologist Gigi Roggero (2011) identifies passion as one of the key elements in the new creative labor market, since "passion allows one to accept the unacceptable, with the more or less illusory hope of being able to conserve or broaden the margins of one's free choice. Passion can therefore be transformed into free labor, the acceptance of precarity, or genuine self-exploitation" (102–3). Through this process of self-exploitation, the dream of the radical democratization of media and total artistic self-realization of every person has, in this sense, been fully co-opted by the logic of the postindustrial economy of neoliberal precarity.

While such a dialectical relationship of the present to the genealogy of nonprofessional film practices certainly deserves a separate treatment in line with recent critiques of the creative economy (McRobbie 2015), it is important to note that the historical cases of amateurism this volume explores took place under radically different economic models of employment and largely still dominant modes of industrial modernity (be they capitalist or socialist). At that historical juncture, amateurism served as a supplement or even a genuine alternative to the hegemonic modes of production (both cultural and economic)—in a way that is different from its current entanglement in the dominant logic of neoliberalism. It is this kind of difference based on the social and political characteristics of each context—rather than purely technological determinations for the development of new media practices—that we take as a fundamental starting point for the way we approach the historiography of our subject, while also placing particular importance of the unevenness of the technological and economic developments on the global scale. The essays in this collection share this emphasis on the specificities of the geopolitical as context of each of the instances of nonprofessional media production they explore, thus contributing to the ever-expanding geographic contours of film and media history.

Rethinking Film History: The Useful Cinema Turn

Such a historical focus on amateur cinema and its social material conditions is certainly not new: the publication of Patricia Zimmermann's seminal *Reel Families: A Social History of Amateur Film* (1995) established the foundations of scholarly work on amateur cinema as a distinct form of film culture. By doing so, it participated in a larger shift within film historiography, which significantly opened up the field in terms of its objects of study and the understanding of what cinema is or has been. In recent years, film studies scholarship has popularized concepts such as *useful cinema, nontheatrical, orphan, industrial,* or—more simply—*noncommercial* to analyze the social, political, and cultural relevance of the medium beyond commercial cinema with theatrical exhibition. This "necessary reorientation of the questions we ask of our film and media history" has opened innumerable avenues for research, introducing into academic discourse experiences and materials previously overlooked by knowledge production (Acland and Wasson 2011, 17). Scholars have begun to reconstruct the powerful effects that these various cinematic practices had on the way modern life was experienced and imagined in the first decades of the twentieth century and beyond. These studies include, for instance, the documentation and analysis of the efforts by colonial authorities to "discipline" the colonized (Stein 2006; Grieveson and MacCabe 2011), the circulation of radical political imaginaries through informal networks of exhibition (Musser 2006; Hogenkamp 2003; Stark 2012; Mestman 2016; Layerle 2008), the intersection of different educational initiatives and cinema (Wasson 2005; Bonifazio 2014; Grieveson and Wasson 2008; Orgeron, Orgeron, and Streible 2012), the use of film in the industrial and military environment (Hediger and Vonderau 2009; Lovejoy 2015; Grieveson and Wasson 2018), or the crossovers between amateur and professional practices since the first decades of film history (Nicholson 2012; Tepperman 2015).

The importance of adopting this expanded understanding of the medium cannot be understated. It helps us see how the assumption that film was largely either a monetary business in search of impressionable audiences or an aesthetic pursuit for the artistic elites has in effect obscured the rich history of cinema's other functions. Institutions beyond production companies, motivations beyond purely commercial reasons or aesthetic pursuits, and uses of film beyond entertainment begin to draw a different—and more complex—picture of the role moving images played throughout the

→ 1. Broadening film studies to non-theatrical.

twentieth century and beyond. This new approach to our objects of study allows us to focus on issues of civic engagement, education, everyday media practices, or political dissent and state control without abandoning questions of aesthetic experience or authorship; instead, we bring these questions into the broader spheres of cultural and social life.

Moving beyond the paradigm of industry-dominated national cinematic histories—and taking a broader view of what constituted film culture in the twentieth century—we can see how amateur (and its intersections with industrial, militant, or educational) film practices around the world have a distinctive historical dimension according to the material, technical, social, and economic factors that marked their emergence and development. We began to explore this global understanding of amateur film culture, and its relationship with the institutional forces that shaped film culture in different contexts, in a special issue of *Film History* that included essays on amateur cinema in Italy, Catalonia, Hungary, Brazil, Iran, and the United States (Fibla-Gutiérrez and Salazkina 2018). The edited collection in *Global Perspectives on Amateur Film History and Culture* significantly expands the reach and breadth of such work, further advancing toward more comprehensive viewpoints on amateur film.

The broader historical reconsideration to which this collection contributes necessarily takes as its starting point not only the conditions of production, but also distribution, circulation, and exhibition of amateur cinema. As part of the spatial turn in film and media studies, one of the more productive approaches to this shifting terrain has been to focus on screening locations beyond the commercial theatrical exhibition. This includes classrooms, museums, military facilities, film societies, city squares, houses, churches, small cinemas, or libraries. Beyond the assumed stable "cinematic ideal" composed of a "large and dark room, celluloid, projector, screen, seated audience" (Wasson 2012, 149), such an expanded understanding of what has constituted the cinematic apparatus historically—including its amateur iterations—brings us closer to recognizing the continuities with our contemporary reality of media's permeation of everyday life. Thus the question of space—understood both as a better historical and theoretical conceptualization of the precise social and cultural spheres in which amateur production functioned, and to which it contributed, and the mapping of its geographic contours—becomes integral to our understanding of the distinctiveness of this mode of filmmaking and its significance for film history.

Together the essays in this collection extend beyond a framework focused exclusively on liberal capitalist democracies and individual creative practices, as has often been the case in the English-language scholarship until recently. This broader scope of geopolitical formations under examination mobilize a more dynamic understanding of amateur cinema as a way to remap the discipline's epistemological and geographic boundaries by not only redefining what cinema *is* (or was) but also showing how *where* and *how* it happened changes radically in different cultural and political contexts. These differences were informed by the cultural sphere in which these media were produced and the political and economic pressures exercised on it by the state, industries, and other cultural institutions. Indeed, as the historical case studies taken from different parts of the world demonstrate here, the spaces, networks, and institutions of amateur cinema intersected with a range of other media practices, often constituting a shared field with experimental productions, forms of political activism, and educational media.

As Charles Tepperman notes in his recent overview of the emergence of amateur filmmaking culture in North America, "beyond the boundaries of the institutions of high art and mass commercial culture there exists an enormous unmapped terrain for creative works" (Tepperman 2015, 2). His research, alongside that of scholars such as Jan-Cristopher Horak (1995) and Alan Kattelle (2000), among others, has charted—in the Anglo-Western context—a "twentieth-century vernacular aesthetic expression that developed at the intersection of popular culture, modernism, and new technology" (Tepperman 2015, 8–9). As Ryan Shand and Ian Craven (2013) mention in their edited collection *Small-Gauge Storytelling*, this vernacular culture not only documented a particular historical time through its films but also constituted a storytelling device in its own right across the globe (1–14). In the French context—and in parallel with the North American and British scholarship—this narrative dimension of amateur cinema was originally conceptualized by Roger Odin (2014) as a "space of communication," bound to familial memory that sometimes circulated beyond the domestic space (15–27). The recent collection *L'amateur en cinéma, un autre paradigme* (Vignaux and Turquety 2016) expands its focus on circulation beyond the familial space, ultimately offering a reconsideration of the amateur as the new subject of film history itself. It aims to position—from a comparative perspective—nonprofessional practices as an equally constitutive part of film history, questioning the methods of analysis that have been entirely based on professional film and are thus incomplete. Seen together with the key volumes published by the Amsterdam University Press's series Film Culture in Transition (Hediger and Vonderau 2009; Elsaesser 2016; Albera and Tortajada 2015), such work demonstrates the serious reconsideration of amateur filmmaking as a social practice that has begun to take place on both sides of the Atlantic (see also Fibla-Gutiérrez and Salazkina 2018).

Defining Amateur Film and Media

Much of this recent scholarship in one way or another seeks to give its own definitions of what constitutes "amateur" cinema. In this volume, however, we take a slightly different approach to our subject. The reader will notice that the definitions and understandings of who can be considered an amateur filmmaker—and what constitutes amateur cinema—differ greatly among the authors and their historical subjects. Rather than insisting on a shared definition, then, what we propose here is a comparative model of analysis for amateur cinema. Nonprofessional film is examined from a historical perspective as a creative practice that inhabits a liminal space between public and private spheres, state institutions and civic platforms, politics and leisure. The model orients itself around the following questions: What have been the intentions behind amateur film production on the ground level? What motivated its institutionalization in different contexts around the globe? What social, cultural, and political spheres has it inhabited? What social, cultural, and political effects did it enable? How can we analyze these developments in relation to each other? In other words, we do not consider the *type* of films that count as amateur (whether made at home or in the public sphere, edited or unedited, with an identifiable title, "authored" or "orphan," etc.) to be decisive, or even what technology is used to produce them (small-gauge formats or professional equipment), but focus instead on the cultural and discursive context of the work vis-à-vis the dominant industrial system of production (meaning widely different things in each context, as the essays in the collection reflect).[1]

As a result, the idea of amateur we propose is necessarily very broad, porous, and rich in its overlaps with other forms of filmmaking (as well as other media more generally). It is precisely this porousness that resists a fixed definition—even one based on specific forms of production, ownership, or sponsorship rather than the properties of the film. For example, despite its noncommercial purpose, institutional and educational media as a whole cannot be referred to as amateur in a traditional sense. And yet excluding sponsored or organized filmmaking from an understanding of what constitutes amateur production would be contradicted by the fact that self-defined amateur filmmakers often formed their own organizations, which in turn sponsored films and events (Mariani 2018; Fibla-Gutiérrez 2018; Tepperman 2018).

Films made by nonprofessionals is an equally imprecise category of definition—what about films made by filmmakers created as private footage or in their free time? And what about other artists making films, despite a lack of professional training or experience in cinema? The boundaries between amateur and experimental film production are therefore particularly difficult to establish, as many of the experimental filmmakers intentionally operated outside of any commercial or institutional structures. And at the same time, as discussions of this specific issue in relation to experimental or avant-garde filmmaking demonstrates very clearly, complete independence from either commercial or institutional structures has always remained more of a discursive horizon than a practical reality of production methods. Perhaps even more paradoxically, historically, amateur filmmaking and film education and forms of professionalization were also often interconnected (as Mestman and Moore's piece in this collection demonstrates), as alternative modes of film education would often arise from amateur experiences. Ultimately, if one were to ignore these contaminations and ambiguous positioning of media makers, operating instead with a clear-cut definition of *amateur*, it would leave out an enormous amount of media production, which, as this collection hopes to demonstrate, has played a very important role culturally, socially, politically, and even aesthetically.

In other words, we see amateur film as a mode of cultural production in which a direct relationship between expressive practices and individual or collective experience replaces commercial goals, regardless of the ultimate objective—political, personal, aesthetic, and so forth (Fibla-Gutiérrez 2019, 177–81). That is, one where an alternative use value for cinema as an everyday expressive tool supplants the production of a commodity and its market exchange value. This is why we continue to use the term *amateur*. Despite its frequent association with dilettantism, the term preserves a connection to an affective charge that plays a decisive role in its production, whether privately or collectively expressed (the same passion that now serves as an operative logic for the postindustrial economy of precarity).

In short, our intention here is not to create a taxonomy or classification of all the different kinds of media that we understand as amateur, or even to provide its broadest possible definition. We leave this task to future researchers, should they see the need for such an endeavor. Instead, here we seek to show its historical vivacity, the fluidity with which media making and media use has always moved across different social, cultural, and economic formations and the multitude of uses and political agencies involved in such film production, all of which emerge with particular force once we broaden our geographic frame of reference. We second here the call expressed in the collection *Asian Video Cultures* (Neves and Sarkar 2017) to "short-circuit" hegemonic narratives of media and to focus instead on "unstable and overlapping media ontologies" that "glide between—and enfold—industrial and amateur, legal and illegal, ratified and renegade, giving rise to multiple mediated globalities" (5).

This shift, in turn, often leads to a necessarily much more varied conception of what constitutes amateur practice and its role in society vis-à-vis other cultural institutions. For example, the work gathered in the 2016 special issue of *Studies in Eastern European Cinema*, "Experimental Cinema in State Socialist Eastern Europe," sheds light on the complex relationship between state-sponsored amateur studios and experimental cinema in socialist Eastern Europe and the USSR from 1960 to 1990 (Vidan 2016; Nae 2016; Vinogradova 2016). Nonprofessional film culture stands here as an alternative term to the avant-garde, which the authors identify with a particularly Western conception[2] of artistic independence and creativity that occludes the context-specific characteristics of alternative filmmaking as belonging to the broader social realm (Gurshtein and Simonyi 2016). These historical cases reflect the complex dynamic of how experimental and oppositional avant-garde and amateur movements often depended on institutional support just as they were striving for creative autonomy from the state. And the study of amateur cinema has become one of the privileged realms within which scholars of Eastern Europe can show how different modes of filmmaking negotiated the tight control of communist bureaucracies, even if they were developed in relatively complicit state-supported cultural spaces such as the Béla Balázs studio in Hungary (Simonyi 2018), the Neoplanta Studio in former Yugoslavia, and the Workshop of the Film Form at the Łódź Film School in Poland.

Such vitality of amateur film culture can perhaps be best understood through the speed with which it can respond to a constantly shifting ideological, aesthetic, and technological terrain. As such it provides particularly useful grounds for a more inclusive and engaged discussion of cinema and media as a form of living cultural practice more generally—in line with Janet Harbord's (2016) critique of cinema as a field "that has become a sacred, spectacularized religion of commodified bodies and desires whose relationship to materiality is buried" (171). An important part of such a reconsideration of cinema as a living cultural practice is dealing with its geography, and this is where the inclusion of amateur filmmaking as a crucial point of reference is capable of radically changing our conceptions of the geopolitical contours of cinema history.

Not only can such an inclusive vision change what is considered marginal in terms of the mode of production and spaces of exhibition, but it also potentially redraws the geographical centers and peripheries of film history itself. This shift provides us with the tools to analyze geopolitical contexts previously ignored by scholarship, which—despite their lack of a strong film industry—have been instrumental for the development of film and media culture through a wide variety of structures, institutions, organizations, cultural groups, and individually lead efforts, many of which fall somewhere in between the state and private realms. In his analysis of noncommercial cinema during the Spanish Second Republic (1931–1936), Fibla-Gutiérrez (2019) describes this phenomenon as "film culture in the absence of film production," providing a framework of analysis for the impact of "everyday media practices, official cultural policies, and transnational networks of collaboration and circulation" in contexts without strong film industries (38–52).

Consequently, what becomes visible through a comparative global analysis is the way that the North American example constitutes the historical exception rather than the norm in regard to the relationship between amateur production and the state as both the guarantor of the institutionalization efforts and the enforcer of ideological pressures. While in the United States this relationship was limited, almost all other historical cases under examination show the state to be a powerful player in this process, as the essays gathered here demonstrate. Similarly, what almost all cases beyond the United States reflect is the force that nationalist rhetoric and its demands for the development, rebirth, and/or strengthening of a national cinema exerted on the institutional shaping of amateur film culture. Here, as elsewhere in the global film history, the conflict between the national(ist) cultural imperatives and the domination of Hollywood creates striking divergent dynamics between the US mainstream film culture, including its amateur reiteration (although certainly not its more politically radical manifestations), and the rest of the world.

In our scholarly reexamination of these developments, we would like to echo Wendy Brown's (2001) call in her book *Politics Out of History* to conduct genealogy as an alternative to progressive and teleological historiography. Film history becomes, then, not a tale of technological/aesthetic advances culminating (or, according to others, reaching its nadir) in the "new media," but a global and transversal reexamination of the uses and circulation of moving images. In the next section, we provide a brief overview of key historical coordinates that have constituted nonprofessional film histories during the twentieth century, establishing points of reference from which we can reconstruct this transversal genealogy of amateur cinema.

Historicizing Amateur Cinema

What moments appear to constitute the key temporal nodes of such an examination? What emerges from the studies brought together here are several key moments in the development of amateur cinema as a distinct media culture and their reflection of broader trends in global history, both cinematic and political.

The first corresponds to the institutionalization of amateur and avant-garde cinema in interwar Europe, North America, and Japan (1920s and 1930s), when the popularization of the first widely accessible nonprofessional cameras (9.5 mm Pathé Baby and 16 mm Cine-Kodak in 1923) allowed for a proliferation of amateur filmmakers' clubs, contests, congresses, and other social structures—often attached to state initiatives (Mariani 2018; Fibla-Gutiérrez 2018). This process can be seen as part of the large process of institutionalizing the avant-garde beginning in the 1920s, which created the spaces and initiatives (clubs, journals, contests, etc.) of film culture more broadly that amateur cinema formed part of, and enthusiastically promoted.[3] As different chapters in this collection show, the proximity of amateur movements to the artistic and political understanding of the term *avant-garde*—attracting individuals and collectives in search of both aesthetic and social ruptures—constitutes a large part of its history. The reduced cost of small-gauge cinema compared to professional equipment attracted educators, scientists, and artists, whose vision of the medium's potential quickly expanded the use of these technologies beyond their initial purpose as a consumer product for wealthy families. The absence of censorship regulations for small-gauge filmmaking provided additional attraction to using them for clandestine and militant political goals. At the same time, this is also the period when state support and continuing institutional legitimization of cinema plays a key role in supporting a wide variety of amateur film initiatives.

While institutionalization of amateur cinema and its expansion in different cultural and social realms continued during the 1940s and into the 1960s—especially given the popularization of 8 mm film (which had appeared in 1934) and the progressive reduction in the price of 9'5 and 16 mm amateur film equipment—it was Cold War politics that shaped amateur film culture of that period, much as it did all forms of cultural work. In the United States, experimental filmmakers like Maya Deren, Jonas Mekas, and Stan Brakhage defended amateur modes of production against the mercantilism of commercial cinema, insisting on their "freedom" from, among other things, explicit political ideologies (Deren 1965, 45–46; Brakhage 1971, 9–10; Mekas and Smulewicz-Zucker 2016, 26). Meanwhile in the Soviet Union and Eastern bloc, amateur film practices were incorporated into worker clubs and state-sponsored artistic studios as a way to promote the participation of workers in the public sphere.[4] In Latin America, amateur film clubs were closely related to the greater institutionalization of cinephilia and the art world, mirroring (and often directly inspired by) similar developments in 1920–1930s Europe.[5] They sought state legitimization but were also constitutive of the gradual development of new, alternative national(ist) discourses, which culminated in the 1960s with the emergence of the New Latin American Cinema.

At the same time, the political use of small-gauge technology became increasingly important for anticolonial movements. It opened a window for both individual and national self-expression and mobilization in the absence of independent national film industries all over the Global South, prefiguring the explosion of nonprofessional media attached to the cycle of global political protests referred as the "Long Sixties." By 1964, the Festival International du Film Amateur de Kélibia (FIFAK) was established in Tunisia, consolidating a network of exhibition and distribution that, in many ways, prefigured the better-known internationalist circuits of Third Cinema (Journées Cinématographiques de Carthage, Pesaro Film Festival, Festival of Latin American Cinema in Viña del Mar, etc.).

The importance and varied uses of small-gauge media for Third Cinema and militant film collectives in the 1960s and 1970s form one of the most vibrant chapters of the amateur film history from a global and transnational perspective. While the way that Third Cinema has been constructed through criticism and university curricula in the English-speaking world has led to its focalization, resulting in a list of famous (male) filmmakers, the actual use of amateur cinema and informal media, such as pirate radios, fanzines, pamphlets, graffiti, and the like, was crucial for this movement and other militant political mobilizations around the world. From grassroots use of film by numerous social movements, including the anticolonial guerrillas trained in Cuba, this critical chapter has been largely unaccounted for in film and media history.[6] The accessibility, portability, and ability of amateur cinema to capture and circulate the very images that official media and commercial cinema were systematically eliding made it a powerful political weapon that was difficult to control. This was especially the case in contexts of tight state control of media, from Latin American dictatorships to Israel-occupied Palestine, in which amateur and nonprofessional cinema became the only way to counter highly manipulated and depoliticized official narratives. At the same time, the distrust of mainstream commercial powers and the cultural and social establishment that formed part of the ethos of the global sixties meant that amateur cinema's status as at least potentially independent from any institutional structures gave it particular appeal on both sides of the Iron Curtain, in Europe / North America and the Global South alike.

By the end of the 1970s and beginning of the 1980s, the popularization of Super 8 mm (which had been initially released in 1965 but reached its peak of consumption decades later) and the irruption of video technologies further expanded and solidified the transnational reach of amateur cinema. The creation of an International Federation of Super 8 mm Cinema in Iran in 1975, and the success of Super 8 mm festivals in Caracas, Kelibia, Barcelona, and Montreal during this period, in many ways prefigured the subsequent emergence of a global media economy in the following decades. It is hardly an accident that these technological and media developments coincide with the move of the global economies toward post-Fordism with its transnational accumulation of capital, heightened reliance on cheap labor outside the economic centers, ascendance of global finance, and a move toward cognitive capitalism with its reliance on immaterial labor in the Global

North, culminating in the rise of neoliberalism of the late 1970s and early 1980s. It is within this context—and fully enabled by these developments—that the ultimate explosion of nonprofessional image-making takes place, marking the beginning of the decisive shift toward the current regime of global participatory (or user-generated) media. As such, it also represents a fascinating transition point in the history of amateur media, and this transition, especially when looked at from a global perspective, provides a highly complex and heterogeneous body of work that is yet to be fully analyzed for a number of reasons.

One of the most obvious ones is that Super 8 mm and video mark a point of no return for the ubiquity of amateur media in society, which could now be found everywhere and in the hands of (almost) anyone. The implications for researchers and archives is significant, as the already massive production of moving images beyond the commercial system since the 1920s now turned into an overabundance of materials with which archives in particular struggle to cope (that is, for the very few who even show interest in amateur cinema, such as the Home Movies—Italian Amateur Film Archive, Catalan Film Archive, Northeast Film, or the East Anglia Film Archive). The unique status of these objects in regard to the practices and theories of preservation and archiving ultimately take us to the present moment, providing further opportunities for considering the relevance of these histories to the kinds of questions with which our field of film and media studies is grappling, both as part of and beyond the new global participatory media regimes.[7]

The Emancipatory Dream of Amateur Media

The images of the infinite and boundless archive, of the totally participatory democratic media enabled by new technologies, and of the truly independent artist whose self-expression seamlessly traverses art and life are all tropes that resonate equally within contemporary culture and the historical case studies that constitute this volume. This continuity provides an uncanny link between the modernist ethos of the 1930s to 1960s and the cybermanifestos of recent decades. The difference lies in the social and economic contexts to which these dreams respond and through which they are (partially) actualized. Discourses on amateur cinema throughout the twentieth century often brought out and intersected with the utopian dimensions of film theory in general, which understands cinema in relation to what it could be—ripe with artistic and political potential yet to be fully realized. The very genre of manifestos, so central to the writing and thinking about cinema throughout the twentieth century, speaks to desired alternative futures, declared to be achievable through cinema. This is particularly the case with the dreams of radical democratization of media and absolute mobilization of the population, which amateur film discourse shares with much of the political avant-garde writings from early Vertov to Zavattini, perhaps finding its most powerful manifestation in the Cuban theorization of Imperfect Cinema. Mestman and Moore, La Parra, and De Leon explore the different reverberations of these ideas in the context of the 1950s and 1960s as linked to political activism in this collection.

Paradoxically, the ideal of total social mobilization through the democratization of media inherent in some conceptions of amateur film production is precisely what gave rise to its rapid institutionalization and the involvement of the state in this process in many historical contexts (see the work on fascist Italy by Andrea Mariani [2018] already referenced, and Guillaumot's essay in this collection). This in turn activated the dream of amateurism often articulated by artists as the highest manifestation of individual subjective artistic creation, free of any institutional or state confines and pressures. The dialectic between these two different utopian strands plays out with particular force in the works here, on the one hand, dealing with amateur filmmaking in the Socialist bloc (Vinogradova, Strupule), and on the other, as they connected to experimental cinematic practices and their conceptualizations (Rosenow, Lerner).

A different, yet equally resonant, configuration between state and independent production, and experimental and amateur cinema as constitutive of the politicized alternative culture of the 1960s and 1970s can be seen in the Mexican *Superocheros* movement, which produced Super 8 mm movies in Mexico during the 1970s and 1980s and are now considered classics of experimental cinema in Latin America (as explored by Lerner).[8] Amateur filmmaking shaped local film cultures through its participation in institutions such as film societies and clubs, specialized publications and archives (both formal and informal), and different forms of oppositional media and artistic experimentation. Many of these initiatives extended internationally through festivals, symposia, and other regular exchanges, creating networks which are yet to be fully accounted for and often placing their centers in unexpected locations—be it Barcelona, Caracas, Kelibia, or Sao Paolo. The aim of *Global Perspectives on Amateur Film History and Culture* is to reflect this global dimension of amateur cinema, adding to the growing body of scholarly work that is decentering the discipline's overwhelming focus on certain Western contexts (mainly the United States, France, Germany, and the United Kingdom). With such an objective in mind, we have gathered essays on China, Mexico, Venezuela, USSR, Latvia, Argentina, Israel-Yiddish, Italy, Spain, and Tunisia that dialogue with recent work on amateur cinema beyond the confines of the Western liberal sphere.

The term *global* in the title of the collection may, indeed, be misleading. By no means do we imagine a total coverage or unified vision of film history, amateur or otherwise. We share Jennifer Bean's (2014) recent claim in the introduction to *Silent Cinema and the Politics of Space* that "'film history' marks a constellation of uneven forces (geographical, economic, political, psychological, textual, experiential) that display neither the coherence of an integral entity nor the continuity of a successive lineage that develops over time" (1). What we propose here is a range of historical studies from different geopolitical vantage points that, instead of seeking to represent a totality (which both "global" and "world" would seem to suggest), move the history of amateur cinema beyond its North American and British experience (which still dominates English-language scholarship) to suggest the relevance and viability of other geopolitical and historical models of its development. At the same time, we are well aware of the impossibility of offering a complete overview of "amateur cinema in the world"—to rephrase a recent important work on queer cinema, which takes a decidedly different approach (Schoonover and Galt 2016). There are crucial omissions of large parts of the world here—for example, the notable absence of work on much of Africa and Asia. We nevertheless decided to keep the term *global* in the title of the collection precisely as an invitation for other scholars to explore the changing geographies of film studies, expanding on the limited contexts and perspectives that can fit into a single edited volume.

Chapter Breakdown

The volume is organized in four sections that emphasize the multiple contexts encompassed by these histories: (1) Medium Specificity and Expanded Media Ecologies, (2) Institutions, Industry, and the State, (3) Politics of Legitimization and Subversion, (4) Transnational Networks: Amateur Cinema Travels. Each of these sections covers a range of geographical and historical contexts with shared conceptual problems and forces shaping the particularities of their development. They highlight the transnational and transhistorical importance of amateur cinema while placing particular emphasis on its relationship to the public sphere and the experience of its participants. Importantly, the essays in the collection enter into implicit dialogue with each other, both within each section and across them.

The first section, Medium Specificity and Expanded Media Ecologies, focuses on the epistemological changes brought about by the inclusion of the amateur in the field of film studies as a distinct realm of cultural expression. The use of specific technologies (Super 8 mm, 16 mm, 35 mm, video, mini DV, iPhone, etc.) and a self-awareness of amateur codes characterize the four essays included in the section. This reflexive dimension highlights an important issue regarding amateur cinema: that this is not a category produced "a posteriori" by film historians and described negatively as "non" professional, theatrical commercial, and so forth, but a distinct film culture already described in positive terms by filmmakers since the first decades of the twentieth century. In "Understanding (Amateur) Cinema: Epistemology and Technology," Benoît Turquety proposes to rethink the epistemological paradigm through which scholars have narrowly understood cinema (based exclusively on commercial fiction films), to include an expanded corpus of technologies and experiences that have informed people's relationship with the medium across the world. The essay offers a model for analysis that surpasses classical film theory and its spectator apparatus.

The self-awareness of amateur cinema was also used to resist assimilation to the categories that continue to structure our discussions of American experimental film in the 1930s, as demonstrated in James Rosenow's chapter "Crossing the Amateur Line: The Lesson of *Even—As You and I*." Here, the author shows how the film *Even—As You and I* (Roger Barlow, Harry Hay, and LeRoy Robbins, 1937) performed its own amateurism to point at the shortcomings of the assumption that the primary aspiration of the American amateur was to enter a Hollywood studio. Moving a few decades further and into the United Kingdom, Graeme R. Spurr's chapter "I Give You a Toast to the Pioneers!"—The *Movie Maker* Ten Best Video Competition 1982–1983" engages with a different kind of self-reflexive discourse on amateur filmmaking practices, this time focused on the anxieties created by the diffusion of video technology into the amateur scene in the early 1980s. The essay uses the 1982/3 *Movie Maker* Ten Best Video Competition to assess the fear that video technology would undermine traditional practice and aesthetics and also calls for an awareness of the archival precariousness of these materials, which are otherwise bound to disappear. The section ends with Margherita Viviani's chapter "From Insiders to Outsiders: Tracing Amateurism in Chinese Independent Documentary of the 1990s and the 2000s," in which the digital video movement that exploded in China in the early 2000s is contextualized by the conscious turn to amateur practices from the 1990s generation of documentary filmmakers, who worked from "inside" the system in China Central Television. The movement to an "outside" of alternative institutions and spaces of film production, exhibition, and discussions allowed the new generation of independent filmmakers to find unexpected opportunities to criticize the reality of a highly controlled state media system.

Viviani's essay offers a perfect segue to the second section of the volume, Institutions, Industry, and the State. Amateur cinema's complex relationship to state institutions and corporations across the world, and the concomitant traversing of public/private spheres entailed by such interactions, stands as a telling example of the medium's impact in society beyond the commercial film industry. In her essay "Seeking Advice: A Political Economy of Israeli Commemorative Home Videos," Laliv Melamed delineates the intrinsic social and institutional framing within which commemorative home videos from Israeli military families are produced and circulated with the support of the state. It offers a critique of the processes of intimacy and professionalization that are associated with amateur media, excavating the home videos' political economy and how they tap into processes of militarization and privatization. In the next essay, "Amateur Film in the Factory: Forms and Functions of Amateur Cinema in Corporate Media Culture," Yvonne Zimmermann focuses on a different yet resonant history of institutionalized memory: in this case the manifold practices and uses of amateur film in corporate media culture. Using the in-house film production of the Swiss company Sulzer Ltd, Zimmermann draws attention to the hybridity and blurred boundaries between amateur and professionally produced films as well as between "corporate home movies" and industrial films.

Moving toward the actual institutionalization of amateur film by state institutions, Julie Guillaumot's essay, "The Ambitions of Amateur Film in Vichy France," looks at the little-known history of the only attempt to set up a state-controlled organization of amateur filmmaking in France, which happened during the Nazi Occupation. The Comité d'Organisation de l'Industrie Cinématographique (COIC) attempted to reorganize the amateur film movement in France and to negotiate the right to film again with the occupying authorities, showing the importance that small-gauge filmmaking had at the time as a means to capture the everyday of life under occupation. The last chapter of the section, Mariano Mestman and Christopher Moore's "On the Amateur Origins of Fernando Birri's Documentary School of Santa Fe," revises one of the most renowned experiences in the history of documentary cinema in Latin America of the 1960s and 1970s: the Santa Fe Documentary School (Escuela Documental de Santa Fe) founded by Fernando Birri in Argentina in 1956. The essay shows how Birri relied on amateur photodocumentary methods that were later incorporated into the institutional model for new Latin American cinema and Third-Worldism initiatives across the continent.

The political uses of amateur film with which Mestman and Moore close their essay are the focus of the third section of the book: Politics of Legitimization and Subversion. The importance of amateur film for militant and countercultural movements, as well as oppositional initiatives in totalitarian regimes, emerges as a key issue from which to trace an alternative history of the medium. Pablo La Parra-Pérez's essay, "The Wind from the South: Experiences of Substandard Filmmaking in Galicia in the 1970s," opens the section by laying out the instrumental role of substandard film technologies (in terms of affordability, independence, and mobility) in the little-known Spanish chapter of the Long Sixties. His call for an expanded and comparative global history of nonprofessional militant film practices is echoed in a section with essays on Spain, Mexico, Italy, the United States, and Latvia. Jesse Lerner's chapter, "Super 8 in Mexico," covers another little-explored history of the Long Sixties, the *superocheros* experimental film movement, and its relationship with both student protest and counterculture movements.

Diego Cavallotti's chapter, "The *Videogiornale*: Social Movements and Amateur Media Technologies in Bologna between the Late 1980s and the Early 1990s," looks at the relationship between amateur media and political struggle within the realm of preservation and historical distance. He poses the question of what kind of archival typology is most suitable for nonprofessional film and video repositories, especially when they are tied to countercultural communities, and offers a dispositive-assemblage model as a tentative answer. In "'A Vital Human Place' for the Counterculture: *Fifth Estate* and Amateur Film Culture in Detroit, 1965–1967," Joseph DeLeon focuses precisely on a short-lived and difficult-to-trace alternative film community based around Detroit's underground press *Fifth Estate*. The essay explores how media "happenings" and experimental films by local filmmaker Emil Bacilla both constituted venues for activism as well as placed the film community in an uneasy relationship with the official spaces and logics of institutions in Detroit, including universities, churches, and the police. The final essay of the section, Inese Strupule's "Ingvars Leitis's Subversive Ethnographic Documentaries, 1975–1989: Cover Stories and National Representation," looks at a series of Latvian ethnographic amateur documentaries to address the ways in which state-sanctioned amateur film production was used to create and uphold ideologies in conflict with those of the Soviet state. Within this section in particular, subversion and legitimation emerge as dialectic categories through which amateur cinema intersected with political struggle throughout the twentieth century.

The final section of the volume, Transnational Networks: Amateur Cinema Travels, addresses the role of amateur film in the creation of networks of circulation and exchange that were especially important for underrepresented cinemas across the world. Samhita Sunya's chapter, "Worldly Matters: Distributed Histories of Tunisian Amateur Cinema and the Screening of Nontheatrical Film," opens the section with an examination of the Festival International du Film Amateur de Kélibia (FIFAK; Kelibia International Festival of Amateur Film), through which Tunisia remained a regional and international hub for nontheatrical film culture. Her essay is an important departure from the usual focus on production of much amateur film scholarship, looking instead at the networks of distribution and exhibition through which the medium traveled. Following these expanded geographies of film culture circulation, Isabel Arredondo's chapter, "Early International Super 8 Film Festivals: The Case of Caracas 1976–1980," analyzes the largely ignored history of the International Federation of Super 8 Cinema (1975–1989), which established Tehran and Caracas as centers of small-gauge film culture in the late 1970s. Focusing on the Festival Internacional de Nuevo Cine Super 8 in Caracas, the essay explores the federation's decentralized network and its interplay between local and global cultural sensitivities.

The last two chapters of the volume delve into the often-ignored geopolitical entanglements stemming from the transnational dimensions of amateur cinema. Maria Vinogradova's essay, "*A Gift to Mother*: 'The Most Universally Appealing Kind of Film That Any Amateur Can Hope to Make,'" looks at cultural diplomacy, analyzing the unprecedented success of the Soviet amateur film *A Gift to Mother* (*Ot vsego serdtsa*, 1964) in the United Kingdom, Canada, and the United States. It demonstrates the scope of interactions between amateur film movements across borders, stressing the internationalist spirit that gave a special pride to members of amateur circles worldwide about their ability to connect with their international counterparts, helping to overcome the tensions of the Cold War. Finally, in "Postcards from *Yiddishland*: Amateur Filmmaking and Vernacular Yiddish Culture," Rachel Webb Jekanowski explores the important role of amateur filmmaking practices and film collecting in Yiddish media. The chapter examines the collection of amateur Yiddish films held at the YIVO Institute for Jewish Research in New York City and contributes to theorizations of the vernacular in amateur film studies and the roles of archival institutions in shaping postvernacular culture.

Together, these essays provide a reflection on the specific configurations and problematics of amateur film culture. Their focus on the past invites us to consider the present. Without romanticizing these earlier practices and ideas of what genuinely popular media could be, these essays illustrate the power and tenacity of such a promise and compel us to reconsider both the conditions of possibility and its potential pitfalls, without entirely giving up on the idea. The desire behind so much of amateur filmmaking is to preserve the past, leaving it for future viewers to endow it with specific meaning and value. In contrast to the relentless presentism of contemporary media scholarship, this body of work, like its subject, gives us a mere glimpse of how much we still don't know about a past that can radically change the way we see the present and think about the future.

Notes

1. These issues of classification are certainly important for the work of archivists, but they become reductive and rather sterile when attempting to conceptualize the place of amateur cinema in relation to film and cultural history in general.

2. For a related critique of the theorization of the "autonomy" of the avant-garde, see Zryd 2006.

3. For more on the institutionalization of the avant-garde, see Hagener 2007 and 2014.

4. See, for example, the exhibition "Enthusiasm" on Polish amateur cinema made in worker clubs from the 1950s to the mid-1980s (Cummings and Lewandowska 2005).

5. For an analysis of this process in Brazil, see Foster 2018.

6. See, for example, the film *Spell Reel* (César 2017), which uncovers the film archive of the anticolonial movement in Guinea Bissau, made up of hundreds of unfinished 16 mm films shot from 1963 to 1973 by a militant collective trained in Cuba in the 1960s.

7. See the special section "Preserving non-fiction films" in the April 1996 *Journal of Film Preservation*, especially the essay eloquently titled "The Massive Mess of Mass Memory" (Baines and Owen 1996, 7–14).

8. See also the special issue of *Wide Angle*, "Superoceros" (Lerner 1999).

References

Acland, Charles R., and Haidee Wasson, eds. 2011. *Useful Cinema*. Durham, NC: Duke University Press.

Albera, François, and Maria Hernández Tortajada, eds. 2015. *Cine-Dispositives: Essays in Epistemology across Media*. Amsterdam: Amsterdam University Press.

Bahr, Fax, George Hickenlooper, and Eleanor Coppola. 1991. *Heart of Darkness: A Filmmaker's Apocalypse*. DVD. Triton Pictures.

Baines, Iola, and Gwenan Owen. 1996. "The Massive Mess of Mass Memory." *Journal of Film Preservation* 25, no. 52 (April): 7–14.

Bean, Jennifer M., Anupama Kapse, and Laura Horak, eds. 2014. *Silent Cinema and the Politics of Space*. Bloomington: Indiana University Press.

Bonifazio, Paola. 2014. *Schooling in Modernity: The Politics of Sponsored Films in Postwar Italy*. Toronto: University of Toronto Press.

Brakhage, Stan. 1971. "In Defense of Amateur." *Filmmakers Newsletter*, no. 4 (Summer): 9–10.

Brown, Wendy. *Politics Out of History*. Princeton, NJ: Princeton University Press, 2001.

César, Filipa. 2017. *Spell Reel*. Spectre Productions.

Cummings, Neil, and Marysia Lewandowska, 2005. *Enthusiasm: Films of Love, Longing and Labour*. London: Whitechapel Art Gallery.

Deren, Maya. 1965. "Amateur versus Professional." *Film Culture*, no. 39 (Winter): 45–46.

Elsaesser, Thomas. 2016. *Film History as Media Archaeology*. Amsterdam: Amsterdam University Press.

Fibla-Gutiérrez, Enrique. 2018. "A Vernacular National Cinema: Amateur Filmmaking in Catalonia (1932–1936)." *Film History* 30 (1): 1–29. https://doi.org/10.2979/filmhistory.30.1.02.

———. 2019. "A Pedagogical Impulse: Noncommercial Film Cultures in Spain (1931–1936)." PhD diss., Concordia University.

Fibla-Gutiérrez, Enrique, and Sasha Salazkina. 2018. "Introduction: Toward a Global History of Amateur Film Practices and Institutions." *Film History* 30 (1): i. https://doi.org/10.2979/filmhistory.30.1.01.

Foster, Lila. 2018. "The Cinema Section of Foto Cine Clube Bandeirante: Ideals and Reality of Amateur Film Production in São Paulo, Brazil." *Film History* 30 (1): 86. https://doi.org/10.2979/filmhistory.30.1.05.

Grieveson, Lee, Colin MacCabe, and British Film Institute, eds. 2011. *Empire and Film*. London: Palgrave Macmillan on behalf of the British Film Institute.

Grieveson, Lee, and Haidee Wasson. 2008. *Inventing Film Studies*. Durham, NC: Duke University Press.

Gurshtein, Ksenya, and Sonja Simonyi. 2016. "Experimental Cinema in State Socialist Eastern Europe." *Studies in Eastern European Cinema* 7 (1): 2–11. https://doi.org/10.1080/2040350X.2016.1112499.

Hagener, Malte. 2007. *Moving Forward, Looking Back: The European Avant-Garde and the Invention of Film Culture, 1919–1939.* Amsterdam: Amsterdam University Press.

———, ed. 2014. *The Emergence of Film Culture: Knowledge Production, Institution Building and the Fate of the Avant-Garde in Europe, 1919–1945.* New York: Berghahn.

Harbord, Janet. 2016. *Ex-Centric Cinema: Giorgio Agamben and Film Archaeology.* New York: Bloomsbury Academic.

Hediger, Vinzenz, and Patrick Vonderau, eds. 2009. *Films That Work: Industrial Film and the Productivity of Media.* Amsterdam: Amsterdam University Press.

Hogenkamp, Bert. 2003. "Léon Moussinac and the Spectators' Criticism in France (1931–34)." *Film International* 1 (2): 4–13. https://doi.org/10.1386/fiin.1.2.4.

Horak, Jan-Christopher, ed. 1995. *Lovers of Cinema: The First American Film Avant-Garde, 1919–1945.* Madison: University of Wisconsin Press.

Kattelle, Alan. 2000. *Home Movies: A History of the American Industry, 1897–1979.* Nashua, NH: Transition.

Layerle, Sébastien. 2008. *Caméras en lutte en mai 68: Par ailleurs le cinéma est une arme.* Paris: Nouveau monde.

Lerner, Jesse. 1999. "Superocheros." *Wide Angle* 21 (3): 2–35. https://doi.org/10.1353/wan.2003.0007.

Lovejoy, Alice. 2015. *Army Film and the Avant Garde: Cinema and Experiment in the Czechoslovak Military.* Bloomington: Indiana University Press.

MacKenzie, Scott. 2014. *Film Manifestos and Global Cinema Cultures: A Critical Anthology.* Berkeley: University of California Press.

Mariani, Andrea. 2018. "The Cineguf Years: Amateur Cinema and the Shaping of a Film Avant-Garde in Fascist Italy (1934–1943)." *Film History* 30 (1): 30–57.

McRobbie, Angela. 2015. *Be Creative: Making a Living in the New Culture Industries.* Cambridge, UK: Polity Press.

Mekas, Jonas, and Gregory R. Smulewicz-Zucker. 2016. *Movie Journal: The Rise of the New American Cinema, 1959–1971.* 2nd ed. Film and Culture. New York: Columbia University Press.

Mestman, Mariano. 2016. *Las rupturas del 68 en el cine de América Latina: Contracultura, experimentación y política.* CABA, Argentina: Akal.

Musser, Charles. 2006. "Introduction: Documentary before Verité." *Film History* 18 (4): 355–60.

Nae, Cristian. 2016. "Reality Unbound: The Politics of Fragmentation in the Experimental Productions of *Kinema Ikon.*" *Studies in Eastern European Cinema* 7 (1): 25–38. https://doi.org/10.1080/2040350X.2016.1112501.

Neves, Joshua, and Bhaskar Sarkar, eds. 2017. *Asian Video Cultures: In the Penumbra of the Global.* Durham, NC: Duke University Press.

Nicholson, Heather Norris. 2012. *Amateur Film: Meaning and Practice, 1927–77.* Manchester: Manchester University Press.

Odin, Roger. 2014. "The Home Movie and the Space of Communication." In *Amateur Filmmaking: The Home Movie, the Archive, the Web*, edited by Laura Rascaroli, Barry Monahan, and Gwenda Young, 15–27. New York: Bloomsbury Academic.

Orgeron, Devin, Marsha Orgeron, and Dan Streible, eds. 2012. *Learning with the Lights Off: Educational Film in the United States.* Oxford: Oxford University Press.

Roggero, Gigi. 2011. *The Production of Living Knowledge: The Crisis of the University and the Transformation of Labor in Europe and North America.* Philadelphia: Temple University Press.

Schoonover, Karl, and Rosalind Galt. 2016. *Queer Cinema in the World*. Durham, NC: Duke University Press.

Shand, Ryan, and Ian Craven, eds. 2013. *Small-Gauge Storytelling: Discovering the Amateur Fiction Film*. Edinburgh: Edinburgh University Press.

Simonyi, Sonja. 2018. "Artists as Amateurs: Intersections of Nonprofessional Film Production and Neo-Avant-Garde Experimentation at the Balázs Béla Stúdió in the Early 1970s." *Film History* 30 (1): 114. https://doi.org/10.2979/filmhistory.30.1.06.

Stark, Trevor. 2012. "'Cinema in the Hands of the People': Chris Marker, the Medvedkin Group, and the Potential of Militant Film." *October*, no. 139: 117–50.

Stein, Eric A. 2006. "Colonial Theatres of Proof: Representation and Laughter in 1930s Rockefeller Foundation Hygiene Cinema in Java." *Health and History* 8 (2): 14–44. https://doi.org/10.2307/40111541.

Tepperman, Charles. 2015. *Amateur Cinema: The Rise of North American Movie Making, 1923–1960*. Oakland: University of California Press.

———. 2018. "'A Recognized Screen': The New York Annual Movie Parties from Parlor to Public." *Film History* 30 (1) 58–85.

Vidan, Aida. 2016. "Irresistible Irreverence: Dušan Makavejev's Amateur Films and the Yugoslav Cine-Club Scene." *Studies in Eastern European Cinema* 7 (1): 53–67. https://doi.org/10.1080/2040350X.2016.1112503.

Vinogradova, Maria. 2016. "Scientists, Punks, Engineers and Gurus: Soviet Experimental Film Culture in the 1960s–1980s." *Studies in Eastern European Cinema* 7 (1): 39–52. https://doi.org/10.1080/2040350X.2016.1112502.

Wasson, Haidee. 2005. *Museum Movies: The Museum of Modern Art and the Birth of Art Cinema*. Berkeley: University of California Press.

———. 2012. "Suitcase Cinema." *Cinema Journal* 51 (2): 148–52. https://doi.org/10.1353/cj.2012.0006.

Zryd, Michael. 2006. "The Academy and the Avant-Garde: A Relationship of Dependence and Resistance." *Cinema Journal* 45 (2): 17–42. https://doi.org/10.1353/cj.2006.0023.

MASHA SALAZKINA is Research Chair in Transnational Media Arts and Cultures and Associate Professor at Concordia University. She is author of *In Excess: Sergei Eisenstein's Mexico* and editor (with Lilya Kaganovsky) of *Sound, Speech, Music in Soviet and Post-Soviet Cinema* (2014).

ENRIQUE FIBLA-GUTIÉRREZ is a Researcher and Writer. He works at the Elias Querejeta Zine Escola in San Sebastian and is the Debates Department Coordinator at the Center of Contemporary Culture of Barcelona (CCCB).

PART I

MEDIUM SPECIFICITY AND EXPANDED MEDIA ECOLOGIES

1

UNDERSTANDING (AMATEUR) CINEMA

Epistemology and Technology

Benoît Turquety

T O WRITE THAT THE DISCIPLINE OF FILM STUDIES was built on the analysis of cinema might seem like a gross truism. However, this statement
does contain an implicit assumption: that for a long time—and perhaps
even today—the term *cinema* has referred primarily to a specific *kind* of
cinema, namely, professional feature films with a commercial (and/or artistic) aim. Even other forms of professionally made films such as animation
or documentaries have been relegated to the margins of what is thought
to constitute the medium. The dominant analytical and historiographical
methods of the discipline of film studies have concomitantly been elaborated mostly on the basis of this professional corpus. Such conflation also
informs the idea that cinema has been organized around apparently stable
frameworks like the distinction between spectator and producer. The spectator is defined here as a subject that views individually the cinematic work
within the apparatus of the dark auditorium but whose aesthetic or cognitive engagement ends as soon as the subject exits the theater. Associated
with this moment when the body is forced to sit still, the spectator is always
essentially suspect of passivity.

As this essay argues, such a framework is greatly problematized when
we think beyond the narrow definition of cinema as commercially exhibited films. Taking amateur cinema as an example, I contest the distinction
between receiver and producer that has informed most scholarly production on cinema. Amateur filmmakers are spectators who cannot be labeled

as passive; they are spectators who imagine themselves as producers and then become one, producers who are still spectators. Certainly, they still watch movies sitting in a dark auditorium, but once out of this space, the engagement with cinema continues in a very active way. For the amateur filmmaker, the theater is only a moment within a continuing cinematic process; it is but one of the nodes in a network of devices and procedures that constitute cinema as a wider and expansive apparatus. Before, after, and even during one's state as a spectator, the amateur filmmaker is a user of machines—cameras, projectors, perhaps film splicers or editing software, and other postproduction applications. The theater itself may constitute one of these machines, an instrument for assessment and experiments, a place for a specific work integrated into a broader creative process. From spectator to user, the amateur is a figure that has the potential to reorganize film studies in a singular way, both in practical and theoretical terms. The epistemological assumptions of the discipline—what is thought to constitute "cinema"—are put in question, supported by an overview of the relationship between amateurs and filmmaking technologies. Then, a distinctive model to analyze the aesthetic and social characteristics of amateur films as artisanal products is posed, based on the concept of "ways of doing" from Michel de Certeau (1984) and the analysis of the film *Le Taillandier* (*The Edge-Tool Maker*), made in 1987 by Claude Bondier.

Technical Transition, Epistemological Crisis

The conflation of *cinema* and *professional cinema* has been an integral part of the paradigm on which film studies have been based—using the definition of *paradigm* that was proposed by Thomas S. Kuhn in 1962 in *The Structure of Scientific Revolutions* (a transposed definition, one might say, as film studies are products of a sociology that is a little different from the hard sciences that constitute Kuhn's model). According to Kuhn (1996, 10), paradigms are characterized by two essential features: "Their achievement was sufficiently unprecedented to attract an enduring group of adherents away from competing modes of scientific activity. Simultaneously, it was sufficiently open-ended to leave all sorts of problems for the redefined group of practitioners to resolve."

Undoubtedly, the precision and breadth of the conclusions and questions posed within the classical discipline of film studies, whether using aesthetic, historical, sociological, cultural, pragmatic, psychological, or other approaches, have been and still are stimulating and inform the work of a large number of researchers. In certain frameworks, though, one can sense that the paradigm has entered into a period of crisis following the massive emergence of digital media.

Today most devices that can play moving pictures and sounds (such as computers, phones, tablets, etc.) can also make and distribute them. Images are made to be shared, each one calling for a response, their circulation constituting the very foundation of social networks such as Instagram, Snapchat, or Flickr. This irruption of digital culture into film studies seems to have upset the discipline, blurring its contours and cracking its foundation,[1] precisely because the concept of the "spectator" has become inappropriate to describe the diversity of contemporary relationships to moving images. The paradigm has been exposed and in the same gesture put under critical pressure. Other models, and other objects on which to build these new problems, are needed. Vinzenz Hediger and Patrick Vonderau (2009) have, for instance, proposed to turn to corporate films, a "genre" that similarly stands outside of professional cinema in the classically defined sense. In this context, as they claim in the introduction of their seminal volume *Films That Work*, "industrial film research might best be understood as part of an epistemology of media in a broader sense" (12).

Everything seems to indicate that digital culture has finally completed a movement that Walter Benjamin (2008) already perceived and associated with film in "The Work of Art in the Era of Mechanical Reproduction," even if there he was characterizing more largely a property of modernity that was born with the extension of the press and the appearance of letters to the editor columns. "Thus, the distinction between author and public is about to lose its axiomatic character. . . . At any moment the reader is ready to become a writer. . . . All this can readily be applied to film, where shifts that in literature took place over centuries have occurred in a decade" (33–34).

The generalization of the division of labor in society brought about a redistribution of expertise, according to Benjamin (2008), and film technics is exemplary in that it allows the amateur to become a producer. In fact, it blurs any essential distinction between amateur and expert, passerby and actor, filmmaker and spectator. Cinema is technically accessible, not requiring the long learning curve required by other mediums; thus, *"any person today can lay claim to being filmed"* (33; emphasis in the original)—or to filming. The medium is not reserved for a rigorously trained and specialized elite but is open to the whole body politic without distinction. The importance of Benjamin's essay could have been to establish the amateur as the paradigm of film. But it required the emergence of digital culture not so as to accomplish his prophecy but rather to illuminate, retrospectively, the historical record testifying to this epistemological gesture.

Today what we understand as "traditional" cinema (projected in a dark auditorium) is clearly perceived as a minor phenomenon compared to other forms of reception of moving images (watching the same film on a digital tablet, a television, a computer, a home cinema screen, in an art gallery or a shopping arcade, etc.). What has been eroded, primarily, is a model in which this reception is entirely isolated from production. Watching films in the conventional apparatus, spectators were nothing more than that; and leaving the theater they became, once again, something completely different (citizens, subjects, individuals). But in the digital environment every received image calls for an image in return, every display comes with a camera, and every spectator is also indissociably a producer of moving images. A reading of Benjamin (2008) suggests that this environment was already in place in 1937, even if the status of cinema in the culture and its association with professional art films rendered the phenomenon invisible, to the extent that it was largely ignored by theorists. It has only been with recent work on the digital episteme that questions or doubts in regard to the old paradigm have been raised. What if the domination of "professional" film in our understanding of cinema has been an epistemological illusion? What if, finally, professional film has always been in the minority?

If we do not, from the outset, restrict the cinematic landscape to films produced by Hollywood, European and non-Western studios, but instead include within the study of cinema all objects produced with motion picture cameras in all domains, it suddenly appears that professional movies constitute a relatively small part of the wide range of film productions that exist. People have always made, alone or in groups (including clubs, associations, unions, political parties, laboratories, etc.), more family films, educational films, scientific and technical films, colonial or religious propaganda films, newsreels, militant films, corporate films, and so forth, than feature films. At the same time, outside large urban zones, "going to the movies" would not necessarily mean watching dominant genre films such as westerns or musicals in commercial movie theaters. Whether in the countryside, in the colonies, or in so-called developing countries, films were most frequently seen in associative, parochial, or governmental meetings, in social spaces modified for the occasion (municipal halls, classrooms, or the town square fitted with a mobile film unit).[2] These sessions were sometimes free, the programs devoid of fiction and composed solely of this "other" cinema that greatly problematizes our epistemological understanding of what constitutes the medium. The projectionists were amateurs, and the films were made by part-time directors. For a large part of the world's population, which classical film theory has cast out to the "periphery," this was the model that framed their concrete apprehension of cinema.[3]

Thus, it is a question of reexamining the whole phenomenon of film not only by including these new objects (the vast and complex domain of non-commercial and amateur productions) into the canon of the discipline but also by asking if this does not ultimately lead to rethinking "cinema" in itself. Opening our understanding to the contributions of amateur directors, actors, projectionists, individually or in families, in clubs, or in festivals, implies not so much the appearance of new facts that can confirm or dispute the old but instead the emergence of new problems in our conception of film, its history, and its technology. If the distinction between spectator and producer is blurred, if the user now emerges as the main figure of the filmmaking apparatus, then the noncommercial uses of technology appear as a valid starting point for a new history and sociology of cinema, based on the epistemological crisis of what has constituted the cinematic apparatus.

Amateur Filmmakers and Technics: Beginning with Kodak

This crisis impacts historians of filmmaking technics on several levels because the issues that amateur filmmakers raise most often involve technological questions. The amateur filmmaker is a user and as such interacts with commercial devices—such as cameras, tape recorders, splicers, and mobile phones. These machines have been designed for a certain purpose, with specific uses in mind. They are inscribed at the same time in their own history, in current amateur practices—real ones, or such as were imagined by their manufacturers—and in the technical network in which they had to integrate themselves.

For example, when Kodak announced that they wanted to make a Super 8 camera again in 2016, they insisted on keeping the specificities of analog film for the connoisseur, but to also integrate the product into the digital universe in the most user-friendly manner possible (connectivity, processing, easy editing, etc.). Kodak then had to take into account the scarcity of photochemical laboratories in the world and organize an efficient network of such laboratories without raising the cost of its Super 8 products prohibitively. On its website, Kodak associated its project with an "Analog Renaissance,"[4] referring to a number of important film professionals who, in the past few years, have been using film again. Amateurs who will buy this new Kodak Super 8 are thus simultaneously spectators and demanding cinephiles, dreaming of having the same tools as the artists they admire—imagining themselves, perhaps, as artisans working within the rules of art, making films that meet the most discerning aesthetic requirements. Of course, the retro feel of this project aims implicitly at transposing to cinema the success of vinyl records and other vintage media forms in the music industry but in reference to a market whose magnitude—or even existence—remains basically unknown.

Amateur technologies—from the Cinématographe Lumière to the Pathé Baby camera, from Kodachrome to Super 8, from the iPhone to the Bolex—trace throughout their functions and histories a coherent and diverse economic and industrial cartography of film, as well as a sociology of spectator-filmmakers. These devices have common features: they adopt the so-called substandard formats (inferior to the 35 mm standard: 16 mm, Super 8, 8 mm, 9.5 mm, 17.5 mm, and also VHS for video, MPEG for digital, etc.), and they are distributed on a sale-based model rather than the rental model of professional equipment. From the technological point of view, they are mainly "closed" machines, using Gilbert Simondon's terminology (2014, 60–69): the simplicity of use and the standardization allowing for repair are prioritized by manufacturers over the adaptability to the operator (although amateur cinema magazines show an affinity for more open machines, which can be dissected, compared, and explained to fellow experts). But beyond these common traits, the different cameras present a remarkable diversity of functions, uses, and cost.

The Bolex H16 was a relatively complex and expensive 16 mm film camera but considered reliable, durable, and versatile; its manufacturer, the Swiss brand Paillard, marketed it to "the professional amateur." By contrast, Kodak Brownies were consumer-oriented, cheap, and extremely easy-to-use cameras that did not require any special settings or adjustments. This marketing policy had been deeply anchored in the history of the Eastman Company since the beginning of Kodak. The firm built its phenomenal success on the slogan "You press the button, we do the rest,"

Fig. 1.1. Bolex Paillard Cine Camera ad, undated (1940s).

coined in 1888 to advertise the first photographic device that functioned with a roll of flexible, transparent film. Before the Kodak camera, amateur photographers needed expensive equipment to develop their glass plates at home and needed to master the chemistry involved in the process, which kept photography in the hands of a specialized public.

Kodak's method radically transformed the field: the photographer now had merely to find an angle and focus, the film being afterward dispatched to a professional laboratory for development, which then sent back the results to the amateur. Eastman needed of course to rely on existing infrastructure (e.g., a working post office, means of transportation) and to create new ones (geographically distributed laboratories employing chemists, etc.). In return, this network entirely disrupted the mode of photographic competence, enabling the massification of a medium on an entirely new basis, which finally redefined what an (amateur) photographer did and what photography was. It is in this way that photography was restricted, little by little, to pressing a button on the camera and the gestures immediately connected to it—framing, focalizing the depth of field—while the chemical development was relegated to the strictly technical domain. Eastman's project of making photography technically available to everyone, without education or training, was transposed to amateur cinema with the Brownie camera. The company also produced high-end amateur cameras for a more specialized customer base. Such was the case of the Cine Kodak Special, Eastman's state-of-the-art rival to Bolex.

Each technological system, in supposing and imposing a certain set of gestures, competencies, and costs, referred to a certain conception of the amateur and to an imagined user of the machine—what Madeleine Akrich (1992, 209), in the framework of actor-network theory, calls the "designer's projected user," which can differ from the real user of the device in its social reception and its concrete culture. Parallel to this, the discourses that surround the machines—mostly generated by advertising—reinforced its social framing and the expectation that the amateur would conform to it, associating each device with a specific social class or a gender: Super 8 cameras, for instance, light and user-friendly, were shown in ads being manipulated by women, while 16 mm cameras were much more likely to be tied to a masculine technophile public.

The history of these devices, understood as integrating the history of their uses within the social and marketing discourses that surrounded them, points to another sociology of cinema and a different understanding of its role in the cultural milieu. The traditional historiography of cinema tended to present it as a radically popular media at the outset, progressively conquered by the higher classes.[5] On the contrary, this history of nonprofessional film devices speaks to the progressive democratization of tools that were initially reserved for the bourgeoisie. The institutionalization of cinema can then no longer be understood solely as a process through which the medium became independent from other forms of performance entertainment of the time—lantern shows, vaudeville, magic, and so forth—but also as a process of specialization within the set of cultural practices prevalent in the different classes of society at a given time. This process established the different functions of cinema as an expressive tool beyond the commercial film industry; amateur photography and film are two of them, but also sound recording, school theater, and others.

Charles Musser (2016) has, for example, analyzed the role played by nonprofessional photographers—notably soldiers of the Filipino war—in the practice of illustrated lectures around 1900. Thanks to "recently developed camera technology—particularly the Kodak camera" (164), these improvised lecturers had sometimes produced slides from their own snapshots or integrated their own films within the show. These uses belong to the history of Musser's "screen practices" but also to a certain moment in the history of the amateur in the then emerging cinematic *dispositif*, when nonprofessional means of image production are incorporated into everyday acts of cultural, social, and political expression. An amateur photographer and filmmaker could become an amateur lecturer, find a stage to present his production to his fellow citizens, and generate change. It is to these different uses of moving image technology that have permeated society throughout the twentieth century, but have been largely ignored by film theory and history, that we now turn, showing how the epistemological shift advocated by this essay is articulated beyond concrete devices and technologies.

From Spectator to User: Ways of Doing

If the cinematic apparatus is no longer centered on the spectator but on a user of machines, we will have to rethink the changes this movement brings about beyond the history of nonprofessional filmmaking devices. The question of use is found at the heart of the historiography and sociology of technology, which have been criticized by feminists for being too centered on the problematic of innovation, giving a specifically creative role to the masculine figure of the engineer. According to the feminist critique, we should envision the users of a device "not as passive receivers but as active participants"

(Oudshoorn and Pinch 2003, 5)—a vocabulary that is familiar to the readers of film criticism and the theory of the spectator, showing how both users and spectators have somehow shared a similar position in film and technology theories. Users can "domesticate" (Silverstone and Hirsch 1992) a technical object, use it as it was meant to be used, follow scrupulously the instructions and the normal uses promoted by the manufacturer. But they also can use it in a bad way, so to speak, by involuntarily or intentionally making it do different things, tinkering with the machine, and so on.

To understand the amateur in this way supposes an analysis of the gestures, the technical operations, and the "ways of doing" that systematically mediate the user's relation with the object. Michel de Certeau (1984), in *The Practice of Everyday Life*, examined those ways of doing and unmasked the capacity for invention hidden in the uses of the devices that surround us. According to Certeau, these ways of using things must be understood in terms of style:

> We must therefore specify the operational schemas. Just as in literature one differentiates "styles" or ways of writing, one can distinguish "ways of operating"—ways of walking, reading, producing, speaking, etc. These styles of action intervene in a field which regulates them at a first level (for example, at the level of the factory system), but they introduce into it a way of turning it to their advantage that obeys other rules and constitutes something like a second level. . . . Similar to "instructions for use," [these "ways of doing things"] create a certain play in the machine through a stratification of different and interfering kinds of functioning. (30)

Conceiving amateurs as users is thus not to submit them to the history of machines but to envision them in the framework of an aesthetics of gesture, of reappropriation, a politics of tactics that is permanently bringing some play within the apparatus, constituting, at the limit, "the network of an anti-discipline" (Certeau 1984, xl).[6] The amateur is a technician and a tactician and therefore a kind of stylist. But the aesthetics in question here are not identical to those of the classic theory of film—for doubtless at this point a new paradigm implies the reworking of the totality of what it has been, including our sensibility itself.

Classical film aesthetics left little room for the amateur, mainly understanding amateurism either as weakness or as a place of utopian freedom. As Maya Deren (2005) wrote in 1959 in "Amateur versus Professional," "The amateur filmmaker is never forced to sacrifice visual drama and beauty to a stream of words, words, words, words, to the relentless activity and explanations of a plot, or to the display of a star or a sponsor's product; nor is the amateur production expected to return profit on a huge investment by holding the attention of a massive and motley audience for 90 minutes" (17).

However, this transgressive aesthetic allows us to understand only a limited part of the works of real amateurs. Most of them do not seek to transgress the rules and codes of "good cinema" but, on the contrary, try to apply them as well as they can. How, then, should we analyze amateur films beyond pejorative (bad aesthetics) or utopian (creative freedom) perspectives? The concept of craftsmanship offers a suggestive departure point from which to devise a new model of analysis for amateur productions.

Let's take for instance a twelve-minute Super 8 sound film titled *Le Taillandier* (*The Edge-Tool Maker*), made in 1987 by Claude Bondier, who had been president of the Annecy Camera Club since 1974.[7] The film is about Saint-Jorioz craftsman Bernard Voisin, and it is illustrative of my arguments for several reasons. First, it displays in an exemplary manner the affinity of amateur filmmakers for craftsmanship. Charles Tepperman (2011, 290) has shown the historical importance of such relations since the foundation of the Amateur Cinema League in the United States in 1926. Second, this "documentary fiction" is based on an elaborate and artisanal method of production.[8] Voisin was in fact long retired, but a friend of his—an acquaintance of the filmmaker—pretended that he needed a tool that Voisin could make. Voisin's son was in the neighborhood to help, so the old man played his part and agreed to make an exceptional return to his trade, supposedly for his friend's needs but in fact for the film. He could thus let his know-how be captured by the camera. The film was postsynchronized, a technique that Bondier had developed during the 1970s with his own do-it-yourself equipment. This creative choice implied a double involvement for Voisin in the film: the toolmaker had to record his voice in front of the edited images in which he appeared, becoming a self-aware actor in the film.

This artisanal process shows the base on which the affinity between amateur filmmakers and craftsmen operates: film- and toolmaking are ultimately two techniques of production that share similar codes. Both makers consider this moment of cinematic creation not as an asymmetrical exchange between the filmmaker and the subject, akin to the painter in front of the passive landscape. Rather, the spectators can perceive how both makers approach the process as technicians, working in common to make this strange object—a film—in the most conscientious manner.

The scenes depicting the toolmaker's expert skills make up more than half of *Le Taillandier* and are not by chance the most "natural" scenes, so to speak—filmmaker and craftsman taking the time to unfold their gestures for one another and for the spectator. Bondier chose to create a semifictional narrative framework around these scenes of craftsmanship that could include educational dialogues about the situation of edge-tool makers in the 1980s. The two protagonists, the old craftsman and the accomplice, were ostensibly staged in scenes that mimic with the greatest precision the conventions of classical fiction. Framing and editing were always "correct," even sophisticated; visual and sound continuity were always respected: matching eyeline and action cuts, no handheld camera, no in camera look, a carefully composed soundtrack featuring all the diegetic sound from the work process, words patiently learned and recited, and so on.

Voisin's performance may be the most touching aspect of the film. Here, the assessment criteria adapted to classical, professional fiction acting become meaningless. Things such as psychological depth and accuracy in the construction of the character are beside the point, replaced by a process of adapting to imagined standards of quality. In fact, style or interpretation in the usual sense of classic film analysis appear as useless concepts. What Voisin's performance shows is the beauty of collective work as well as the effort and humility that the maker puts into a particular technical process, and the sort of ambition that is not of stylistic singularity but simply of having done a technically good job. What Certeau teaches us is to still understand this benevolent actor's technicality as style within the framework of everyday technicality.

The important historical parallel between the amateur filmmaker and the craftsman, proposed by Tepperman, seems to us the place from which an aesthetic model for amateur cinema is to be constructed. To be able to appreciate an amateur film, a scene, a gesture, a certain virtuosity in the highly coded art of selfies, food porn, or didactic films, one has to develop a sensitivity that may be closer to the assessment of technical objects or gestures than to classical high art. Appreciating the beauty of a well-sewn dress made of expertly chosen cloth or a sturdily built wooden table relies on a quite specific expertise. As Certeau mentions, there is a real stylistic dimension to this kind of work, which is no less remarkable even though it is based on technical expertise. Film analysis must then adapt accordingly to this new framework based on craftsmanship in order to fully integrate amateur films within the discipline and give them their full due.

Fig. 1.2 and 1.3. Stills from *Le Taillandier*, Claude Bondier, Super 8, 1987. Collection
Cinémathèque des Pays de Savoie et de l'Ain, from the film *Le Taillandier* by Claude Bondier.

Conclusion

The complexity of amateur cinema as an object of study is manifold. Part of its difficulty is certainly connected with the epistemological imbalance that this essay aims to correct. That the term *cinema* has referred primarily to a specific *kind* of cinema (namely professional feature films with a commercial and/or artistic aim) led to an undervaluation of amateur filmmaking's cultural and historical importance. For instance, one can argue that the Lumières' Cinématographe was the first machine truly defining the cinematic era because it allowed for projection in front of a large audience. But it may also be because it was first conceived as an amateur device, contrarily to the Edison Kinetograph for instance. In the first months of its exploitation, the Cinématographe was restricted to professional use; but it was again sold to amateurs as early as 1897. This hesitation between professional and amateur is crucial; its echoes have reappeared throughout film history, as Walter Benjamin (2008) saw, and as is now clearly emerging as a major characteristic of digital cultures, from Hollywood to Lagos or Tehran.

Reconsidering film history from this new perspective entails epistemological and methodological problems. For instance, contrary to the classical film studies approach, amateur film history is largely an anonymous history, whose contexts and motives have to be reconstructed through other means. As a complement to film analysis, the archaeology of technical objects can participate in describing that complex system, allowing for an understanding of filmmakers as socially, economically, and culturally determined users of machines. But it remains difficult to appreciate the unstable balance between normal and singular uses or between misinterpreting instructions and transgression. The question that remains may be which epistemological value these differences should be given in a potentially new paradigm, yet to be constructed. After that, other problems will emerge. For instance, do we have to consider that, in a user-centered paradigm, the spectator has disappeared? Should we think of the digital environment as incompatible with spectatorship?

But *spectator*, along with *user* and *machine*, are not universal concepts. They should be situated, historically and geographically. The relations with technical objects or with images are not the same everywhere. Machines, gestures, and expectations are sensitive to place, climate, and social environment. From the traditional professional context to the amateur realm, cinema has been displaced, and thus maybe transformed. We have to follow it through its other displacements between cultures, and observe how the concepts are being redefined by local contexts or diasporic movements. In contrast with traditional film culture, amateur cinema is not only user-centered, it is also decentralized, involving new relations with local technical systems, cultures, media, arts, traditions. This new paradigm does indeed seem to be "sufficiently open-ended to leave all sorts of problems. . . . to resolve" (Kuhn 1996, 10).

Notes

1. See, among others, Elsaesser and Hoffmann 1998; Gaudreault and Marion 2015; Casetti 2015.
2. For more about these "cinema vans" showing noncommercial films, and their importance in Nigeria during and after the colonial era, see Larkin 2008, 86–98 and 119–22.
3. The issue of the periphery has recently been developed, particularly within transnational approaches. See, for example, Iordanova, Martin-Jones, and Vidal 2010.
4. Kodak.com, "Kodak Super 8 Camera: Designed for Creating," accessed February 6, 2020, https://www.kodak.com/consumer/products/super8/super8-camera/default.htm.
5. This is partly the thesis of Noël Burch (1990).
6. On "tactics" as opposed to "strategies," see the definitions given in Certeau 1984, xlvi.
7. It is difficult to provide a concrete example of amateur production from this perspective, since isolating a particular film inevitably disrupts the essential tension between the "normal" and the "singular".
8. To quote the category proposed for the film by the Cinémathèque des Pays de Savoie et de l'Ain, which preserves it.

References

Akrich, Madeleine. 1992. "The De-Scription of Technical Objects." In *Shaping Technology/ Building Society: Studies in Sociotechnical Change*, edited by Wiebe E. Bijker and John Law, 205–24. Cambridge, MA: MIT Press.
Benjamin, Walter. 2008. *The Work of Art in the Age of Its Technological Reproducibility and Other Writings on Media*. Edited by Michael W. Jennings, Brigid Doherty, and Thomas Y. Levin. Cambridge, MA: Belknap Press of Harvard University Press.
Burch, Noël. 1990. *Life to Those Shadows*. Berkeley: University of California Press.
Casetti, Francesco. 2015. *The Lumière Galaxy: 7 Key Words for the Cinema to Come*. New York: Columbia University Press.
Certeau, Michel de. (1980) 1984. *The Practice of Everyday Life*. Translated by Steven Randall. Berkeley: University of California Press.
Deren, Maya. 2005. *Essential Deren: Collected Writings on Film by Maya Deren*. Edited by Bruce R. McPherson. New York: Documentext.

Elsaesser, Thomas, and Kay Hoffmann, eds. 1998. *Cain, Abel or Cable? The Screen Arts in the Digital Age.* Amsterdam: Amsterdam University Press.

Gaudreault, André, and Philippe Marion. 2015. *The End of Cinema? A Medium in Crisis in the Digital Age.* New York: Columbia University Press.

Hediger, Vinzenz, and Patrick Vonderau, eds. 2009. *Films That Work: Industrial Film and the Productivity of Media.* Amsterdam: Amsterdam University Press.

Iordanova, Dina, David Martin-Jones, and Belén Vidal, eds. 2010. *Cinema at the Periphery.* Detroit: Wayne State University Press.

Kuhn, Thomas S. 1996. *The Structure of Scientific Revolutions.* Chicago: University of Chicago Press.

Larkin, Brian. 2008. *Signal and Noise: Media, Infrastructure, and Urban Culture.* Durham, NC: Duke University Press.

Musser, Charles. 2016. *Politicking and Emergent Media: U.S. Presidential Elections of the 1890s.* Oakland: University of California Press.

Oudshoorn, Nelly, and Trevor Pinch. 2003. *How Users Matter: The Co-Construction of Users and Technology.* Cambridge, MA: MIT Press.

Silverstone, Roger, and Eric Hirsch, eds. 1992. *Consuming Technologies: Media and Information in Domestic Spaces.* London: Routledge.

Simondon, Gilbert. 2014. *Sur la technique.* Paris: Presses universitaires de France.

Tepperman, Charles. 2011. "Mechanical Craftsmanship: Amateurs Making Practical Films." In *Useful Cinema*, edited by Charles R. Acland and Haidee Wasson, 289–314. Durham, NC: Duke University Press.

BENOÎT TURQUETY is Associate Professor at the University of Lausanne. He is author of *Inventing Cinema: Machines, Gestures and Media History* and of *Medium, Format, Configuration: The Displacements of Film.*

2

CROSSING THE AMATEUR LINE

The Lesson of Even—As You and I

James Rosenow

IN EARLY 1937, ROGER BARLOW, LEROY ROBBINS, AND Harry Hay found an advertisement in *Liberty* magazine. It read: "These gates guarding the entrance to the mighty M-G-M Studios, will open wide with welcome to the winners in the *Liberty*-Pete Smith Amateur Movie Contest" (*Liberty* magazine correspondence). This ad appears in and provides the narrative catalyst for their 1937 film *Even—As You and I*. With scraps of film stock, the three filmmakers shot and starred in this overtly self-reflexive work as an entry for the "*Liberty*-Smith" contest. The one-reel, twelve-minute film depicts the events around the making of an experimental short, a film-within-a-film, titled *The Afternoon of a Rubberband*. The limited scholarship on this film refers to it exclusively as an amateur production, "a good natured spoof on Surrealism" (Stein 2005) with, perhaps, a "more complex" relationship to Soviet avant-gardism (James 2005, 51). At first glance, *The Afternoon of a Rubberband* looks like pastiches of European and Soviet examples popular among the Little Theatre cinephiles of the 1930s. Indeed, *Even—As You and I* is ostensibly about three amateur filmmakers making an amateur film for an amateur contest. So why question—as this essay aims to—its amateur status?

We acknowledge the entangled origins of American *amateur* and *avant-garde* filmmaking, yet we cling to the principle that it was not until after World War II—with Maya Deren's "specifically and *aggressively* amateur practice" (James 2005, 51; emphasis added)—that the true tradition of avant-gardism was born in the United States. The historiographic justifications for this pre– versus post–World War II divide vary. While the two generations do differ, as Jan-Christopher Horak (1996) has pointed out, in terms of material conditions and social distance from the Industry, it is not true that *only* the later generation defined their practice in terms of personal expression and considered their production as "art" (14–15). Granting authorial expression only to post–World War II practice flattens our conception of 1930s production. The earlier generation did not collectively view itself as amateur, especially in our typical understanding of the term. For artists like Barlow and Robbins—each of whom earned his living behind either still or moving cameras for over six decades—it *mattered* that they and their work were called amateur.

The term *amateur* lacked firm definition throughout the interwar era, and the frequent failure to grapple with its inchoate form has had lasting consequences. The 1930s witnessed both the concretization of Hollywood's classical style and the canonization of European avant-garde art, as well as multiple debates regarding cinematic and artistic classifications and hierarchies of taste.[1] Experimental filmmakers like Barlow, Hay, and Robbins were questioning American artistic identity while texts like *Have We an American Art?* (1939) were being published. They debated the terms *documentary* and *kitsch* before they were firmly defined. They were in the first classrooms, as students or teachers, in which film and photography were taught alongside painting and sculpture. Yet we rarely consider this apropos their cinematic authorship. By trying to define American amateur cinema, we have, in some sense, lost what *amateur* might have meant to those same so-called amateurs.

As Charles Tepperman (2015) has demonstrated, in amateur filmmaking publications throughout the era, the term *amateur* was publicly debated and rarely universally agreed on (53–65). For example, in the May 1933 *American Cinematographer*, opposite an identically formatted insert announcing amateur "Prize Winners Coming to Hollywood," a full-page advertisement page declares: "You Are Not an Amateur! You are a Cinephotographer . . . Cinegrapher . . . Cinegraphist or have you a better name. . . . To us the word Amateur when used in connection with any of the arts implies someone who is sort of a bungler . . . at least rather awkward. From the fine specimen of pictures we see from the hobby-ists in the motion picture field, we know they are far from awkward. We know they have advanced far enough in the art to be given a more dignified name" ("You Are Not an

Amateur," 31). Readers were invited to make suggestions that evaded the "the stigma . . . the popular conception the word implies" (31). The write-in results were posted in the subsequent issue. "Cinephotographer" won with a landslide of 1,116 out of 1,563 votes. With results, the editors included feedback praising the publication for its attempt to rebrand the practice, one anonymous contributor writing, "deep down in my heart I always hated to admit that I was an amateur" ("Cinephotographer Leads . . . ," 66). However, the journal never adopted the new designation. The "amateur movie" section stayed "amateur" for the remainder of the decade, only occasionally designating the more formally expressive works as being achieved by an "advanced amateur."

Before discussing *Even—As You and I* itself, it is important to realize that its narrative is also its fiction. It is *not* an amateur film—not really. Rather, the film aggressively and reflexively performs a false amateurism that calls into question strict cinematic taxonomies and the status of the American independent filmmaker at the end of the 1930s. At stake in affording aesthetic ambition to independent filmmaking prior to World War II is a new and deeper understanding of the interwoven role experimental cinema played in the larger threads of American modernism.

Consider that twelve years before Deren ([1959] 2005) urged her fellow American amateur filmmakers to use their artistic and personal freedom to contest the "amateur" classification's "apologetic ring" (17), the independent filmmaker and theorist Lewis Jacobs attempted to account for the damage the amateur distinction already wrought on American experimental filmmaking in the decade prior. Jacobs (1947) begins his essay, "Experimental Cinema in America: Part One 1921–1941," with issues of perception before moving to formal distinctions: "In Europe the term for experimental efforts, 'the avant-garde,' has an intellectually creative connotation. But in America, experimenters saw their work referred to as 'amateur,' an expression used not in a laudatory, but in a derogatory sense. Lack of regard became an active force, inhibiting and retarding productivity" (111). For Jacobs, what distinguished experimental filmmaking from all other productions—including amateur—was that it privileged form over content in its endeavor to develop motion pictures as an artistically expressive medium. In many ways, the experimental filmmaker's objection was simply that *amateur* mistook their own vision of their practice. These ambitious artists—who worked seriously across mediums but oftentimes outside both Hollywood and avant-garde institutions—used filmic languages and their own critical distance from filmmaking institutions to articulate their own position. In what follows, I propose that we see *Even—As You and I* as part of Barlow's and Robbins's career-long attempt to use photographic mediums to resist assimilation into the very categories that were forming then and that continue to structure our discussions today. Once we realize they were familiar with diverse artistic circles and critically dissatisfied with their relation to established modes of filmic art making, the tone of the film's address changes. While often parodic, *Even—As You and I* is not solely broad parody but also says something pointed and constructive about cinema's formal possibilities. It insists on its makers' self-identification as modernist artists.

Let's approach this film about amateur filmmaking through an in-depth consideration of its makers' circuitous careers and diverse formal upbringing, unbound by disciplinary or medium restrictions. I hope to eschew the notion that their necessary "work for hire" or transmedium "dabbling" undermines their artistic legitimacy (Horak 1996, 15). My argument begins by examining the generalizing assumption informing the *Liberty-Smith* contest and the ways *Even—As You and I* subverts it. Namely, that the primary, mutually exclusive aspiration of the ambitious American amateur filmmaker was to pass through the gates guarding Hollywood, *not* to make thoughtful works of art. This professional/amateur dichotomy is as misleading as the other founding cinematic binary the film directly addressed—the opposition between American commercial production and the European avant-garde.[2] Through close visual analysis and a series of interviews with the makers, the work's sophisticated exchange between formal idioms emerges, as well as its dense network of citations from a variety of sources. Making sense of the film (and the film-within-a-film) requires that viewers mimic the visual literacy of its makers. In order to get the makers particular spin on a chase scene, one had to understand the medium well enough to be able to identify the traits and meaning of Eisensteinian montage. In order for many of the jokes to land, viewers needed to be relatively fluent in both "high" surrealist art and popular specialty franchises. Furthermore, *The Afternoon of a Rubberband*'s placement within *Even—As You and I*'s overarching diegesis affords the viewer the opportunity to compare supposedly irreconcilable approaches, determine their common ground, and expand on their expressive potential. Parsing these individual strands of thought—treating seriously a deceptively complex work that appears to be anything but serious—we can begin to see how *Even—As You and I* articulates its

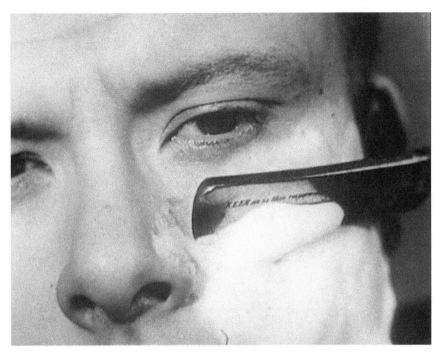

Fig. 2.1. Still from *Even—As You and I*. LeRoy Robbins cuts free from celluloid chrysalis. From *Avant Garde: Experimental Cinema of the 1920s and '30s* (Films from the Raymond Rohauer Collection), Kino Video 2005.

critical position both in relation to and outside other filmmaking modes, consistently asserting its own alterity not on the grounds of its amateur status but on its developed and thoughtful means of creative expression.

False Amateurs and Surreal Encounters

Even—As You and I opens with Barlow, Robbins, and Hay seeking an idea for the contest. And failing miserably. After much head-scratching and chain-smoking, Robbins discovers a series of articles on Dada and surrealism. Ideas finally spill out onto their scraps of paper, and the three begin assembling their shots. Unlike the confident struts and cranks performed by Mikhail Kaufman in Dziga Vertov's *Man with a Movie Camera* (1929)—which *Even—As You and I* undeniably references here—the cinematographic efforts of these cameramen appear clumsy and inexperienced. Barlow awkwardly straddles a telephone pole, Hay dangles a camera down a dark manhole, and Robbins chases cats. The blunders continue into the

Fig. 2.2. Still from *Even—As You and I*. Harry Hay takes swipe at *Un Chien Andalou*. From *Avant Garde: Experimental Cinema of the 1920s and '30s* (Films from the Raymond Rohauer Collection), Kino Video 2005.

editing room, where Robbins cuts the film stock in a way that seems less about editorial choices than about freeing himself from a celluloid chrysalis. Finally, the men gather to view the product—*The Afternoon of a Rubberband*. For nearly four minutes, the viewer is assaulted by a string of quick cuts, the shots averaging three seconds, that take us from frying a light bulb, to a dapper De-Chirico-esque bust and his guest dining on a baby, to overkilling a snail with a steamroller as a woman (the screaming likeness of the schoolmarm on Sergei Eisenstein's Odessa steps from *Battleship Potemkin* [1926]) watches in horror. The film-within-a-film ends with a handwritten title card: "This is where we came in." The lights come on and the men appear satisfied with their work. Until they discover they have actually missed the submission deadline. This final snafu resolves quickly with another fortuitous find—a new ad: "Tricks & Gadgets, Another Contest." Thus *Even—As You and I* ends with the charmingly naive filmmakers recommencing the creative cycle.

The "*Liberty*-Smith" and "Tricks & Gadgets" contests actually ran in *Liberty* magazine from December 1936 through early summer 1937 (*Liberty* magazine correspondence), roughly when *Even—As You and I* was shot. Promotional contests were pervasive across the 1930s mediascape, but for filmmakers entrenched in experimental film culture as Barlow, Robbins, and Hay were, the choice to highlight the "*Liberty*-Smith" contest seems odd. First, because of the silent, eponymous cosponsor. As instantly recognizable as the film's references to *Battleship Potemkin* or *Un Chien Andalou* were and are for an avant-garde-inclined eye, "Pete Smith," evoked in *Even—As You and I*'s second shot, would have been just as familiar to a seasoned Hollywood viewer. Smith's one-reel, often comedic *Specialties* were an MGM staple beginning in 1931. This popular genre depicting bumbling husbands and wives attempting to become proficient spouses transformed Pete Smith into a household name. His protomocumentary form of direct address can be observed throughout *Even—As You and I*.

The second feature that makes the *Liberty*-Smith contest an odd choice for our filmmakers is the host publication itself. Unlike cinema-specific publications that Barlow subscribed to—*Photoplay, American Cinematographer, Movie Makers*—*Liberty* was a general-interest magazine. Accordingly, *Liberty* contests were democratic appeals, inviting amateurs of all sorts to get in the game: "$10,000, Has Been Set Aside for Unknown Authors." "A $5,000 Home-Life Snapshot Contest You Can Win!" "Invent a Laughable Alibi and Win Your Share of the $250 Cash Prize Fund." Although offered monetary incentive, *Liberty*'s film contests were less interested in courting those so-called advanced amateurs whose experimental work challenged cinematic norms than they were in discovering a potentially profitable attraction. Moreover, unlike, say, *Movie Makers*, which helped organize local screenings of winning submissions, *Liberty*'s promise of exposure, to "open the gates of Hollywood," was hollow. Winning film submissions received little more than a mention, noting only the maker's name and hometown.

Consider the actual wording of the call for participation, as it was printed in the January 9 issue, the very same issue we see in *Even—As You and I*: "These gates guarding the entrance of the mighty M-G-M Studios, will open wide with welcome to the winners in the *Liberty*-Pete Smith Amateur Movie Contest. Everyone who owns or can borrow a 16mm or 8mm amateur movie camera is eligible to compete for cash prizes totaling $1000 and for real Hollywood contracts which may be awarded to amateurs who demonstrate directorial talent, originality, and effectiveness in story treatment" (*Liberty* magazine correspondence). Research suggests that its makers never entered *Even—As You and I* in this or any contest. Two issues, again, are raised here that deserve attention. First, in violation of the contest rules dictating that amateur-gage film be used, *Even—As You and I* was done on 35 mm. Second, this call for participation seems to perpetuate the misconception that the guiding motivation for independent productions at this time was a desire for professionalization and the accompanying fame and glory. And for filmmaking, going pro meant going Hollywood.

Barlow, Hay, and Robbins did in fact meet one another in Hollywood, but each arrived in Los Angeles via different means and for different purposes. Harry Hay, born in 1912 in England, was raised in Los Angeles after his family emigrated in 1919. At twenty-one, Hay dropped out of his Stanford theater program and returned to Los Angeles to establish the activist Hollywood Theatre Guild with his boyfriend and fellow actor Will Geer.

Native Minnesotan Roger Barlow joined the navy at seventeen as a "means of getting out into the broader world, [where] there were going to be pretty girls and foreign automobiles" (Barlow 1980). In 1929 he was stationed off the southern California coast. He served as the ship's sole Photographer First Class, recording experimental aviation landing tests with his personal 35 mm hand-cranked Bell & Howell camera.

> It was just me, a one-man apprentice photographic laboratory, and I did everything. . . . There wasn't anything else I really wanted to do. I read everything. I bought all the photographic books that I could find and just lived, worked, thought photography. . . . I came across a book called *The Film Till Now*, by an English writer, a film historian, Paul Rotha. It was like a religious person discovering the Word of his God. It was almost like a blinding flash of something. . . . I moved, perhaps naturally into the more creative aspects of filmmaking. *That is, really making motion pictures. Not just doing motion picture photography.* (Barlow 1980; emphasis added)

Upon his release from duty, Barlow went to live with Robbins in a bungalow on their mutual friend's—architect Richard Neutra—Silverlake property. Barlow had met Robbins during a shore leave a year prior and was instantly taken by the bespectacled photographer's recent exploits on an expedition to the Yucatan peninsula. As fate would have it, the twenty-seven-year-old's year south of the border overlapped with the location shooting of none other than Sergei Eisenstein. As Robbins (1975) tells it, "When I met [Eisenstein] he was working on *Que Viva Mexico*. It was a casual meeting. I watched him work. I saw him at his hotel. I was enormously impressed with his aesthetic, his film work . . . regardless of subject matter, his film had form." To this chance encounter, Robbins largely credits his decision, when the expedition broke up, to hitch a ride aboard a Los Angeles–bound fishing boat, rather than return to his hometown of St. Louis.

Once in Los Angeles, Robbins sought out local photographic and film circles that shared his ideas about the mediums' formal capabilities. "You see, photography was barely acceptable as an art in those days. Stieglitz was the first to make a dent in photography as an art in this country. Later, of course. Weston" (Robbins 1975). In the right place at the right time again, Robbins found himself by the end of 1932 within Edward Weston's artistic circle. "By accident, or the gods or whatever, I ran into the Westons. And this gave a much clearer, and much more defined, much greater fundamental concept as to the fact that the camera is a creative tool . . . I was an artist so I used it in that sense" (Robbins 1975). While it was with Weston that Robbins held long discussions on photography's expressive potential, it was Weston's son Brett who helped Robbins secure work on some Sam Goldwyn projects and on a variety of still and moving promotional shoots, from Shell Oil advertisements to architectural documentation for local design firms. Robbins often recounted both his formal discussions and commercial practice in his correspondence with the then-ship-bound Barlow.

While they faced bouts of unemployment during the height of the Depression, by the time Barlow, Robbins, and Hay set out to shoot *Even—As You and I*, each had stable, and even successful, employment. Barlow was shooting and editing footage for the Federal Theater Project, the Los Angeles County school district, and the California Conservation Corps. Hay was engaged with progressive theater and the queer art scene. In 1937 he was coming off his leading role as Dr. Barnes in the West Coast premiere of Clifford Odets's *Waiting for Lefty*, for which he garnered praise from the theatrical world broadly and from the actor Edward G. Robinson personally (Timmons 1990, 46). Robbins was nearly a year into an eighteen-month stint with the California Federal Art Project (FAP). Along with the photographer Hy Hirsch (who has four cameos in *Even—As You and I*) and the Westons, Robbins (1975) produced "creative . . . not documentation" photography on a biweekly basis for the FAP.

Most accounts of Robbins's and Barlow's occupational history say no more than broadly that both were employed by the Works Progress Administration (WPA), which oversaw a variety of New Deal initiatives. When discussing his and his project-colleagues' work, however, Robbins is ever careful to distinguish the FAP's creative photographic endeavor from the WPA's better-known documentation work under the Farm Service (FSA) and Resettlement Administrations (RA), which were producing breakout photography stars the likes of Dorothea Lange and Walker Evans. "Ours," stated Robbins (1975), "was a different concept entirely. Though we all worked in photography, we were like another artist who worked in another medium." This awareness that his own photographic practice was fundamentally *not* what was being done and celebrated elsewhere is a subtlety that is rarely afforded to histories of 1930s artistic production. It is generally assumed that in the larger 1930s mediascape, aesthetic concerns took a back seat to political and social content. Robbins (1975), however, believed that while he was certainly politically oriented and socially motivated, his work was driven by his desire for formal expression. "I feel that my activity, my energy simply went in *other* directions. In an aesthetic direction." After contrasting FAP's approach to photography with FSA's and RA's approaches, Robbins stresses that the latters' photographic collection was often fed directly into national magazines, like *Life*. "But *Life* wasn't an ART magazine. It was photojournalism and that is a sumptin' different. That's very different, the major impact was content, the major impact was not form" (1975). Even here, Robbins is careful not to imply that, say, a Margaret Bourke-White photograph was somehow formally deficient—merely that in the context of *Life*, which rarely mentioned the names of photographers alongside their photographs, the photograph's emphasis unavoidably became content instead of form. Almost echoing Barlow's "making motion pictures versus doing motion picture photography," Robbins caps off his interview with one final and particularly pertinent clarification: "I think today [1970s] with this latest resurgence of, or renewed, or maybe initial interest in photography as an art . . . there is still confusion as to what part of it is art and what part of it is history. There is an awful lot that is history. There is an awful lot that is art. And I think there's some confusion, which is which? [chuckles]" (1975).

Whereas Robbins returns to "which-is-which" distinctions on the level of the work, emphasizing the work's motivation or function—form versus content, art versus journalism, aesthetic pleasure versus historical document—Barlow's anthem touches on labels applied to a film's maker. When asked whether he preferred his role as a director, cinematographer, or cameraman, Barlow (1980) pithily responded, "We thought of ourselves simply as makers, film makers." The "we" being filmmakers like him and

Robbins—as well as Lewis Jacobs, Slavko Vorkapich, Willard van Dyke, and Ralph Steiner—who spent the decade traversing the "professional" and "amateur" divide, producing works in a variety of mediums and styles, and continuing to defy canonical classifications. Rather than identify with a job title, and therefore define their work by ill-fitting industry or fine-art terms, Barlow and these likeminded makers related their artistic work to the medium itself. They were makers, makers of film.

Moreover, these makers deeply engaged the questions that define modernism, American art, and experimental film history. In this era in the United States, definitions were in exciting disarray—before disciplinary, canonical, and medium boundaries became entrenched. These difficult-to-pin-down filmmakers played pivotal, but largely forgotten, roles across the mediascape throughout these interwar years. Instead of defining the 1930s American modernist cannon according to subsequent acts of institutional or critical or popular inclusion, I propose we identify works through attention to formal means and ambitions, as these filmmakers tried to do. Thus we can re-view *Even—As You and I* as an example of pre–World War II experimental filmmaking in which form subserves institutional critique and the kind of self-critical reflection on the nature of the medium that shortly thereafter came to be associated with modernism itself. We can also move from seeing *Even—As You and I* as a film mocking Hollywood continuity or Soviet montage or surrealist absurdity to a film whose makers were comfortable enough to employ all cinematic modes of address.

Upon close analysis, even those superficial, "parodic" references to European avant-gardism turn out to demonstrate the relevance of their techniques and theories to the American context (James 2005, 51). Form had its place, even in a decade where content seemingly reigned supreme. Take an explicit example of the film refusing to place narrative content ahead of reflexive means: the seventh shot of *Even—As You and I* depicts a close-up of hands scribbling "Script no. 17. Boy meets girl." Immediately upon inscribing the words, the hand, frustrated, releases the pencil. The camera cuts to a close-up of an overflowing wastebasket where two more balls of crumbled paper fall on the pile. Three shots later the camera returns to a close-up on the hand. This time it writes, "Script no 34. Girl meets Boy." Thus after multiple starts, the idea for the film's plot remains fixed on a formulaic meeting between two individuals of opposite sexes. "No. 34" joins the others in the wastebasket. The filmmakers opt for a more creative premise.

It matters that the characters encounter "real works of art" not as objects but as mass media reproductions. The articles we see Robbins discover in the film were from *Life* and *Time*'s coverage of the Museum of Modern Art's (MoMA) new exhibition: *Fantastic Art, Dada and Surrealism*. The articles briefly mention the film program that ran alongside the MoMA show. The most notable inclusions in this program were René Clair's *Entr'Acte* (1924), Hans Richter's *Vormittagsspuk* (1927), and Luis Buñuel and Salvador Dalí's *Un Chien Andalou* (1929), all of which are referenced in *The Afternoon of a Rubberband*. But, these references appear to have a critical bite. Similar to Dada photomontage simultaneously using and mocking cubist techniques, the avant-garde section of *Even—As You and I* adopts certain images, tropes, and practices and highlights their perceived contextual impotence. These national publications explained these artistic modes to American audiences as *having been* aggressive gestures in a post–World War I Europe but not as having relevance domestically.

After this initial surreal encounter, the camera focuses on reproductions of famed surrealist works including René Magritte's *False Mirror* (1935), Meret Oppenheim's *Object* (1936), and both Dalí's *Persistence of Memory* (1931) and *Femme à tête des roses* (1935). The only painting reproduction to appear in the film more than once is *Femme à tête des roses*, which appears five times, calling attention to a specific, not general, aspect of surrealism informing the filmmakers. *Femme à tête des roses* isn't Dalí's most notorious work, but it nevertheless exemplifies Dalí's paranoiac-critical method, which stresses that the mind perceives connections between things that have no logical connection. The more seemingly illogical the juxtaposition, the more the mind strives to metaphorically link the two images. This creates a stronger image that can develop into a chain of images. While Dalí's theories have no historical connection to Eisenstein's, the makers of *Even—As You and I* seem here to conflate them cleverly. Dalí's recurring painting and references to Eisenstein clearly invoke both theories as disparate images calling on the beholder to supply the connections.

By framing *The Afternoon of a Rubberband* with a traditional Hollywood narrative structure, the film highlights the demand both commercial and avant-garde films place on their viewer to construct intelligibility from successive images—be they crumpled scripts landing in a trash heap or a statue salivating over a well-seasoned baby. This inclusive gesture sets the present work in critical relation to multiple filmic modes. Instead of being consumed or steamrolled by either cinematic behemoth, instead of relying on one filmic mode or another, these filmmakers use both, juxtaposing them. With their "playful" film, Barlow, Hay, and Robbins provide a possible critical position from within which film art in the United States could flourish unencumbered by artistic classifications and institutional boundaries.

Titles Matter

One of modern art's defining features is that arguably for the first time in history, the determination of "what constitutes art" rests solely on an artist declaring it to be so (e.g., Marcel Duchamp's *Fountain* and Richard Mutt's justification for it). But what if the work's maker is not called an artist, but an amateur? Does that make her resulting work any less art? Filmmakers like Barlow and Robbins found themselves both temporally and institutionally in that difficult-to-navigate no-man's-land. They were caught between the camps of the Hollywood professionals and the European avant-garde film-artists. This particular neither/nor status of independent American production needs to be reconsidered, beyond center-and-periphery binaries. Barlow's suggestion that he and other so-called amateurs used the medium of film to resist assimilation into either category perhaps provides a way forward by asking to what—if not the medium itself—these categorical designations appealed. For its full subversive weight to be felt, *Even—As You and I* ultimately demands to be considered as a work that intentionally defies neat identification.

If this work is, as I believe it to be, a series of challenges to cinematic and artistic classifications, a final question must be raised: what the *hell* is going on with its title? Regardless of how many times one watches the film, the eponymous "you" and "I" remain untethered from any diegetic referent. What's more, any attempt to interrogate the title plunges us down yet another rabbit hole of densely layered citationality. Much like the film, the seemingly unrelated quotations operate with at least some semblance of thematic, albeit absurd, unity.

The conspicuous dash, holding "even" at bay from "you" and "I," recalls other examples of punctuation play, such as Duchamp's *The Bride Striped Bare By Her Bachelors, Even*. Sans dash, *Even as You and I* was the title of a popular early twentieth-century collection of parables, which included such gems as "All Very Good: The Sweet Uses of Perversity." "Even as You and I" was also the title of a chart-topping Broadway musical number from *Everybody's Welcome* (1931). This romantic and raunchy duet features a couple who, presumably to reconcile themselves to enormous amounts of imminent premarital sex, asks why a label like "marriage" can alone render acts acceptable. This was not, however, the first, nor second, time "even as you and I" is used as a passionate refrain to question repercussions.

In his 1897 poem "The Vampire," Rudyard Kipling repeats "even as you and I" on six occasions as a man laments once good intentions now lost, because a callous woman fed on his romantic naiveté. In 1914, Kipling's "The Vampire" inspired a six-stanza parody published by *Photo Era*: "The Gummist, with Apologies to Rudyard Kipling." In a way that should, by this point, feel familiar, the poem's author adopts the voice of a disenfranchised photographer whose artistic approach of gumming—the practice of creating brushy, artistic effects through the use of gum bichromate—is perceived as "other than" art, universally snubbed by the purveyors of taste.

> O, the paint we did waste and the "tears" we did waste
> And the prints that were always "slammed,"
> By "would-be" critics who did not know
> (and now we know that they never could know)
> And did not understand.
>
> A "gummist" there was and his coin he spent
> (Even as you and I!)
> Paper and paint to his last red cent
> (While his land-lady dunned him for "past-due" rent)
> But a "gummist" must watch "development"
> (Even as you and I!) (Weston 1914)

At the risk of explaining away the joke, this poem—like Barlow, Robbins, and Hay's film—falsely performs its amateurism in two ways. First, this depiction of a blubbering, penniless, would-be photographer was penned by none other than Edward Weston, Robbins's aesthetic father figure, whom he credited as the only photographer apart from Stieglitz to "make a dent in the cause of photography as an art" (1975) before the 1930s. The central role Weston played in independent filmmaking, especially on the West Coast, remains all but ignored and deserves a more thorough handling elsewhere.[3] However, just as *Even—as You and I*'s makers were not actually inept, struggling neophytes, Weston at the time of *The Gummist* was gaining an international reputation for his high-key portraits and eager to move toward more "expressive" practices. While history recognizes Weston's shift in the 1910s as the start of the distinctive practice that would earn the photographer his place in the halls of modernism, it is clear from the articles published about him at the time, few knew just what to do with his new photographic approach and whether or not it could be called "art." The deeper irony of the poem is that prior to this 1910s moment—in which both Stieglitz and Weston turned away from the practice—photographic gumming was held in high regard. It was associated with the pictorialist school. Originating as early as 1869, pictorialism seemed for decades to be photography's most viable path toward acceptance as art. The pictorialist movement was also largely championed by so-called amateur photographers and was considered, until the advent of amateur filmmaking, to be "perhaps the only [art] in which the amateur equals, and frequently excels the professional in proficiency" (Wilson and Reed 1994, 4). Amateur status in photography parallels its later film corollary in many ways. Despite its brevity, Weston's poem not only tackles issues of technological advancements and availability, questions of anonymous appropriation and reproduction, and conflicts of commercial or federal sponsorship. But perhaps most significantly in this context is the point the *Gummist* seems to make with its feigned amateurism, a point that will again be made with *Even—As You and I.*

The "gummist" he sweat through his foolish hide
(Even as you and I)
While the highlights he scrubbed till they almost cried—
(with a bristle-brush none too softly applied)
When the print was "done," friends threw it aside
(Even as you and I) (Weston 1914)

On the one hand, the message is for the foolish maker who rests his work's claim to art status on superficial surface effects. The other message echoes the first but addresses the public: instead of insisting that a work meet established expectations and occupy familiar critical categories, take the time to look. What was actually made might even surprise you and I.

Notes

1. The ur-example of these 1930s cultural debates, in my mind, would be the publication of Clement Greenberg's (1939) infamous "Avant-Garde and Kitsch." An argument could (and likely should) be made elsewhere regarding Greenberg's role in skewing, for multiple generations, our understanding of this era's diverse transmedia practices. By stating early in his essay that while a single culture or society may produce works that fall under the categories of "avant-garde" and "kitsch," but no further connections between the two

camps are possible, he ostensibly removed a large body of 1930s production—particularly independent filmmakers—from critical formal consideration.

2. One of the prime examples of deliberate canon construction from this era is the Museum of Modern Art (MoMA). MoMA, which opened its doors to the public in November 1929, was the first museum to include the mediums of film in its permanent collection. Without diminishing the sincere and singular effort MoMA exerted in assuring photography's and film's global acceptance as art, one must also consider the perhaps unintended impact this first film library had on the reception of early independent film production in the United States. The library was more or less divided in those early years into two categories: American Hollywood and European avant-garde. In her book, Haidee Wasson (2005) thoroughly attends to the many outside forces that effected MoMA's first film acquisitions but leaves the question of lasting consequences unanswered.

3. Another example, parallel to the Robbins's case, is the career and formal practice of Willard Van Dyke. Van Dyke gave up his rising career within the Shell Oil Corporation to apprentice with Weston. He went on to become a founding member and leading proponent of F.64 photography (a name given to the movement by Van Dyke, not Weston), document the execution of WPA murals, codirect a commercial documentary—*The City*—for the 1939 World's Fair, produce wartime propaganda for the Office of War Information, produce early television programing, and later become the director of MoMA's film library, where he spearheaded the effort to establish the library as an autonomous museum department.

References

Barlow, Roger. 1980. *Reminiscences of Roger Barlow.* Columbia Center for Oral History Archives, Rare Book and Manuscript Library, Columbia University, New York.

"Cinephotographer Leads. . . ." 1933. *American Cinematographer,* June 1933, 66.

Deren, Maya. (1959) 2005. "Amateur versus Professional." In *Essential Deren: Collected Writings on Film,* edited by Bruce McPherson, 17–18. Reprint. New York: McPherson.

Greenberg, Clement. 1939. "Avant-Garde and Kitsch." *Partisan Review* 6, no. 5: 34–39.

Horak, Jan-Christopher. 1996. "The First American Film Avant-Garde, 1919–1945." In *Lovers of Cinema: The First American Film Avant-Garde 1919–1945,* edited by Jan-Christopher Horak, 14–66. Madison, WI: University of Wisconsin Press.

James, David. 2005. *The Most Typical Avant-Garde: History and Geography of Minor Cinemas in Los Angeles.* Berkeley: University of California Press.

"Leroy Robbins." 1975. Video recordings relating to New Deal art in California. Archives of American Art, Smithsonian Institution, Washington, DC.

Liberty magazine, correspondence 1936–1937. MGM Legal Department Collection, Margaret Herrick Library, Academy of Motion Picture Arts and Sciences, Los Angeles, CA.

Stein, Elliot. 2005. "Film Notes." *Avant-Garde: Experimental Cinema of the 1920s and '30s.* DVD. New York: Kino Video.

Tepperman, Charles. 2015. *Amateur Cinema: The Rise of North American Moviemaking.* Oakland: University of California Press.

Timmons, Stuart. 1990. *The Trouble with Harry Hay: Founder of the Modern Gay Movement.* Boston: Alyson.

Wasson, Haidee. 2005. *Museum Movies: The Museum of Modern Art and the Birth of Art Cinema*. Berkeley: University of California Press.

Weston, Edward. 1914. "The Gummist, with Apologies to Rudyard Kipling." *Photo Era* 32, April 1914, 182.

Wilson, Michael, and Dennis Reed. 1994. *Pictorialism in California: Photographs 1900–1940*. Malibu: Getty Museum.

"You Are Not an Amateur." 1933. *American Cinematographer*, May 1933, 31.

JAMES ROSENOW is Assistant Professor of Film Studies at the University of Rochester.

3

"I GIVE YOU A TOAST TO THE PIONEERS!"

The Movie Maker
Ten Best Video Competition 1982–1983

Graeme R. Spurr

Pioneers

The purpose of this chapter is to broadly survey the key issues surrounding new video practice, creativity, and aesthetics for British amateur cinematographers of the early 1980s through examining one of the first video competitions in the United Kingdom. Announced in 1982, the *Movie Maker* Ten Best Video Competition 1982–1983 emerges in British amateur media culture sitting between profound shifts in analog and digital equipment. The competition's historical importance arises from its underreported nature, representing the diffusion and use of early video equipment in the mainstream UK amateur cine publication *Movie Maker* and its affiliated competition, the Ten Best (Rose 1982, 248–49). Perceptions of anxiety surround the rise of home video technologies however, and the competition, its initial reporting, as well as the entries themselves give testament to contestations over this "new" technology.

This anxiety surrounding the competition can be further defined into specific concerns: consumer discomfort over the arrival of video, its impact on a "cine-traditional" discipline, and its integration into an already existent type of amateur media practice. Retrospective evaluations of the competition's historical importance also indicate a "preservation anxiety," with the competition sitting between the Institute of Amateur Cinematography's own Film and Video Library and the East Anglian Screen Archive. These "video-movies" are on the periphery of the archive and they exemplify the unfortunate economic limit of the sector, as well as the denigrated status of early video formats (Martin 2005; Hetrick 2001). The entries and their reporting therefore present a series of acute critical, cultural, and technological issues for research.

During the early 1980s, domestic amateur video equipment neared a general level of affordability in the United Kingdom, but this was just one factor in the shift away from traditional forms of amateur film practice. For a few commentators, the UK cine scene of the 1970s and 1980s was plagued with a growing sense of disinterest locally and internationally from companies, such as *Norris* and *Eumig*, involved in the production of amateur film technology: "Most people were glad to say goodbye and good riddance to 1981, a year of recession, redundancies, bankruptcies and urban unrest. It was a pretty bleak year for amateur movie-making too, with a sharp drop in sales of cine equipment, aggravated by the rapid growth of video as well as the economic climate. Companies large and small went out of business, and when Eumig went bust in Vienna, it seemed as though the writing was on the wall. Cine's days were outnumbered" (Watson 1982, 282).

Such reporting indexes a transitory period in the cine movement, with video equipment's domestication a market response to dwindling cine equipment sales. The state of the market at the time was, in contrast to journal reports of "industry death," not entirely unprofitable (Watson 1984, 7; "Cine a £15 million-a-year UK Market" 1982, 14). Sales of cine equipment had been decreasing since the late 1960s however, and combined with a poor economic climate, the manufacturing shift toward video was a route of escape from the stagnation of the market. Dissident voices mocked the movement toward video, but the economic benefits of the development were evident (Watson 1984, 8). Also, the shift to video systems was visible within parallel professional developments reported a few years earlier in the *British Kinematograph Sound and Television Journal* with technical "simplicity" being a key facet of this "video" development (Harris 1977, 77).

"Simplicity" would be a crucial cause of the cine movement's apprehension around video however, with the video industry perceived to be simplifying equipment in favor of the domestic and family user. The innovation being offered by microprocessor and microcomputer technology was both practical and economically sound by making the equipment smaller, less specialized and easier to use. This could be problematic for those with more creative intent and aspiration: "Do you ever pine for the days when we had a few things ourselves? Older readers will recall that, once upon a time, a light meter was an essential accessory. You had to measure distances or make a good judgement. If having done most of it yourself, you got a good result, the old ego expanded and you felt you were into a wonderful hobby. Not so now. The electronics have taken over. Anyone can do it. Thank goodness they haven't yet devised an electronic script writer" (Watson 1982, 283).

Such comments from cine journalists index larger concerns around liberal notions of western individualism and the impact of technology on consumers' agency and creative control. Cine enthusiasts' anxiety of video stemmed from the fear that the "democratizing" technology would undermine a traditional and conservative type of practice sustained through both prewar and postwar periods. This reluctance around video was a trend that continued through the decade: "One senses a growing unease over the direction the amateur film is taking and the threat posed by video" (Malthouse 1989, 33). Certain writers also expressed concerns about commercial interests "muscling in" on the amateur scene, and tensions between consumer and manufacturers were not only evident, but significant: "Film and camera manufacturers are out for a mass market, and if that market shows signs of stagnation—as it must be—then out they will come with a new idea and equipment to keep the tills ringing. It's not your artistic ability they are interested in, only your money. That's business and progress" ("Video Take Over" 1979, 16).

These initial projections of video's negative impact on amateur filmmaking, characterize much of the early discourse and discussion around video in the UK amateur cine movement: "There's a five-letter word going the rounds of cine circles at the moment; the pundits smile knowingly, the purists throw up their hands in horror and the novices just get confused. No prizes for guessing—the word is of course VIDEO" ("Video" 1980, 49).

Despite this, one of the first national amateur video competitions is announced in the April 1982 issue of *Movie Maker*: the Ten Best Video Competition. In its inauguration, rhetoric around the competition appears to carefully balance the introduction of this new video technology, with notions of traditional film creativity. As Tony Rose (1982), then managing editor of *Movie Maker* stated, while video technology was materially different to cine cameras, the process of producing and editing movies for a video competition, the "film-language" or technique used to construct a narrative, would remain unchanged and static: "The deployment of long-shots, medium-shots and close-ups to tell a story or expand an idea will remain the same. The use of parallel cutting to show simultaneous events taking place in different locations will remain the same, as will the use of lighting and music to convey atmosphere. Not even the punctuation marks—the fades and dissolves are going to change" (248–49).

Rose was explicit in legitimizing the competition, with appeals to tradition appearing to negotiate readership carefully: "The inauguration of the video competition is not just an attempt to be trendy and it is certainly not a denigration of film" (1982, 248–49). Regardless of this, there were still a range of practical reasons that restricted a dual competition featuring both cine and video entries:

> So why, you may ask, should we have a separate competition on video? The answer lies in the nature of the end product. A film, by its nature, is designed to be shown to a large audience and half the point of the Ten Best Films contest is that it brings winning films before an audience of thousands, the initial screenings taking place in the impressive auditorium of the National Film Theatre. A video tape, by its nature, is designed to be shown to a small audience in a domestic setting—and the few attempts at large screen video presentations I've seen tend to confirm rather than deny this. (Rose 1982, 248–49)

Parallel to this call for "budding video enthusiasts," Rose commented on potential entries for the new competition tentatively, with expectations of quality appearing distant and unlikely: "To judge from the few amateur-produced videotapes we have chanced to see so far, the art is in its infancy" (1982, 248–49). It is therefore astonishing when, in the February 1983 issue of *Movie Maker* introducing the winners of the competition, Rose (1983) states: "When I introduced the competition in our April 1982 issue, I struck a slightly sceptical note by mentioning that we did not expect the number of entries to be vast or their quality to be outstanding. My forecast has proved to be half right" (78). While the majority of entries adhered to initial expectations, other material proved to oppose many of the then-current attitudes to video: "Somehow, their producers have all managed to overcome the handicaps that we tend to think of as inherent in video. They are edited, for example, quite as fluently as well-made films and without any noticeable sacrifice of picture quality—a reminder, if it were needed, that there are no technical problems in the world that can't be conquered by creative ingenuity" (Rose 1983, 78).

Initial accounts of video had placed it in opposition to film and film-practice, but the *Movie Maker* competition counters many of these early attitudes. There are, as Rose makes clear, limitations to the initial three-way video technology (portable packs consisting of camera, recording device, and battery pack), such as projection and editing, but it is possible to overcome these through "creative ingenuity."

The initial reporting and announcement of the *Movie Maker* video competition 1982/3 place it between broadly traditional and modern conceptions of amateur video equipment. The competition marks the diffusion of early, and considerably bulky, three-way video systems; and this use in amateur productions would be prior to the release of smaller camcorders and cheaper video technology in the mid-1980s. The competition, therefore, exemplifies the potential and limitations of the new medium, while also being a measure of the success of the technology for amateurs. While prior reporting of the competition was marked by hesitation around video, there were occasional attempts to offer a humorous negotiation of the competing and "contested" voices: "On the one hand there are the baleful head-shakings of the 'cine-is-dead-brigade' and the blandishments of the video hype merchants, and on the other the confident claims by the dedicated cineastes that film is the only way to do it if you want to finish up with anything worthwhile" (Cleave 1983, 61).

The *Movie Maker* Ten Best Video Competition 1982–1983

Judged by *Movie Maker* staff, the competition had five winners and, as stated by Rose (1982) in his opening speech, the competition "is a significant milestone in the history of amateur movie-making and video" (248–49). Earlier questions had been raised in the journal as to why the Ten Best was not open to video, with "the present state of video technology" not being favorable for large-scale projection (248–49). Video was not rejected outright, as anecdotal reports predicted, and attempts such as this competition were made to integrate it into established patterns of behavior and creativity. As two of the winning competition entries—*Hong Kong* and *Civic Week*—will exemplify, practice would stay incredibly familiar and, to quote the end of Rose's introduction, "video and film would indeed progress hand in hand" (*The Movie Maker Ten Best Video Competition* 1983).

Hong Kong: A Memorable and Established Experience

This first winning entry, *Hong Kong*, can be broadly characterized in the holiday and travel film genre: an already established amateur film category.

Heather Norris Nicholson, a social historian working on pre-, inter-, and postwar cine material, has stated that amateur holiday and travel films occupy an "intriguing position" within traditions of travel representation, extending historically established links between tourism, photo-mechanical technology (both moving and still), and memory (2009, 93). Nicholson's argument will be echoed, with *Hong Kong* defined as a video production that has predominantly remained with the formal, aesthetic, and generic characteristics of the 1930s cine material she discusses. This video, arguably, continues the visual motifs and themes associated with early amateur travel film and its connection to memory and tourism. While emulating the conventions of the cine material, it is not identical; and there are occasions where the possibilities and practicalities of a distinct video aesthetic arise.

Produced by Stephen King of Wilmslow, Cheshire, *Hong Kong* was shot using a U-Matic camera, the JVC KY1900, and a Sony 4800S recorder. King chose to shoot *Hong Kong* on the U-Matic format, stating that his reason for selecting the format was because it "had the advantages of quality reproduction, ease of editing and adding soundtrack" (Rose 1983, 80). Unlike other prize winners, King had no previous history of involvement in the amateur cine movement or participation in a regional club. He had worked as a professional still photographer, and at the time of the competition had been in advertising for "a number of years" (80). As a result of being involved in professional photography, it was reported in *Movie Maker* that King had become increasingly interested in moviemaking (78). Having previously planned a trip to the Far East, King had thought that *Hong Kong* would make an "interesting topic" for a documentary-type production (78).

Discussing King's entry, *Movie Maker* reported that he found it "essential to plan his shooting schedule in advance," so that no time was wasted in Hong Kong, indicating the considerable planning and energy put into production (Rose 1983, 78). King also researched the culture thoroughly, which helped him to select shots before going (78). Upon returning from the holiday, King cataloged all his shots, which amounted to two and a half hours of material, and began editing on a JVC editing suite (78). Having completed most of the work and organization prior to shooting, King stated that the tape came together with only a few corrections being necessary (78). This editing efficiency was a consequence of the nonlinear editing offered by the professional JVC suite. Nonlinear editing was a significant move away from traditional analog methods and, importantly, allowed a nondestructive editing process on original source material.

In discussing the movie, King said that he was quite pleased with the "way the tape turned out" and producing it had taught him extensively about location shooting (Rose 1983, 78). After entering *Hong Kong* in the competition, several commercial sponsors contacted King wanting to use the video for marketing. He and *Hong Kong* remain an "anomaly" in light of this "commercial interest," with a distinction between his work and that of the cine-clubs. His professional identity and employment in professional photography evidently sets King apart from the "amateur/professional distinction" inherent in cine-clubs and other enthusiasts of the time. The commercial interest in his film then indicates differing motivations and self-identification with a "perceived" moviemaking community (78).

The movie starts with a video title; in an exotic font, the words "Hong Kong" are repeated vertically in six rows as the camera pulls away. A slow panning shot from right to left of Hong Kong's skyline begins. The movie commentary, read by the producer's wife, describes the skyline: "Hong Kong's famous skyline hardly needs any introduction to the world at large, it symbolizes the wealth of a western way of life mixed with the mystery and excitement of the far-east" (*Hong Kong* 1982). This opening shot and commentary set one of the film's main themes and problematize Hong Kong as a stereotypical, cultural, and economic meeting point of East and West. It is a theme that is reiterated throughout the rest of the documentary. Cutting to a medium shot of a traditional Chinese junk vessel sailing down the harbor channel, the camera follows the boat through the water as other vehicles cross in and out of the picture at varying speeds and rhythms. "This first classic view of the waterfront shows the contrast between modern life and the traditional Chinese way of live on the junk. The theme of the old and new, which is repeated time and time again in Hong Kong. The junks move in and out amongst hydrofoils, cargo ships, speedboats and yachts in this one of the world's busiest channels" (*Hong Kong* 1982).

Emphasis is then turned to a boat journeying toward Hong Kong island with the scene being shot from the vessel. The stationary shot from the boat captures the rhythm of the water, as the camera is transported into the city. The video then moves to night shots of different cooking stalls. This section features one of the most interesting and unexpected visual "effects" with the lights of the cooking stalls creating an intensive reddening of the image. After discussing the food, we are taken to the neon-filled night scenes of the city: "At night the signs are illuminated and light up the city in a blaze of color. Some are very intricate and artistic, all are advertising their goods or services" (*Hong Kong* 1982).

Hong Kong finishes with a section on the floating Jumbo restaurant: a culinary house with its own jetty. The camera, once again, takes the trip across the jetty before closing on a symmetrical and balanced shot of the restaurant from across the water. With this shot and narration, the video entry ends. In this summarizing comment, the relationship Nicholson outlines in earlier amateur travel films between tourism, memory, and image is visible, beside the evident "promotional" intent of the production commentary: "Hong Kong: a most memorable experience and this is just one of the many treasured memories that you will take home with you. There is no other place like it in the world and we hope you have a good holiday" (*Hong Kong* 1982).

Hong Kong resonates with the 1925 to 1950 material that Nicholson examined (2009) in the North West Film Archive and Yorkshire Film Archive, characterized by an excess of continuity with traditional amateur travel representations. Consequently, this video entry is only pioneering in its use of new equipment, rather than creating a novel viewing experience. Prior conventions of the travel film can be viewed quite clearly in the imposition of narrative structure onto *Hong Kong*. Nicholson, when discussing the holiday film, writes of how there are varying degrees of narrative, with a common feature being the inclusion of the start and end of a journey: "Not surprisingly, holiday films involving a journey often start and finish their narratives with scenes of departure and arrival . . . the tendency to include opening scenes of half-packed bags, leaving the house, and even details of the journey to a destination, indicate more considered attempts to structure narrative" (2009, 93).

While King and his wife do not feature in *Hong Kong*, and there are no scenes of departure and arrival, the content of the video is excessively structured. By mimicking the journey into Hong Kong, a tourist perspective is constructed and presented as an experiential window, eliciting the perspective or gaze of being there. The linear temporality of *Hong Kong* also assists in creating an experience of day and night. *Hong Kong's* "visual journey" can all be considered effects of King's imposition of structure onto the footage. This element of storytelling indicates King's comprehensive understanding of the aesthetics associated with narrative structure and form. With his knowledge of still photography and a career in advertising, it is easy to conclude that King would be visually literate with these types of motifs. The narrative structure of *Hong Kong*, along with King's extensive planning and preproduction, position it within the kind of serious practice associated with earlier forms of amateur travel, as recognized by Nicholson (2009). She identifies how British amateur travel films (from 1925 to 1950) demonstrated advanced formal characteristics and narratives despite being "home movies" (93–127). *Hong Kong* continues this combination of advanced form, narrative, and "serious leisure," used to distinguish the much earlier filmic practice (Stebbins 1977, 582–606).

The inclusion of particular journeys, such as the harbor and Jumbo ride, add an ellipsis to the narrative that is in keeping with the technical ability of older amateur travel material. *Movie Maker*, when discussing the entry, reported that: "*Hong Kong* has the look of a glossy commercial but it's given a touch of the amateur (not amateurish) informality by the commentary which is spoken with infectious enthusiasm by the producer's wife. Quite a model, this, for all makers of holiday travelogues" (Rose 1983, 81). The near professional quality of the movie would appear to be bound up in the exhibition intention of the entry. The absence of the couple from their own holiday film is also connected to this facet: its intended function as promotional material. This entry is not a family holiday film, but a well-executed and consciously planned attempt at a travel documentary.

Production notes from the movie hint at significant practical difficulties concerning the weight of the U-Matic equipment. Humor is even made of the fact, with it stated in Rose's introduction that King should get an award for "just" carrying the equipment. It is evident that issues of weight and bulk still plagued early video technology, even for creatives with serious intent. Particular aesthetics of video technology do begin to benefit the image, such as the excessive burning of red and green color sections. This adds illumination to the evening shots of Hong Kong's neon signs, tantalizing the viewer in the latter part of the movie: "The picture quality is superb throughout, notably in some glowing night scenes" (Rose 1983, 81). However, aside from aesthetic benefits, *Hong Kong* features representations that, though praised in *Movie Maker*, are inherently problematic: "*Hong Kong*, of course, is the documentary and an excellent one of its kind. Colourful, entertaining and non-controversial, it tells us what the inquisitive tourist, rather than the political student would want to know" (Rose 1983, 81).

Congratulated for its apolitical tone, the assumption by the competition judges is that *Hong Kong* succeeds because of its apparent neutrality. However, in its theme of the "inquisitive tourist" the movie avoids issues of social inequality, overhousing, nationality, and colonialism. In positioning the video toward promotion and tourism, it follows a well-tread colonial path and gaze. Fallacies surrounding the exoticism and mystery of the East are as intrinsically controversial as the "political student." The colony's political and social issues are sidetracked in keeping with the promotional and exhibition agenda of the film.

Hong Kong and the travel genre it represents stay well within the realms of previous cine production, exhibiting formal and aesthetics traits familiar to 8 mm versions of the entry. Local detail and reporting are the focus of the movie, with the material providing significant historical description and explanation of expansive local phenomenon. *Hong Kong* does reiterate a series of ideological issues, however, regarding colonialism, nationality, and representation, which ironically allow it to establish continuity with previous filmic forms of the genre. *Hong Kong*'s tone, while informative, subjugates the very buildings, people, and items it tries to represent. Combined with its commercial aspects, the video unfortunately parallels Nicholson's argument about holiday films fifty years prior: "Such material may subsequently provide a wealth of socio-cultural, economic and historical 'evidence,' albeit mediated through the organising optics of the cinematic gaze, and the always inherently politicised process of representing other localities and lifestyles" (2009, 94).

Hong Kong while successful in both "amateur" and "professional" terms, still carried elements of the Eurocentric, conservative, and wealthy past from which such leisure activities emerge. While *Hong Kong* represents the professional emulation that certain amateurs aspired to, the next entry indicates something of the opposite: an "authentic" expression of locality.

Civic Week: Posterity and Local Custom

Civic Week charts a local event, also titled "Civic Week," in the small Northern Irish town of Ballyclare, Country Antrim. It is arguable that *Civic Week*, while made on video equipment, is a continuation of the amateur posterity production form. Its content and style echo John Grierson's 1949 appeal to amateur moviemakers in *Amateur Cine World*, for a civic form of amateurism: "This is a challenge to all of you as local citizens. General information from a national point of view does not fill gaps. It is up to the local amateur cinematographer to play his part and provide a local information service. You have great power in your hands" (Grierson in Malthouse 1949, 151).

Similar in form to earlier amateur films documenting public celebrations, *Civic Week* is concerned primarily with the recording of the community unmediated. It was produced by Archie Reid, a senior teacher who had been making amateur films since university (Rose 1983, 80). Having worked on 16 mm, standard, and Super8 mm, video was a natural continuation of already established leisure patterns. Reid was well known within the amateur scene, being the winner of three "Ten Best" cine trophies, with *Journey into Russia* (1969), *Inherit the Earth* (1969), and *Other Days around Me* (1973). These cine competitions were a template for the later "Ten Best" video competition. In addition to local competitions, Reid was also successful in international competitions (Rose 1983, 80). He was made a fellow of the Institute of Amateur Cinematography (IAC) in 1981 and had written for a variety of the amateur publications, such as *Movie Maker, Film Making* and *Amateur Film Maker*. In contrast to King, Reid was an already involved member of the cine movement prior to entering the competition. He started using video technology in 1982 for educational purposes in his school: "In many ways it's like starting with 8 mm all over again, inventing ways to lift off, and replace sound, remembering to fill the frames with close-ups, cutting on action" (Rose 1983, 80).

Civic Week was shot on a Panasonic 3030 camera and edited on a Panasonic 3000 and 7000 recorder. This was, as Rose says when introducing *Civic Week*, "strictly amateur equipment" and quite different in quality from the industrial and commercial format of U-Matic. Footage from over forty events was shot during one week in Ballyclare. The final edit was an attempt to create a collage of images, colors, and sounds to represent the "full week in a few minutes" (Rose 1983, 80). One of the problems, noted by Reid, in using domestic video for editing is that the method he uses (source material copied from one recorder input to another master recorder) loses quality due to the duplication process: "With 8 mm it was fighting the quality loss as the pictures are enlarged, with video as they are copied. I enjoy the ability to watch the effects on the screen as I cut, but find tape is as vulnerable as film. One slip of the finger and instead of wiping sound to dub in commentary—the precious original picture can be erased" (Rose 1983, 80). Unlike the nonlinear editing enabled by the U-Matic equipment in *Hong Kong*, Reid had to edit the *Civic Week* footage in a linear fashion from one recorder playing the source material to a master tape being recorded on another device. There were significant differences in the possibilities offered by just "strictly" amateur editing equipment.

The video begins with an emblem of Ballyclare Civic Week, with the logo *"Industria et Probitate,"* Latin for "By Work and Integrity," the motto of this Irish community. A voice-over from Reid then begins while we see images of a marching band: "To the rest of the world Ulster may seem a place of violence and bitterness but to those of us that live here there is another image. These are the people of one small community coming together to enjoy themselves in a week in May. These are the images and sounds of Civic Week in Ballyclare" (*Civic Week* 1982). The movie focuses on people of varying ages enjoying themselves. Much of the pleasure of the film comes from the footage's unmediated quality, giving the viewer a sense of intimate access to this event and community. Shots of the motorcycle racing event, which run through the film, act as a point of connection in the video entry.

Later scenes focus on dancing, a daycare center for young babies, elderly couples singing, and fancy dress. Several games are also filmed, such as musical chairs. *Civic Week* ends with a closing commentary from Reid where he says: "For seven days in May one Ulster community has found time to remember the happier things in life" (*Civic Week* 1982). The film presents an intimate "inside" view of Ballyclare, while also preserving the event for national memory. It represents the kind of civic amateurism Grierson discusses, and in doing so integrates the diffusion of truly amateur video equipment alongside the formal and civic discourses of prior cine practice (Grierson in Malthouse 1949, 151).

Civic Week, while well received, faced criticism from one competition judge for its quick succession of shots: "Bernard Ashby, the professional film editor on our panel, said that many of the shots were just a bit too short for his taste" (Rose 1983, 82). The quick pace of the shots is one of *Civic Week*'s strengths and provides the viewer with an immersive experience of the event that feeds into the civic discourses of the production. The "vividness and freshness" offered by the amateur cinematographer in 1949 is no different to the qualities that *Civic Week* presents with its accelerated editing: "So it was not surprising that those early films should have been vivid and sincere, even though they might have lacked the glossy veneer of later productions" (Malthouse 1948, 502). Compared to *Hong Kong*, *Civic Week* certainly lacks the glossy commercial aesthetic of King's production, but its emphasis as a local record with its own visual style of fast editing, quick close-ups, an excess of coverage, nonnarrative, and simplicity attribute it with both value and historical continuity. *Movie Maker* described it in similarly positive tones: "A brisk no-nonsense record of a local event, made with all the pace and 'attack' that we've long associated with Archie Reid's films. The change to tape has certainly not affected his style" (Rose 1983, 82).

Civic Week, like *Hong Kong*, stays within a familiar amateur tradition of recording and preserving local customs, events, and community but lacks the professional emulation of *Hong Kong*. Considering intended functions and exhibition circumstances however, such differences are evidently related to these divergent aims. *Hong Kong* is promotional and *Civic Week* is a local record. In spite of divergent aims, both winning entries present familiar amateur forms, continuing the travelogue and posterity production genres rather than departing from them.

Contrary to some of the concern reported at the start of this chapter around the demise of amateur cine practice, video's integration into already established patterns of cine production was relatively unproblematic (Mee 1982, 3). Certain issues are highlighted by the selection of two nonfictional documentaries. First, at this point in time only industrial and commercial equipment such as the U-Matic was offering nonlinear editing. The advantages of this can be seen in *Hong Kong*'s editing, which was completed on JVC suites achieving professional results. Linear editing was not an unsurpassable obstacle however, and Reid evidences efficient use of the duplication method. Regardless of this, linear editing was visibly of a much poorer quality, and the difference in U-Matic and VHS formats is evident. The second issue is production time. While preproduction was generally the same as if using film, shooting schedules on video were significantly shorter, with some of the entries being shot in three to five days. The cost of one entry on film (16 mm), at £2000, also indexes the economic and cost benefits of early video. On a practical level, the benefits of video can also be viewed in terms of performance. With the ability to instantly play back, actors are capable of honing and refining performances for the first time in amateur productions, as opposed to waiting for rushes, or film processing, which could take days. This kind of advantage is demonstrated well in the winning fictional short of the competition, *One of Them Picture Things* by Peter Wilson, in which the acting is significantly enhanced by the ability to instantly rewatch performances from actors (Rose 1983, 80). *Movie Maker* would go onto emphasize in its afterthoughts that four out of the five winners had learned their craft on film but was less than sympathetic to the runners-up: "It would perhaps be merciful not to dwell on these tapes that didn't make the grade" (Rose 1983, 82–83).

In conclusion, the *Movie Maker* video competition was innovative in UK moving-image history, but notions of it being truly pioneering are dampened by its adherence to the conventions of previous amateur film production codes. Certain discourses and voices criticizing the then video equipment's picture quality and weight are most likely confirmed by the competition, especially if one looks at the qualitative difference between U-Matic, Beta, and VHS entries. The competition entries do overcome these difficulties, and if editing is used as an example, in very ingenious ways. The winning video entries, then, promote the ideas present in Rose's introductory speech emphasizing that content was far more significant than medium in the evaluation of amateur texts. The competition does showcase the possibilities of video for the amateur movement, indicating that similar results are more than possible with equipment that, like earlier postwar equipment, had been considered "substandard." A host of interesting aesthetic effects emerges from the video entries, but the reporting of these nuances, such as the "burning" of colors in the night scenes of *Hong Kong*, are considered mistakes, as opposed to new creative effects.

In contrast to comments at the start of this article, video would not cause the demise of the UK cine movement, and, as is evidenced by the competition, it was supplementing already existent amateur film forms and practices rather than supplanting it. While video had caused initial fear and anxiety, particularly in the threat it posed to more conservative historical notions of amateur filmmaking, much of the technologies' dissemination into amateur spheres saw it retain strikingly similar form, genre, and aesthetics. In this sense the introduction of a new technology did not significantly alter the cultural and social shape of Western bourgeois amateur filmmaking, but provided instead new expressive possibilities that were soon taken up by "inquisitive tourists" and enthusiasts of the "happier things in life."

References

"Cine a £15 million-a-year UK Market." 1982. *Amateur Film Maker* 4:14.
Civic Week. 1982. Directed by Archie Reid. NI, VHS.
Cleave, Alan. "Comment." 1983. *Movie Maker* 21:61.
Hong Kong. 1982. Directed by Stephen King. UK, U-Matic.
Harris, Raymond. 1977. "Comment." *The British Kinematograph Sound and Television Society Journal* 59:77.

Hetrick, Judi. 2001. "Amateur Video Must Not Be Overlooked." *The Moving Image: The Journal of the Association of Moving Image Archivists* 6:66–81.

Malthouse, Gordon. 1948. "Grierson on Amateur Filmmaking." *Amateur Cine World* 3:502–7.

———. 1949. "John Grierson Discusses the A.C.W. 'Commended' Films." *Amateur Cine World* 13:150–53.

———. 1989. "Three of the Best." *Amateur Film Maker* 4:33.

Martin, Jeff. 2005. "The Dawn of Tape: Transmission Device as Preservation Medium." *The Moving Image: The Journal of the Association of Moving Image Archivists* 5:45–66.

Mee, Gerald. 1982. "Let the Jubilation Commence." *Amateur Film Maker* 4:3.

The Movie Maker Ten Best Video Competition. 1983. "Introduction to the competition." Tony Rose. UK, Betamax.

Nicholson, Heather Norris. 2009. "Holiday Recording and Britain's Amateur Film Movement." In *Home Movies on Home Ground*, edited by Ian Craven, 93–127. London: Cambridge Scholars.

Rose, Tony. 1982. "Movie Maker's New Video Contest." *Movie Maker* 16:248–49.

———. 1983. "I Give You a Toast to the Pioneers!" *Movie Maker* 17:78–83.

Stebbins, Robert. 1977. "The Amateur: Two Sociological Definitions." *Pacific Sociological Review* 20:582–606.

"Video." 1980. *Film Making* 18:49.

"Video Take Over." 1979. *Amateur Film Maker* 1:16.

Watson, Ivan. 1982. "There's Still Plenty of Gold in "Them Hills." *Movie Maker* 16:282.

———. 1984. "8mm Video: Has Kodak Backed the Wrong House?" *Amateur Film Maker* 7:7–8.

GRAEME R. SPURR works at London College of Fashion, University of the Arts London.

4

FROM INSIDERS TO OUTSIDERS

Tracing Amateurism in Chinese Independent Documentary of the 1990s and the 2000s

Margherita Viviani

THE POPULARITY OF AMATEUR DOCUMENTARIES IN CHINA IS related to the flood of digital video (DV) that swept over the country at the end of 1990s.[1] In this chapter, I offer an account of the emergence of amateurism in Chinese independent documentaries, looking in particular at the legacy of those early 1990s professional or semiprofessional documentary pioneers who introduced a new "amateur attitude" into Chinese independent documentary cinema. It was this group who first saw the opportunities offered by digital technology and created a parallel system of filmmaking with its own forms of production and film style. After providing the context of this era of filmmaking, we will turn to the career of Wu Wenguang. His professional-turned-amateur film and video activity became a model for independent filmmakers, greatly informing the vibrant amateur documentary scene that is such a prominent feature of present-day Chinese cinema.

Academics and filmmakers generally use the term *independent* (*duli*) rather than *amateur* (*yeyu*) to refer to unofficial documentaries in China. Before the arrival of digital cameras, feature and nonfeature films were produced by a few central production companies and directly supervised by organs of the party-state; in this sense, *independent* generally refers to those documentary films produced and screened outside television and film institutions, with the implication that they did not follow the party-state line nor the mainstream media rules (in a country where media censorship, including the internet, is still extremely active and pervasive). Later, in the 2000s, the preferred term for such documentaries became *minjian* (*popular or grassroots*) (Deprez and Pernin 2015, 8), which tacitly detached style from the political connotations of "independent" and also indicated stronger interest in the means of production introduced by new technology: these films could be shot by anyone, screened more easily (not needing cumbersome exhibition technology), shared through online platforms, and, finally, used as a tool for social activism. However we label these documentaries, most of them share the following characteristics: they are made by filmmakers or camerapersons who do not operate within a professional capacity (regardless of whether they have professional associations or education in film); thematically, these films are concerned with changes in Chinese society, with a focus on marginalized groups or forgotten histories; these films are not intended to make a profit; due to the nature of their production and distribution, they are not submitted to the state for censorship and are therefore exhibited in noncommercial and unofficial venues; and, lastly, the films are marked by what I call an "outsider quality" (shaky cameras, minimal editing, long running-time, lack of voice-over or theme music, etc.) that distinguishes them from the documentaries aired on television (which rely on more standardized stylistic norms).

Bearing these qualities in mind, and thinking, too, about how amateurism as a technological or aesthetic mode is defined differently depending on context (era, culture, nation) (Zimmermann 1995, 55), these independently produced, popular documentaries are taxonomically recognizable as the products of an amateur film structure—an outsider structure that provides entrance to filmmakers who are willing to operate independently of the state or market. Usually when amateur practices are recognized by academic research, they are connected to the rise of individuality and the new culture of self-expression in China, and thus linked to the emergence of public citizenship—a theme to which we shall return at the end of this chapter.[2] However, the material history of DV amateur documentary with its recent socially engaged mode did not arise programmatically from the heads of like-minded individuals, but instead came out of important changes in the economic and technological context in which Chinese media has operated since the dawn of economic reforms and liberalization. In the next section I will look at the early development of Chinese documentary cinema and its bearing on the evolution of outsider documentary-making.

The Rise of the "Independent Documentary" Filmmakers: From Professional to Amateur

With the launch of the socialist market economy in 1992, China witnessed a great acceleration of the economic and social transformations that were first initiated in 1978. Decisions about what to produce increasingly depended on what would garner a large share of the TV audience, and the quota of imported films from outside of China was also gradually raised: the endogenous Chinese media slowly established itself as a self-sufficient enterprise in competition with enormously popular Western products. In the mid-1990s, Chinese Central Television (CCTV)—founded in 1978—adopted a producer responsibility system, permitting program producers to recruit their own crew, outsource projects to freelance filmmakers, and manage their own budgets. This encouraged film professionals to achieve new goals and standards; it stimulated technical advances in filmmaking and the decentralization of the control on documentary films. CCTV also invested in new technologies, such as the electronic news-gathering camera invented in 1986 (Chu 2007, 90); such technology allowed for easy outdoor shoots, less rehearsal time, and less reliance on scripts. Thus, Chinese documentarians were suddenly able to experiment in ways quite unlike earlier propaganda films and studio products, both of which informed traditional documentary filmmaking.

Documentary cinema continued to serve the state's political ideology; however, in time, the ideological influence on the content became less evident. The key word for content became *ordinary* (*pingmin*) that is, the life and problems of normal, ordinary people. These developments and changes in Chinese television proved to be extremely influential in the emergence of an independent amateur film culture. Documentaries were featured in programs hosted in a television studio, often in the presence of an audience and filmmakers. These programs anticipated new possibilities of film produced independently outside the work units[3] of the state-owned and state-controlled television system.

The interest in amateur documentaries coincided with radical changes in Chinese society, as the socialist market reforms made the Chinese economy boom. With rapid economic development and industrialization, a new inequality manifested itself in multiple dimensions—regional, class, and gender—and the social problems it gave rise to (such as mass displacement, poverty, lack of education, and poor living conditions) caught the attention

Fig. 4.1. TV professionals shooting independent documentaries. Photograph by author.

of photographers, filmmakers, and artists who began documenting this changing society, often outside of official institutions. Among them was a group of professional and semiprofessional filmmakers who, in the early 1990s, started producing documentary films with private funds, outside the reach of CCTV and other television stations. Instead of educational or professional values, what was important to this group was a love of improvisation, independence, marginal and self-selected subjects, and defiance of the production values inherent to mainstream film. These documentary films are referred to as the "new documentary movement" (*xin jilupian yundong*) or "independent documentary" (*duli jilupian*).

Independent (*duli*) signifies films made outside both the control of official organs of ideology and the state as well as outside the control of the market. The distance from the government meant that there was no formal distribution of their work and no submission to any formal censorship process.[4] The nonprofit status meant that these documentaries were not commercial vehicles, even if they were sometimes entered into the overseas documentary festival circuit. These documentaries were mostly unknown

Fig. 4.2. Caochangdi Workstation during an interval of documentary screening. Photograph by author.

to the general public, as they were neither aired on television nor widely distributed, and their domestic circulation was limited to film students, circles of intellectuals and friends, and others who were invited to screenings in private venues, a sort of "dining room theatre".[5]

The main focus of these Chinese independent documentaries was on the "other" in contemporary China, the "weaker" or "disadvantaged" social groups (*ruoshi qunti*) who were bearing the costs of rapid industrialization and urbanization. Filmmakers explored the life of the rural population migrating to metropolitan areas to find more highly remunerated employment (*liudong renkou*, or "floating population"), like the young maids moving to Beijing featured in Li Hong's award-winning documentary *Out of Phoenix Bridge* (1997). They also touched on the controversial issue of the status of minority nationalities (often residing in remote and poor regions of western China), like the Tibetan community portrayed in Duan Jinchuan's *No. 16 Barkhor South Street* (1996), or the topic of elderly people coping with the rapid economic and social change, as depicted in Yang Lina's *Old Men* (1999).

Independent documentaries refused to be overtly didactic. Most notably, this meant purging the films of the voice-over, that omniscient presence that organizes spectator response in the standard TV documentary film. The function of the voice-over is not only to impose a value framework on the content but also to explain the context and the central actions, thus creating continuity and unity as well as point of view. The disappearance of the voice-over dislocated documentary's strongest mediating device, allowing viewers alone to confront the images shot and edited by the filmmakers. In similar fashion, extra-diegetic music (added music soundtrack) that cues the viewer into the emotional tone of documentary sequences is replaced with silence or diegetic sound. In doing away with the superstructure of production values and voice-over, documentarians offered contradictions on screen without directly commenting on them, thereby creating a space for a more active and autonomous spectatorship. They defined their independence as separate from not only party-state discourse but through the independence of interpretation elicited in the audience. The films generally favored long shots, with handheld cameras, interspersed with close-ups of bodies and landscapes. The techniques and content of these films are clearly marked by an interest in documentary films made outside of China: the Chinese "on the spot realism" (*jishizhuyi*) style is heavily influenced by cinéma vérité's stylistic tags, such as long shots, the absence of voice-over, and minimal editing.

However, given these influences and the training of the documentary filmmakers, it is evident that the concept of amateur must be extended to include their activities. Filmmaking technology, even of the analog video variety, was far too expensive for an average private individual to own and too complex for the untrained to operate. To shoot a documentary, one therefore had to borrow equipment and have access to cameras and editing suites, which required having direct access to or contacts inside the television system (Robinson 2013, 20). Moreover, using cumbersome and heavy equipment in public places would have attracted questioning by the authorities, unless the filmmaker was working inside the system. As a result, predigital filmmakers were mainly TV professionals—even if their amateur film works were dramatically different in terms of shooting style, editing, distribution, exhibition, and treatment of the subjects on screen from what they produced in their day jobs as insiders of the system—following the urge to document the tremendous changes that Chinese society was undergoing. These filmmakers were working autonomously, outside the professional model of investment, production, distribution, and consumption, as well as from political ties of any kind. They were insiders making film on the outside, blurring the boundary between what we usually think of as amateur and professional.

Free from ideological pressure and commercial values, these insiders showed that the independent amateur shouldn't be defined against the state-run professional film culture but rather should be viewed as a distinct, more free, and individual realm of film culture. Amateur filmmaking in China emerged, then, from the party-state media it was ideally distancing itself from, as insiders with positions and training in the mainstream television model used their professional tools and knowledge to make amateur films. However, this porosity between professional and amateur soon evolved and changed with the advent of digital technology.

The Digital Video Documentary

At the end of the 1990s, digital cameras entered the Chinese market and were immediately adopted as a cheap substitute for the expensive and cumbersome analog camera. Filmmaker Wu Wenguang (2002) has a concise take on this transformation:

> Digital video cameras swiftly became a cheap, portable, convenient tool requiring only one person to operate. They could also be connected to a personal computer, which only requires a video capture card to become a video editing workstation. . . . Since 1998, numerous individuals have shot work using these small machines. From 1999 to 2000, the number of DV works boomed. In addition to professionals, a wide range of people was involved, including visual artists, company employees and students. The works they produced included documentaries, experimental short films, dramas and various shorts which are hard to define at present. (135)

The introduction of digital technology into documentary-making brought about two important changes. First, digital documentary-making escaped administrative control and regulation at the production level because the camera was a personal, portable tool that didn't belong to a professional work unit, as was the case with first generation, or predigital, independent documentary films. Second, digital recording proved to be a powerful tool of self-expression, as its built-in mobility allowed it to record reality as it unfolded around the cameraperson, offering a seemingly less mediated vision of Chinese society. It increased the choice of subjects, since filmmaking did not require elaborate setup and the camera could be operated without the attention of those on which it was directed. At the same time, it was able to produce technologically accomplished results that could be either easily shown to audiences or downloaded. The digital camera blurred the line between professional and amateur production values, allowing a greater degree of independence than with analog technology. Similarly, given its relatively low cost, digital film also made the filmmaker more independent economically, significantly cutting down on production costs. Digital technology allowed anyone, including the amateur, to offer their own perspective on society, and it directed collective attention to the detailed modes of life experienced by marginalized social groups.

The second, or digital, generation's claims to truth are symbolized by the statement "my camera doesn't lie,"[6] which aims to debunk institutionalized filmmaking and stress individual experience of and adherence to reality against the supposed lies of a mainstream media in the service of official ideology (Wang 2005, 23). Given the mobility allowed by their equipment, independent filmmakers were more likely to look for opportunities to portray aspects of society not shown elsewhere, rather than explicitly debate the negative sides of the party-state system. In other words, they didn't question the government-supervised limitations to the circulation of information but opted instead to test the boundaries of the limitations, which is known in Chinese as "playing edge ball" (*da cabianqiu*) (Stern and O'Brien 2012). Moreover, TV stations, cinema, and other information network organizations must have the contents of digital video censored before screening. Therefore, censorship affects the distribution, but not the production, of digital-video works, which includes feature films. Since there was virtually no official domestic distribution of these digital documentary videos, they simply did not undergo the censorship machine—in the government's eyes, the films lingered in a sort of limbo of semihome-video production.[7] As long as films were confined to private viewing or to the small circuit of the independent community and overseas screenings, they did not incur any major problems.

Contrary to the first generation of independent documentaries, amateur digital documentaries started circulating in very small, unofficial film-festival circuits and public screenings.[8] These screenings were facilitated by changes in exhibition technology: a cheap LCD projector now allowed people to organize screenings in cafeterias or bookshops, providing small "theatrical spaces" for independent feature and nonfeature films (Gao 2015, 170). These newly emergent venues were therefore independent too, since the screenings were exempt from the state's governing mechanism of censorship, as discussed earlier.

Amateur documentaries showed class, gender, and ethnicity in ways that deviated from the official narrative. The variety of filmed subjects was a natural development and continuation of the first phase of the new documentary movement, as easy-to-use digital cameras gave filmmakers the possibility to immerse themselves, at little cost in terms of equipment, in various social situations and to edit their films at home. They made a virtue out of technological limitations by locating realism (rough footage, minimal editing, etc.) at the center of their aesthetic approach. These films were made to create a visual archive of nonofficial popular culture for the future.

This archive relies heavily on new modes of digital circulation and consumption such as internet and wireless broadband mobile phones, DV websites,[9] blogging, and online video platforms (such as *Tudou.com* or *Youkou. com*, along with *YouTube* and *Vimeo*), which have had a strong influence on the independent filmmaking scene. However, Chinese documentaries are not supported by any independent distribution system, and filmmakers themselves generally choose to concentrate on production rather than on distribution and exhibition. My impression, after attending several independent film festivals in China and personally spending time with documentary makers, is that independent documentarians do not seem particularly interested in reaching an audience wider than the attendees at small venues and underground film festivals. One possible explanation for this would be that the documentary films have an intrinsically amateur attitude: they are not meant to be commercialized or used to enter a film career but rather to document and express oneself, just like if it was a private or home video.[10]

Twenty-first-century independent documentary filmmakers operate, then, in a media environment that allows them to exert a stronger amateur identity than filmmakers in the 1990s. The first generation of independent documentary filmmakers was mostly composed of media professionals who decided to become independent from the state media apparatus. The second generation of digital documentary makers consists of amateurs from all walks of life: poets, painters, students, clerks, and free entrepreneurs. They can be described as falling in between the enthusiast, who invests in technology and creates artistic finished products, and the everyday user, who owns relatively inexpensive technology and does not plan or edit their films (Buckingham, Pini, and Willett 2007, 190). The first generation of documentary filmmakers, with their cinéma verité credo, their early adaptation of new, cheaper technologies, and their choice of marginalized social types as documentary subjects, paved the way for the rise of the amateur video makers, both in terms of style, content, and creating spaces of exchange. I conclude this chapter with an example of this legacy: the most prominent figure of independent and amateur documentary in China.

Wu Wenguang: From Indie Documentary Maker to Amateur Video Curator

Wu Wenguang, one of the most famous Chinese independent documentary filmmakers, shot his first documentary while working inside the system of the CCTV. *Bumming in Beijing: The Last Dreamers* (*Liulang Beijing, Zuihou De Mengxiangzhe*, 1990) is a compilation of videotaped interviews and daily-life scenes of six disaffected artists and intellectuals much like Wu himself, who came to Beijing in search of fortune. Set in Beijing a few months after the Tiananmen crackdown, the documentary reveals their lives, their dreams, and their current situations. There is a complete lack of didacticism (going against the norm of TV documentaries at the time). Instead, there is a profound need to document what is happening around the filmmaker, even down to the most unpleasant details. The film has no voice-over or music, and a series of long shots communicate the deep alienation and depression that pervades the life of these artists. Even though Wu was a young TV worker back then, his documentary was deliberately conceived as an amateurish home video: Wu borrowed a cheap camera from work and self-taught himself to use the editing facilities at CCTV in order to show what would never be included in official media: the psychological effects of state oppression on the life of intellectual drifters. *Bumming in Beijing*'s raw quality and unscripted filmmaking process, together with its not-for-profit motivation, was quite unique in China at the time.

Fundamental references for the majority of independent documentary makers of the time, by their own admission, were Frederick Wiseman, with his direct cinema approach of fly-on-the-wall style and long takes, and Japanese documentarian Ogawa Shinsuke, who used to live among the subjects of his films to the point of becoming part of their lives—a feature Chinese documentarians rapidly adopted and have yet to abandon. Wu met both Wiseman and Ogawa, learned from their particular approaches to documentary filmmaking, and shared this knowledge upon his return to China.[11] The result is that both filmmakers, filtered through Wu's own work, have been highly influential in the development of the new wave of Chinese independent documentary films from the 1990s onward.

In 1999, Wu embraced digital technology for the first time to shoot *Life on the Road (Jiang Hu)*, a semiethnographic work about a performing-art troupe. Wu describes the shooting of *Life on the Road* as a casual and independent activity that moved him further toward a rougher, more spontaneous form of filmmaking. He was always hanging around the art troupe "carrying the camera like a pen" (Wu 2010, 53), something he could not have done before with heavy and conspicuous machines, which required elaborate set-up and inevitably affected the attitude of the subjects being filmed. Using a digital camcorder made him lose interest in making documentaries in the traditional sense, where an implicit narrative unifies the work; instead, he started videotaping the world around him, such as a friend's wedding, dinner with friends, or rock concerts. In his own words, "all kinds of people and things, entirely without theme, intention, or plot, crowd together onto the DV tapes. [This material] is part of my visual diary" (Wu 2010, 53).

Embracing the codes of amateur filmmaking (with its heightened proximity to the subject of the film, its dwelling on everyday dramaturgical occasions, from parties to concerts) is, for Wu, motivated by his privileging of authenticity and autonomy as hallmarks of a filmmaking aesthetic that is resolutely on the outside of the institutional film culture and system in which he was initially entrenched. *Jiang Hu* is not explicitly linked to any broader social agenda, even if, by the very act of using "amateurish" filmmaking as a path to one's own subjectivity, Wu is implicitly endorsing a certain position of individualism (Johnson 2006, 66). As Wu put it, "DV saved me," because it allowed him to be free from the rules and constriction of the party-state and the increasing marketization of the TV station (66). DV technology changed not only the way the documentary was recorded, edited, and distributed in China; it also changed the lives of many who embraced this technology as a tool of self-expression and individuality: DV "freed" the professionals and opened new possibilities to the nonprofessionals. It allowed Wu, together with other filmmakers of the time, the chance to "maintain a relationship with documentary making which is more than just a status" (66). In other words, he found an alternative to professionalism (*zhuanye*) in amateurism (*yeyu*).

This newly found freedom also gave Wu the chance to be increasingly involved in participatory and amateur projects as a curator and producer. This

Fig. 4.3. Stills from *China Village Documentary Project*, Caochangdi Workstation.
Photograph by author.

was made possible in part thanks to the opening of Wu's own documentary studio in 2005. The studio is based at Caochangdi Workstation (*Caochangdi gongzuozhan*), a Beijing independent nonprofit art space involving performance art, documentary film/video, and video art, founded by Wu himself and his partner, choreographer Wen Hui, and thanks to the help of public and private funders and organizers, both domestic and, especially, international.[12] Caochangdi quickly became a meeting, film screening, and discussion place for Chinese and international filmmakers, amateurs and scholars, and also the headquarters of important participatory video projects under Wu's supervision. In this way, Wu has encouraged and helped several digital filmmakers to pursue their own video works by creating a new institutional space for amateur film culture to develop in China.

One example is the *China Village Documentary Project*, which was launched in 2005 as part of a joint China-European Union-sponsored program. The project focused on village governance, and the villagers were asked to follow and record the village elections. Notwithstanding the novelty of Wu's participatory video project, the village documentary project is still very much an authorial work supervised and even edited by professional filmmakers. A more mature and well-organized spin-off of the village documentary project is the *Folk Memory Project* started in 2010, where Wu sent a group of young amateur filmmakers back to their villages to interview the elderly and collect data about those who died during the Great Famine, one of the most traumatic episodes in Chinese history.[13] The *Folk Memory Project*'s intention is to shed some light on China's past and reconcile the official history taught in school with the families' own histories and memories. Different from the other independent documentary makers, who normally work on their own as artists, the young filmmakers would return from their fieldwork to Caochangdi (where they lived and worked together) to transcribe interviews, post photos of village elders, upload excerpts and comments on the internet, and edit their documentaries. They usually exhibited their first versions to an engaged audience that consisted of fellow documentarians, graduate students (and sometimes foreign visitors)—and they received critiques in order to revise their work. Some of these films were invited to domestic and foreign exhibitions (Chiu and Zhang 2014, 199–200).

Wu encouraged them to work on their subjects using the expression "*qu Wu hua*" (literally, "getting rid of Wu"), with his surname "Wu" standing for the Chinese independent documentary professional tradition (Chiu and Zhang 2014, 199–200). By using this expression, it looks like Wu himself was trying to distance himself from his own so-called elitist and artistic work (where the main subjects were intellectuals and artists, like in *Bumming in Beijing*) to engage more closely with the lower strata of society, as shown in *Jiang Hu*. Yet, he also moved away from his role as the main filmmaker/director/artist/professional behind the camera to act instead as facilitator and supporter—both physical (with Caochangdi workspace and facilities) and intellectual (coordinating the project and advising the young amateur filmmakers) and in an institutional space for independent and amateur film culture. As Johnson (2014) points out, behind Wu's work with amateur filmmakers there are transnational forces generally overlooked by observers and researchers, such as funding organizations and nongovernmental organizations (NGOs), which are in fact shaping participatory and grassroots video projects in China. "Getting rid of Wu" can also be seen as distancing a part of Chinese independent filmmaking from the formula of direct-cinema style (with its minimal intrusion, long shots, very long running times, and focus on the marginalized) in favor of an aesthetic that is more transnational and socially engaged. Not by chance, participatory, activist, and more socially engaged documentaries seem to be a dominant trend among the Chinese independent film community (Viviani 2014, 107–8). Whatever the case may be, there is a legacy to the new amateur generation: independent filmmakers from the first generation, like Wu, are now supporting amateur digital-video making, and can also be, as in Wu's case, mentors for new socially engaged video projects.

Wu's career is only one of the many personal stories that can be recounted regarding the spread of amateur film culture in China since the 1990s. Yet, due to his reputation and his status (not only as a filmmaker but the creator of a hub of filmmakers), he embodies perfectly the development of amateur documentary making in China and its complex play of insider/outsider positions. The history of this film culture shows that it arose, first, from filmmakers who operated inside the system as TV professionals, which gave them the cultural references and connections to seize the moment with the arrival of digital technology. These first documentarians in the 1990s introduced an amateur aesthetic of production and style into China for the first time, where professionalism was identified with mainstream, censored, and commercialized television documentaries that were elaborately produced (i.e., traditional voice-over, music, and higher production values). In contrast, the hallmarks of amateurism included independent funding, narrative structures unified by an authorial ideology that nevertheless lacked an institutional core (they tended to be collages, video "diaries," and other examples of subjective cinema), and exhibition in noncommercial spaces like private homes, bookstores, and other small venues.

There is a strong tendency among amateur documentarians to sympathize with the freedom to express individuality rather than the highly centralized and politically driven media mainstream. It is against this background that we can identify the specificity of Chinese film amateurism through a group that consciously structured their work outside the professional core. Thus, it was not the filmmakers' identity (that is, a lack of any professional training or connections), but rather their film product and the lack of distribution through official channels that defined the amateurism of the first generation of independent filmmakers. However, as cheap digital-video technology became widely available in China, a second generation of independent filmmakers emerged. They were even more distant from professional film institutions, working autonomously as amateurs who identified with previous forms of independent documentary making while expanding the limits of digital filmmaking culture.

Mainstream media and the party-state can be seen as fundamental actors in the rise of amateur documentary cinema. I prefer to look at documentary as a social-technical network of individuals, technologies, and institutions, instead of considering independent documentary in conflict with the authority and the marketization of society. As a consequence, even with the advent of digital cameras, the amateur identity overlaps and is often intertwined with that of the professional, and so do the films, as we have seen with Wu's collective filmmaking projects—which are often financed by foreign institutions and NGOs and screened to larger audiences. The ambiguous and porous status between amateurism and professionalism (going back and forth from mainstream to independent, from "inside" to "outside") is unique and has allowed Chinese amateur documentaries to thrive today amid the post-socialist Chinese media environment.

Notes

1. Digital video (DV) is an inexpensive, high quality audio/visual format, where information is presented as a sequence of digital data, rather than in a continuous signal as analog information.

2. Amateurism is discussed in Jaffee 2006, Zhang 2006, and Yu 2017, 273.

3. Apart from employment, the *work unit* (*danwei*) in urban China also provided health care and free housing and schooling, therefore the work unit was not only where an individual worked during the period when the Chinese economy was still more heavily socialist, but it was also where he or she lived and belonged, creating a situation in which individuals depended on their work unit for almost anything.

4. There were a small number of full-time professional censors who reviewed the final cut of TV-commissioned documentary or investigative programs before they were broadcast or distributed. Even if a film produced by and for a TV network was rejected by censorship, it was simply not aired, and its maker usually incurred no further trouble.

5. A typical screening of Wu Wenguang's documentaries would include friends watching his film while he was cooking dinner for them in the kitchen (Gao 2015,170).

6. The implication of this statement is discussed in depth in Zhang (2006).

7. Unless filmmakers use bigger HD cameras or the shooting involves (very rarely) more than one person, even shooting in public zones can be regarded as amateur recording. However, the local authorities always keep an eye on filmmaking activity, and filmmakers occasionally experience confrontation or pressure from the police if the local authorities suspect they are filming something that might harm the image of local authorities or expose their wrongdoings.

8. In China, independent film festivals are advertised as a "film exchange week," so that organizers do not need to submit the films to the state prior to viewing, thus bypassing any

formal censorship. The government is generally tolerant of these informal public screenings, as they attract a relatively restricted crowd of festival goers, intellectuals, overseas academics, and so on. Nonetheless, independent festivals in some cases really "played edge ball," and lost, with the government: a few of them were shut down permanently.

9. Until 2012 there were several websites linked to independent film festivals and DV workspaces (Beijing Independent Documentary Festival and Caochangdi Workstation, for example), which acted as digital-video archives and forums. Sadly, in the last few years they have all been closed down.

10. Nonetheless, a few of them made their way to international film festivals, thanks to occasional foreign coproductions or interested scholars, entering a circuit of foreign university screenings. They consist, however, of a very small number of documentary films shot by professional and semiprofessional filmmakers who, similar to the first generation of independent filmmakers, consciously adopt an "amateur attitude."

11. Wu had the chance to work for Wiseman in the editing of one of Wiseman's documentaries, *Belfast, Maine*, during his stay at Wiseman's residence. He also met Ogawa in Japan in 1991 during a workshop at the Yamagata Independent Film Festival.

12. Among the international supporters there were Kampnagel (Germany), Zürcher Theater Spektakel (Switzerland), Borneoco (Netherlands), and Asian Culture Council (United States).

13. In China, the Great Famine (1959–1961) remains a taboo topic; official Chinese figures report that around fifteen million Chinese people died of starvation, while unofficial estimates are as high as forty million.

References

Buckingham, David, Maria Pini, and Rebekah Willett. 2007. "'Take Back the Tube!': The Discursive Construction of Amateur Film and Video Making." *Journal of Media Practice* 8 (2):183–201. https://10.1386/jmpr.8.2.183/1.
Chiu, Kuei-fen, and Yingjin Zhang. 2014. *New Chinese-Language Documentaries.* New York: Taylor and Francis.
Chu, Yingchi. 2007. *Chinese Documentary: From Dogma to Poliphony.* London: Routledge Media.
Deprez, Camille, and Judith Pernin. 2015. "Introduction." In *Post-1990 Documentaries: Reconfiguring Independence,* edited by Camille Deprez and Judith Pernin, 1–19. Edinburgh: Edinburgh University Press.
Gao, Dan. 2015. "Chinese Independent Cinema in the Age of Digital Distribution." In *DV-Made China: Digital Subjects and Social Transformations after Independent Film,* edited by Zhen Zhang and Angela Zito, 163–73. Honolulu: University of Hawai'i Press.
Jaffee, Valery. 2006. "The Ambivalent Cult of Amateur Art in New Chinese Documentaries." In *From Underground to Independent: Alternative Film Culture in Contemporary China,* edited by Paul Pickowicz and Yingjin Zhang, 77–108. Lanham, MD: Rowman and Littlefield.
Johnson, Matthew David. 2006. "Wu Wenguang and New Documentary Cinema's Politics of Independence." In *From Underground to Independent: Alternative Film Culture in*

Contemporary China, edited by Paul Pickowicz and Yingjin Zhang, 47–76. Lanham, MD: Rowman and Littlefield.

———. 2014. "Bringing the Transnational Back into Documentary Cinema: Wu Wenguang's China Village Documentary Project, Participatory Video and the NGO Aesthetic." In *China's iGeneration: Cinema and Moving Image Culture for the Twenty-First Century*, edited by Matthew D. Johnson, Keith B. Wagner, Kiki Tianqi Yu, and Luke Vulpiani, 255–98. London: Bloomsbury Academic.

Robinson, Luke. 2013. *Independent Chinese Documentary: From the Studio to the Street.* Basingstoke, UK: Palgrave Macmillan.

Stern, Rachel E., and Kevin J. O'Brian. 2012. "Politics at the Boundaries: Politics and the Chinese State." *Modern China* 38, no. 2 (March): 174–98. http://www.jstor.org/stable/23217439.

Viviani, Margherita. 2014. "Chinese Independent Documentary Films: Alternative Media, Public Spheres and the Emergence of the Citizen Activist." *Asian Studies Review* 38 (1):107–23. http://dx.doi.org/10.1080/10357823.2013.873016.

Wang, Yiman. 2005. "The Amateur's Lightning Rod: DV Documentary in Postsocialist China." *Film Quarterly* 58, no. 4 (Summer): 16–26. doi:10.1525/fq.2005.58.4.16.

Wu, Wenguang. 2002. "Just on the Road: A Description of the Individual Way of Recording Images in the 1990s." In *The First Guangzhou Triennial Reinterpretation: A Decade of Experimental Chinese Art (1990–2000)*, edited by Hung Wu, Huangsheng Wang, and Boyi Feng, 133–38. Chicago: Art Media Resources.

———. 2010. "Individual Filmmaking." In *The New Chinese Documentary Film Movement: For the Public Record*, edited by Chris Berry, Xinyu Lü, and Lisa Rofel, 49–54. Hong Kong: Hong Kong University.

Yu, Tianqi. 2017. "An Inward Gaze at Home: Amateur First Person DV Documentary in Twenty-First Century China." In *Amateur Filmmaking: The Home Movie, the Archive, the Web*, edited by Laura Rascaroli, Barry Monahan, and Gwenda Young, 271–87. New York: Bloomsbury.

Zhang, Yingjin. 2006. "My Camera Doesn't Lie? Truth, Subjectivity and Audience in Chinese Independent Film and Video." In *From Underground to Independent: Alternative Film Culture in Contemporary China*, edited by Paul Pickowicz and Yingjin Zhang, 23–45. Lanham, MD: Rowman and Littlefield.

Zimmermann, Patricia Rodden. 1995. *Reel Families: A Social History of Amateur Film.* Bloomington: Indiana University Press.

MARGHERITA VIVIANI is an independent scholar and translator.

PART II

INSTITUTIONS, INDUSTRY, AND THE STATE

5

SEEKING ADVICE

A Political Economy of
Israeli Commemorative Home Videos

Laliv Melamed

In 2010, the Office of Families and Commemoration (OFC), under the state of Israel's Ministry of Defense, published a booklet titled *Paths of Commemoration*. The booklet provides guidance for families of soldiers who have died during their military service, prompted by appeals to the office on behalf of families who were seeking ways to commemorate their loved ones. The resulting document is a product of "thorough research in which various private commemorative activities were reviewed, studied, mapped and catalogued" (Ministry of Defense 2010).[1] Among the activities offered to families is a "personal commemorative movie." Providing an initial definition of what such a work of media might be, the booklet's authors contend: "A personal movie tells [the spectators] about your loved one and yourselves—his family—through stills, videos, interviews with family and friends, and the documentation of memorial ceremonies" (ibid.). The authors, an anonymous and abstract voice of the state, then describe the process of production, listing film professionals that the family might want to consult with, accounting for distribution options, and providing a few cautious notes on costs and the challenging aspects of making a family movie.

The booklet provides a rare opportunity in which the family-made video is scrutinized by a state institution. It refers to video productions put together by Jewish-Israeli families to commemorate soldiers who died during the decades-long military conflict in the area.[2] These videos began surfacing on the Israeli media sphere as early as the 1990s when Israeli television networks started allocating special time slots during the National Memorial Day to allow families to broadcast their own personal commemorative projects. Thus, family-video productions done within the intimate sphere of the home became oddly tied to the institutions of media. Using the term *movies*, the booklet seems to imply the public resonance of these otherwise intimate forms. While this word choice is telling, throughout this chapter I will refer to them as *videos*, underlining both technological and ontological dimensions of domestic media practices.

Indeed, personal commemorative videos entail intricate formations in which the public (media) sphere and the private one entangle. They are initiated, funded, and produced—to a certain degree—by families, responding to the families' internal feeling of loss, and are part of the families' habitual media practices (Chun 2016). The videos are then circulated via television, a media institution tightly tied to the state. Yet, neither television nor any other state institution participated in the production, funding, or archiving of the videos. Their relation to larger operations of national security and national ideology is likewise obscured. While death is a consequence of military conflict, the videos themselves omit any violence—violence being embedded in military action and in the apparatuses of state ideology—and are focused instead on the intimacies of family life. This obscuring of occupation and colonial violence is true for families that, through other channels, publicly criticized the army or the government. Are these home productions a means for individuals to negotiate forms of power and resist a reality of constant crisis, or are these videos a tool that makes violence endurable?

In this chapter I rethink the relations between the state and the home video from the perspective of the state, asking how the state refers to a form of media production that is allegedly outside its regulation and control. On the surface, there is no reference: *Paths of Commemoration* was written after personal video memorials had already been being produced and circulated by families for almost two decades. Moreover, the booklet is not a policy statement but a sheet of information, a service provided to the citizen. The state's intervention is postured as advice, as merely surveying instruments for personal commemoration. Thinking the practice of the home video as an instrument to manage family feelings and conventionalize state's violence, my question is what is the advice and what does it do? In a manual-like manner, the booklet underlines utility, reducing the political complexity of memory into a self-forming technique, a thing one wants to do for one's self. Furthermore, it implicitly directs the bereaved toward a privatized film knowledge configured by the freelance filmmaker. The terminology of support and the focus on techniques, invite reading the personal commemorative video as a form in which subjectification and technology meet, what Michel Foucault terms "technologies of the self" (1988, 16–49). In the booklet the personal use of video by the family has formative and integrative ends, however it is the state that delimits such formative space.

Although home videos are mostly associated with a bottom-up perspective of power, by looking at a state-issued protocol I suggest that this interplay between affective media forms and the sovereignty of the state can be traversed. In this scheme the all-incorporating nature of sovereign power subsumes individuated expression of affinity and creativity. Introduced as an evocation of intimacy, what is at play here is a pervasive form of power that erases both the family implication in the structure of the state and the violence itself—the brutality of the Israeli occupation and suffering endured by Palestinians and Lebanese subjects. While my critique aims at destabilizing the oppressive mechanisms inflicted by the Israeli regime, my focus is not colonial violence as such but the most internal mechanisms that normalize and legitimate it.

Through the scrutiny of the state, the family video becomes a form that organizes and preserves social formations. It designates a particular mode of production, to be allocated outside the spectrum of institutional and commercial film production; at the same time, it also reaffirms a certain film knowledge, figured by the film professional, and shaped through a neo-liberal political economy of private services. Framing an intimate mode of production, the state reinforces a constructed division between institutionally inflicted culture of memory and memories that are mundane and effective. Yet it is precisely this sanctioning that inscribes the act under the state purview, even if indirectly. Put differently, in guiding the bereaved toward the personal video production, cultural, economic and political categories are retained, putting into order what can be otherwise contingent and unstable. While the state withholds its power through the rhetorical form of "advice," the freelance filmmaker emerges as a constellation of labor and creativity through which mourning is formed while acts of governance are privatized and rendered intimate. Thus, family video making becomes an extension of the apparatus of state power and regulation.

Lastly, focusing on the governmentalization of everyday practices offers a new perspective on the correlation between the institution and the home video, one that moves us away from the methodological fixation on the archive and its implications of foundness and retrospective reevaluation. Instead, *Paths of Commemoration* is an antecedent to a home video, a speculative and suggestive attribution through which conventions of media forms, work, and citizenship are shaped.[3] In this chapter, the object of formal analysis is not the videos themselves but rather the booklet, as a protocol of production that organizes a discursive space and regulates the visual form. My close reading of this document and its generic rhetoric of services aims both to illuminate the politics of the personal commemorative video within the cultural constellation of Jewish-Israeli memory formations and to offer a methodological framework for situating the home movie in relation to sovereignty. Rather than being concatenated into national-cultural histories and aesthetics through archival excavation and reevaluation, I argue that the home movie is a technique of self-formation and self-representation implemented by the state.

The Office of Families and Commemoration: Reproducing the Personal

The Office of Families and Commemoration (OFC) is part of the Unit for the Commemoration of Soldiers, housed under the Ministry of Defense. Under the umbrella term of commemoration, the unit facilitates the establishment and maintenance of military cemeteries, the erection of commemorative monuments, the publication of books, the designing and maintenance of a web platform, and the observance of fallen soldiers' memories. Overseeing institutional memory as a state-appointed entity notwithstanding, the Unit for the Commemoration of Soldiers' missions cross over to private activities induced by individual families. The OFC maintains that it does not initiate or promote personalized commemoration of individual soldiers. Indeed, the production of a commemorative video was never the subject of any state policy, official or ad-hoc. However, the office provides families with a small grant for the purpose of personal commemoration (as indicated on the OFC website, in 2017 the amount was 7,663 shekels, equivalent of approximately 2,185 USD). It also keeps itself up to date with practices and trends of family commemoration and keeps in touch with the families themselves. The office being informed of private practices, together with families repeatedly requesting such information, lead to the writing of the 2010 booklet.

Although the OFC relates to private commemorative activities only through the rhetoric of services, that is, advising families per request, the space of private commemoration is in itself a category formed by the OFC. Put differently, what is designated as private or personal is not a-priori, but a sphere that is realized through the OFC's policies of memory and its typological and administrative scheme. Its elastic jurisdiction, catering to both public and private commemoration, anchors the discursive categories of public and private in concrete domains, while at the same time putting them on a continuum. The political structure of separation on the one hand and extension on the other hand is essential when considering the office's sensitive task. Approaching a family that has suffered loss, the OFC functions as a governing agency that supports the family as it faces an enormous crisis and incorporates the family's mourning into the social texture and collective memory. The personal emerges as a balancing paradigm that retains the social order and, by allowing the family a space for mourning and introducing meaning through social acceptance, keeps the family and its mourning closer to the state. The OFC's work of mediation and translation of personal loss into social formulations or vice versa enables a pervasive and multifaceted form of governing that implements state power into the domain of intimacy while providing institutional care.

Memory, either institutionalized, cultural, or private (Sturken 1997; Mayzel and Shamir 2000) has been intrinsic to the formation of Jewish-Israeli identity since the establishment of the state, whereas the state's culture of mourning and its emphasis on military power are interdependent. The predominance of memory and mourning for the national narrative has encompassed individuated losses, yet those were traditionally instrumentalized as avatars of national ideals, commemorating the single soldier as a metonym of collective identity rather than a particular intimate loss. Over the years, the overlapping emergence of new media technologies and new political paradigms brought new subjects of memory. These are evident in the OFC's definition of its own mission and its elucidation of what constitutes personal commemoration. An apparent shift in rhetoric and trends notwithstanding, the state continuously valorized the personal as a venue for commemorative work.

The OFC started collecting information on private commemorative activities as early as 1975, when it published an earlier version of *Paths of*

Commemoration (Ministry of Defense 1975). That year marked a sea change in the state's treatment of bereaved families in the aftermath of the 1973 War, also known as the Yom Kippur War or the October War. The chaos that spread by the war's break, and the high numbers of missing, wounded, captured, and dead, lead the army and the Ministry of Defense to acknowledge family bereavement and formulate it as a matter of state policy. In the 1975 edition, the family is positioned as the grounds for the work of memory, rather than its subject. In the introduction to the 1975 booklet, Professor Efraim A. Aurbach articulates an ideology of memory that is closely tied to national causes:

> [The people] will not give away the greatest accomplishment of political independence and the people's freedom. The fallen had fallen for this, and their memory demands that we shall follow their ways. And it should be made clear: their memory does not grant us, those who remember—be it bereaved parents, widows or orphans—any special rights, but the right to remember more, and to be able to pass on this memory to those who owe gratitude for not being personally and intimately affected. . . . This memory, if perceived as right, can forestall hopelessness, weakening of the spirit, and provide our generation and the ones to follow a source of encouragement and faith. (Ministry of Defense 1975, 1)[4]

The decades that passed from 1975 and the change in rhetoric and technologies of memory lead the OFC to publish a second guidebook in 2010. The stress on statehood as an emancipatory means in the 1975 introduction has no trace in the 2010 edition. While the 1975 introduction equates nation-building with freedom and situates memory as an instrument of sovereignty, casting the bereaved in the role of those who secure the strength of national morals, the 2010 edition concerns the well-being of the family and the home. It is perhaps not by chance that Aurbach's opening words, coming from the perspective of the intellectual (Aurbach was a professor of Judaism at the Hebrew University and himself a bereaved parent), tie commemorative activity to sovereign ends, are substituted in 2010 by the brief of the administrator, the head of the OFC, Arye Mu'alem. The proposition that commemoration is a private activity conducted in the locus of the family separates it from acts elicited by the state. Packaged as an informative brochure, inspired by self-help genres of writings, the 2010 edition is about channeling the pain of loss into meaning and production, or even a product.

The emergence of new technologies, their commodification, and their inscription into a social organization in which individuation and personification are in excess, seems to be going hand-in-hand with the relocation of the personal. The 1975 edition lacks any reference to video-making as a practice of memory. Personal commemorative activities, even if dedicated to a single dead, are geared toward the sphere of civil society and take place in public space, activities such as the beautifying of outdoor spaces, editing an anthology of writings, launching educational programs or a scholarship fund, and others that stretch across the fields of leisure, culture, religion, and science. In contrast to this wider cultural denotation, the 2010 edition sticks to forms of biographical representation, listing video-making and the production of a memorial book first and, further down the list, designing a personal website. The introduction describes commemorating as telling a story and adds: "Naturally, there will arise differences between tellers, and between different atmospheres and different characters" (Ministry of Defense 2010). The plurality of tellers, characters, and atmospheres further enhances the notion that the state as a unifying mechanism steps back and that memory is individuated.

In accordance with the OFC's typology, the phenomenon of family-made commemorative video emerges when both private and public media markets lean toward the personal. The developing of digital video as a mass-consumed product in the 1990s allowed more possibilities for personal media usages, as media became instrumental for self-formation (Renov 2004; Newman 2014) and engraved into everyday life. Specific to Israel, in the 1990s the public media market was going through privatization, and commercial broadcasting entities entered a media sphere thus far governed by a state-owned broadcasting authority. Within the logic of commercial media, the self is at the center as both consumer and commodity. The emerging broadcasting system showed particular appetite for the personal, translating hegemonic identity positions into popular individuated "stories" packed into TV formats, such as reality TV or the character-driven documentary (Yuran 2001). Further into the first decade of the twenty-first century—the context in which the 2010 *Paths of Commemoration* was written—the commodification of the self was enhanced through new media technologies and spheres that catered to self-use and self-branding (Clough and Willse 2011; Shah 2015). The booklet taps into this economy of the self, reproducing the personal by an existing culture of memory brought together with new forms of subjugation.

When the 2010 edition reckons the benefits of video commemoration, it highlights its embodied qualities and its auto-usability. It describes video as generating "a live and visceral documentation of the fallen soldier, and allow the family and the next generations to have a visual memory of their loved one, to hear his voice and experience feelings and descriptions told by his friends and acquaintances" (Ministry of Defense 2010). Video emerges as a technology that best configures the permeate nature of an expanded self, a subject that is individuated, embodied, and affective yet, at the same time, commodified, formulated, reproducible, and liable to the state.

From Excavation to Regulation

When the practice of video commemoration is introduced, the booklet's authors indicate two types of movies: a personal movie and a documentary or fiction film. The personal video is defined as being facilitated by family members and as being composed of materials that are mostly, if not entirely, products of family media, such as video segments, still images, and homemade documentation of commemorative gatherings. The definition of documentary or fiction film describes them as cultural texts that incorporate the individuated story into the narrative of historical events and involve a complex and expansive production done by professional production companies. In conclusion, it is noted that most movies done today are personal ones. The underlying logic of the typology designates productional categories that correlate with the assigning of memory to different social spaces. The home video is defined vis-à-vis professional filmmaking. The gesture of defining attests to the instability and obscurity of the home video, and at the same time inscribes it into social formations.

Thinking the home movie through the premise of "national cinema," Liz Czach (2014, 27–38) probes the appropriation of the amateur movie as indicators of social and aesthetic configurations. Although for Czach the main question is one of cultural value and not governance, her inquiry clearly demonstrates the main conundrums involved in making amateur cinema an object of archival and scholarly scrutiny. Differentiating amateur film and home movies, Czach contends that the amateur film enters the national canon mostly due to its aesthetic value, predicated on the conception of national cinema as formally distinctive. The home movie, on the other hand, is valorized as a visible evidence of everyday life, deemed important due to its sociological and historical record. Interestingly, the criterion for entering a canon is either production value or historical resonance, two aspects that the booklet identifies as constituting the documentary/fiction film. According to Czach, recuperation of amateur/home cinema relies on applying a set of characteristics or values that were developed in relation to mainstream canonical cinema, such as the texts' authors, subjects, genres, and so on. Taking Czach's argument one step further, assigning value through preexisting social, historical, and ideological categories, the work of archivization and critique echoes the logic of the state, extending and reproducing hegemonic discourses.

Czach's essay helps frame the dominant methodological premises in home-movie literature. Attempting to decipher a visual expression that is often obscure, redundant, unimportant, and banal, a few analytic patterns were established. First, the archive, with its typological structure, emerges as the main nexus between the obscurity of the home movie and an institutional history. Situating the debate in the locus of the archive and using a terminology of recuperating limits our approach toward amateur and home movies to a temporal structure of retrospective revaluation and dictates a particular positioning of these materials in relation to sovereignty. Through the prism of the archive, history and ideology are traced and excavated, rather than being situated as instigating motors.

Another framework has to do with situating amateur and home movies in relation to discursive formations. This often leads to a binary scheme of public-private, outside-inside, professional labor-playful leisure, affirmative-alternative. As argued by Patricia Zimmermann (1995) in her seminal book *Reel Families*, such binary schemes are themselves discursively constructed. Attempting to stabilize meaning through such categorization is problematic because the home movie is never completely outside of social systems, labor definitions, or dominant ideologies, but always, and already, in reference to them. In their introduction to *Mining the Home Movie*, Zimmermann and Ishizuka (2008) suggest that the home movie offers an alternative insight into history, highlighting the creative and nonconformist aspects of everyday practices. However, the essays in this important intervention into the field address homemade productions that are already ordered by sovereign forms of knowledge, be it artistic practices (although avant-garde) or the archive. Additionally, writing on home movies shot by marginal communities—European Jews, American Japanese, or Chinese immigrants in Trinidad—shows that while the movies can be read as an insurgent history, their making often used to retain the subjects' social and economic status, reinscribing them into normativity in the face of exclusion and state violence.

In contrast to Zimmermann and Ishizuka's suggestion of alterity, there are the ways in which the home movie is interpreted and instrumentalized. Analyzing a state-issued document, and moreover one informed by a utilitarian approach (like the one discussed here), articulates a political logic in which the home movie can be thought of as an instrument of normativity, a liminal production that is integrative and extensive to the dominant order. *Paths of Commemoration* also evaluates the home movie after the fact, responding to a phenomenon that is almost two decades old, yet its formulation as advice has a preemptive nature. By defining and describing what the personal commemorative video is, and what it should set out to do, the booklet produces normative dispositions, stating the form's "oughts" and "shoulds" and implementing standardization. This opens an entire terminology of regulation through which to think about the political economy of the home video.

Informed Affinities: Freelancing and the Privatization of Film Knowledge

Making film knowledge available to the family, *Paths of Commemoration* translates production labor into applied practices, underscoring efficiency and accessibility. The production of a personal video is synopsized as collecting and organizing available footage, planning the shooting, putting together a script, editing, and distributing the video. The authors corroborate that each of these practices can be done by the family itself or with the help of professionals. The need of prerequisite technical knowledge is more heavily stressed when it comes to the stages of shooting and editing, however the booklet does mention available user-friendly do-it-yourself technologies. Considerations for professional film knowledge are put forward in a segment titled "To Give a Thought" (literally translated as "preliminary thought"). Central to the format of self-help writing, this segment appears in each of the booklet's subsections and is designed to be preparatory, a "friendly" warning about potential affective costs that the labor of memory may charge from the family. In the video section, families are made aware that going over family footage might trigger difficult feelings and are advised that the process of making a video is an elongated one with relatively high financial costs. Considering such challenges, families are encouraged to hand the work to "a person with some *affinity* for this field, who will be able to meet your expectations and who will know how to include *qualitative parts* and integrate them into the overall context." This will guarantee "true partnership in the work of commemorating your loved one" (Ministry of Defense 2010; emphasis mine). The booklet's suggestive terminology leaves indeterminate the nature of "true partnership," the measures of affinity, and the quality of the work done by the designated person. Therapeutic and aesthetic objectives are confusingly mixed, leaving unclear what the family can gain from exporting its memory work: a less painful production process or a more quality product? Professionalization, if that is what is intended by the tacit language, is only advised or informed on.

What effect, if any, did the booklet have on the videos themselves? The booklet does not really engage with formal aspects, neither specifying how the videos actually looked like nor how they should look. By not addressing formal matters the booklet either assumes that amateur productions are not aesthetically distinct or that the formal conventions are by now commonplace and do not need to be articulated as guidance. The booklet briefly describes the videos as composed of found media combined with interviews, a description that can easily apply to commercial documentary rhetoric. The interview functions as a liminal formal expression that crosses from family documentation to documentary by organizing ephemera or mending fragmented reminiscences while also demanding—at least in the technological environment of the late 1990s and early 2000s—a more complex and specialized mode of production. Indeed, the talking head, whether it is amateurly or professionally framed, has been a prominent part of the personal commemorative video. Production taken over by freelance film professionals, a shift that took place even before the 2010 booklet was written—yet was certainly reinforced by it—brings the family commemorative video even closer to mainstream documentary. This way distinction becomes merely discursive.

The freelance filmmaker, a category of labor mostly obscured in film and video histories, anchors formal mastery and artistic values in economic ones and emerges in moments of transition. For example, the freelance work of avant-garde and experimental filmmakers at the service of movements such as the British documentary movement in the United Kingdom, New Deal documentaries in the United States, among others (Kahana 2008; Swann 1989), was instrumental to the emergence of the social documentary. That said, freelancing is mostly associated with currents of privatization in an era of free-media markets. In the context of Israel, freelancing thrives with the privatization of the Israeli broadcasting system in the early

1990s and with it the unproportional opening of film departments and film schools in the privatized system of Israeli higher education. The combination of a new economy of production and an inflation of creative labor had filmmakers zigzagging their way between family, industrial, and television markets. Thus, the freelance filmmaker mediates between the sphere of institutionalized knowledge and the domestic one. Through the figure of the freelance filmmaker, the categories of family movie and mainstream media coalesce.

Steering families toward professionalized services, the booklet's prose obscures a production niche that by 2010 was already commonplace in the realm of commodified family media. Despite the trending of the family video and the rising market of film knowledge on demand, work done by freelance filmmakers did not easily lend itself to industrial and formal analysis. Pitching their work as intimate and process-based, and the final product as tailored according to each family's needs, the language of private services makes it hard to assess standards and currencies of production and form (see, for example, Keren Production "Private Customers," n.d.; Aluma Films, n.d.). For the freelance filmmaker each family is an exception, therefore there are no rules. Specific to commemorative home videos, production costs are further obscured under the moralistic caveat of translating mourning into profit-driven industries. Framed through the personal family video, love and loss prevail as authentic and idiosyncratic, despite their formulaic branding.

The nebulous suggestion to transpose the family work of mourning to "a person with some affinity for the field" relocates what can be thought of as a labor of love to the realm of professional knowledge. Adding "qualitative parts" means incorporating loss into a structure of coherence and communicability, which is integrative—both therapeutically and aesthetically—by keeping the crisis of loss tamed and contained. "Each commemorative video for a loved one who died has a different story," the booklet's authors assert, "therefore, each movie is of different character, that emanates from the personality of the dead, the family's preferences and the way it chooses to commemorate its loved one" (Ministry of Defense 2010). Personal commemoration is predicated on singularity, and the services provided by the freelance filmmaker to a particular family singularize the process of filmmaking. With a system of privatized production services in place, the result is uniformity through individuation, or a plurality of singular expressions. Lastly, embedding expertise into a structure of affinity obscures material wages, standardization, and the sovereignty of professional knowledge itself. Ostensibly, with no need to worry about funding, distribution, or reception, the privatized video production has no need to conform to hegemonic narratives. Yet these aspects, related to more direct infliction of social conventions that come with institutional media or the regulatory power of the state, are not missing but suppressed. The state allegedly remains an uninvolved, uninterested party that mainly advises.

Seeking Advice: Toward a Rhetoric of Service

Where is the work of power in the advice? What mode of governance can be drawn from the service of informing the citizen? The state's gesture of advising ostensibly diminishes a vocabulary of governing. In a cautious and didactic way, the booklet introduces into the emotional structure of the reader the world of forms, techniques, and efficiency. A rhetoric of service carefully omits any implications of authority, designating acts of private mediation as beyond the state's regulation. Instead, there is benevolent pragmatism that addresses questions like how to prepare, what to expect, how long it will take, who are the professional authorities to consult with, and what difficulties—emotional or financial—might arise. The media production, being a complex technological, formal, and cultural object, and being grounded in a particular industrial, economic and artistic "field," indeed begs for an advice.

Structured as a self-help guide, the state-authored document indicates the relocation of sovereignty to the technocratic or psychocratic. In such a scenario, the state's most viable intervention is regulation, but here a more subtle, dissociative paradigm prevails, the aim of which is not power as such but the administration and monitoring of life and subjecthood, what Michel Foucault refers to as biopower. Biopower applies to various state mechanisms whose subject is life—biological, psychic, and social. Here, loss and mourning are administrated in the level of the individual subject and the social body, and the state functions as a source of mental support. More specifically, the political structure at work can be read along the lines of Foucault's concept of governmentality (1991, 87–104). Emerging with modern statehood, and with the economizing of political life, Foucault terms governmentality a way of managing the population through means that are essential to it, such as wealth and security. He writes, "The population is the subject of needs, of aspiration, but it is also the object in the hands of the government, aware, vis-à-vis the government, of what it wants, but ignorant of what is being done to it" (100). Foucault describes a system of governing grounded not on the force of law or explicit forms of sovereign power, but technical expertise, the managing of needs, the tacit rhetoric extended by the state, and the displacement of certain state affairs to the private domain.

The idea that certain conducts are situated outside state sovereignty, but are in fact an extension of it, is central to my argument. Later in his lecture, Foucault notes that the governmentalization of the state is "at once *internal and external to the state*, since it is the tactics of government which makes possible the continual definition and redefinition of what is *within the competence of the state and what is not, the public versus the private and so on*" (1991, 103; emphasis mine). At this point, Foucault discerns two forms of power, making the distinction between sovereignty and governmentality. Sovereignty preserves power through the direct infliction of authority via concrete laws, regulations, and institutions. Governmentality, on the other hand, assures the survival of the state not through the centralization of power but through "disposing things" and employing tactics, which serve a "plurality of specific ends" (95). Returning to the question of where to locate media objects and means of production, either as amateur or institutional, Foucault's concept of governmentality explicates the indirect and pervasive links of amateur cinema and state's hegemony.

The plurality of ends—which in this case secures the plural singularity of the dead—highlights personal needs and choices. Advising, offering practical solutions, and securing benefit and well-being are all subsumed under the booklet's rhetoric of service. Such rhetoric is salient for the way different private venues of memory productions (e.g., freelance filmmakers) introduce themselves to the family. Put differently, the state and the market conform under the same rhetoric. The slip from the state to the market has much to do with the fact that in the booklet the state concerns itself with the formation of memory through private activities. Here Foucault's notions of tactics seem germane.

For Foucault tactics are what enable the art of government as a means of inflicting power and maintaining order. Can we think of "paths of commemoration" as a set of tactics the ends of which are governmentality? Ostensibly, these are offered by the OFC as what is practiced by individuals in order to serve their own individuated needs. The terminology itself, the choice of the word *paths*, rather than the literal *means* or *practices*, disassociates power or utilities from one's own selfhood. And yet, the circumventing of direct means of power into "tactics" done on and by the subject echoes Foucault's delimiting of a theoretical framework that ties methods of self-care and self-knowledge to political life. As a result, self-care and self-knowledge become forms of subjugation that derive directly from the configuration of power (Foucault 1982, 1988). Concerning the meeting point between psychic life, technology, and the apparatus, the booklet's "to give a thought" section is where the relations between self and power become the most articulated.

The state's official standpoint—according to which personal commemoration is not a policy but a privatized practice that corresponds with individuated needs and on which the state can only inform—equivocates the issue of authority and preserves an autonomy of commemoration. With most of its listed techniques already formalized by the time of its publication in 2010, the booklet seems to suggest that a certain conduct and a certain need came before the official response. Indeed, the booklet does not open up new venues or advocate new techniques, yet it establishes those techniques as a norm and signals a process of standardization and institutionalization of certain paths of commemoration. The rhetoric of service stands for the administration of the subject's self-realization, while delimiting the subject's own sphere of autonomy. Allegedly autonomous, the personal is at once stripped from its politics and regulated by the state through its mapping of techniques.

While it carefully eschews any act of directing and uses pragmatism to enhance a naturalized and neutralized language, the booklet offers a glimpse into the ways the state perceives itself as assisting its citizens in implementing their roles as state subjects. The advice is an intricate and tacit interpellating mechanism, a gesture that organizes the self through formulating and standardizing ways to mourn and to express pain. Read critically, the booklet offers a glance into the way a certain institution or an organization explains itself and its actions to itself. Such analysis entail reading the booklet against itself, making explicit not only the subject of the address, but the systematic rational that positions the subject vis-à-vis expertise, professionalism, and techniques.

In conclusion, the booklet's brief note on distribution uncovers the extent to which the home movie is an expansive object that permeates through different social constellations. In this section the authors suggest screening the video to family members, friends, and acquaintances, as well as "targeted audiences" of different groups of which the deceased was a member, such as military units and youth movements. If wishing to reach a larger audience, television and the internet are listed as possible venues.[5]

Seeking to locate the home movie in relation to sovereignty, we must attend its appending and implementing powers and the fraught inflictions of normalcy through gestures of everyday intimacy. These are often untraceable from the fetishistic perspective of archival resurrection but are discernable through a systematic discourse formed by the governing apparatus of the state. Indeed, as a technique the home video entails many aspects in which the state, the market, or institutional media disavow their formative role. Ultimately, the sphere of homemade video production, and specific to Israel, personal memory production, is not an antidote to the state operations but is its necessary precondition.

Notes

1. Original in Hebrew. All translations in this chapter are mine.
2. Israel has been engaged in conflict with its Arab neighboring countries since it was established. More specifically, I refer to the Israeli-Palestinian conflict and to the Israeli occupation of the south of Lebanon, which started with the first Israel-Lebanon war in 1983 and ended in the early 2000s, with another eruption of military conflict in the summer of 2006.
3. Similarly, discursive analysis of manufacturers manuals and amateur filmmakers' journals highlight the constructive work of the advice. See, for example, Zimmermann 1995; Fung 2008, 29–40; Howe 2014, 39–50.
4. The essay originated from a paper given at a conference held by the Public Committee for the Commemorating of the Soldier, Tel Aviv, 1975.
5. As far as I know, none of these family memorial videos was ever broadcast or screened as a "legitimate" cinematic artifact outside the specific frame of the National Memorial Day designated media slots/pages.

References

Aluma Films. "Documentary" and "Personal Films." Accessed October 25, 2017. http://www
    .aluma-films.com/.
Chun, Wendy Hui Kyong. 2016. *Updating to Remain the Same*. Cambridge, MA: MIT Press.
Clough, Patricia Ticineto, and Craig Willse, eds. 2011. *Beyond Biopolitics: Essays on the
    Governance of Life and Death*. Durham, NC: Duke University Press.
Czach, Liz. 2014. "Home Movies and Amateur Film as National Cinema." In *Amateur
    Filmmaking: The Home Movie, the Archive, the Web*, edited by Laura Rascaroli and
    Gwenda Young, with Barry Monahan, 27–38. New York: Bloomsbury Press.
Foucault, Michel. 1982. "The Subject and Power." *Critical Inquiry* 8, no. 4 (Summer): 777–95.
    http://www.jstor.org/stable/1343197.
———. 1988. "Technologies of the Self." In *Technologies of the Self: A Seminar with Michel
    Foucault*, edited by Luther H. Martin, Huck Gutman, and Patrick H. Hutton, 16–49.
    Amherst: University of Massachusetts Press.

———. 1991. "Governmentality." In *The Foucault Effect: Studies in Governmentality*, edited by Graham Burchell, Colin Gordon, and Peter Miller, 87–104. Chicago: University of Chicago Press.

Fung, Richard. 2008. "Remaking Home Movies." In *Mining the Home Movie: Excavation in Histories and Memories*, edited by Patricia Zimmermann and Karen L. Ishizuka, 29–40. Berkeley: University of California Press.

Howe, Maija. 2014. "The Photographic Hangover: Reconsidering the Aesthetics of the Postwar 8mm Home Movie." In *Amateur Filmmaking: The Home Movie, the Archive, the Web*, edited by Laura Rascaroli and Gwenda Young, with Barry Monahan, 39–50. New York: Bloomsbury Press.

Kahana, Jonathan. 2008. *Intelligence Work: The Politics of American Documentary*. New York: Columbia University Press.

Keren Productions Film and TV. "Private Customers." Accessed January 15, 2018. http://www.kerenpro.com/.

Mayzel, Matitiahu, and Ilana Shamir, eds. 2000. *Patterns of Commemoration*. Tel Aviv: The State of Israel, Ministry of Defense.

Ministry of Defense 1975. *Paths of Commemoration*. Tel Aviv: The State of Israel, Ministry of Defense.

———. 2010. *Paths of Commemoration*. Tel Aviv: The State of Israel, Ministry of Defense.

Newman, Michael, 2014. *Video Revolutions: On the History of a Medium*. New York: Columbia University Press.

Office of Families and Commemoration. n.d. "Private Commemoration Grant." The State of Israel, Accessed January 14, 2018. https://www.mishpahot-hantzaha.mod.gov.il/mhn/parents/memorial/Pages/maanak_vealvaa_lemimun_anzaha_pratit.aspx.

Rascaroli, Laura, and Gwenda Young with Barry Monahan, eds. 2014. *Amateur Filmmaking: The Home Movie, the Archive, the Web*. New York: Bloomsbury Press.

Renov, Michael. 2004. *The Subject of Documentary*. Minneapolis: University of Minnesota Press.

Swann Paul. 1989. *The British Documentary Movement 1926–1946*. Cambridge, MA: Cambridge University Press.

Shah, Nishant. 2015. "The Selfie and the Slut: Bodies, Technology, and Public Shame." *Review of Women's Studies* 1, no. 17 (April). https://www.epw.in/journal/2015/17/review-womens-studies-review-issues/selfie-and-slut.html.

Sturken, Marita. 1997. *Tangled Memories: The Vietnam War, the Aids Epidemics and the Politics of Remembering*. Berkeley: University of California Press.

Yuran, Noam. 2001. *Channel 2: The New Statehood*. Tel Aviv: Resling. [in Hebrew]

Zimmermann, Patricia. 1995. *Reel Families: A Social History of Amateur Film*. Bloomington: Indiana University Press.

Zimmermann, Patricia, and Karen L. Ishizuka, eds. 2008. *Mining the Home Movie: Excavation in Histories and Memories*. Berkeley: University of California Press.

LALIV MELAMED is Research Fellow at the Goethe University at Frankfurt.

6

AMATEUR FILM IN THE FACTORY

Forms and Functions of Amateur Cinema in Corporate Media Culture

Yvonne Zimmermann

O VER THE LAST FIFTEEN YEARS, AMATEUR FILM HAS developed into a vibrant research field. While pioneering studies by Patricia R. Zimmermann (1995) or Roger Odin (1995) mainly focused on home movies and family films, recent scholarship has pointed to the manifold amateur film cultures outside the home and has started to explore the institutional, technological, social, and aesthetic specificities of these "out of home" amateur cinemas. In so doing, the main focus has been placed on amateur film clubs and festivals (see Tepperman 2014). Other social and institutional contexts in which amateur film played an important role have received little attention so far. Among these rather overlooked fields is amateur film in the factory. There has been some occasional scholarship on footage of home moviemakers, mainly from the middle class, who took industry as subject matter for their zest for making movies (see Nicholson 2008), but these filmic forays into the factory and working-class lives were made by and for factory outsiders. My interest here lies in amateur film produced and used in the institutional context of corporations. This approach implies a shift in amateur film studies from individual amateur filmmakers, amateur film organizations, and amateur film collections to the decidedly non-amateur institution of corporations that generally are not associated with amateur film culture or film culture at all.

While the making (and watching) of amateur films and home movies is usually perceived as a hobby and leisure-time pursuit, the boundaries between leisure and work in regard to amateur film have been anything but firm. This chapter further complicates ongoing discussions on the relationships between amateur and professional movie making (see Mattl et al. 2015). I also wish to draw attention to another border area that I locate between amateur cinema as a leisure-time pursuit and a workplace occupation. In what follows, I examine the configurations of leisure and work in amateur film practice in the institutional context of corporations and the role amateur film played in the organization and management of work processes and workers. In doing so, I insert the study of amateur film in a broader context of the burgeoning field of useful cinema studies.

Recent scholarship into amateur film in socialist states, among them Maria Vinogradova's (2017) dissertation on amateur cinema in the Soviet Union, Ralf Forster's (2018) monograph on amateur film in the German Democratic Republic, and Veronika Jančová's dissertation project on amateur films made in the context of Czech worker clubs, has opened up new avenues to explore the relationship between leisure and work in amateur film practiced in socialist states, where amateur filmmaking was usually organized around amateur film studios that were affiliated with work places. This chapter focuses on the place of amateur cinema in capitalist business organizations in the Western world. It studies how amateur film contributed to corporate media culture but was also part and parcel of popular media culture, and how it was put to use for corporate purposes of marketing and corporate governance.

While Vinzenz Hediger and Patrick Vonderau (2009) have hinted at the formal analogy of private films and certain forms of industrial films and the similar functions that films can have in families and industrial organization, it is Brian R. Jacobson's (2017) essay on amateur films made by two company owners in New England, Henry Sturgis Dennison and Charles B. Hinds, between 1926 and 1941, that, to my knowledge, is among the first to undertake a foray into amateur film that served factory insiders as a business strategy. Jacobson is mainly interested in the aesthetics of those amateur films of the company owners that very much reproduce established forms and narratives of industrial films, such as the factory gate film and the process film.

In this case study, amateur films by the company owner also play a crucial role, but they are only one aspect among many others. The object of my inquiry is Sulzer Ltd., a globally active industrial engineering and manufacturing company founded in Winterthur, Switzerland, in 1834. For its large variety of amateur film (and photo) practices in the first half of the twentieth century, Sulzer may not be representative for other corporations, but it lends itself as an exemplary case to study the configurations of corporate amateur film in relation to industrial film, corporate media culture, and colonial visual culture as well as in relation to corporate governance. The following topics, all under debate in amateur film studies, will be addressed: (1) the relationship between amateur and professionally produced films, (2) the relationship between amateur filmmaking as leisure pursuit and work practice, and (3) the distinctions between amateur film and home movies or family films.

Amateur Film Production in the Factory

Amateur film laid the foundation of Sulzer's in-house film production in 1937 when Jules Bichsel, engineer in the pump department, switched to the newly founded film department to write and direct—as a pump expert and film amateur—*Wasserversorgung mit Sulzer-Pumpen* (Water Supply with Sulzer Pumps). Bichsel's debut film qualifies as amateur cinema since filmmaking was not (yet) Bichsel's principal occupation. Although the work of an amateur, the film reproduces the structure and rhetoric of one of the classic types of industrial film, the process film (see Gunning 1997). Step by step, *Wasserversorgung mit Sulzer-Pumpen* shows the fabrication, the worldwide export, and the use of pumps in daily life and in agriculture. Water is the motif and framing element of the film, and its taming and cultivation with the help of pumps is depicted as a benefit for humankind. This rhetoric of the company's rendering service to society (while its real objective—to make profit—goes unmentioned) is a basic strategy in corporate films (and other forms of corporate media) for legitimizing the existence of capitalist corporations. Apparently, amateur filmmaker Bichsel had been familiar with the conventions of professionally produced process films, possibly from seeing them in commercial cinema (where they would be part of the program of shorts) or at trade fairs, and sought to emulate them—or, as an expert in pump engineering, had internalized the basic narrative of industrial capitalism and intuitively followed the production steps with his camera. Unfortunately, for lack of sources, we do not know which one was the case (while both could have been).

Naming Bichsel an expert amateur, to use the term Jacobson (2017) proposes to designate the company owners in his study, seems quite adequate, not least because the term resonates with a certain tension in historical discourses on the relationship between professional filmmakers and corporate

Fig. 6.1. Screenshot from *Wasserversorgung mit Sulzer-Pumpen* (1937). Sulzer Corporate Archive in Winterthur.

sponsors. Bichsel *was* an expert in pump engineering, and he put his expertise in the service of the company when he shot his first amateur industrial film. In many corporations, among them Sulzer, technical expertise was more appreciated than cinematic skills, whereas professional producers of industrial films were often blamed by corporations for capturing visually attractive objects or processes while lacking technical expertise and knowledge of work procedures. In that sense, professional filmmakers, once they entered the factory, were also expert amateurs—experts in filmmaking, but amateurs in engineering.

From this perspective, who is deemed expert and who is considered amateur is not based on factual skills but on the respective appreciation of different kinds of skills. This of course questions the concept of skills that, in film and media studies, puts a habitual emphasis on amateur films' aesthetic and narrative qualities. In the course of further films, autodidact Bichsel turned filmmaking into his main occupation and gradually professionalized the production of industrial films in Sulzer's film department,

Fig. 6.2. Shooting at Sulzer in Oberwinterthur, Switzerland, gas turbine plant Hainaut (undated). Sulzer Werkmitteilungen, no.1 (1956): 4.

Fig. 6.3. Editing of a film at Sulzer (undated). Sulzer Werkmitteilungen, no.1 (1956): 5.

Fig. 6.4. Projection booth in the Sulzer Building 1934 (undated). Sulzer Werkmitteilungen, no.1 (1956): 5.

together with Max E. Trechsel, himself also an engineer, who became direc-tor of the so-called propaganda and patent division at Sulzer in 1941.[1]

Even though both film division and propaganda department profession-alized over time, amateur film remained a main pillar in the corporation's image production for both external and internal communication. Amateur image production at Sulzer had started with photography. Since the 1920s, the company equipped assembly operators with cameras in order to cap-ture images of installations and facilities in foreign countries. Sulzer offered to pay for the production of all slides that were related to products of the company,[2] and even prizes had been instituted for this aim.[3] This makes clear that Sulzer was avid to use amateur images as a method of rational-izing the company's marketing processes.

In a similar vein, in 1944, Sulzer organized an in-house information event to familiarize Sulzer engineers with the work and workings of the propaganda department. In a paper on "The Film in the Service of Propa-ganda," Trechsel explains Sulzer's practice of mandating the company's rep-resentatives and technicians abroad to shoot film footage for integration in professionally produced industrial films. For that matter, Sulzer instructed its representatives, technicians, and installers how to shoot films that would serve the company—and what to avoid.[4] Home movies and souvenir films are explicitly mentioned as don'ts. Instead, Sulzer advised its staff to capture scenes that present the plant, its functioning, and, if possible, its different application areas. Employees were particularly instructed to pay attention that there is always movement in the image. Special advice is given for shooting assembly abroad: utmost care should be taken that the "character" of the respective country would immediately be apparent. To achieve this, the lecturer recommends shooting "landscapes with native people or native people as machine operators."[5] At the same time, it is stressed that native people should not just be positioned next to machines, but assigned appropriate work.[6] There is an obvious tendency in this advice to stage native people and workers in foreign countries as markers of "otherness," which is also evident in the films that resulted from this practice (see below).

The idea of turning professional engineers into amateur filmmakers and exploiting their skills was a principle that applied to the entire Sulzer marketing strategy. Trechsler induced employees in foreign countries "to shoot film material and send it to us, just as we do with photo material," with the aim to create a film library that would allow the compilation of corporate films for all possible purposes at any time.[7] The reason for this strategy was that in 1944, due to the indeterminacy of the outcome of World War II, Sulzer, domiciled in a country with formally neutral political status, did not have a targeted propaganda strategy. Instead, the company collected as much advertising material as possible so that once things were sorted out, Sulzer would, as Trechsel put it, "only need to push the button to get the thing going in any desired direction."[8]

Collaborations between Amateur and Professional Filmmakers

With employees providing stock footage for professional filmmaking (and photo making) and marketing, corporate visual media production at Sulzer was a collaborative work between amateurs and professionals. One result of this practice is the 1939 corporate film *Die Erzeugnisse der Firma Gebrüder Sulzer Aktiengesellschaft auf dem Weltmarkt* (Sulzer Products on the World Market). The opening titles acknowledge that Sulzer engineers and service technicians were behind the camera. The compilation film opens with a short review of the company's history and continues with a presentation of contemporary images—both still and moving—of machines and works to document the global activities of the corporation and its range of products.

The film is utterly static, with a gesture of showing rather than telling, and sticks to the principle of itemization. There is no discourse, no explicit argument; instead, the film presents itself as an illustrated and—to some extent—animated catalog of Sulzer products. The film was meant to premiere at the Swiss National Exhibition in Zurich, but the exhibition's official film selection committee rejected it for its poor quality.[9] Also in-house, the film was deemed "botched" because the responsible experts were absent for military service.[10] Nevertheless, it would be screened on occasion, always accompanied by a lecture.[11] The lecture manuscript refers explicitly to the fact that: "The pictures do not come from the studio of a film production company, but were made by Sulzer engineers and service technicians, and therefore do not claim to be up to the standard of a highly developed film art."[12] The statement underscores how Sulzer's amateur film culture took care to distinguish itself from contemporary "amateur filmmaking as art" discourses proliferating in Western societies.

Obviously, while taking profit from photographic and filmic amateurism in the company, Sulzer also took a certain pride in its amateur image production. Also the "flaws" of the first corporate amateur industrial films—such as "no accomplished cinematic craftsmanship, no brilliant photography that makes full use of light and shadow effects"—were openly acknowledged and presented as evidence of "simple, human-artistic and lively dedication," or, as testimony of authenticity.[13] In a certain way, Sulzer promoted amateurism as an unpolished, yet authentic and thus more efficient mode of industrial film and photo production and endorsed it as a decidedly collaborative operating mode between amateurs and professionals. Viewed from this perspective, amateur film culture helped convey to industrial production the sense of collective practice.

Corporate Amateur Cinema, Colonial Visual Culture, and the Travelogue

There are at least four amateur films in the holdings of Sulzer Corporate Archive in Winterthur that attest to the practice of Sulzer representatives and technicians shooting amateur films abroad for the corporation.[14] These films were probably never (meant to be) exhibited in full length in the context of the corporation but used as resources for the company's marketing efforts. Some shots from the four films have indeed been included in the 1939 film *Die Erzeugnisse der Firma Gebrüder Sulzer Aktiengesellschaft auf dem Weltmarkt*. Even though their historical purpose was to feed the company's visual reservoir, the films deserve closer attention as works in their own right, despite—or rather because of—their precarious status as work in the traditional sense, for all four films lack titles and credits and some also lack closure. The labels on the film cans and the titles in the corporate list of archived films hint at the countries in which the shooting took place and at the topics filmed: "Egypt," "Romanian Oilfields," "Argentinian Oilfield Ship," and "Argentinian Refrigerated Slaughterhouse." All films are in black and white, silent, and shot on 16 mm reversal film stock (which gives a positive image directly when processed). Their length is between six and a half minutes and nine minutes (at a speed of twenty-four frames per second). Dating these moving images is difficult, as is typical for nonfiction films in nontheatrical circuits where films largely remained not only black and white and silent, but well into the 1950s also stayed faithful to the gesture of showing (rather than telling) in the tradition of nonfictions in early cinema (see Y. Zimmermann 2011a, 82–83). As a raw guess, the films were made between 1930 and 1938. They illustrate that the term *amateur film* designates a specific mode of film production and exhibition that developed beyond film industries and theatrical-cinema circuits rather than a genre category. Amateurs made all kinds of genre films. While Sulzer rejected home movies from its workforce because they did not serve the corporation's marketing strategy, the company welcomed travelogues, as is the case with the examples discussed here. Charles Tepperman (2014), among others, has noticed that amateur cinema shares many similarities with films of the cinema's first two decades, both in terms of subject matter and visual rhetoric. This holds true also for the films Sulzer technicians shot abroad, for they reproduce the motifs and aesthetics of early travelogues. In two of the films, modern means of transportation open and close the films and give them the framing structure of arrival and departure typical for travelogues, while phantom rides from ships and other vehicles, lavish pans and long takes shot with a fixed camera put landscapes and locals before the camera as objects to be looked at. While the films demonstrate many features in common with "the cinema of attractions," in the sense that they display the images for visual consumption, they also replicate the problematic colonial regime of looking as a form of visual appropriation and possession of the world through images—at the expense of turning foreign places and cultures and local inhabitants into exotic "others."[15] Following the advice from the corporate headquarters mentioned above, the films do not focus on the work of native machine operators as manual labor but present native workers as extras to the machines. They signal cultural difference and illustrate the international distribution of Sulzer appliances. The stars in the films are the machines, whereas native workers serve as stereotypical representations of their respective foreign and "exotic" countries and thus as indicators of both "otherness" and the global outreach of the corporation.

It is with the same technique of looking that the films visually appropriate touristic sites and industrial objects. In doing so, they rehearse patterns of popular types of early industrial films, such as the process film and the factory tour film. They display an ambivalent tension between the picturesque and modern infrastructure in that they take particular interest in technical installations and industrialized landscapes, which in "Argentinian Oilfield Ship" and "Argentinian Refrigerated Slaughterhouse" are captured in phantom rides from a cargo vessel the same way Alexandre Promio, in his 1896 *Vue Lumière,* captured the panorama of the Canale Grande in Venice from a gondola. As far as they depict industrial processes (as does "Argentinian Refrigerated Slaughterhouse," which follows the trajectory of live cattle from the meadows to the slaughterhouse and to cold storage), these industrial amateur films exhibit a somewhat similar generic overlap with the popular film form of the travelogue that Frank Kessler and Eef Masson (2009) identify in early cinema. However, despite the tense entanglement of both tourist and industrial sightseeing, there is a certain predilection for technical installations and operations that the films visually appropriate and, in an imperial gesture, take into possession with the same techniques that travelogues use to conquer "the world as picture."[16] As such, and not surprisingly, they also evidence how corporate moving images from amateur filmmakers, alongside films from popular visual culture, are interwoven with modern imperialist ideologies.

Amateur Film in the Factory between Leisure and Work

While amateur filmmaking as thus far considered was part of work practice at Sulzer, it also extended into leisure time. A striking example is Martin Kürsteiner, head of social security administration and health care at Sulzer. His enthusiasm for amateur cinema was aroused when in 1942 Sulzer's film division produced a film about the construction of a boiler plant. At that time, Kürsteiner was a boiler engineer, and it was in this capacity that he suggested that animated scenes be included in the film to give it a relaxed feel. This was the beginning of a "career" of hobby cinematography beyond the factory that spanned more than two decades. As the company magazine, *Sulzer SLM Werkmitteilungen*, reported in 1969, it was to no small extent Jules Bichsel, head of the film division, helped pave the way for Kürsteiner's filmmaking passion in that, besides giving him advice, Bichsel lent Kürsteiner his camera when the latter wished to record his trip from Vienna to Venice in moving images.[17] Kürsteiner joined the local amateur film club to improve his technological skills. Until 1969, he made approximately thirty films, mostly home movies. It should therefore come as no surprise that none of Kürsteiner's hobby films are to be found in Sulzer's archival film collection.

Sulzer apprentices took a somewhat different approach to amateur film in the factory when they made a film in their spare time about the first day of their apprenticeship at Sulzer and about everyday work life in the engineering school in the late 1960s. The company's in-house magazine lauds the result as "unconventional, almost 'nouvelle vague' à la Sulzer apprentices," and appraises certain shots for evoking French films by Cocteau and Clair from the 1930s.[18] There is no trace of this film in the corporate film archive either. The closing sentence in the report makes clear in what sense the corporation might profit from their apprentices' first steps into the world of film art: "It is . . . a wonderful leisure activity whose use lies not least in its encouraging teamwork."[19] Amateur film was greeted as a teacher of teamwork, a soft skill highly welcomed in the workplace. Thus, leisure-time amateur filmmaking was appreciated at Sulzer as a training ground for working environments.

While Kürsteiner and the apprentices expanded their work occupation into a leisure-time pursuit, the opposite direction was equally possible: When in 1965 the Winterthur city council launched a competition, initiated by Jules Bichsel, on the topic of Winterthur, Sulzer employees ranked first to fifth.[20] The winner, Herbert Breitenmoser, turned his hobby into his profession and from the 1970s until 1995 headed the photo and audio-vision division at Sulzer.

The Company Co-Owner's Expert Work as Film Amateur: The Case of Robert Sulzer

The work of company co-owner Robert Sulzer (1873–1953), grandson of company founder Johann Jakob Sulzer, presents yet another case that deserves a closer examination than can be made here. Patron Sulzer was an ardent photo and film amateur in his own right—just like Henry Sturgis Dennison and Charles B. Hinds and probably a considerable number of other company owners, among them also Rudolf Sprüngli, the owner of the Swiss chocolate factory Lindt & Sprüngli (see Y. Zimmermann 2011b, 332).

A certain overlap between industrial and travel films also characterizes Robert Sulzer's amateur picture production, albeit his spectrum is broader, and his film work is said to date back to the earliest years of cinematography, when he experimented with the first photographic dry plates produced by the Lumière company.[21] Sulzer acquired the necessary technical skills and developed dry plates, made prints from photographs, and produced his own projection slides, thus epitomizing the self-taught ethos that may be included among the features of the amateur production mode. He was also familiar with the "Autochrome Lumière" process and shared his knowledge on color photography in numerous lectures.[22] The Lumière brothers were held in high regard at Sulzer, and both Louis and Auguste were honored with detailed obituaries in the company magazine in 1948 and 1957, respectively.[23] This fascination with the Lumière brothers may be explained by their inventive talent, a core quality in engineering business. It is probably also related to the kind of "enlightened paternalism" that, as Jacobson (2017, 199) holds, is often associated with nineteenth-century company owners like the Lumière brothers. Sulzer shared this enlightened paternalism with them, as we will see in more detail. Unfortunately, none of his photos and films could be retraced. According to written sources, Sulzer documented his world trips with the photo camera and shot moving images on the island of Bali.[24] Next to scenic pictures, he experimented with scientific photography and made micrograph images of bacteria as well as time-lapse color films on the growth of plants.[25]

The borders between the professional life and the private life of a company owner like Robert Sulzer are hard to determine. His travels around the globe that he captured with his photo and film cameras as a film amateur, for example, were professional business trips. If one wants to declare Sulzer's passion for photography and cinematography a leisure-time pursuit, it is crucial to acknowledge that he put his hobby to use in the workplace to the benefit of the company: Sulzer would show and live-comment his travelogue from Bali, the micrograph images of bacteria, and the time-lapse color films in programs that also included the (semi) professional industrial films of the corporation and actualities about the construction of new production sites or the social life in Sulzer apprentice camps shot by the company's expert amateur workforce. Some of Robert Sulzer's illustrated lectures were open to the public; others were reserved for Sulzer employees and pensioners. If one trusts the enthusiast recounts published in local newspapers and the company magazine from the 1930s to the 1950s, patron Sulzer was an exceptionally gifted master of ceremonies, which would help explain the popularity of these screenings among the workforce.

It is remarkable that not all of these events were organized by the company; some were also arranged by employees. When Sulzer's Employees' Association invited its members and relatives to a film and slide lecture evening about the "installations and products of our company today and yesterday" to the Casino Winterthur in 1947, the demand for tickets was so high that the event had to be repeated the next day. Each night, the illustrated lectures hosted an audience of around six hundred people—and still more than one hundred people had to be turned away.[26] At these events, in-house-produced industrial films were screened, while Robert Sulzer presented his own slides on the development of the company. On other occasions, the patron showed his travel and scientific images—to the great pleasure of his audiences, it seems: an article in the company magazine on lectures and screenings for pensioners by Robert Sulzer and Max E. Trechsel in July 1951 provides a vivid description of the patron's time-lapse films: "Right before our eyes, beans germinated and grew upwards, flowers blossomed and withered; an amaryllis opened its buds, developed a calyx, and slowly scrunched up its withered leaves. It was very impressive to experience this process, which otherwise takes weeks, in such a short time-span."[27]

The Bali travelogue is also recounted in some detail and supplemented with information on how the film was exhibited: "In the second film we followed Dr. Robert Sulzer on his trip to Bali, a small island in Indonesia. The pertinent and humorous comments of the scenes made us forget that it was a silent film. Some records played the original music and accompanied the peculiar temple dances that the Balinese people perform to worship their Gods. Images from daily life and festivities gave us some impressions of the life of these cheerful islanders, and great applause thanked Dr. Robert Sulzer for his interesting screenings."[28] This description illustrates once more the colonial gaze inherent in Sulzer's amateur film culture outlined above.

Amateur Films in the Factory as "Corporate Home Movies"

To grasp the particular experience of such screenings for the audience and to recognize their usefulness to the corporation, it is helpful to turn to phenomenology and Vivian Sobchack's (1999) understanding of home movies. Drawing on Belgian psychologist Jean-Pierre Meunier's phenomenology of cinematic identification, Sobchack challenges the common notion that different types of films are completely discrete categories or fixed objects. For Sobchack, a home movie, like a documentary or a fiction film, is not a mere cinematic object but rather a specific viewing modality and effect of film reception.[29] A home movie, then, is "less a *thing* than an *experience*," an experience that is defined by the particular subjective relation to an objective cinematic or televisual text (241). With Meunier, Sobchack argues that the form of cinematic identification does not necessarily depend on the type of film screened. Rather, it is existential knowledge and forms of attention that structure cinematic identification with, and of, the cinematic object. "Thus, a fiction can be experienced as a home movie or documentary, a documentary as a home movie or fiction, a home movie as a documentary or fiction" (246). Sobchack uses the phrase "home-movie attitude" to describe that any type of film can be experienced as a home movie, holding that the structure of identification in the home-movie attitude is essentially one of evocation.

From this perspective, it can be argued that the amateur films, but also the (semi) professionally produced Sulzer films, regardless of whether they belong to the category of industrial films, travelogues, actualities, or scientific films, were experienced as *home movies* of the corporation when screened in the context of the business organization. From a sociological point of view, the evocative home-movie attitude of the viewers of Sulzer films (whether professional or amateur) in screenings such as described above contributed to the creation of a sense of a "work family." As Alexandra Schneider (2004) has argued, home movies do not just represent family. As a decidedly performative practice, they *produce* family, both in the course of *making* home movies and in the moments of *watching* home movies in the family. Somewhat similar observations can be made in regard to the organizational context of the corporation. The collaborative making and the collective consumption of these "corporate home movies," whether amateur or professional, whether industrial or not, *produced* the corporation as a socially coherent entity.

From a corporate governance perspective, the production, exhibition, and collective consumption of corporate home movies can be seen as a social technique that Sulzer used to bond with employees and to integrate the workforce into the corporation. This technique of community-building is reminiscent of what German sociologist Max Weber (1990) calls *Verge-meinschaftung* (communitization), which he understands as a construc-tivist process of manufacturing social bonds based on subjective senses of togetherness on emotional, affective, or traditional grounds.

Corporate amateur cinema and home-movie film culture at Sulzer, to-gether with Robert Sulzer's work as an expert amateur, can therefore be considered a management strategy to promote positive worker relations. Films were just one tool among others in the corporate media mix that served this aim. For example, the first issue of the company magazine, pub-lished in 1919, declares as its objective the strengthening of the connection between the management and the staff.[30] For, as the seventh issue quotes from shoe company Bally's first house magazine, "only if all manpower, from the management to the last worker, stick together, the prosperity of our factory and as a result the welfare of each individual is possible."[31] As not only the enthusiastic reports on patron Sulzer's lectures and screenings attest but also the obituaries speak of, Robert Sulzer's so-called enlight-ened paternalism seems to have been particularly successful in bridging the gap between management and staff and helped create a good working atmosphere. Upon his death in 1953, Sulzer was acknowledged even by left-oriented newspapers as a "patriarchal leader" and appreciated, in particu-lar, for his management of the nonprofit society for the building of cheap housing for workers that his father had founded in 1872.[32]

Conclusion

The study of amateur film in the non-amateur institutional context of corporations has brought to light a decidedly professional use of amateur film. This may seem like a contradiction. However, as the Sulzer case il-lustrates, amateur film in the factory turns upside down common ideas in film and media studies of the professional-amateur relationship. The expert amateur—expert in business management and engineering and amateur in filmmaking—questions the common notion of skills in reference to film-making rather than to the knowledge of what the film is about. Also, the case draws attention to the different levels or meanings of amateur cinema in the factory if we look at it from the perspective of production, exhibition, and reception. Films were made in an amateur production mode by both the workforce and the management, out of passion and/or with a view to rationalization and were professionally used by the management for mar-keting and the management of employees.

The Sulzer case also shows that amateur film has been part and parcel of useful cinema culture. At the same time, it uncovers the overlaps between corporate media culture and popular media culture and amateur film's participating in a visual culture that from a Western-centric perspective has appropriated the world with a colonial gaze. To turn this argument around and toward the discipline of film and media studies, the study of amateur film in the factory makes clear that amateur film produced and used within corporations is not something "other" to be segregated behind the factory walls—it is a part of visual media culture.

Notes

1. Herbert Wolfer, "Würdigung des beruflichen Wirkens," in *Zur Erinnerung an Max E. Trechsel 1893–1978*, 11–13, 1978.

2. E., "Lichtbilder-Abend," *Sulzer Werk-Mitteilungen*, no. 1 (1933): 16.

3. J[ohannes] Fülscher, "Die Bedeutung der Photographie in der Industrie," *Sulzer Werk-Mitteilungen*, no. 4 (1931): 58.

4. Lehner, "Der Kinofilm," in *Vorträge über Sulzer-Propaganda Januar/Februar 1944 gehalten vor GS-Propaganda-Personal*, January 19, 1944, unpublished typescript, 4 (Sulzer Corporate Archive Winterthur, 113).

5. Ibid.

6. Ibid.

7. [Max E. Trechsel], "Der Film im Dienste der Propaganda," in *Vorträge über Sulzer-Propaganda Januar/Februar 1944 gehalten vor GS-Propaganda-Personal*, January 19, 1944, unpublished typescript, 2 (Sulzer Corporate Archive Winterthur, 113).

8. [Max E. Trechsel], "Diskussionsabende über Sulzer-Propaganda," in *Vorträge über Sulzer-Propaganda Januar/Februar 1944 gehalten vor GS-Propaganda-Personal*, January 19, 1944, unpublished typescript, 2 (Sulzer Corporate Archive Winterthur, 113).

9. In connection with the exhibition, Zurich hosted the 5th UNICA International Amateur Film Congress, which took place from June 5–11, 1939. See "Tagesprogramm," *Offizielle Ausstellungszeitung der Scheizerischen Landesausstellung 1939 Zürich*, no. 32 (June 5, 1939): 6. On film's role in the exhibition see Y. Zimmermann 2014.

10. Sulzer responding to Georg Fischer's survey on films sponsored by other companies, October 28, 1948 (Corporate Archives, Georg Fischer Ltd., 15/01/0829).

11. For example, the film was screened at the end of a meeting of the Technical Society Winterthur on January 12, 1940, and accompanied by a lecture. See "Mitteilungen der Vereine," *Schweizerische Bauzeitung* 115, no. 10 (1940): 120.

12. "Sulzer-Propagandafilm 1939: Wegleitender Begleittext für einen Vortrag," unpublished typescript, June 18, 1940, 1 (Sulzer Corporate Archive Winterthur, 113).

13. "Nur ein Werkfilm . . . ," *Sulzer Werk-Mitteilungen*, no. 6 (1940): 46.

14. On this topic, see also Luca Peretti's (forthcoming) case study on amateur films that geologists and geophysicists made when they were sent to Iran in the late 1950s and early 1960s to look for oil on behalf of the Italian oil company, ENI.

15. On the intersections of amateur film and travel film as a form of "safari" and its particular forms of visual appropriation, see Schneider 2002. See also Gunning 1995.

16. I am alluding here to Martin Heidegger's (2002, 71) dictum in "The Age of the World Picture" (1938) that "the fundamental event of the modern age is the conquest of the world as picture" (2002, 71). The notion of "world picture" stated in the title of the book means the world grasped *as* picture, rather than a picture of the world (67).

17. Kä [Ursula Kälin], "Hobby: Filmen," *Sulzer SLM Werkmitteilungen*, no. 11 (1969): 28.

18. K., "'Die neue Welle:' Sulzer-Zeichnerlehrlinge filmen sich selber," *Sulzer SLM Werkmitteilungen*, no. 4 (1967): 24.

19. Ibid.

20. "Filmamateurwettbewerb," *Sulzer SLM Werkmitteilungen*, no. 2 (1965): 32.

21. G. Golliez, "Auguste Lumière," *Sulzer Werk-Mitteilungen*, no. 2 (1957): 55–59.

22. Ibid., 58.

23. G. Golliez, "Louis Lumière," *Sulzer Werk-Mitteilungen*, no. 11 (1948): 84–87; G. Golliez, "Auguste Lumière," *Sulzer Werk-Mitteilungen*, no. 2 (1957): 55–59.

24. Golliez, "Auguste Lumière," 58.

25. Ibid.

26. Hb., "Film-und Lichtbilder-Vortragsabend der Angestellten-Vereinigung," *Sulzer Werk-Mitteilungen*, no. 2 (1947): 14.

27. G. Böhler, "Filmvorführung für unsere Pensionierten," *Sulzer Werk-Mitteilungen*, no. 5 (1952): 47.

28. Ibid.

29. On other attempts to differentiate between home movies and amateur films as objects rather than as experience, see P. Zimmermann 2008; McNamara and Sheldon 2017.

30. Gebrüder Sulzer Aktiengesellschaft, "An unsere Mitarbeiter!" *Sulzer Werk-Mitteilungen*, no. 1 (1919): 1.

31. "Werk-Mitteilungen," *Sulzer Werk-Mitteilungen*, no. 7 (1919): 1.

32. Karl Ketterer, "Erfülltes Lebenswerk," *Die Tat* (June 22, 1953).

References

Forster, Ralf. 2018. *Greif zur Kamera, gib der Freizeit einen Sinn: Amateurfilm in der DDR*. Munich: Edition text + kritik.

Gunning, Tom. 1995. "'The Whole World within Reach:' Travel Images without Borders." In *Cinéma sans frontiers 1896–1918: Images across Borders*, edited by Roland Cosandey and François Albera, 21–36. Lausanne: Éditions Payot.

———. 1997. "Before Documentary: Early Nonfiction Films and the 'View' Aesthetic." In *Uncharted Territory: Essays on Early Nonfiction Film*, edited by Daan Hertogs and Nico de Klerk, 9–24. Amsterdam: Stichting Nederlands Filmmuseum.

Hediger, Vinzenz, and Patrick Vonderau. 2009. "Record, Rhetoric, Rationalization: Industrial Organization and Film." In *Films That Work: Industrial Film and the Productivity of Media*, edited by Vinzenz Hediger and Patrick Vonderau, 35–49. Amsterdam: Amsterdam University Press.

Heidegger, Martin. 2002. *Off the Beaten Track*. Edited and translated by Julian Young and Kenneth Haynes. New York: Cambridge University Press.

Ishizuka, Karen L., and Patricia R. Zimmermann, eds. 2008. *Mining the Home Movie: Excavations in Histories and Memories.* Berkeley: University of California Press.

Jacobson, Brian R. 2017. "The Boss's Film: Expert Amateurs and Industrial Culture." In *Amateur Movie Making: Aesthetics of the Everyday in New England Film 1915–1960,* edited by Marta J. McNamara and Karan Sheldon, 198–218. Bloomington: Indiana University Press.

Kessler, Frank, and Eef Masson. 2009. "Layers of Cheese: Generic Overlap in Early Non-Fiction Films on Production Processes." In *Films That Work: Industrial Film and the Productivity of Media,* edited by Vinzenz Hediger and Patrick Vonderau, 75–84. Amsterdam: Amsterdam University Press.

Mattl, Siegfried, Carina Lesky, Vrääth Öhner, and Ingo Zechner, eds. 2015. *Abenteuer Alltag: Zur Archäologie des Amateurfilms.* Vienna: Synema.

McNamara, Martha J., and Karan Sheldon. 2017. "Introduction." In *Amateur Movie Making: Aesthetics of the Everyday in New England Film 1915–1969,* edited by Martha J. McNamara and Karan Sheldon, 1–13. Bloomington: Indiana University Press.

Nicholson, Heather Norris. 2008. "'As If by Magic:' Authority, Aesthetics, and Vision of the Workplace in Home Movies, circa 1931–1949." In *Mining the Home Movie: Excavations in Histories and Memories,* edited by Karen L. Ishizuka and Patricia R. Zimmermann, 214–30. Berkeley: University of California Press.

Odin, Roger. 1995. "Le film de famille dans l'institution familiale." In *Le film de famille: Usage privé, usage public,* edited by Roger Odin, 27–42. Paris: Méridiens Klincksieck.

Peretti, Luca. Forthcoming. "'There Exists No Life More Daring and Adventuresome than That of an Oil Drigger.' ENI's Geologists-Filmmakers in Iran." In *Films That Work Harder: The Global Circulations of Industrial Cinema,* edited by Vinzenz Hediger, Florian Hoof, and Yvonne Zimmermann. Amsterdam: Amsterdam University Press.

Schneider, Alexandra. 2002. "Autosonntag (Switzerland, 1930)—A Film Safari in the Swiss Alps." *Visual Anthropology* 15:115–28.

———. 2004. *Die Stars sind wir: Heimkino als filmische Praxis.* Marburg: Schüren.

Sobchack, Vivian. 1999. "Toward a Phenomenology of Nonfictional Film Experience." In *Collecting Visible Evidence,* edited by Jane Gaines and Michael Renov, 214–54. Minneapolis: University of Minnesota Press.

Tepperman, Charles. 2014. *Amateur Cinema: The Rise of North American Moviemaking, 1923–1960.* Berkeley: University of California Press.

Vinogradova, Maria. 2017. "Amateur Cinema in the Soviet Union: History, Ideology and Culture." PhD diss., New York University.

Weber, Max. 1990. *Wirtschaft und Gesellschaft: Grundriss der verstehenden Soziologie.* Tübingen: Mohr.

Zimmermann, Patricia R. 1995. *Reel Families: A Social History of Amateur Film.* Bloomington: Indiana University Press.

———. 2008. "The Home Movie Movement: Excavations, Artifacts, Minings." In *Mining the Home Movie: Excavations in Histories and Memories,* edited by Karen L. Ishizuka and Patricia R. Zimmermann, 1–28. Berkeley: University of California Press.

Zimmermann, Yvonne. 2011a. "Dokumentarischer Film: Auftragsfilm und Gebrauchsfilm." In *Schaufenster Schweiz: Dokumentarische Gebrauchsfilme 1896–1964,* edited by Yvonne Zimmermann, 34–83. Zurich: Limmat.

———. 2011b. "Industriefilme." In *Schaufenster Schweiz: Dokumentarische Gebrauchsfilme 1896–1964*, edited by Yvonne Zimmermann, 241–381. Zurich: Limmat.

———. 2014. "The Avant-Garde, Education and Marketing: The Making of Nontheatrical Film Culture in Interwar Switzerland." In *The Emergence of Film Culture: Knowledge Production, Institution Building, and the Fate of the Avant-garde in Europe, 1919–1945*, edited by Malte Hagener, 199–224. Oxford: Berghahn.

YVONNE ZIMMERMANN is Professor of Media Studies at Philipps—University Marburg. She is author of *Bergführer Lorenz: Karriere eines missglückten Films* and editor of *Schaufenster Schweiz: Dokumentarische Gebrauchsfilme 1896–1964*.

7

THE AMBITIONS OF
AMATEUR FILM IN VICHY FRANCE

Julie Guillaumot

IN FRANCE, AMATEUR FILM WAS TRADITIONALLY STUDIED IN relation to home movies and their role within the family. As a result of Roger Odin's pioneering work (1995), research has since extended into other domains, further refining the concept of amateur film (Turquety and Vignaux 2016), including explorations of contemporary uses of video stemming from mobile phones and the web (Allard, Creton and Odin, 2014), as well as creative practices that reutilize amateur images. However, since Gilles Ollivier's first articles (1991), the French amateur filmmakers' clubs and the discourses of its members have not been at the center of such critical historical reevaluation.[1] In France, amateur filmmakers gathered in local organizations from the 1920s mainly to share technical knowledge and to see and comment on each other's films. Although these clubs only brought together a small part of active filmmakers, their influence spread in France through specialized magazines and textbooks, bringing practical and technical codes to amateur cinema.

This oversight and the difficult access to amateur films[2] have prevented scholars from analyzing the extent to which small-gauge filmmaking was involved in key moments in the country's recent history. While, for example, Jean-Pierre Bertin-Maghit's work (2015) has provided in-depth analysis of films shot by the French soldiers during the Algerian War and what they reveal about how these men perceived and experienced the conflict, similar exploration of amateur films during the Second World War has not been carried out yet despite the general interest of historians in French cinema of that period (Bertin-Maghit 1989; Lindeperg 2013). This is a serious omission both with respect to the history of amateur cinema and of that particular moment. After the German invasion of France in June 1940, the country was divided into several parts, all under authoritarian rules. While a government-in-exile led by General de Gaulle and named Free France set up in London to continue resistance, a demarcation line crossed the territory: the North under the control of Germany, known as the "occupied zone," and the South, named the "free zone," remaining no more as a republic but a "French state." Settled in Vichy, this government—hence known as the Vichy regime—rejected parliamentarianism and advocated a renewal of the values of French society through the "National Revolution," a doctrine inspired by French nationalist extreme-right movements and their will to "collaborate" with Nazi Germany. In the first months of the German occupation, which lasted until 1944, amateur film unexpectedly came to the center of discussion twice. First, the German military authorities forbade filming in small-gauge formats, a medium mainly intended for amateurs. Next, an amateur film division was created in May 1941 within the Organizing Committee for the Cinema Industry (COIC). It was the first and only state-supported organization ever devoted to small-gauge filmmaking in France. The COIC as a whole had been created in December 1940 by the French state under two laws: one "concerning the provisional organization of French industry" passed on August 16, 1940 (*JORF*, August 18, 1940, 4731–33); the other, "regulating the cinematographic industry" passed on October 26, 1940 (*JORF*, December 4, 1940, 58–59). It aimed at limiting German control of this economic sector and its actors, but also implementing a new national policy of supervision and support of cinema. Despite Vichy's ambitions for autonomy, the COIC ultimately allowed the German authorities to keep close watch on professionals in the film sector from both occupied and nonoccupied zones, since they were now grouped into one central organization.[3]

This chapter focuses on the attempts of the Vichy administration to control and institutionalize small-gauge film culture during the German occupation, highlighting the cultural and political significance of amateur cinema at such an important moment in the country's history.

Before the war, amateur filmmakers were still exploring the possibilities of the medium, imagining the role that it could play in society. They exchanged ideas with their peers in a Europe that was gradually being impacted by totalitarian ideologies that elsewhere instrumentalized and even controlled amateur cinema (e.g., Germany, Italy) ("Italie" 1936). By the late 1930s, the growing importance of amateur filmmakers in the French cultural milieu opened possibilities for institutionalization. In this context, what ambitions led to the creation of an amateur department within the COIC? What roles did amateur filmmakers play in this development? What was the outcome of this initiative alongside the war?

The analysis of the official publications of the German and French state administrations, as well as in the corporatist newspaper *Le Film,* allow us to reconstruct the regulatory context in which this amateur film division was created. Two objectives emerge: the first one was to allow amateurs to film again, through negotiation with the occupying forces. The second one, which was even more ambitious, was to reorganize amateur film on a national level by creating one central organization. The inspirations for the latter project are evident in the department's press releases in 1941 and can be traced back to the 1930s through the journal *Ciné Amateur,* the leading French publication in this field. As editor-in-chief, Pierre Boyer (named director of the amateur division of the COIC in 1941) published monthly editorials between 1931 and 1939. He reported on the growing practice of amateur film among the French bourgeoisie, the technical advances being made, and the application of multiple techniques that were not merely confined to family chronicles. The magazine reported on the development of dozens of amateur filmmakers' clubs in France, as well as the organization of a national amateur filmmakers' movement and its first international connections. Although the realities of war did not allow for the formation of a national organization, the COIC's initiative and Boyer's texts testify to the strong hopes aroused by small-gauge filmmaking practices at the beginning of the Second World war, which seemed to widen the possibilities of cinema at that time by creating new users and new practical applications beyond the limited scope of the commercial film industry.

The Weight of Prohibition

The initial prohibitions on photographing and on representing public spaces through images emerged early in the German occupation. A student from Tours writes in his war diary in June 1940, three days after the invasion of his city: "They [the Germans] have put signs up everywhere. Some say that the plunderers are subject to the German law of war. Others

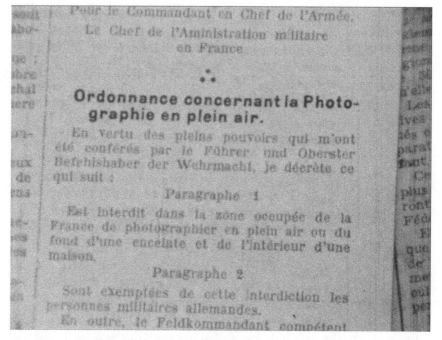

Fig. 7.1. Announcement of the ban of September 16, 1940, in a local newspaper, shot by the amateur filmmaker René Imbault. Screen shot from *A l'ombre de mon clocher*, courtesy of Ciclic.

forbid painting, drawing or photographing the ruins" (Chauvin 1940). These early warnings soon became official with the publication of several German ordinances. These were issued by the German military command in Paris (Militärbefehlshaber in Frankreich), which administered the occupied zone. Its propaganda service (Propaganda Abteilung) was placed directly under the authority of the German Ministry of Information and Propaganda (Bertin-Maghit 2004, 41–42). On September 16, 1940, the ban was first applied to "outdoor photography" and to shooting "from the bottom of an enclosure and from inside a house" (*VOBIF* 10, October 5, 1940, 96). These orders were disseminated through the regional press as well as in specialized journals. Some amateur films produced during this period emphasized this situation. In his film about the war years at Pithiviers, René Imbault included a shot of the insert from his local newspaper that announced the ban (fig. 7.1).

From October 22, 1940, filmmakers were entirely deprived of their tools since "the shooting of small gauge films of any kind and of any dimension was forbidden." (*VOBIF* 14, November 4, 1940, 120–21) The same decree also included all screenings of small-gauge films now subject to authorization. These measures were specified in May 1941 by an official statement from the German authorities to merchants. Only members of the German armed forces could purchase film stock and small-gauge motion picture cameras, as well as order film to be developed and printed (*Le Film* 1941c, 7).

These restrictions were more severe than the rules imposed in other Nazi-occupied territories. A part of northern France was administered by the German command in Belgium. This meant that some ordinances, including the regulation of amateur cinema, could differ. Indeed, Belgium and the north of France had a much more flexible regulation in place. Not only was it possible to shoot and show small-gauge films after obtaining the proper authorization, but an April 25, 1941, ordinance also provided exceptions for family home movies. Thus, it was not necessary to obtain authorization to shoot films "concerning family life" or to screen films in meetings "that do not go beyond the family" (*Le Film* 1941b, 85). In comparison to these territories, it is clear that a much more stringent regulatory control was employed in the area of occupied France controlled from Paris.[4]

The Vichy regime's May 1941 creation of an official division to regulate amateur filmmaking seems rather unexpected. Why was it necessary to oversee a prohibited practice? It should be remembered that, in September 1940, the German military authority linked all professionals in the French film industry to a single organization divided by branches, in order to control this sector, its members and their activities, as well as to enforce the new regulations. Thus, the Germans could also delegate to the French onerous tasks such as providing information for professionals, managing authorization requests, establishing professional files, and so forth. These functions were taken over in December 1940 by the COIC, whose establishing decree mandated the creation of "implementation groups," which were exact copies of the organizational structures initiated by the German authorities. Even though the COIC and its divisions were now applying the new policy of the Vichy regime in cinema, their administrative mandate was also inherited from the previous organization set up by the Germans. In light of these circumstances, it seems logical that an office was created within the COIC, which was exclusively responsible for the enforcement of the ordinances about amateur film that the German military command had issued earlier.

A Breach in the German Regulations

The practice of small-gauge filmmaking being prohibited, the desire to change this situation was therefore the first ambition of the amateur film division of the COIC. Its mission was officially announced in *Le Film* (1941d) in its July 15, 1941 issue: "To envisage, in agreement with the occupying authorities, the possibilities of its resumption of activity." Regarding this point, it is probable that negotiations began immediately with the Germans. In comparison to the aforementioned text that prohibited merchants from developing small-gauge films for general customers, these discussions brought real progress that loosened these restrictions. Subject to authorization, 8 mm, 9.5 mm and 16 mm films shot before October 1, 1940, could now be developed if they were of a familial nature. In addition, families could request permission to organize private screenings for an unlimited period (*Le Film* 1941e, 8).

If the freedoms conceded appear thin, they nonetheless represented a breach in German regulations. Authorization to develop films shot before the autumn of 1940 enabled merchants to serve the general public and, most certainly, to close their eyes to the exact date when films were shot. Hélène Mariette shot five family films between 1941 and 1943 in Amboise (occupied area). All the boxes carry a stamp indicating that the reels had been authorized by the amateur film section of the COIC (fig. 7.2). These family pictures were, however, shot well after October 1940. This example demonstrates the flexibility of the COIC in relation to the rules it was responsible for enforcing. Nevertheless, it is difficult to qualify this flexibility given the scarcity of available sources. How many applications for permits were submitted to the amateur film division? What were the responses? Unfortunately, the archives of the division have not been preserved.

It is also difficult to determine with certainty the scope with which these rules were applied. Despite the division of France, the Vichy government still defended its sovereignty over the entire country. When the COIC was created, its rules concerned all French professionals across both zones, although its decisions had to be validated by the German command. In this context, on July 21, 1941, the COIC issued a communiqué reminding "in a clear and complete manner" the general framework in which "resellers of amateur cinematographic material" were expected to operate (*Le Film* 1941e, 8). However, the text was ambiguous. It referred to the ordinances of the occupying authorities, but it came from an institution that exercised its powers over the whole country. Moreover, it never clearly stated which territory was impacted by these ordinances and reminded that "the making of

Fig. 7.2. A box carrying a stamp indicating that the amateur reel inside had been authorized by the amateur film section of the COIC. The Hélène Mariette collection, Ciclic Film Archive. Author's photography.

amateur films, in all places and in all its forms, is prohibited until further notice." Although certain restrictions existed in France even before the declaration of war (no images of members, equipment, or installations of the French army), no official text was then decreed by the Vichy regime (*JORF* and *JOEF* 1940–1944) to forbid all amateur filmmaking, as the Germans did in the occupied zone.

It is likely that the ambiguities within the communiqué caused confusion among French amateur filmmakers. Even without official prohibition within the free zone, the magazines *Photo Cinéma* and *Cinéma-Spectacles*, sold in the South after 1940, spoke of amateur film as a "suspended" activity (Monier 1941) and even extinct or dormant (Saramito 1942b) until 1944.

A Fight for the Recognition of Amateur Film

These circumstances did not prevent the head of the amateur film division of the COIC, Pierre Boyer, from developing a project aimed at creating a national organization for amateur filmmakers that he called a General

Union (union générale) of amateur cinema. Indeed, the first mission of the division was "the reorganization of amateur film at the national level." An article in *Le Film* (1941f, XI) presented the thrust of the project in December 1941. Basing itself on French amateur filmmakers' clubs, the aim was to bring together amateur filmmakers and those who had never joined a club before into a single organization that would be financed by member contributions. The funds collected would make it possible to supply the groups "with equipment and laboratories, study centers, and places for screenings, debates and training," as well as help create a "National Amateur Film Library" to facilitate the circulation of films. This infrastructure would allow filmmakers to meet and exchange in order to improve their practice. It would have social virtues by contributing to a "healthy, intelligent distraction" as well as by ensuring an egalitarian access to the technical means necessary for the making of a film. The text emphasized the educational nature of this activity, likened to a "professional training ground," citing several professional technicians and filmmakers that had originated from the amateur film movement (*Le Film* 1941f, XI).

While the article made Raoul Ploquin, the director of the COIC, responsible for the decision to integrate amateur cinema into the COIC, the text also made frequent mentions to Boyer, who was probably the driving force in the creation of the amateur division and in the definition of its objectives. As mentioned earlier, the publication *Ciné Amateur*, where Boyer served as editor-in-chief until 1939, contributed to the structuring of the amateur film movement in France. It was the official publication of the French Federation of Amateur Film Clubs (FFCCA), founded in 1932, and of the Club of French Amateur Filmmakers (CACF), a large Parisian club. In 1936, it published the first official bulletins of the International Office of Information and Documentation of Amateur Cinema, which foreshadowed the International Union of Amateur Cinema (Union Internationale du Cinéma d'Amateur, UNICA). An amateur filmmaker himself, Boyer joined the CACF in 1931 and won awards in national and international competitions.

Boyer was already a fervent promoter of amateur film, even in the face of public authorities. He led a campaign to carve out a place for amateur film at the International Exposition of Arts and Technics in 1937 and obtain state support for the organization of the 3rd International Congress of Amateur Film in Paris. After publishing an open letter in *Ciné Amateur* to the Minister of National Education in September 1936, he explained in an

October 1936 editorial that this appeal "had a considerable impact in the official spheres." Similarly, in May 1939, Boyer used the pages of *Ciné Amateur* to report on the steps taken by amateur Parisian filmmakers to have the specificity of their activities be taken into account in the new Cinema Regulation Act that was being prepared by the French government. These initiatives were not always successful. The archives of the Department of Fine Arts contain the FFCCA's grant application letter for the 1937 International Congress, as well as the negative reply that it was given.[5]

However, these same archives also testify to the capacity of amateur filmmakers in Paris—mainly from the bourgeoisie—to mobilize their political networks in order to bring their demands to the highest level of the state. In 1939, they initiated exchanges between the Ministry of the Interior, the Department of Fine Arts (Ministry of National Education), and the National Assembly, in order to retain the right to film in public spaces and gather together for screenings without being required to follow rules designed for commercial films.[6] While the political sympathies of club members are difficult to establish, a note written in 1939, kept in the archives of the Department of Fine Arts, reveals that in order to obtain an exemption within the new Cinema Regulation Act, club representatives would have no scruples as to no longer screen "any political, religious or tendentious film," and particularly all Soviet films.[7] Conservative political opinions among members of the clubs may have later facilitated exchanges with the Vichy regime. In 1940 and 1941, these links and convergences were probably useful in defending amateur film in the face of the leaders of the COIC.

In 1941, Boyer merely continued with the quasi-missionary work he had begun in the 1930s in support of amateur film. The texts of the amateur film section of the COIC and the *Ciné Amateur* editorials from before the war use the same vocabulary, identical arguments, and are inspired by the same sincere faith in the future of amateur cinema. In his October 1936 editorial, Boyer (1936c) made the following emphatic declarations: "It must be finally known everywhere, quickly, definitively, without surprise, that amateur cinema is not a negligible joke but, on the contrary, a very strong movement that is growing every hour; an intense artistic faith that every country concerned about its culture must organize, fortify and guarantee."

This language is reminiscent of the superlatives used to describe the screening of July 30, 1941, organized to present "the most remarkable achievements of amateur cinema" and "to demonstrate, right under the nose of the 'big' cinema, what [amateur filmmaking] is, what it can do" (Michaut 1941).

More generally, in the texts introducing the amateur cinema section of the COIC, statements about "the tremendous importance of the amateur film movement" and "the strength, the dynamism, the artistic faith that amateur cinema represents" (*Le Film* 1941f, XI) resonate with Boyer's vision.

Sources of Inspiration for the Project Promoting a National Organization for Amateur Filmmakers

Beyond Boyer's enthusiastic words in favor of amateur cinema, his texts for *Ciné Amateur* also make it possible to draw parallels between the ambitions of the project of General Union and Boyer's previous experiences reported in the magazine. In October 1936, when Boyer (1936c) wrote in his editorial about "every country concerned about its culture," he was certainly referring to Germany. In July 1936, he represented France at the 2nd Congress and the 5th International Amateur Film Competition organized in Berlin by the Bund Deutscher Film Amateur (BDFA). Boyer was dazzled: not only did the BDFA receive regular financial support from the film agency in Germany, but sixty thousand marks had been devoted by the German government to the congress and personalities of the regime saluted the importance of amateur cinema. In August 1936 Boyer (1936b) wrote in his editorial: "How can one fail to see that the extraordinary development of German amateur cinema and its brilliant, well-earned, extremely rapid successes stems from the fact that it is not taken lightly by our neighbors. . . . The Third Reich applauds amateur cinematographic research and also supports them. . . . And you, France, little-known cradle of cinema, what are you doing for us?" Consequently, Boyer always cited the German model for amateur film organizations as an example to be followed. This state-supported structure was certainly an inspiration for him when the General Union was conceived.

The 1941 project also seems built on Boyer's personal reflections about the role of a national federation of amateur filmmakers clubs in the late 1930s. The year 1937 was marked by a rupture between the national federation and the CACF, to which Boyer belonged. In the context of this rivalry, Boyer (1938b) presented his vision of the mission that a national federation should have in his October 1938 editorial. He insisted on the development of exchanges between the Paris clubs and those in the rest of the country. In this respect, he valued two initiatives of the CACF: the creation in 1936 of a film library and the organization in 1938 of "a vast documentation . . .

creating an inventory of the names and addresses of all those who practice amateur cinema in France . . . so that filmmakers . . . can quickly find, without research, an important list of names of inestimable value for their projects," especially those related to creating new clubs.

There is no doubt that these reflections inspired Boyer to imagine the aforementioned National Library of Amateur Film in 1941. Similarly, they also served to help define the role of "clubs or sections of the general union" as "places for screenings, debates and training" (*Le Film* 1941f, XI). Regarding the proliferation of new associations of filmmakers, which he judged sometimes too small and fragile, Boyer (1938a) wrote in his August 1938 editorial: "Would it not be desirable for the clubs of the major cities to undertake this regrouping by region? . . . It is necessary to organize the amateur film network of the country. . . . It is possible because everything is ready, including the members. It is only necessary to find bit of logical spirit, a spirit of union and mutual understanding."

Thus, Pierre Boyer's contribution to the national organization of amateur film in 1941 seems obvious, considering the description of similar, almost identical, projects in his writings during previous years.

Such organization also echoed the German organization of amateur film, which was based on a single grouping that consisted of local sections. It was also similar to the structuring of amateur film in Italy, where amateurs had been obligatory members of the cinematographic sections of the fascist university groups (GUF) since 1934 ("Italie" 1936). Moreover, the tensions that had divided the French movement between 1937 and 1939 were so important that Boyer used them as an argument in presenting his own project. Indeed, the article in *Le Film* in December 1941, which describes the plan for a new national organization in detail, presents it as a remedy for "the state of anarchy which, in the same city, has made different clubs rivals, enemies" (*Le Film* 1941f, XI). This strong will to unite the different amateur clubs was the fruit of years of disagreements experienced by the filmmaker inside the French amateur film movement.

A Stillborn Project

After these difficult years, which resulted in an underrepresentation of France in the international competition in Zurich in 1939, Boyer probably saw the creation of the COIC as an unexpected opportunity to implement the unifying institution he had dreamed of. After convincing Raoul

Ploquin, the director of the COIC, he circulated information on the devised institution through his network of contacts. In May 1941, *Photo Cinéma* published a short article titled "Towards a Regulation Act for Amateur Film?" In parallel, Boyer organized events to promote amateur cinema. In July 1941, a gathering was held with two hundred guests, professionals, but also "German *Propaganda-Staffel* authorities, [and] the directors of the COIC," to view eight amateur films "ranging from simple sketches to strange films, from pure photographic aesthetic research to narrative short films and the most complete documentaries" (Michaut 1941). In its report, *Le Film* highlighted the surprise and interest of the spectators, including the German authorities (Michaut 1941). Films were not only shot by members of the CACF but also by other Parisian clubs. Boyer seemed to be gradually reconnecting with the French clubs. The minutes of the Board of Directors of the French Society of Photography and Cinematography (SFPC) show that this association was requested by the COIC in October 1941 to complete a questionnaire regarding its activities for the unification project (Proceedings SFPC 1932–1944, 157–60). These exchanges with the clubs probably encouraged Boyer to unveil his program in *Le Film* in the aforementioned December 1941 article (*Le Film* 1941f, XI). This was to be the highlight of this initiative, which did not come to fruition.

In the months and years that followed, no issue of *Le Film* spoke of the activities of the amateur film division of the COIC until March 1944. At this date, *Le Film* announced the authorization given to CACF and SFPC to once again organize screenings reserved for their members. A few months before the start of the liberation of France, Boyer's dream project was not even mentioned, and all the films shown had been made before the war (Boyer 1944, 12). However in March 1942, Roger Saramito (1942a), a journalist of *Cinéma-Spectacles*, explained how amateur cinema practice was a great way to learn technique as well as develop "an artistic sensibility, an eye." This argument was similar to one of Boyer's reasons for supporting a national organization (*Le Film* 1941f, XI). Saramito's article concluded by highlighting the government's commitment to amateur film through the COIC. Two months later, in another article in the same journal, Saramito (1942b) no longer spoke of the future. He praised the role of "amateur film clubs" in the artistic development of cinema but concluded by suggesting that the movement would be reborn "once the hostilities were over."

Meanwhile, Ploquin left the leadership of the COIC on May 25, 1942, replaced by a steering committee as desired by the Vichy government (*JOEF*,

May 26, 1942). It is likely that the national organization project did not survive the change of direction. In October 1942, the board of directors of the SFPC gave an update on the project and noted that "due to the current circumstances that are unfavorable to the development of amateur cinema, it has been decided not to proceed with the project" (Proceedings SFPC 1932–1944, 170). The circumstances were indeed unfavorable. For historian Jean-Pierre Bertin-Maghit, the year 1942 was pivotal. Due to the defeats that Nazi Germany was experiencing, the occupying authorities toughened the restrictions on raw materials, in particular for film and chemical products (Bertin-Maghit 2004, 38–39). Manufacturers had great difficulty in sourcing film stock. Consequently, the state already struggled to implement its own propaganda policy. Under these conditions, it seems logical that Boyer's grand project was not a priority for the authorities.

Conclusion

One year passed between the creation of the amateur film division of the COIC in May 1941 and the departure of Raoul Ploquin in May 1942. It was the lifespan of a strange institutional project, that was both a tool aimed at regaining rights for amateur filmmakers and a stepping stone for the implementation of a public organization of amateur cinema. How could Pierre Boyer believe in the future of a "general union of amateur cinema" in a time of war? It was as though the development of the amateur film movement in the 1930s had prevented him from taking a realistic look at the situation in France after the German invasion. Did he think that the German leaders would welcome a model similar to that of fascist Italy or the German BDFA, which had integrated the Austrian filmmakers after the *Anschluss* of 1938? Did he think that this project would serve the National Revolution? In a context of shortages, with a French economy under guardianship, heavily taxed by the Germans, his efforts were unable to strike a chord among the leaders of the COIC, the Vichy regime, or the German authorities. The organization of amateur film by the state in France did not take place, and when the National Center for Cinema (CNC) was founded in 1945, amateur film had no place in it.

Involved in amateur cinema since 1931, Boyer seemed to be the main figure behind the ambitious amateur filmmaking project. His intriguing trajectory deserves to be better known and researched. Despite his clear involvement with the Vichy regime, he never experienced any significant backlash after the liberation. His attitude paralleled the state of mind of a part of the French population until 1942: benevolent toward the Vichy policy, ready to make do with the occupation. By the end of 1942 this attitude changed, especially after the invasion of the southern "free zone" by the Germans in November. Boyer reappeared only in 1944 by participating in amateur films on the liberation of Paris. In 1947 he took over the reins of *Ciné Amateur* once it had reemerged and was the head of a production company for institutional films. At that time, the idea of a state-supported national organization had disappeared, but Boyer was still a regarded figure in the amateur filmmaking community.[8] He remained editor-in-chief of *Ciné Amateur* until his death in 1964, continuing to support the development of amateur cinema.

The 1941 project is actually indicative of the ambitions and dynamism that characterized the first attempts to institutionalize amateur film in France. During the interwar period, the French press was full of positive comments regarding this new medium. Boyer was not alone in seeing amateur film as a powerful tool to spread ideas and allow for broader individual and collective expression. Amateur film was used extensively by teachers, doctors, as well as by members of different movements across the ideological spectrum. In 1935, the French right-wing movement *Croix-de-feu* had a photo-cinema group that filmed the movement's major events—mainly impressive parades of supporters and commemorations of the Great War.[9] Various workers' movements around the world made use of this technology in collectives, such as in France, Japan, the United States, and various European countries, to defend the labor movement (Hogenkamp 1981, 129–30). These examples reveal how small-gauge films allowed for the emergence of intriguing film production experiences yet to be explored. Considering this growing use of amateur film, sometimes with political ideas in mind, it was maybe natural that Boyer found an attentive ear in the COIC and that authoritarian regimes were trying to control it.

As the existence of hundreds of films kept in the French regional archives shows, many amateurs filmed between 1940 and 1944 throughout France. These previously inaccessible documents constitute a new ground for research. Despite the legal and material obstacles, people made home movies in which a seemingly normal everyday life under war was recorded, sometimes reflecting the small daily upheavals and prohibitions that their risky activity entailed. Children and family life still had a prominent place, but some filmmakers integrated wartime situations in their family films. Fifty-year-old Henri Lecerf, who lived with his wife in Montargis, made a diary of the couple's life in the war between 1940 and 1944, filming the place of their exile during the German invasion of 1940, the ruins on the way back, German soldiers in front of their house, a harvest of apples, a new homemade shelter in the garden, and so forth. Some filmmakers even used cinema to joke about their living conditions. Louis Le Meur made a humorous film about his daughter's birthday in October 1940, staging the lack of money and food and the black-market arrangements. In 1943, Jacques Pénin filmed his six-month-old daughter, Agnès, eating a meal. Before filming Agnès, he made numerous shots of plugs, lamps, and light bulbs. With a touch of irony, this gives the baby a star status. It is also a way to make fun of the many power outages that affected Parisians at that time.

Others filmmakers chronicled local events (sports, charity fairs in aid of French prisoners in Germany), sometimes even official events of the regime like Jacques Griffon's filming of the head of the French State Philippe Pétain's visit to Châteauroux in 1942. Many wanted to leave a testimony about their wartime experience, filming first of all the desolation of ruins after 1940s raids just like Pierre Staub in Beauvais, then the German presence or Nazi flags in the public space at the risk of being detected and arrested. René Imbault even captured the removal of public statues in 1941 in Pithiviers with a hidden camera.[10] Although few documents are accessible, films were also made to support the Vichy regime. For example, Pierre Villiaume and friends filmed the vocational training centers (*centres de jeunesse*) set up by the regime in the Orleans area. Their images were produced to be shown in a local exhibition promoting these new facilities. Without a doubt, the future identification and analysis of these films and practices should therefore provide new insights into the French public opinion during the Second World War and the uses of amateur film, adding to the growing scholarship on the multiple lives of moving images beyond the commercial screen and professional filmmaking.

Notes

1. In other countries, amateur film movements are beginning to be studied, as Charles Tepperman (2014) has done with regard to amateur filmmaking in North America.

2. These films have long been neglected by film archives. In France, the first regional amateur films collections weren't created until the 1980s.

3. With the agreement of the Germans, the COIC had official authority over both zones, in order to harmonize in most of the country decisions about professional cinema and the new rules (professional files, cinema exhibitions). An important issue was also to avoid dividing the commercial film market.

4. It would be interesting to set up a collaboration between European researchers to compare these ordinances with those taken in other European Nazi-occupied countries, in order to understand the logic of these differences.

5. "Congrès cinématographiques, juin 1937-septembre 1945," Archives from the Department of Fine Arts—Cinematographic Affairs (1920–1950), F21/8670, National Archives, France.

6. "Statut du cinéma (1934–1939)," Archives from the Department of Fine Arts—Cinematographic Affairs (1920–1950), F/21/8656, National Archives, France.

7. "Note pour monsieur le directeur général des Beaux-Arts" dated April 13, 1939, from the cabinet of the Minister of National Education, "Statut du cinéma (1934–1939)," F/21/8656, National Archives, France.

8. From the first issue published in 1947, *Ciné Amateur* becomes again the "official organ" of the FFCCA. After the 6th International Congress of Stockholm in August 1947, the journal also becomes that of the UNICA. See Boyer 1947a; Boyer 1947b.

9. Twenty films shot by this group between 1934 and 1936 have been preserved by the National Centre for Cinema (CNC), France.

10. In 1941, to overcome the lack of metals, Vichy government organized the removal and the melting of a number of French public bronze statues.

References

Primary and Archival Sources

Archives de l'administration des Beaux-Arts, politique du cinéma [Archives from the Department of Fine Arts, Cinematographic Affairs] (1920–1950), F21/8670 and F/21/8656, National Archives, France.

Chauvin, Jean. 1940. Papers. Sous-série 40J, Departmental Archives of the Indre-et-Loire, France.

Proceedings of the French Society of Photography and Cinematography (1932–1944), French Society of Photography (Société française de photographie, SFP), France.

Official Publications

JOEF (*Journal officiel de l'État français. Lois et décrets*) [Published by Vichy government between January 5, 1941, and August 25, 1944].

JORF (*Journal officiel de la République française. Lois et décrets*) [Until December 1940].

VOBIF (*Verordnungsblatt des Militärbefehlshabers in Frankreich*) [Official newspaper containing the ordinances adopted by the military governor for the French occupied territories between July 4, 1940, and October 20, 1944].

Periodicals

Ciné Amateur

Boyer, Pierre. 1936a. "Éditorial," June 1936, 17.
———. 1936b. "Éditorial," August 1936, 13.
———. 1936c. "Éditorial," October 1936, 13.

———. 1938a. "Éditorial," August 1938, 7.

———. 1938b. "Éditorial," October 1938, 7.

———. 1939a. "Les amateurs et le statut du cinéma (2)," May 1939, 7.

———. 1939b. "Raisons et leçons d'une défaite," July 1939, 7.

———. 1947a. "Renouer," August 1947, 5.

———. 1947b. "Réussites françaises," September 1947, 3.

Delbonnel, Jean-Jacques. 1938. "Pierre Boyer," March 1938, 16.

"Italie." 1936. *Bulletin officiel du centre international de renseignements et de documentation du cinéma d'amateur* (inserted in *Ciné Amateur*), June 1936, 11.

Cinéma-Spectacles

Saramito, Roger. 1942a. "Le cinéma d'amateur: école du bon cinéma professionnel," March 28, 1942, 12.

———. 1942b. "L'action des ciné-clubs d'amateur dans le développement de l'art cinématographique," July 4, 1942, 8.

Le Film

1941a. "Vers un statut du cinéma d'amateur?" May 1941, 104.

1941b. "Nouvelles officielles," June 7, 1941, 85.

1941c. "Réglementation de la vente au détail d'appareils cinématographiques, de pellicule, et de tous accessoires pour formats réduits," June 21, 1941, 7.

1941d. "L'activité du cinéma d'amateurs rattachée au comité d'organisation," July 15, 1941, 4.

1941e. "Droits et obligations des revendeurs de matériel cinématographique d'amateurs," August 30, 1941, 8.

1941f. "Vers l'organisation officielle du cinéma d'amateurs en France," December 20, 1941, XI.

Boyer, Pierre. 1944. "Deux clubs d'amateurs parisiens ont fait leur réouverture," March 18, 1944, 12.

Michaut, Pierre. 1941. "La Section de Cinéma-Amateur du Comité d'organisation de l'industrie cinématographique a donné une très intéressante séance d'information," September 27, 1941, XXVII.

Photo Cinéma

Monier, Pierre. 1941. "Films du passé, sachons vous conserver," January 1941, 22.

Films

Griffon, Jacques. 1942. *Visite du Maréchal Pétain à Châteauroux*, 9.5 mm film, from Ciclic, MPEG video, memoire.ciclic.fr/1974-visite-du-marechal-petain-a-chateauroux.

Imbault, René. 1939–1945. *À l'ombre de mon clocher*, 8 mm film, from Ciclic, MPEG video, 25:30, memoire.ciclic.fr/3106-a-l-ombre-de-mon-clocher.

Lecerf, Henri. 1940–1946. *La Libération de Montargis*, 9.5 mm film, from Ciclic, MPEG video, 66:42, memoire.ciclic.fr/9568-liberation-de-montargis-la.

Le Meur, Louis. 1940–1941. *La famille Le Meur 1940/1941*, 16 mm film, from La Cinémathèque de Bretagne, MPEG video, 21:30, www.cinematheque-bretagne.bzh/base-documentaire-famille-le-meur-1940_41-_La_-426-4760-0-1.html.

Mariette, Hélène. Family films made between 1941 and 1943. Ciclic Film Archive.

Pénin, Jacques. 1942–1944. *Agnès 31 octobre 1942; Gilles 30 novembre 1944*, 9.5 mm film, from Cinéam, MPEG video, 6:57, www.cineam.asso.fr.

Staub, Pierre. 1940. *Beauvais, ville martyre*, 9.5 mm film, from Le Forum des images, MPEG video, 4:08, collections.forumdesimages.fr.

Villiaume, Pierre. 1942–1943. *Centres d'apprentissage dans le Loiret sous l'Occupation*, 16 mm film, from Ciclic, MPEG video, 16:21, memoire.ciclic.fr/11380-centres-d-apprentissage -dans-le-loiret-sous-l-occupation.

Books and Articles

Allard, Laurence, Laurent Creton, and Roger Odin, eds. 2014. *Téléphone mobile et création*. Paris: Armand Colin.

Bertin-Maghit, Jean-Pierre. 1989. *Le Cinéma français sous l'Occupation*. Paris: Olivier Orban.

———. 2004. *Les Documenteurs des années noires: les documentaires de propagande, France 1940–1944*. Paris: Nouveau monde éditions.

———. 2015. *Lettres filmées d'Algérie: des soldats à la caméra (1954–1962)*. Paris: Nouveau monde éditions.

Hogenkamp, Bert. 1981. "Le mouvement ouvrier et le cinéma." *La Revue du cinéma* 366 (November): 125–35.

Lindeperg, Sylvie. 2013. *La Voie des images: quatre histoires de tournage au printemps-été 1944*. Lagrasse: Verdier, 2013.

Odin, Roger. 1995. *Le Film de famille: usage privé, usage public*. Paris: Méridiens Klincksieck.

Ollivier, Gilles. 1991. "1928–1959: idéologies, structures et évolutions des clubs de cinéastes amateurs." *Archives* 40 (April): 1–12.

Turquety, Benoît, and Valérie Vignaux, eds. 2016. *L'Amateur en cinéma, un autre paradigme: histoire, esthétique, marges et institutions*. Paris: AFRHC.

JULIE GUILLAUMOT is a professional archivist and a PhD candidate at the University of Caen. She is preparing a thesis on French amateur cinema during World War II at the University of Caen (research team LASLAR).

8

ON THE AMATEUR ORIGINS OF FERNANDO BIRRI'S DOCUMENTARY SCHOOL OF SANTA FE

Mariano Mestman and Christopher Moore

THE DOCUMENTARY SCHOOL OF SANTA FE AND ITS founder, Fernando Birri, are inescapable references in the story of the New Latin American Cinema. The school grew out of a brief course offered by Birri in 1956. The young Argentine had recently returned from studies at the Centro Sperimentale di Cinematografia in Rome, and he was asked to help organize a course on film with the Instituto Social at the Universidad Nacional del Litoral (UNL) in Santa Fe, Argentina. The course was deemed a great success and, soon thereafter, Birri and the UNL institutionalized their efforts by establishing the Instituto de Cinematografía (Institute of Film, or IC), which began offering classes in April 1957. In the years that followed, the IC would further consolidate itself, becoming known across Argentina and throughout Latin American for its focus on social issues of the time.

At this moment in the late 1950s and early 1960s, other film schools were then cropping up in other Argentine cities, part of a broader movement that was progressively revamping the national cinema. This was a particularly crucial political and cultural moment in Argentina, a moment perceived by many artists and intellectuals as an "opening" for the arts. The democratic-popular government of Juan Domingo Perón (1946–1955) had been overthrown by a civic-military coup in September 1955. Hopes that the new government might better service the arts were quickly dashed, however. Instead, the coup inaugurated a period best characterized as politically

Fig. 8.1. Work at the office of the Instituto de Cinematografía of the Universidad del Litoral in the 1960s." Colección Museo Histórico, Universidad Nacional del Litoral.

instable with a contradictory "modernization" of cultural fields and higher education. Many middle-class and intellectual sectors similarly grew frustrated by the repressive actions of the military government (1955–1958) and by the so-called treason of the democratically elected Arturo Frondizi (1958–1962)—a man who abandoned his original political program and his promises to reincorporate the at that time banned Peronist party (and, with it, the working class) back into Argentine political life.

When Frondizi was himself removed by a subsequent military coup in 1962, Fernando Birri left his position as director of the UNL's Instituto de Cinematografía, and departed Argentina the following year to go to Brazil with a group of his collaborators. This brought an end to many of the IC's initial efforts. Although the IC would continue to make films and offer classes after Birri left, his departure somehow put an end to that initial impulse that so characterizes the Documentary School of Santa Fe today.

This chapter returns to 1956 and the beginnings of that experience. There, the local converged with the transnational, and an internationally renowned film program was born out of a faith in amateurs—their knowledge, their perspective, and their capacity for self-expression. In Part I, we show how Birri's initial effort—an introductory course on documentary, offered at the university's margins (as part of its extension program, out of the social sciences division), and counting among its enrollees painters, schoolteachers, lawyers, even social workers—drew inspiration in equal parts from professional and amateur realms. In Part II, we analyze a key aspect to the filmmaker's early approach: the use of *fotodocumentales*—photo-documentaries or photo essays—as a first step for those learning to make films. We reconsider this practice of using photography and social surveys as borrowing from the possibilities of the amateur. The act of taking a picture or asking a question made the filmmaking effort accessible to enrollees with little or no background in production, and it was an adequate first step given the limited initial resources of the IC. Most important, fotodocumentales helped focused students' attention on the capturing of local realities and on the social possibilities of the cinema. As such, although clearly part of a certain (socially and politically conscious) professionalization project, these practices belong to the broader field of amateur cinematic cultures for providing an alternative vision of cinema's social function and an alternative means of institutionalizing nonindustrial cinematic practices. In Part III, we focus on the well-known documentary *Tire-dié* (1958–1960). We look at the project's evolution from a student-made fotodocumental to the IC's first documentary film, finished in 1958. We pay special attention to the film's deliberately noncommercial character, both in terms of how it was produced and how it was used socially, across informal networks of exhibition, through community screenings and postscreening audience surveys. Finally, in Part IV, in order to show their impact in later professional film production at school, we return to those unpublished surveys. We note that Birri and his team utilized commentaries from nonfilmgoing audiences to assess their successes in film and to develop the next set of films—a series that, as with the others, featured almost exclusively amateur actors.

Birri himself was no "amateur," and his film school quickly became a point of cinematic reference in Latin America, but the initiative, at least in its origins, stemmed from a bottom-up approach, one that drew inspiration, where not direct investment, from local, amateur practices and bases of knowledge. In many ways, it was the IC's incorporation of amateur participants, from its students and its film subjects to the neighborhood audiences with whom it shared its films, as well as their association with alternative film cultures, such as local "foto" or "cine-clubs," that proved an ideal means for training future professionals, thus demonstrating the fluid and productive boundaries between the amateur and the professional. In so doing, the IC's particular approach charted a new path for the institutional-ization of innovative cinematic practices.[1]

Part I

In November 1956, the Documentary School of Santa Fe offered students a brief hybrid course on film studies and film production, which lasted for four days and was hosted by Fernando Birri. Birri had been invited to give the class by Angela Romero Vera, then the director of the Insti-tuto Social. Her invitation was hardly accidental; Romero Vera shared Birri's enthusiasm for using photography, film, and social surveys in the classroom.

Born in Santa Fe, Birri first arrived at UNL as a student in the 1940s. Before leaving Argentina to study in Italy, he served as director of UNL's university theater and, later, for a local puppeteering ensemble. Romero Vera, a lawyer and sociologist who had fled the Spanish Civil War, was also an active participant in the academic and social life of UNL. She regularly pushed for interdisciplinary exchanges among the social and juridical sciences, and she, too, was interested in using social surveys and even documentary photography as a means for understanding local realities and circumstances.[2] When Romero Vera became director of the Instituto Social in 1956, just as Birri was returning from Italy, the two immediately collaborated to create the Instituto de Cinematografía. Initially just an idea—that film and photography were increasingly media of choice and that the cinema offered UNL an additional means by which to integrate the surrounding community—the concept quickly spawned a physical center, with buildings, chairs, libraries, studio space, laboratories, dedicated fac-ulty, and even publishing capacities.[3]

The contours of that initial idea can be traced back through documents of the era, to before the IC was institutionalized. In those documents, the theoretical-practical teaching that the fotodocumental method offered emerges as a particularly useful tool, however "amateur" or "precari-ous" the effort might have appeared. The brief course that Birri offered in 1956, in a borrowed classroom at the university's law school, was, Birri recalled, a sort of "homemade" workshop, and notably "modest." Despite its humble beginnings, more than one hundred students enrolled. Many of them came from outside of the university and from nontraditional back-grounds; enrollees included young writers, painters, and local musicians,

"Cineclub" enthusiasts, independent playwrights, students, social workers, and teachers (Birri 1956, 5).

For the first class Birri borrowed a shabby magic lantern from the chemistry department and projected a pair of fotodocumentales that he had brought with him from Italy. With scant resources, the classes were held in an informal setting, divorced from the standards of school schedules and lecture times, which allowed for conversation and debate to continue until dawn. The course's informality was central to the early successes of Birri's teaching; he later acknowledged that the students generated the classroom's energy. Lessons designed by the teachers became "collective dialogues," where students brainstormed potential fotodocumentales they could produce themselves. In the span of just a few days, students secured material support from the local Foto Club Santa Fe, and within a week they premiered initial fotodocumentales of their own—"still approximate" and "incomplete," their works led to more classes and more projects (Birri 1956, 5).

In that initial moment, the fotodocumental was thought of as a kind of "notebook" (texts, themes, profile shots, landscapes) that would then inform future documentaries and fictional films. The fotodocumental emerges, then, as a perfect solution to their situation, perfectly adequate for the extreme scarcity of resources during that time. Though the IC did not have the means to provide industry-standard equipment, Birri believed that his students did not need such things for their training. Instead, they needed to rely on their passion and enthusiasm, two key concepts traditionally associated with amateur practices. Each student chose the subjects of their fotodocumentales freely, but sociopolitical issues were strongly emphasized and far and away the most common themes chosen by the first wave of participants: misery, flooding, poor children following the trains, overcrowding in the convents, precarious housing in the city's shantytowns, issues of electricity and water in the barrios, the abandoned elderly, harsh working conditions—as Birri put it, "the daily difficulties in the struggle for life" (Birri 1956, 6).

Romero Vera similarly underlined the social dimension of the practice, and she identified the ethics at the core of the IC's mission. The IC's ethics continued a tradition of union and compromise between the Universidad Nacional del Litoral and the people, one that also called to mind the establishment of the Instituto Social in 1928. Romero Vera liked to point out that the UNL envisioned extension programs not as some "simple education of lower classes by an elite," but instead as "an exchange"; and the film program, in particular, was described as "a new form of communicating with our people in their local environments" (Romero Vera 1956, 3–4). Even in those early stages, Romero Vera, like Birri, was already thinking about the social uses of fotodocumentales and documentary film and their ability to question or persuade a spectator. Birri hoped spectators would be "moved" or "outraged" by what they saw, and might then understand that "things can't go on this way," and act accordingly (7).

Part II

Where, exactly, did the idea of the fotodocumental come from? Most histories of the Documentary School of Santa Fe are based on Birri's own writings and frequently mention the school's two principle influences: the British Documentary School, created by John Grierson, and Italian Neorealism—"the great ally of documentary in fiction," according to Bill Nichols (Nichols 1991, 167). The Neorealist collaborations between Cesare Zavattini and Vittorio De Sica are of particular importance.

To suggest that there were ties between the Documentary School of Santa Fe and the two European movements is not to imply that it simply imitated them—rather, the commonalities were more direct and profound. By the late 1950s, the IC was actively in dialogue with the British and Canadian documentary movements (both were promoted by Grierson). The IC often projected the British and Canadian documentaries, republished their writings, and offered courses and conferences on the significance of their work. Grierson felt a similar affinity for the people from Santa FE. He called the fotodocumental *Tire-dié* (1956) a "simple but profound" contribution, and he applauded Birri's use of the fotodocumental as a teaching tool (Mestman and Ortega 2014, 229).

Grierson recognized that Birri had made the fotodocumental a central component of his educational project. In Birri's preface to his 1956 text, *Fotodocumentales,* he reflected that he drew on his prior experiences at the Centro Sperimentale in Rome in his quest for "utility" over "originality" (6). For his course the same year, Birri used writings from the classes offered by Luigi Chiarini, the Centro Sperimentale's director, and screened two fotodocumentari (Italian original name) that he brought with him from Rome: *Un paese* and *I bambini di Napoli,* both from 1955.[4]

The history of *Un paese* is a long one. By way of synthesis, it represents an encounter between the famous North American photographer Paul

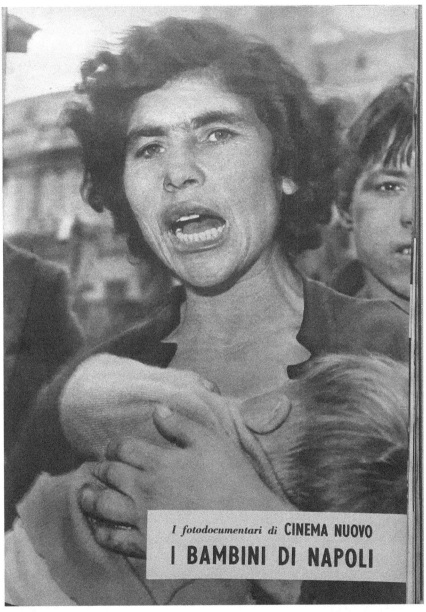

I *fotodocumentari di* CINEMA NUOVO
I BAMBINI DI NAPOLI

Fig. 8.2. Fotodocumentario *I bambini di Napoli*, photos by Chiara Samugheo and texts by Domenico Rea. *Cinema Nuovo*, no. 63 (July 1955): 57–64.

Strand and Cesare Zavattini. In 1952, the two met in Rome to do a joint photo-and-essay project (fotodocumentario) on the Italian village of Luzzara, the town where Zavattini had been born. One part of the book had been published beforehand as a fotodocumentario. Under the name *25 persone*, it appeared in the film magazine *Cinema Nuovo* in July 1955.[5] In fact, it was just one among many fotodocumentari published in successive issues of the journal between 1954 and 1956. *Cinema Nuovo*, edited by Guido Aristarco, published fotodocumentari from noted writers, historians, and filmmakers; along with Zavattini and Strand, there was filmmaker Vittorio De Sica on the protagonists in his film *Il tetto* from 1956 (a film on which Birri collaborated), Ernesto De Martino on his ethnographic work in Lucania and on southern Italian culture, the Napolese writer Domenico Rea on poverty in Naples, and the American photographer and filmmaker William Klein on the nighttime creatures of 42nd Street in New York, among others.

In those years, both Aristarco and Zavattini maintained close ties to the cinema of Latin America. The relationship between Italian fotodocumentari (1954–1956) and Birri's fotodocumentales is also significant. In addition to the evident influence of the former on the latter, it is striking the degree to which they seem to be in conversation with one another, with their shared sentiments, beliefs, and approaches. Both practices were centered on predominant themes of local, social significance, and both thought the fotodocumentario/fotodocumental a method for teaching, which further bridged the divide between "amateur" and "professional" realms.

Despite there being a common structure to them, the photographic and literary/journalistic treatment of the fotodocumentari in *Cinema Nuovo* varied from one issue of the journal to the other.[6] There are also various themes: from work in the port of Genoa and misery in Naples and Rome, to daily life in cities and villages to New York nightlife, the Venice Festival, or the world of cinema. Still, the Italian fotodocumentari that documented social problems and those that focused on the local daily life enjoyed more privileged treatment than others. These two aspects—the social and the local—as we have seen, was also prominent in the initial impulses of the school of Santa Fe.

In this context, when we consider the incorporation of the Italian fotodocumentario into Birri's initial course and, later, as a teaching method at the Instituto de Cinematografía, perhaps the aspect that we might emphasize most is the method's usefulness as a means of collective and straightforward expression, one that remained within reach for the amateur practitioner. Although the fotodocumentari of *Cinema Nuovo* included prominent photographers, writers, and filmmakers, Zavattini's project, at its core, aimed to expand beyond this select group. Zavattini (1955) himself expounded on this in an introduction that he wrote for a special *Cinema Nuovo* compilation of already-published fotodocumentari: a 1955 collection of all twenty-four series published between issues 49 and 72 of the journal.[7] Penned as a sort of letter directed to Aristarco, Zavattini begins by reflecting on the fact that the photographic camera had, by then, become a rather household item and that millions of people were using cameras on a daily basis. Why, then, he continued, had no one to date thought of introducing still cameras into schools, for example, as a means of breaking down certain barriers between the things students studied and the realities that awaited them after school? Zavattini believed, even if only for technical reasons, that this would oblige teachers to pursue a pedagogy further ingrained in reality (*più calzante*). He implied that this technical teaching, on the basis of images, might similarly help overcome a certain fear that he himself felt in front of the camera, which would then assist in the formation and development of the students' personalities and perspectives. In this context, he ruled: "One day, dear Aristarco, you will publish fotodocumentari from the young, [and] not just the old guard." Of course, he added, "this will mean that you will have to dedicate more pages to the fotodocumentari, lest we believe that the only topics worthy of tackling are those included in the twenty-or-so fotodocumentales included in that original volume." Quite the contrary, he continued, there exist "three million" potential stories out there. "Why not consider," Zavattini asked Aristarco, "a school trip, where students have the cameras? Why not propose that some lab or photography store lend some cameras to an elementary school and we see what happens."

May a thousand flowers bloom! Or millions of fotodocumentari, even—and especially!—if they came not from great authors but instead, from school exercises, from more precarious forms of local youth's technical training and apprenticeship, as per Zavattini's utopian vision of total, social, and artistic participation. Perhaps Birri wondered, too: Why not use the fotodocumentales as a method for teaching his students at the Instituto de Cinematografía?

Fig. 8.3. Cover of the first issue of the Cuaderno de
Fotodocumentales Santafecinos, edited by the Instituto
Social and the Instituto de Cinematografía, Universidad
Nacional del Litoral, December 1956. (Diagrammed by
Jorge Planas Viader, Juan H. Croppi, and Edgardo Pallero,
from the Instituto).

Part III

Tire-dié, the School of Santa Fe's first documentary film, began as a student
fotodocumental and was included in the school's first published collection,
Fotodocumentales (santafecinos). The fotodocumental, much like the film,
focused on children of the "Tire-dié" neighborhood, located at the city's out-
skirts, as well as their families. There, where trains passed through town at
a slower pace, children ran at perilously close proximity to passenger trains
and begged "*Tire-dié!*" or "*Tire-diez*" ("Toss a dime!") of the tourists aboard.
Both versions of *Tire-dié* take this stunning (and photographic/cinematic)

act of risk as their starting point, even as both also detail the many political, psychological, and related barriers to the survival of the poor in Santa Fe.

As a film, *Tire-dié* borrowed more than just its subject matter from the earlier fotodocumentales—and, thus, from their Italian predecessors. The project, in its genesis, its production, and its exhibition, closely adhered to the precepts of the School of Santa Fe. As with earlier fotodocumentales, shooting was preceded by an extended period of research and community outreach. Students were encouraged to leave the classroom and enter the community, with cameras, to ask questions, take pictures, and see what happened next. In the case of *Tire-dié*, those early explorations grew into a film. First, students and faculty engaged residents in extended conversations—recorded on paper and, eventually, on tape—on issues faced by the community. Then, nonprofessional actors were recruited from among the train-chasing children in the neighborhood and their parents. Finally, Birri partnered his filmmaker colleagues with students and began production. In this way, the fotodocumentales were more than just notes for future films, as Birri at one time characterized them: not only were they testing visuals, but they were also making connections, engaging subjects, and securing future partnerships. More than simple inspiration for future efforts, producing the fotodocumentales actually laid the logistical groundwork for the film to be made and, in turn, for the students to progressively professionalize themselves.

This amateur-though-progressively-professionalizing quality of the IC's work also extended to the film's exhibition. Although UNL hosted Birri, his students, and his film subjects for a formal premiere of *Tire-dié* on campus, the group almost immediately commenced a neighborhood-by-neighborhood tour of Santa Fe with the film. Beginning on October 2, 1958, Birri and his students presented the film at nineteen venues in twenty-three days.[8] They premiered *Tire-dié* to five hundred santafesinos at the popular Sociedad Vecinal de la Zona Sud. On October 3, while high school and university students across the country took to the street in response to presidential decrees regarding higher education, another five hundred watched the documentary at the Sociedad Vecinal General Arenales. On October 10, more than four hundred showed up for an open-air screening at the city's Club Social y Deportivo. We could cite many other examples of these sorts of events.

Even as local media, including Santa Fe's daily *El Litoral*, lamented "technical deficiencies" in the project, suggesting that *Tire-dié* could not compete with more polished work from the capital city or from overseas, reporters were nonetheless forced to acknowledge the surprising support that the film received, noting that some screenings required a second showing to accommodate those left outside one or another venue.[9] For Birri, who wrote about the premieres in an editorial in 1959, "The culturally revolutionary phenomenon owed not to the quantity of people but to the distinct sectors of the city from which those people came and whose respective opinions, curiosities, and interests they represented."[10] As the director and his collaborators took the film off campus and into the community, each screening provided additional opportunities for locals to represent themselves, their opinions, and their interests.

More than simply showing *Tire-dié* to audiences, Birri pushed his students to think of the screenings as opportunities for conversation. With this in mind, he assigned students to conduct surveys with audience members after each of the neighborhood premieres. The surveys that have survived, which number more than eight hundred and which are housed today at UNL, offer valuable insight into the ways that the Tire-dié and other Santa Fe neighborhoods understood the project. Unlike the local and national press, they saw the effort not just as an amateurish hobby or a film-school exercise but also as an important opportunity for local individuals and institutions to break through barriers of industry and "professionalization" and participate, themselves, in the world of film.

Structured on the basis of three simple questions—(1) Did you like the film? [*¿Le gustó o no el film?*], (2) Why? [*¿Por qué?*], and (3) What kind of issues would you like to see us make films about? [*¿Sobre qué argumento le gustaría a Ud. que hiciésemos una película?*]—the surveys primarily functioned to encourage conversation among IC participants and their neighbors, also the intended public for *Tire-dié*. In case after case examined, conversation on the film provoked reflection on topics ranging from the proper aesthetics of the documentary genre to adequate means for addressing child poverty. This contact that Birri pursued—what he called the social moment of both production and distribution—ultimately drew the IC away from the university, even during a moment like October 1958, when national politics again predominated and the student movement had again captured the nation's imagination.[11] With time, popular reactions to *Tire-dié* similarly drew the filmmakers away from the documentary genre, despite enthusiasm for the film. The majority response in the neighborhoods understood the real as fluid, situated *Tire-dié* as more *local* than *documentary*, and saw in the cinema not so much an opportunity to capture reality as one to help santafesinos tell their story, making ideal use of tools and perspectives unique to their surroundings.

Though many popular, Buenos Aires-produced films and novels of the time shared the concerns of *Tire-dié* and did their part to encourage public conversation on questions of housing and poverty, santafesinos tended to agree that *Tire-dié* offered something more. In an emblematic exchange, one audience member—a thirty-year-old clerk—told one student, "I'm more satisfied than I was with other films that are being offered at the cinema. There's more reality." She even mentioned having seen Lucas Demare's *Detrás de un largo muro*, a hugely popular feature from 1958 on shantytowns in Buenos Aires. "There is reality," she offered, "but there is not reality like in this one, here there is more reality." When someone nearby suggested that Birri's film was not as technically sound as others—perhaps alluding to Demare's—the young woman insisted that she didn't mind: "That doesn't matter to me, the technical defects, the subject is what matters, I didn't even notice [the defects]."[12]

Even as some saw "technical defects" in *Tire-dié*, from underexposed visuals to muffled sound, the film overall endeared itself to local audiences. Instead of citing personal ties to the campus, many expressed admiration for their work—less for the film's aesthetics than for moral reasons. Birri called *Tire-dié* "a moral and technical product" (Birri 1964), and many in the audience seemed to agree. Well over one hundred of those polled (116 out of the 806 extant surveys) made a point of distinguishing the work of the filmmakers. Many noted the "effort" or the "will" required of the students.[13] Others called it an "audacious" film,[14] and admitted that they probably would not have dared do such work themselves, given the opportunity (or challenge).[15] A thirty-three-year-old "employee" replied that she appreciated "the filmmakers' effort, and I applaud it, because I like that in Santa Fe they are doing something for ourselves."[16] A forty-two-year-old schoolteacher, watching the film for the second time in as many weeks, offered that, "I can see that you have good people,"[17] and so trusted that future work would go well on this basis alone.

Though much of the conversation between student-hosts and subject-audiences focused on the recently completed *Tire-dié*, at least one of the three questions focused on the future and on what kinds of films the

Instituto de Cinematografía should make as a follow-up to *Tire-dié*. In this sense, Birri was using this "social moment" to explore future collaborations with the people. This provided yet another direct linkage between Birri's filmmaking and the fotodocumental method. Just as he had done with his students' fotodocumentales, Birri valued *Tire-dié*, the film, for its utility—a utility measured in terms of the conversations it stood to produce.

What, then, did the conversations and encounters do, for Birri and the IC? What projects did the audience-subjects suggest? In one memorable exchange, a *bufetero* (buffet tenant) at one of the screening venues was interviewed. Stealing himself away from duties at the bar, he had only been able to catch random portions of the film. But he had worked in the neighborhoods surrounding Tire-dié before, he was familiar with the "problems" there, the "misery" there, and he appreciated the "truthfulness" of the work. Asked what sort of films the IC could or should make, he replied, "There are so many beautiful subjects—at this moment, what can I tell you. Subjects based on reality, based on [our situation], all of the good and all of the bad, show it."[18] While acknowledging, as many did, that he was hardly a filmmaker himself, he asserted that there were many local topics on which to make local films, and that one needn't only make films on the sad or the depressing. Others took the bufetero's argument even further, suggesting that the IC need not even stick with the documentary genre. A twenty-six-year-old housewife, with nine children, loved *Tire-dié* "for showing the truth." But when asked about future films the IC might make, she suggested, "A drama, a family drama, a love story, but simple, true things, like this one."[19] The door seemed entirely open.

Logic of this sort could lead to any number of potential films or film genres. "Truth" might assume the form of a dramatic story, a family story, or a simple love story. Although more than half of those interviewed urged the filmmakers to either continue their collaborations with locals (187 answers, or 27 percent of those providing an answer to question 3) or continue with "the same [*lo mismo*]" or "something similar [*algo similar*]" (185 answers, or 27 percent), audiences seemed to approach notions of "the same" from a diversity of interpretations. "Lo mismo" could mean "neighborhood topics,"[20] or "popular films,"[21] films aimed at policy change,[22] or "more or less *lo social*."[23] What was clear was that, for many of those interviewed, "lo mismo" did not necessarily mean another film like *Tire-dié*, or even something of the documentary genre. One seventeen-year-old student asked,

"Why don't you continue tackling the same topic, just with a different focus [*distintos enfoques*]? I don't mean that you should do the same thing, but with the same thing . . . you can do a lot of different things [*con lo mismo . . . se pueden hacer cosas diferentes*]."[24]

Part IV

With *Tire-dié*, the IC had developed a practice that truly "fit," and was very much in line with the aspirations of Zavattini and others for a new cinematic culture closely tied to social realities in its production, exhibition, and representation. The way in which the film was made, as well as circulated, not only provided Birri and his team with a chance to make shared use of the IC's resources. The noncommercial, collaborative process also pointed the way forward, toward subsequent projects. While in the following years the school continued with additional fotodocumental series, as well as documentary films on different topics (among them, the well-known *Los cuarenta cuartos*),[25] and even as it continued to further institutionalize and professionalize,[26] Birri began a new film project: *Los inundados*. *Los inundados* was not a documentary film but instead a sort of testimonial fiction: a satirical take on how local politicians and popular classes responded to regional floods. It was, in Birri's terms, "The first film made for, by, and of santafecinos." Though the filmmaker pitched the film and the ideas behind it as "a national, realist, critical and popular cinema,"[27] *Los inundados*, like *Tire-dié*, might more accurately be defined by the methods used. As with *Tire-dié* and *Los cuarenta cuartos*, *Los inundados* used local actors (nonprofessionals, though many with stage experience) and local crew members to revisit a popular local story written by a popular local author. What most defined *Los inundados* was its local integration, an integration that was itself rooted in earlier community efforts pushed by Birri and the IC.[28]

Tire-dié, like *Los inundados*, was not so much about discovery as about integration, collaboration, and providing a means of self-expression for local "experts." Neighborhood audiences were already perfectly aware of the brutal realities facing locals. Many of them knew the characters featured in the film or were familiar with the neighborhoods depicted. They valued *Tire-dié* less because it taught them something new but because it helped them tell their story. At a time when many artists had grown interested in the "real" Argentina, when novels such as *Villa Miseria también es América* (1957) and films such as *Detrás de un largo muro* (1958) allowed audiences in the city to "see" them for the first time (Auyero 2000, 102), *Tire-dié* somehow offered "more reality" than the others.

The degree to which Birri achieved a locally popular cinema impeded its incorporation on a national scale. In 1962, the national film institute (INC) sounded the death knell when it qualified *Los inundados* as a "B"— or, commercial screening not required. At around the same time, *Los cuarenta cuartos* was censured by the national government. The government further stunted Birri's ambitions by stalling the creation of a national film school.

Fernando Birri was no amateur. He received formal training from the giants of Italian Neorealism, and he arrived in Santa Fe with considerable filmmaking experience already under his belt. To his great credit, he understood well the significance of a Zavattini, or a De Sica. Birri liked to describe Neorealism as a moral attitude more than a cinematographic style, as many Italian critics often said. In Santa Fe, in 1956, he used the teaching and practice of fotodocumentales (linked to Zavattini´s experiments with "investigative films" [*film inchiesta*] throughout the 1950s and the "flash-films" [*film-lampo*]) (Parigi 2006, 283) to instill in his students a desire to use the camera, but as a means for engagement, for encounter, for interaction, and for a mutual education. In so doing, he made a deliberate choice to break away from the predominant model of film education. Birri's methods instead taught *fotodocumentalistas* and *documentalistas* to exist in the real, to contribute to it, and to respond to it. Similar to the goals and the role of the Instituto, as defined by Angela Romero Vera, Birri felt he was preparing his students for the honest realities of their professions the best way possible. This decidedly noncommercial program, he thought, would prove an ideal means for training future professionals.

Notes

1. A brief oral version of this chapter was presented by the authors at the VI International Congress of Argentine Association of Audiovisual and Film Studies, Santa Fe, Argentina, March, 2018. Among texts that discuss the initial period of the IC, we would like to credit certain texts as key sources for our work: Birri 1956, 1964; Peralta 2011 (especially chap. 2); Neil and Peralta 2008 (especially pages 14–34, on the period from 1956–1962); Scarciófolo and Centurión 2014. We would also like to express our thanks to Sergio Peralta and Oscar Vallejos for their insights regarding the history of the IC and of

the UNL, as well as the collaboration from Vanesa Coscia and Masha Salazkina. At the Universidad Nacional del Litoral, Stella Scarciófolo and the staff at the Museo y Archivo Histórico "Marta Samatán" were very welcoming and helpful to us, especially as related to the *Tire-dié* "surveys" of 1958. Additional research for this essay was done in the Fernando Birri Collection at Brown University. We would like to thank Patricia Figueroa for all her help with accessing the collection materials. By the end of 2019, when this chapter was already finished, David Brancaleone published a key two-volume work on Neorealism and Zavattini's influence in Cuba, Mexico, and Argentina. The input of this profound and well-researched text includes many references to Italian photodocumentaries, on Birri's experience, and his relationship with Zavattini. Brancaleone's volumes also include the letters between Birri and Zavattini.

2. Costa and Scarciófolo (2015, 247–50) argue that, into 1946, as director of University Extension at UNL's Instituto Social, Romero Vera "oversaw the purchase of cameras, film, and development chemicals to open a photography wing at the College of Law and Social Sciences, intended to be used by students of her department . . . in social surveys."

3. See Birri 1964, 9.

4. *Un paese*, texts by Cesare Zavattini, photos by Paul Strand (Torino: Einaudi, 1955). *I bambini di Napoli*, texts by Domenico Rea, photos by Chiara Samugheo. *Cinema Nuovo*, no. 63 (July 1955): 57–64.

5. See *Cinema Nuovo*, no. 53 (July 1955): 137–44.

6. This variety of subject matter also appears, of course, in the Santa Fe fotodocumentales. Luis Priamo, who included photographs from IC fotodocumentales in the book *Fotogramas santafecinos,* makes special reference to their diverse character. He compares the "pretty notable differences" between images taken by the photographer Oscar Eduardo Kopp (for the fotodocumental version of *Tire-dié*, 1957) and those taken by others, such as Luis Blanche. He points out "the careful compositions and treatment of light" in Kopp's work, which he associated with his extensive experience and activity in photo-clubs, against a work like Blanche's, "correct" in certain senses but lacking "a carefulness and equivalent formal refinement." Priamo also remarked that the teamwork of those early years for the IC did not continue later on, "when the fotodocumental was adapted as the individual first-year practicum, assigned in Introduction to Cinema." And so, he suggests that "it's reasonable to suppose that the images in fotodocumentales after Kopp and Blanche, realized individually by first-year students, would suffer from a lesser photographic quality" (Priamo 2008b, 84). See also Priamo's (2008a) own memories of his experience with fotodocumentales in "Relato con fotos fijas y *raccontos*," featured in the same book.

7. In September 1958, at the opening of the Second Exhibition of Fotodocumentales, Birri recognized the great debts that his project owed to "those fotodocumentales that appeared in the pages of *Cinema Nuovo* toward the end of the great Neorealist moment, [and which] ended up here [Santa Fe], used as a method, the first stage of an Argentine, Latin American experience" (Birri 1964, 31). Mariano Mestman is currently working on the relationship between Santa Fe and Italy's photodocumentaries.

8. This number is based on a cross-referencing of articles in *El Litoral* with IC archives housed at UNL's Museo Histórico. Elsewhere, Chris Moore has worked on a complete reconstruction of the film's projections during those days, the surveys conducted, and the debates that unfolded (Moore 2017; especially chap. 2).

9. "Exhibióse el documental 'Tire-die,'" *El Litoral*, September 28, 1958.

10. Fernando Birri, "Universidad y cine," in *Ojo del mundo* (Santa Fe, Argentina: Instituto de Cinematografía, 1959), 13.

11. Many attendees made mention of the national university conflict debate in their conversations with students coordinating the screenings. See Moore 2017.

12. "Escribano, 30, fem." Folder: "Proyección República del Oeste, Esc. López y Peames (4 October 1958)." "Encuestas," Museo y Archivo Histórico "Marta Samatán," hereafter UNL-MyAH.

13. "Empleado de correo, 22, masc." Folder: "Barrio Progresista, Guemes 4189 (9 October 1958)." "Encuestas," UNL-MyAH; and "Empleado, Puerto S. Fe., 18, masc." Folder: "República Los Hornos [No date]." "Encuestas," UNL-MyAH.

14. "Carpintero, 27, masc." Folder: "Función Gral. Arenales (3 October 1958)." "Encuestas," UNL-MyAH.

15. "Empleado, 18, masc." Folder: "Proyección Sociedad Vecinal 'Villa del Parque, El Triángulo,' (6 October 1958)." "Encuestas," UNL-MyAH.

16. "Empleada de comercio, 33, fem." Folder: "Proyección República del Oeste, Esc. López y Peames (4 September 1958)." "Encuestas," UNL-MyAH.

17. "Maestro, 42, masc." Folder: "Proyección Sociedad Vecinal 'Zona Sud, Barrio Candioti (Esc. Mariano Moreno),' 7-x-58." "Encuestas," UNL-MyAH.

18. "Bufetero del Club Los Hornos, 53, masc." Folder: "República Los Hornos [No date]." "Encuestas," UNL-MyAH.

19. "Casada, 9 hijos, quehaceres, 26, fem." Folder: "Función Gral. Arenales (3 October 1958)." "Encuestas," UNL-MyAH.

20. "Estudiante, 16, masc." Folder: "Barrio Progresista, Guemes 4189 (9 October 1958)." "Encuestas," UNL-MyAH.

21. "Arpicero, 42, masc." Folder: "Barrio Progresista, Guemes 4189 (9 October 1958)." "Encuestas," UNL-MyAH.

22. "Empleado, 22, [no gender given]." Folder: "Barrio Progresista, Guemes 4189 (9 October 1958)." "Encuestas," UNL-MyAH.

23. "Electrotécnico, 42, masc." Folder: "Barrio Progresista, Guemes 4189 (9 October 1958)." "Encuestas," UNL-MyAH.

24. "Estudiante, 17, fem." Folder: "Proyección '7 Jefes' (Escuela Amenabar) (17 October 1958)." "Encuestas," UNL-MyAH.

25. *Los cuarenta cuartos* (1962, dir. Juan Oliva) also began as a fotodocumental on Santa Fe's derelict housing. Birri called the film the "second filmed social survey" after *Tire-dié* (*El Litoral*, January 30, 1963).

26. The IC began to develop its plan of studies for 1960 and beyond. See the analysis by Neil and Peralta 2008, 29–32.

27. Poster for *Los Inundados*, Brown University, Fernando Birri Collection.

28. Even though, at the time of the film's beginnings (1961), the topic had already been tackled in a 1958 fotodocumental and in a 1959 documentary short, both titled *La inundación de Santa Fe* [Santa Fe flooding], the screenplay for *Los inundados* was based on a story from the 1930s, by the santafecino writer Mateo Booz. The project was conceived of by Birri and Adelqui Camusso (director of the IC from 1962–1969), back when they worked together in Rome in the 1950s.

References

Auyero, Javier. 2000. "The Hyper-Shantytown: Neo-liberal Violence(s) in the Argentine Slum." *Ethnography* 1, no. 1 (July): 93–116.

Birri, Fernando. 1956. "Nace una experiencia cinematográfica." In *Instituto de Cinematografía e Instituto Social de la UNL: Fotodocumentales*. Santa Fe, Argentina: Universidad Nacional del Litoral.

———, dir. 1958–1960. *Tiré-dié*. Trigon-film.

———. 1964. *La Escuela Documental de Santa Fe*. Santa Fe, Argentina: Editorial Documento.

Brancaleone, David. 2019. *Zavattini: Il Neo-realismo e il uovo cinema latino-americano*. 2 vols. Parma, Italy: Diabasis.

Costa, María Celia, and Stella Maris Scarciófolo. 2015. "La UNL, impulsora del cine documental latinoamericano." In *Santa Fe en la gestación y desarrollo de la Argentina*, edited by Graciela Agnese, 247–50. Santa Fe, Argentina: Espacio Santafecino Ediciones.

Giménez, Manuel Horacio. 1961. *La escuela documental inglesa*. Santa Fe, Argentina: Editorial Documento.

Instituto de Cinematografía e Instituto Social de la UNL: Fotodocumentales. 1956. Santa Fe, Argentina: Universidad Nacional del Litoral.

Mestman, Mariano. 2011. "From Italian Neorealism to New Latin American Cinema." In *Global Neorealism 1930–1970. The Transnational History of a Film Style*, edited by Saverio Giovacchini and Robert Sklar. Jackson: University Press of Mississippi.

Mestman, Mariano, and María Luisa Ortega. 2014. "Grierson and Latin America. Encounters, Dialogues and Legacies." In *The Grierson Effect: Tracing Documentary's International Movement*, edited by Deane Williams and Zoë Druick. London: Palgrave-Macmillan/BFI.

Moore, Christopher. 2017. "*Cine local*: Argentine Documentary Film and the Politics of Presence, 1948–1978." PhD diss., Indiana University, Bloomington.

Neil, Claudia, and Sergio Peralta. 2008. *Fotogramas santafesinos: Instituto de Cinematografía de la UNL, 1956–1976*. Santa Fe, Argentina: Universidad Nacional del Litoral.

Nichols, Bill. 1991. *Representing Reality: Issues and Concepts in Documentary*. Bloomington: Indiana University Press.

Parigi, Stefania. 2006. *Fisiologia dell´immagine. Il pensiero di Cesare Zavattini*. Torino: Lindau.

Peralta, Sergio. 2011. "Cine y política en el Instituto de Cinematografía de la Universidad Nacional del Litoral." PhD diss., Universidad Nacional del Litoral.

Priamo, Luis. 2008a. "Relato con fotos fijas y raccontos." In *Fotogramas santafesinos: Instituto de Cinematografía de la UNL, 1956–1976*, edited by Claudia Neil and Sergio Peralta, 97–126. Santa Fe, Argentina: Universidad Nacional del Litoral.

———. 2008b. "Sobre los Fotodocumentales del IC de la UNL." In *Fotogramas santafesinos: Instituto de Cinematografía de la UNL, 1956–1976*, edited by Claudia Neil and Sergio Peralta, 83–83. Santa Fe, Argentina: Universidad Nacional del Litoral.

Rea, Domenico, and Chiara Samugheo. 1955. "I bambini di Napoli." *Cinema Nuovo* 63 (July): 57–64.

Romero Vera, Ángela. "Prólogo" [*Prologue*]. 1956. In *Instituto de Cinematografía e Instituto Social de la UNL, Fotodocumentales*. Santa Fe, Argentina: Universidad Nacional del Litoral.

Scarciófolo, Stella, and Jorgelina Centurión. 2014. *Ojo del Mundo. Orígenes y las primeras producciones del Instituto de Cinematografía de la Universidad Nacional del Litoral.* Santa Fe, Argentina: Universidad Nacional del Litoral.

Zavattini, Cesare. 1955. "Introduzione." In *I fotodocumentari di Cinema Nuovo*, 3. Milano: Cinema Nuovo Editrice.

Zavattini, Cesare, and Paul Strand. 1955. *Un paese.* Torino: Giulio Einaudi Editore.

MARIANO MESTMAN is a social sciences researcher at the Gino Germani Institute in the Universidad de Buenos Aires.

CHRISTOPHER MOORE is a documentary filmmaker and historian.

PART III

POLITICS OF LEGITIMIZATION AND SUBVERSION

9

THE WIND FROM THE SOUTH

Experiences of Substandard Filmmaking in Galicia in the 1970s

Pablo La Parra-Pérez

THIS CHAPTER FOCUSES ON XORNADAS DO CINE (CINEMA ENCOUNTERS), a film showcase and seminar that took place annually between 1973 and 1978 in Ourense, a midsize city located in Galicia in northwest Spain.* The Xornadas became an important space of discussion and political experimentation with nonprofessional modes of film production. Instead of approaching this event as a local curiosity, I propose a larger analytical framework, both geographically and chronologically. My aim is to reevaluate its relevance in a global history of nonprofessional film cultures in the Long Sixties.

My analysis draws on the concept of *ciné-geography*, coined by Kodwo Eshun and Ros Gray. To describe how militant cinema developed during the 1960s and '70s in the form of a transnational network, Eshun and Gray observe a series of "situated cinecultural practices in an expanded sense, and the connections—individual, institutional, aesthetic and political— that link them transnationally to other situations of urgent struggle." In this atlas of radical filmmaking, they call attention to "the invention of

*This essay was in part made possible by support from the Social Science Research Council's International Dissertation Research Fellowship, with funds provided by the Andrew W. Mellon Foundation. Thanks to Xan Gómez Viñas, Margarita Ledo Andión, and Ramiro Ledo Cordeiro, and to the editors of this volume for helpful exchanges. Special thanks to Llorenç Soler, for his dedication and generosity.

discursive platforms," that is, the gatherings, meetings, and festivals that became fundamental spaces of encounter and discussion (Eshun and Gray 2011, 1). I would like to approach the Xornadas as one of these discursive platforms. Not by chance, one of the most promising developments of recent film scholarship of this period is the analysis of film encounters as privileged standpoints from which to reconstruct transnational circuits (Djagalov and Salazkina 2016; Mestman and Salazkina 2015; Moine 2014; Kötzing and Moine 2017).

The timespan of the Xornadas coincides with one of the most turbulent periods of recent Spanish history. After four decades of dictatorial rule, general Francisco Franco died in 1975. Anti-Franco opposition had grown stronger since the late 1960s and the mid- and late '70s saw an uncertain and violent transition to parliamentary democracy. The "peripheral nations" became one of the most active fronts of contestation: in the Basque Country, Catalonia, and Galicia the struggle for democratic rights converged with historical claims to political and cultural autonomy. The agendas were anything but homogenous: they ranged from negotiated demands to political devolution to national-popular movements that envisioned the establishment of sovereign socialist states.

Radical Left nationalists in Galicia often drew upon an anticolonial rhetoric as they challenged the authority of Madrid. Economically underdeveloped, with massive emigration rates and industry largely confined to furnishing raw materials to other Spanish regions, Galicia also suffered cultural repression, the public use of the Galician language being outlawed under Franco's rule. Influential authors such as Xosé Manuel Beiras, a founding member of the Galician Socialist Party (PSG, Partido Socialista Galego), described the situation in terms of "internal colonialism" (Beiras 1972). The Marxist-Leninist party Galician People's Union (UPG, Union do Povo Galego) would push further the colonial analogy. Founded in 1964 with major involvement of exiles in Latin America, the UPG was largely influenced by Third-Worldist referents including Maoism, the Cuban revolution, and Algerian independence. As UPG's literature argued, "the oppression of a State over a nation is colonialism, therefore Galicia, the Basque Country, Brittany or Ulster are colonies just as Angola or Mozambique are" (quoted in Vivero Mogo 2001, 1026).[1] In the 1970s, what was known as the "National-Popular Galician Movement" (a front of worker, peasant and student organizations under rigid control of the UPG) engaged in the most relevant social mobilizations of the time, rivaling the Galician branch of the Spanish CP, traditionally the most articulated anti-Franco force (Núñez Seixas 2015, 82–86).

The consolidation of radical Galician nationalism had a major effect on cultural theory and practice. The Xornadas were no exception, and became the epicenter of a series of a "highly politicized, sustained debate on the conditions of possibility of Galician cinema" (Colmeiro and Gabilondo 2016, 101). Unlike Catalonia or the Basque Country—where public and private funds for "vernacular" film production were available[2]—in Galicia this debate was essentially *noninstitutional* and *nonprofessional*. In an interstitial moment between the end of the dictatorship and the first Galician autonomous government (formalized by the 1981 Statute of Autonomy), the protagonists of the Xornadas were amateur and militant filmmakers, activists, writers, students, and moviegoers who got involved in a series of self-managed experiments in film production, distribution, and exhibition.

Any discussion about nonprofessional film cultures in Spain in this period must start by acknowledging that small gauges (8, Super 8, and 16 mm) were not only affordable, easy-to-use film formats, but also a space of creative freedom. While 35-mm films were subject to stringent censorship under Francoist laws (Gubern 1981), substandard formats were in a legal limbo, being de facto more refractory to repression. Film censorship was removed in 1977, after the first democratic elections since 1936 were held in Spain. However, the same decree that abolished censorship also denied any public subsidy to films "made with more than 50% of archival footage or including spectacles, interviews, surveys or chronicles of current events in the same proportion" (quoted in Trenzado Romero 1999, 158). This provision prolonged the subversive potential of substandard, low-cost filmmaking beyond the temporal limits of Francoism.

In the specific context of Galicia, these fundamental advantages of substandard cinema (affordability and expressive freedom) intertwined with additional layers of symbolic and practical meaning. Stimulated by the Third-Worldist inspiration of radical nationalists, substandard filmmaking evoked the anti-colonial guerrillas largely brought into focus by Third Cinema, a constellation of referents associated especially with Latin America. These transatlantic dialogues were hardly new: after steady waves of migration and exile to the Americas, modern Galician culture has operated in an expanded transnational space—what José Colmeiro (2009) terms "the Galician Atlantic" (217). Additionally, in the largely agrarian and geographically dispersed Galician society, the lightness and mobility of small-gauge cameras and projectors were perceived as a fundamental asset for bringing film culture to the countryside in a context in which Galician radicals perceived the overexploited peasantry as the central political subject of national-popular struggles.

The Awareness of (Filmic) Underdevelopment

The genesis of the Xornadas is to be found in a series of clandestine, or semi-clandestine, meetings in film clubs. In Ourense, the activities of film clubs such as Miño in the 1960s and Padre Feijoo in the 1970s converged with a heated political atmosphere. While dictatorial rule strictly restricted the rights of assembly and discussion, in late Francoism film clubs were *counter public spheres* of extraordinary relevance, creating spaces for informal film pedagogy and political subjectivization.[3] Members of Galician film clubs often ended up forming amateur cinema groups such as Equipo 64 (founded by members of the Santiago-based SEU Film Club) or the collectives Lupa, Enroba, and Imaxe, active in the early 1970s (Gómez Viñas 2014, 141–45). Starting in 1973, the Xornadas would provide a stable meeting point for these nonprofessional film formations.

Conscious that Galicia lacked a professional film infrastructure and tradition, the opening declaration of the Xornadas was an explicit recognition of filmic underdevelopment, famously stating that "Galician cinema is the awareness of its own nothingness. And that is already something" (Gómez Viñas 2014, 135). In the twilight years of the dictatorship, the Xornadas aimed to lay the foundations for a film culture adapted to the social, cultural and linguistic specificity of Galicia. The subversive potential of the encounter did not escape the notice of the Francoist authorities: the police seized some of the amateur Galician films screened in the first meetings, showing that the expanded spectrum of freedom of nonprofessional filmmaking still had its limits (Martí Rom 1976, 88).

The Xornadas gained momentum in 1976. In a climate of political euphoria after Franco's death, the fourth encounter brought together filmmakers from the Basque Country, the Canary Islands, Valencia, and Catalonia to discuss the problem of "national cinemas" in stateless nations. The delegates issued a joint "Declaration on National Cinemas" published in Basque, Catalan, Galician, and Spanish. With national-popular undertones, the declaration defined national cinemas as "the instrument of the ideological struggle of the exploited classes of the different nationalities of the Spanish state." It also called for the promotion of minoritized languages, and envisioned the creation of self-managed structures for film production and distribution.[4] The convergence of radical film practice and

Fig. 9.1. Cover of *A Xornada*, a journal edited during the last edition of the Xornadas, published as a supplement of the newspaper *La Región* (January 10, 1978). The image features a still from Llorenç Soler's film *Highway: A Gash Carved into Our Land*, discussed in this chapter. Courtesy of the Archivo Histórico do Nacionalismo (Fundación Bautista Álvarez de Estudos Nacionalistas).

national liberation struggles situates the Ourense declaration, at least in rhetorical terms, in the orbit of recent international events such as the International Encounters for a New Cinema held in Montreal in 1974 where the anti-colonial tradition of Third Cinema found "its correlate in a new kind of national cinema that aimed to 'democratize the structures of film'" (Mestman and Salazkina 2015, 4). Not by chance, detailed reviews of Montreal '74 were quickly included in books edited in Spain which would be addressing the same readership as the participants of the Xornadas (Linares 1976, 273–81; Hennebelle 1977, 2:509–11).

The Ourense declaration had an ephemeral but considerable influence. It inspired debates and film projects on national cinemas in other territories of Spain and attracted a great deal of attention to the Xornadas. As film critic Juan Hernández Les put it,

> The Xornadas have become the only serious film festival . . . happening nowadays in Spain. The public attending the screenings . . . is interested in culture; hence their youth, their beards, their bohemian look; hence as well why the bourgeoisie is absent. The Xornadas is an unofficial festival, marginalized by the public authorities; and there lies its force, its sincerity, and its future. (1977, 69)[5]

Beyond a shared interest in promoting Galician cinema, however, the Galician contingent at the Xornadas soon broke up into two opposing factions, summarized by Margarita Ledo Andión (2009) as an argument between "militant cinema and commercial cinema" (151). One of the most vocal agitators in this discussion was Carlos Varela. A rank-and-file militant of the UPG, from 1971 Varela directed the Valle-Inclán film club in Lugo, where Soviet cinema was screened along anti-imperialist films such as Gillo Pontecorvo's *La battaglia di Algeri* (*The Battle of Algiers*, 1966) and Jorge Sanjinés's *Yawar Malku* (*Blood of the Condor*, 1969). Varela was yet another example of a film-club activist who would take up the small gauge movie camera, proposing a model of revolutionary film culture largely inspired by Third Cinema.

Carlos Varela: Towards an Urgent Cinema

The revitalization of Galician culture was perceived by some as an opportunity to lay the foundations of a professional film industry. The architect and entrepreneur Víctor Ruppen sponsored a series of films shot in 35 mm in the hope that a new generation of Galician filmmakers, most of them coming from amateur groups, could have an impact on the commercial screen

(Gómez Viñas 2015, 112–13; Folgar de la Calle and Martín Sánchez 1998). With Varela at the helm, the most radical delegates at the Xornadas contested this position head on, advocating a militant film culture, produced apart from industrial or commercial structures and engaged in the Galician national-popular movement. As Varela put it in 1977,

> Here and now, we must break with "standard" 35- and 70-mm formats. If necessary, we must invent and create an aesthetic expression suitable for small formats. A new way of conceiving film practice in its entirety, to put cinema at the service of its owner: the people. . . . I think that short films are today in Galicia the only real alternative. In our circumstances, this film practice has social and political dimensions impossible to achieve with feature-length films. (González 1992, 223)

Varela further underlined that this was not a stopgap measure until more sophisticated films could be produced in Galicia, but rather a deliberate political project envisioning the democratization of film culture. Beyond sharing an "anti-colonial" ethos, his discourse echoed some of the fundamental assumptions of Third Cinema as originally conceptualized by Argentinian filmmakers Fernando Solanas and Octavio Getino. Their influential 1969 essay "Towards a Third Cinema" was, among other considerations, a critical reflection on the ideological implications of film production methods. While in earlier texts Solanas and Getino were rather indecisive regarding film formats,[6] in 1969 they unambiguously rejected professional-commercial film structures ("the 35 mm camera, 24 frames per second, arc lights, and a commercial place of exhibition for audiences") as imperialist in essence. In contrast, they saw in substandard lightweight cameras, portable recorders and high-sensitivity film stock a crucial opportunity to "demystify" and democratize film practice (Solanas and Getino 2014, 237, 240).

It is well known that the idea of Third Cinema evolved over time and, by the mid-1970s, it included postcolonial national film industries that had little to do with insurgent experiments in small-gauge filmmaking (Chanan 1997). Spanish critics such as Julio Pérez Perucha were sarcastic about the contrast between the scarcity of Galician film structures and the "prestigious 'Third-Worldist' films . . . most of them shot in 35 mm and supported by governmental institutions" that Varela and the like praised and screened at the Xornadas (González 1992, 239). Perucha's criticism overlooked that Third Cinema literature always acknowledged the necessity of adapting film practice to heterogeneous material conditions, ranging from precarious oppositional film practices against authoritarian regimes to the collaboration with revolutionary governments that provided radical filmmakers with the means to engage in more ambitious projects. For instance, in 1972 Cuban filmmaker and theorist Julio García Espinosa—whose texts circulated in Spain—simultaneously defended state-supported Cuban films and "a short film shot in the agitated streets of Montevideo" as different expressions of the same project (1976, 42–43). Indeed, with many countries in the Southern Cone suffering dictatorial regimes in the '70s, a concept of "urgent cinema" associated with the versatility of Super 8 was perceived by some Latin American critics as the most promising development of the original radical spirit of Third Cinema (Gumucio-Dagron 1980).

Varela, indeed, chose Super 8 to develop his singular film practice. He produced a vast homemade film archive of the Galician national-popular movement, shooting the demonstrations, assemblies, and clashes with police in which he participated himself. Edited in camera and shot in reversal film stock, Varela's pieces could be screened shortly after the events, becoming low-cost film-tracts for ready use. His tactical use of Super 8 situates him in what Sebastien Layerle (2016, 165) describes as an understudied "Super 8 moment" in the history of radical filmmaking.[7] Varela's premature death in 1980 cut short any further development of his project. And, although he would be remembered in radical milieux as "perhaps the greatest representative of militant cinema in our homeland," as the poet Darío Xohán Cabana put it (González 1992, 261), the full recognition of his work had to wait until 2005, when filmmaker and researcher Ramiro Ledo Cordeiro rescued Varela's footage from almost complete oblivion.[8]

Varela's ultralight film gear allowed him to nimbly follow political agitation across Galicia, which points to another fundamental feature of substandard filmmaking: its portability. Although film clubs and universities provided alternative screening spaces in urban areas, in Galicia's largely agrarian society, scattered smallholdings and hamlets frequently lacked any infrastructure for film exhibition. Many discussions at the Xornadas thus revolved around the development of mobile structures for distribution and exhibition. Interestingly, the idea of a mobile rural film culture had been articulated decades ago by one of the most distinguished Galician filmmakers of all time, Carlos Velo.

Carlos Velo: The Longstanding Utopia of Rural Film Action

In 1977 the Xornadas paid homage to Carlos Velo. The presence of the veteran cineaste in Ourense raised excitement high, particularly when he took sides in the heated discussions of the encounter. An established

Fig. 9.2. Carlos Varela with his Super 8 camera, photography included in his obituary published in the nationalist journal *A Nosa Terra* (August 29 1980).

documentary filmmaker since the 1930s, Velo was among the many central figures of Galician politics and culture who, in the wake of Republican defeat in the Spanish Civil War (1936–1939), sought asylum in Latin America. He became a major figure in the Mexican film industry and maintained strong ties with anti-Franco dissidents—being, in fact, one of the cofounders of UPG.[9] In sum, Velo personified the circuitous network that connects the postwar Galician exile, Latin American radicalism, and the rebirth of Galician nationalism in the 1960s.

As early as 1956, during the First Congress of Galician Emigration held in Buenos Aires, Velo had proposed the creation of a Galician Film Center (CCG, Centro Cinematográfico Galego). The CCG would be headquartered in the Argentinian capital, charged with the acquisition and distribution of a catalog of "educational, documentary and informational" films and the production of a regular "Galician newsreel." As Velo further observed, "one of the most important missions of the CCG will be the organization of Rural Film Action Groups that will bring to small villages and farmhouses the cultural message of the cinematograph" (Velo 1956, 186).

Although neither the Argentinian section of the CCG nor the rural film groups operating on Galician soil (a nearly impossible operation in 1950s Spain) came to fruition, Velo's project was anything but forgotten and would pervade the Galician filmic imagination for decades. The idea of rural film action echoed different experiments in mobile cinema that Velo knew firsthand. For one, he was among the filmmakers and photographers who actively participated in the Pedagogic Missions (Misiones Pedagógicas) sponsored by the Spanish Second Republic between 1931 and 1936 to disseminate the progressive pedagogical and civic values of the new Republican regime. As Jordana Mendelson observes, it "was probably the most significant government venture in the 1930s to utilize film and photography, both to record the experiences of the *misioneros* and the realities of rural Spain and to create an audience for film in the countryside" (2005, 94). Equipped with a panoply of portable projectors, accumulators, rotary converters, transformers, epidiascopes, cameras, radiograms, and amplifiers, the Misiones brought a wide catalog of films—mostly educational and documentary—to rural areas of Spain, including Galicia (García Alonso 2013). The debates held at the Xornadas make clear that the memory of the Misiones was still vivid four decades later. In the context of a discussion regarding the creation of a commission to distribute Galician films in the countryside in 1974, the delegates explicitly evoked La Barraca, an ambulant theater group codirected by poet Federico García Lorca, which worked with the Misiones (González 1992, 177). Later discussions on mobile cinema were explicitly linked to the versatility of substandard formats. As Luís Álvarez Pousa, the driving force behind the Xornadas, observed in 1975, Super 8 and 16-mm projectors "could be moved from one village to another, from one *parroquia* to another," advising Galician filmmakers to "produce substandard cinema" (González 1992, 185–87).[10]

Velo's rural film action echoed other experiments in mobile cinema, such as those undertaken by Cuba Sono Film (CSF) between 1938 and 1948. An initiative of the Cuban Popular Socialist Party (Partido Socialista Popular), CSF produced a series of militant documentaries directed at peasant and worker audiences. With the help of a modest mobile unit (a van equipped with a 16-mm Kodaskope projector), CSF's volunteers organized screenings in urban and rural areas, including sugar refineries and cane fields (Sacerio 1984). It is likely that Velo was familiar with this practice, since CSF produced some films paying homage to other Galician exiles.[11] The understudied experience of the CSF set an important amateur precedent for the institutional initiatives in mobile cinema famously supported by the Cuban Institute of Cinematographic Art and Industry (ICAIC, Instituto Cubano del Arte e Industria Cinematográficos), established in 1959.[12] In fact, Velo advised Alfredo Guevara (the first director of the ICAIC until 1982) on matters concerning the first steps of the institute and the conception of the ICAIC's *cine-camión*.[13]

Closing an intricate circle of transatlantic crossings, Velo brought Cuba to the table with his interventions at the Xornadas in 1977. Fueling an atmosphere already thick with Third-Worldist fascination, Velo drew parallels between the situation in Cuba in 1959 and the filmic underdevelopment of Galicia in the 1970s. Galicia, Velo argued, could draw inspiration from ICAIC, an institution that made the most of Cuba's scarcity of means while forging ties with international filmmakers. He recommended for Galicia "a structure of documentary filmmaking with minimum means, requiring the minimum apparatus, envisioning the support of other film groups, such as the Catalan ones" (Hernández Les 1977, 70). For Velo, the goal was to produce militant newsreels ("the more political, the better"), calling on fellow filmmakers to portray the lives and struggles of the Galician popular classes (González 1992, 214).

Although the construction of an ICAIC-inspired Galician Film Center was still unfeasible in the late 1970s, Xan Gómez Viñas is right in observing that Velo's utopian idea of rural film action would find a compelling afterlife in two self-managed film projects coordinated by another regular delegate at the Xornadas: the Barcelona-based filmmaker Llorenç Soler (2006, 79).

Llorenç Soler: The Filmmaker as Organizer

When Llorenç Soler arrived in Galicia in 1976, his trajectory represented that of the underground history of militant filmmaking in Catalonia. Despite the uneven filmic and economic development of Catalonia and Galicia, Galician radical film activists saw their Catalan counterparts as examples from which to drawn valuable lessons, a perception influenced by a shared opposition to Spanish centralism. Since the mid-1960s Soler had combined his salaried work as an autodidact industrial filmmaker with a fruitful clandestine film activity. He was present in early experiments in informal film education that sprang up in Barcelona in the late 1960s, such as the ephemeral Aixelà school, where he taught the technical basics of 16-mm filmmaking (Portabella 2001, 123–24); he was a member of the Central del Curt, a cooperative specialized in the distribution and production of militant and alternative cinema (García Ferrer and Martí Rom 1996, 46–51); and he was working on a groundbreaking history of independent cinema together with film historian Joaquim Romaguera i Ramió.[14] With the help of Helena Lumbreras—another pivotal figure in militant film culture in Spain (La Parra-Pérez 2018)—Soler's films reached international film encounters. In 1969, Soler's *Largo viaje hacia la ira* (*Long Journey to the Rage*, 1969) won the Fipresci award at the Leipzig Film Festival, a true mecca for militant filmmaking. As part of the Central del Curt contingent, between 1976 and 1978 Soler brought his firsthand knowledge of European and Latin American radical film cultures to the Xornadas.

While in Galicia, Soler became involved in six film projects. I will focus on two of them: *Autopista: Unha navallada a nosa terra* (*Highway: A Gash Carved into Our Land*, 1977) and *O Monte e Noso* (*The Land Is Ours*, 1978). With these films Soler aligned with the more radical positions taken in the Xornadas. He explicitly situated *Autopista* "in the wider framework of a national liberation struggle," observing that the gravity of the "Third-World and colonial situation of Galicia" was "incomparable to any other nation in the Spanish State" (Soler 1977, 19). Moreover, to contribute to the development of alternative networks in rural areas, he crafted collaborative modes of film production and distribution in 16 mm, observing that it was impractical to "distribute 35 mm films allegedly linked to the Galician reality when in most of the *parroquias* they can't be shown because they don't have the necessary projectors" (Martí Rom 1979, 60).

Both of these films engaged with two emblematic chapters of the national-popular Galician movement. *Autopista* approached the struggle against the "Atlantic Highway," an infrastructure promoted by the Spanish government that split Galicia in two, disrupting traditional uses of the land. In turn, *O Monte* portrayed the peasant mobilizations clamoring for the restoration of the *man común*, a regime of communal property abolished by Francoist laws (Cabana Iglesia et al. 2013, 128–29). Heading each of these mobilizations was an assembly movement, or *Coordinadora*, that funded the films with the help of donations. In a series of assembly meetings, Soler's film crew discussed the scope, form, and content of the films with activists and neighbors in affected areas (Soler 1994, 45). Soler made the most of the portability of lightweight film gear (often carrying himself both the 16-mm camera and a Nagra recorder) to gather testimonies on site and follow the moving actions of the protesters through the forests. The result were two powerful pieces of agit-prop. One of the most striking features in both films were a series of tightly framed shots of peasants at work or expressing their political views and grievances. Through parallel montages, their presence and testimonies were contrasted to the capitalist (or rather *colonial*, as the voiceover emphasizes in *Autopista*) exploitation of the land, illustrated by the ravages of logging or the heavy machinery involved in demolition and clearance. This resistant portrait of the countryside was praised by the press in the sphere of the UPG, finding in these films a compelling illustration of the project, tinged with Maoist undertones, to both praise and raise the revolutionary awareness of the Galician peasantry. As an enthusiastic review in the radical nationalist journal *A Nosa Terra* observed, by giving the floor to the peasants themselves, Soler's films "turned the protagonists of history into its own narrators" (González 1992, 247).

Aware of the scarce exhibition structures available, Soler trained the Coordinadoras' activists in the use of mobile 16-mm projectors (Soler 2002, 83). To use Velo's term, a series of itinerant *groups of rural film action* circulated the films in villages, turning hay lofts, barns, and taverns into improvised screening spaces (Gómez Viñas 2006, 79). These sessions often led to impromptu assemblies to discuss the ongoing struggles and raise funds and support. That is, they became what Solanas and Getino described as

Fig. 9.3. Llorenç Soler and Mireia Pigrau during the shooting of *O monte e noso* (ca. 1978). Unknown author.

film-acts: meetings in which "the film is the pretext for dialogue, for the seeking and finding of wills" (2014, 248). Once again, the Argentinian film-makers are not a formulaic reference. In 1978 Soler wrote a report about the making of *O Monte*. With Third Cinema connotations, he observed that the collective production and distribution of this film "broke the traditional relations of production of the capitalist film industry." Just as Solanas and Getino's essay called to integrate film and politics into an impure hybrid praxis that *proletarianizes* the filmmaker (2014, 244), for Soler, his Galician film projects "put into question the function of the filmmaker as auteur." By negotiating every detail with the people involved in the struggle, Soler concluded, he was just an "organizer" (Soler 1994, 45).

Conclusion

I have explored the discussions and practices that flourished around the Xornadas as an important contribution for an expanded and comparative global history of nonprofessional film practices. The reconsideration of film culture beyond the commercial screen problematizes our understanding of what constitutes film history, raising compelling questions about the social and political dimensions of film practice. In Galicia in the 1970s, a subnational context lacking a strong film industry, has, so to speak, no credentials to be included in dominant film histories. However, at the juncture of a country's troubled transition from dictatorship to liberal democracy, it became a fertile ground for experimentation with nonprofessional modes of film practice. Although these experiences were firmly anchored in local specificities, I aimed to resituate them into a wider ciné-geography. This gesture not only demands attention to an understudied scenario of struggle, but also tests the outermost chronological and geographical boundaries of established narratives. Even sophisticated periodizations, such as Fredric Jameson's (1984), identify a decline of "Third Worldism"—that is, a fundamental element of the radical wave of the Long Sixties—in the early 1970s. In contrast, when decentering the US–France axis that informs this perspective, an expanded chronology surfaces and the pervasive influence of Third Cinema in the Galician radical film imagination in the late 1970s requires us to reflect on a series of belated aftershocks. Likewise, looking at militant practices through the prism of amateur filmmaking reveals a history of political small-gauge film culture that has been obscured by the untenable cliché that considers amateur cinema as a mere expression of a dilettante consumer culture circumscribed to wealthy circles. As I have argued, small-gauge film had many uses beyond the bourgeois home as early as the 1930s and 1940s. Decades later, radical movements with scarce resources would be fully aware of this political potential. By analyzing different projects inextricably linked to national-popular struggles in Galicia in the 1970s—from the production of a home-made political film archive (Varela) to the planning of revolutionary film institutions (Velo) or the development of activist film projects together with social movements (Soler)—I aimed to sketch some specific film practices in which the affordability, independence, and mobility of substandard film technologies were instrumental. These case studies are not just humble vestiges of a radical past—but also milestones in a long struggle for the democratization of film practice; a struggle at once present and distant from current events.

Notes

1. I have no space to unravel the many problematic aspects of such a claim. Suffice it to say that *colonial misidentifications* were recurrent in Western radical left at the time (Kornetis 2015). All translations are mine unless otherwise indicated.

2. For instance, the Barcelona council supported the production of a newsreel in Catalan (*Noticiari*), while in the Basque Country Caja Laboral and the Orbegozo Foundation sponsored the film series *Ikuskak* (Trenzado Romero 1999, 77–78).

3. My conception of film clubs as public spheres in Oskar Negt and Alexander Kluge's sense draws on Andersson and Sundholm (2010). For a genealogy of radical film clubs in Spain, see Fibla-Gutiérrez and La Parra-Pérez (2017).

4. On the 1976 Xornadas, including a transcription of the declaration, see Gómez Viñas (2015, 212–14).

5. The reference to the "beards" of the attendees unwittingly points to the problematic patriarchal bias of the Xornadas, where all-male panels and manifestoes were the norm.

6. In 1968 they still considered 35 mm a valid medium for a "new cinema" (Solanas and Getino 1973, 13).

7. Layerle focuses on film collectives based in French Brittany. Breton and Galician nationalists had strong ties at the time; a great deal of further research is needed to determine if specific filmic exchanges also took place.

8. Ledo Cordeiro's compilation film *CCCV: Cine Clube Carlos Varela* (2005) is made with restored and digitalized film and print materials from Varela's archive. See also Ledo Cordeiro's essay on Varela (2006).

9. For an overview of Velo's trajectory, see Fernández (2007).

10. The *parroquia* is a traditional Galician territorial division that comprises several small villages.

11. That is, *Homenaje a Castelao* (*Hommage to Castelao*, 1938), dedicated to Alfonso Daniel Rodríguez Castelao, a major figure of modern Galician nationalism, or *Un héroe del pueblo español* (*A Hero of the Spanish People*, 1946), a tribute to the anti-Franco *guerrillero* José Gómez Gayoso (Redondo Neira 2004).

12. On the forgetting of prerevolutionary film experiences in Cuba, see Vincenot (2011).

13. During his Mexican exile, Guevara worked in Velo's production company, were both established a long-lasting friendship (Fernández 2007, 159).

14. This essay would only be published forty years later (Romaguera i Ramió and Soler 2006).

References

Andersson, Lars Gustaf, and John Sundholm. 2010. "Film Workshops as Polyvocal Public Spheres: Minor Cinemas in Sweden." *Revue Canadienne d'Études Cinématographiques / Canadian Journal of Film Studies* 19 (2): 66–81. https://doi.org/10.3138/cjfs.19.2.66.

Beiras, Xosé Manuel. 1972. *O atraso económico de Galicia*. Vigo: Galaxia.

Cabana Iglesia, Ana, Alba Díaz Geada, Daniel Lanero Táboas, André Taboada Casteleiro, and Victor Manuel Santidrián Arias. 2013. "Dinámicas políticas de la sociedad rural gallega: entre la agonía de la dictadura y la implantación de la democracia: (1970–1978)." *Historia del presente* no. 21: 123–44.

Chanan, Michael. 1997. "The Changing Geography of Third Cinema." *Screen* 38, no. 4: 372–88. https://doi.org/10.1093/screen/38.4.372.

Colmeiro, José. 2009. "Peripheral Visions, Global Positions: Remapping Galician Culture." *Bulletin of Hispanic Studies* 86, no. 2: 213–30.

Colmeiro, José, and Joseba Gabilondo. 2016. "Negotiating the Local and the Global. Andalusia, the Basque Country, and Galicia." In *A Companion to Spanish Cinema*, edited by Jo Labanyi and Tatjana Pavlović, 81–110. Malden, MA: Wiley-Blackwell.

Djagalov, Rossen, and Masha Salazkina. 2016. "Tashkent '68: A Cinematic Contact Zone." *Slavic Review* 75 (2): 279–98. https://doi.org/10.5612/slavicreview.75.2.279.

Eshun, Kodwo, and Ros Gray. 2011. "The Militant Image: A Ciné-Geography." *Third Text* 25 (1): 1–12. https://doi.org/10.1080/09528822.2011.545606.

Fernández, Miguel Anxo. 2007. *Las imágenes de Carlos Velo*. Mexico DF: Universidad Nacional Autónoma de México.

Fibla-Gutiérrez, Enrique, and Pablo La Parra-Pérez. 2017. "Turning the Camera into a Weapon: Juan Piqueras's Radical Noncommercial Film Projects and Their Afterlives (1930s–1970s)." *Journal of Spanish Cultural Studies* 18, no. 4: 341–62. https://doi.org/10.1080/14636204.2017.1380148.

Folgar de la Calle, José M., and Rita Martín Sánchez. 1998. "Víctor Ruppen e o cine galego contemporáneo: unha entrañable utopia." *Semata* 10:475–82.

García Alonso, María. 2013. "Intuiciones visuales para pueblos olvidados. La utilización del cine en las Misiones Pedagógicas de la Segunda República Española." *Cahiers de civilisation espagnole contemporaine. De 1808 au temps présent*, no. 11. https://doi.org/10.4000/ccec.4861.

García Espinosa, Julio. 1976. *Por un cine imperfecto*. Madrid: Castellote.

García Ferrer, J. M., and Josep Miquel Martí Rom, eds. 1996. *Llorenç Soler*. Barcelona: Associació d'Enginyers Industrials de Catalunya.

Gómez Viñas, Xan. 2006. "Llorenç Soler na Galiza. Un cinema de man común." *A Trabe de Ouro* 66, no. II: 75–80.

———. 2014. "Cinema in Galicia: Beyond an Interrupted History." In *Companion to Galician Culture*, edited by Helena Miguélez-Carballeira, 135–56. Woodbridge: Boydell & Brewer.

———. 2015. "Do amateur ao militante: implicacións políticas e estéticas do cinema en formato non profesional na Galiza dos anos 70." PhD diss., Universidade de Santiago de Compostela.

González, Manuel, ed. 1992. *Documentos para a historia do cine en Galicia: 1970–1990*. Santiago de Compostela: Centro Galego de Artes da Imaxe.

Gubern, Román. 1981. *La censura. Función política y ordenamiento jurídico bajo el franquismo (1936–1975)*. Barcelona: Península.

Gumucio-Dagron, Alfonso. 1980. "Vers un Cinéma Urgent." *CinémAction* 10–11: 190–95.

Hennebelle, Guy. 1977. *Los Cinemas nacionales contra el imperialismo de Hollywood: nuevas tendencias del cine mundial, 1960–1975*. Vol 2. Translated by Xavier Aleixandre. Valencia: Fernando Torres.

Hernández Les, Juan. 1977. "V Xornadas Do Cine: Ourense. La resistible ascensión del cine gallego." *Cinema 2002* 27: 69–74.

Jameson, Fredric. 1984. "Periodizing the 60s." *Social Text* no. 9/10: 178–209. https://doi.org/10.2307/466541.

Kornetis, Kostis. 2015. "'Cuban Europe'? Greek and Iberian Tiersmondisme in the 'Long 1960s.'" *Journal of Contemporary History* 50, no. 3: 486–515. https://doi.org/10.1177/0022009414556663.

Kötzing, Andreas, and Caroline Moine, eds. 2017. *Cultural Transfer and Political Conflicts Film Festivals in the Cold War*. Gottingen: Vandenhoeck & Ruprecht.

La Parra-Pérez, Pablo. 2018. "Workers Interrupting the Factory: Helena Lumbreras's Militant Factory Films between Italy and Spain (1968–1978)." In *1968 and Global Cinema*, edited by Christina Gerhardt and Sara Saljoughi, 363–84. Detroit: Wayne State University Press.

Layerle, Sébastien. 2016. "'Une mémoire populaire des luttes': modalités d'appropriation militante du Super 8 selon le groupe de réalisation breton TORR E BENN (1972–1975)." In *L'amateur en cinéma. Un autre paradigme. Histoire, esthétique, marges et institutions*, edited by Benoît Turquety and Valérie Vignaux, 149–66. Paris: AFRHC.

Ledo Andión, Margarita. 2009. "Anos setenta: elipse e cinema." In *Portas de luz. Unha achega ás artes e á cultura na Galicia dos setenta*, edited by Fernando Agrasar Quiroga, 149–55. Santiago de Compostela: Centro Galego de Arte Contemporánea.

Ledo Cordeiro, Ramiro. 2006. "Na memoria de Carlos Varela Veiga. Lugo, 1945—Malpica, 1980." In *Entrecruzar: itinerarios icónicos de ida e volta*, 74–81. Santiago de Compostela: Centro Galego de Arte Contemporánea.

Linares, Andrés. 1976. *El cine militante*. Madrid: Castellote.

Martí Rom, Josep Miquel. 1976. "Aproximación al cine gallego." *Cinema 2002* 17–18: 87–89.

———. 1979. "Lorenzo Soler: De los pocos que han logrado cerrar la puerta del pasillo." *Cinema 2002* 57: 57–60.

Mendelson, Jordana. 2005. *Documenting Spain: Artists, Exhibition Culture, and the Modern Nation, 1929–1939*. University Park: Pennsylvania State University Press.

Mestman, Mariano, and Masha Salazkina. 2015. "Introduction: Estates General of Third Cinema, Montreal '74." *Revue Canadienne d'Études Cinématographiques / Canadian Journal of Film Studies* 24 (2): 4–17. https://doi.org/10.3138/cjfs.24.2.FM.

Moine, Caroline. 2014. *Cinéma et guerre froide: histoire du Festival de films documentaires de Leipzig : 1955–1990*. Paris. Sorbonne.

Núñez Seixas, Xosé M. 2015. "¿Colonia o champú? El nacionalismo gallego en la transición democrática." *Historia del presente*, no. 25, 81–96.

Portabella, Pere. 2001. "Sesión continua o la rutina del acomodador." In *Historias sin argumento. El cine de Pere Portabella*, edited by Marcelo Expósito, 121–41. Valencia: La Mirada.

Redondo Neira, Fernando. 2004. "Las imágenes de la Guerra Civil y la lucha antifranquista en la Cuba Sono Film." In *El documental, carcoma de la ficción*, 1:237–38. Córdoba: Filmoteca de Andalucía.

Romaguera i Ramió, Joaquim, and Llorenç Soler. 2006. *Historia crítica y documentada del cine independiente en España, 1955–1975*. Barcelona: Laertes.

Sacerio, Mirian. 1984. "¿Qué fue la Cuba Sono Film?" *Bohemia* 26 (June):14–19.

Solanas, Fernando E., and Octavio Getino. 1973. *Cine, cultura y descolonización*. México, D.F.: Siglo XXI Editores.

———. 2014. "Towards a Third Cinema: Notes and Experiences for the Development of a Cinema of Liberation in the Third World (1969)." In *Film Manifestos and Global Cinema Cultures*, edited by Scott MacKenzie, translated by Julianne Burton and Michael Chanan, 230–50. Berkeley: University of California Press.

Soler, Llorenç. 1977. "Unha navallada a nosa terra." *Userda* 3:19.

———. 1994. "A propósito de *O monte é noso*." In *Llorenç Soler, dunha beira a outra*, edited by Manuel González, 45. A Coruña: Centro Galego de Artes da Imaxe.

———. 2002. *Los hilos secretos de mis documentales.* Barcelona: CIMS 97.

Trenzado Romero, Manuel. 1999. *Cultura de masas y cambio político: el cine español de la transición.* Madrid: CIS-Siglo XXI.

Velo, Carlos. 1956. "Proposta de creación do Centro Cinematográfico Galego." In *Primeiro Congreso da Emigración Galega*, 185–87. Buenos Aires: Nós.

Vincenot, Emmanuel. 2011. "Jocuma: un caso olvidado de cine comprometido en tiempos de Batista." *ArtCultura* 13, no. 22: 9–24.

Vivero Mogo, Prudencio. 2001. "As referencias internacionais da UPG (1964–1980)." In *Entre Nós. Estudios de arte, xeografía e historia en homenaxe ó Profesor Xosé Manuel Pose Antelo*, edited by Xesús Balboa López and Herminia Pernas Oroza, 1023–35. Santiago de Compostela: Universidade de Santiago de Compostela.

PABLO LA PARRA-PÉREZ is Coordinator of the Department of Research at Elías Querejeta Zine Eskola (EQZE) and Principal Investigator on the research project "Zinemaldia 70: All Possible Histories" funded by the San Sebastian International Film Festival and EQZE. He received his PhD from New York University in 2018 with a dissertation on militant film cultures in Spain in the Long Sixties.

10

SUPER 8 IN MEXICO

Jesse Lerner*

IN JULY OF 1972, AN ECLECTIC GROUP OF Mexican filmmakers published a remarkable manifesto entitled *Eight Millimeters versus Eight Million*. In it, the authors attack the directors and producers of big-budget feature films who adopt the label "independent," even while practicing a type of industrial filmmaking that "implies subordination to all the norms of censorship existing," and, according to their manifesto, a "total acceptance of the systems which we have criticized through cinema" (*Manifesto: Eight Millimeters versus Eight Million* 1999 [1972], 37). They single out the film *Zapata* (dir. Felipe Casals, 1970), a biography of the revolutionary leader starring popular singer Antonio Aguilar in the title role, shot in 70 mm with hundreds of extras in period costumes and a budget of twelve million pesos. For twelve million pesos, the authors state hyperbolically, "we could have made 10,000 super 8 films which would represent everything of our historical, social and artistic context." The signatories of the *Eight Millimeters versus Eight Million* manifesto included not only committed Super 8 filmmakers of the era (e.g., Oscar Menéndez, Sergio García), but also directors known for their works shot in 35 mm (e.g., Luis Buñuel, Rubén Gámez) as well as writers and poets (Juan de la Cabada, Leopoldo Ayala). Their manifesto represents a key document for understanding the polemics surrounding small-gauge filmmaking in Mexico, one which brings into sharp focus a number of issues and conflicts between amateur film and commercial cinema, between state-approved

*The author would like to thank Álvaro Vázquez Mantecón, Pablo Marín, Luciano Piazza, Sergio García Michel, Alfredo Gurrola, and Gregorio Rocha for the generous sharing of materials.

filmmaking and *engagé* art, and between contrasting modes of production, ideological goals, and visions of the film medium's social role.

The origins of small-gauge filmmaking in Mexico have never been researched thoroughly, and only a handful of biographical sketches of some of the principal figures outline the first few decades of 9.5 mm and regular 8 mm productions. Perhaps best known of these early practitioners is a medical doctor who immigrated at the beginning of the twentieth century from Spain to the provincial city of Papantla, in the north of Veracruz: Dr. José Buil Belenguer, who in 1924 acquired a 9.5 mm Pathé Baby projector, and then a year later, a 9.5 mm Pathé camera with which he filmed hundreds of home movies over the course of fifteen years (Buil 1997). Unlike most similar collections of amateur films, the doctor's movie reels were neither lost nor discarded, but rather rescued by his filmmaker grandson, José Buil, who used them as the basis for a feature-length documentary, *La línea paterna* (1995). Often choosing domestic and quotidian subjects, not unlike the Veracruzano doctor, any number of amateur filmmakers using 8 mm, 9.5, and later Super 8 were active in Mexico between the 1920s and 1980s, largely from the middle class, which grew during the "Mexican miracle," a period of sustained economic growth between the 1940s and 1970s. The Cineteca Nacional and other media arts institutions have in recent years held open screenings for International Home Movie Day, and the National University's Filmoteca is releasing a series of DVDs of regional filmmakers, each focused on a different state, which include many amateur, didactic, touristic, and ephemeral films, *Colección Imágenes de México*, bringing more of this hidden history of nonindustrial production to light. The amateur color footage gathered together as *Imágenes Típicas de Michoacán*, for example, in the volume devoted to that state is richly suggestive. Similarly the filmmaker and archivist Gregorio Rocha has released a DVD entitled *Amateurs*, with digital copies of early films by the likes of Joaquín Amaro, José María Labarga Santamaría, Luis Rodríguez Breillard, and Humberto Ruíz Sandoval. Other significant collections of amateur films made in Mexico are in archives outside the country (Acosta Urquidi 2013).

If the Super 8 filmmakers who wrote the *Eight Millimeters versus Eight Million* manifesto have an antecedent in these small-gauge amateurs, other key influences on the *superocheros* (a neologism these filmmakers used to describe themselves; it could be translated as the "super-eighters") were political and social movements rather than cinematic ones. Key among these was the student movement of the late 1960s, whose protests against the government culminated in a deadly confrontation with the state's repressive force on October 2, 1968. Based at the National University (Universidad Nacional Autónoma de México, UNAM), and with active associates at the National Technological Institute (Instituto Politécnico Nacional, IPN) and other schools throughout the city and the nation, the student movement began in response to the brutality of the riot police, or *granaderos*, who interrupted peaceful student protests with violence. Activist students formed the National Strike Committee (Consejo Nacional de Huelga, CNH) in response and demanded freedom for all political prisoners, the abolition of the *granaderos* and the law of sedition (a catchall used to justify the imprisonment of dissenters), and a pardon for all victims of state repression. News coming in from Paris, Prague, Tokyo, and Chicago contributed to the students' sense that a global sea change was imminent. The authoritarian president Gustavo Díaz Ordaz responded by rejecting "public dialogue," and sent the military to occupy the campuses of UNAM and the IPN. Further raising the stakes was the fact that Mexico was slated to host the 1968 Summer Olympics, a first for the so-called developing world, scheduled to begin on October 12 of that year. The prospect of civil unrest and mass protests as an international spotlight shined on Mexico was more than the administration could bear. Tensions escalated and tentative alliances between radicalized students and workers groups were negotiated, often across class divisions, until at a mass protest on October 2 at Tlatelolco Plaza, where thousands of students, workers, and sympathizers had gathered, the government's paramilitary snipers opened fire on the crowd, killing between two hundred and three hundred individuals, by most estimates. This episode, narrated in the words of the eyewitnesses and victims in Elena Poniatowska's *La noche de Tlatelolco: Testimonios de historia oral* (1971), remained a central point of reference for the *superocheros* and more generally a landmark in the history of twentieth-century Mexico that endures as a generational trauma. Luis Echeverría, the secretary of the interior during the Tlatelolco massacre and sometimes identified as one of its intellectual authors, succeeded Díaz Ordaz as president at the end of 1970. Though President Echeverría spoke of democratic reforms and released some political prisoners, he maintained a heavily repressive hand against all dissenters. On June 10, 1971, the government again massacred its own citizens when members of the special forces dressed as civilians and opened fire on student protesters at an event that became known as the Corpus Christi Massacre or *Halconazo.*

Following the Tlatelolco massacre, many activists were incarcerated and tortured, first in Campo militar #1 and then later in the infamous Lecumberri prison (the Porfirian panopticon that today houses the National Archives). Family members were able to smuggle Super 8 cameras and cartridges in and out of Lecumberri thanks to their compact size, and the resulting footage formed the basis for the French-Mexican coproduction denouncing the treatment of these political prisoners, *Historia de un documento* (Óscar Menéndez, 1971). This experience pointed to the format's ability to elude censorship; while the government could relatively easily keep track of the film being processed at the relatively few labs that handled 16 mm and 35 mm, the infrastructure of Super 8 was decentralized, as it could be purchased and developed at hundreds of camera stores across the country. Around the time of this film's release, the strengths of the Super 8 format had been discovered by other groups of nascent filmmakers who banded together under the banner of their medium. These emergent filmmakers converged around a series of competitions, the first of which was convened by the regulars at a coffee shop in the capital's historic center. The Café de arte y galería Las Musas was a countercultural meeting point run by the impresario, musician, gallerist, jeweler, and Aquarian insider Victor Fosado, a venue which hosted concerts, exhibitions, and happenings. In late 1969 his bohemian hangout coffee shop closed, and Fosado struggled to find an alternative location that was viable. Reluctant to give up his role as a cultural promoter, Fosado joined with the filmmaker Menéndez to convene the Primer Concurso de Cine Independiente premio Luis Buñuel (the First Competition of Independent Cinema for the Luis Buñuel Prize), the first of many national forums for short films in this format. The stated theme was "Our Country" ("Nuestro País"). Five unranked prizes, consisting of a diploma signed by the acclaimed refugee from Franco's fascism, Luis Buñuel, were given to the winners. In a country where the experimental cinema of the interwar years had largely been lost and forgotten and where the commercial film industry had such a powerful influence, Buñuel was the most immediate model of a filmmaker who had used the medium as a way to skewer the repressive roles of family, religion, military, morals, and state, even from within that industry. Buñuel had previously shown interest in the work of young Mexican filmmakers; in Alberto Isaac's entry in the 1965 First Experimental Cinema Competition, *En este pueblo no hay ladrones* (adapted from Gabriel García Márquez's eponymous short story), the militant atheist makes a cameo as the village priest.

The submissions to the first Luis Buñuel competition were diverse in style and intentions, and included a handful of shorts with touristic and mainstream sensibilities—*Baja California Sur, paraíso perdido* (dir. Romero Hernández), for example. The majority of the entries however were characterized by social criticism and a countercultural sensibility, often making allegorical condemnations of the oppressive functions of religious, government, military, and educational institutions, as well as economic inequalities and the generalized indifference to them. The regularity of these themes, and the use of popular music from the United States and England (e.g., The Doors, Janis Joplin, The Rolling Stones), led one critic to characterize the event as one marked by certain recurrent images and the filmmakers' musical choices: "idylls with bearded guys, repression in the streets, aggression against the symbols of power, and the reverent solidarity with the folklore of youthful rebellion in the USA . . . this repetition of references and external signs began to mix in the viewer's memory from so many scenes in the films. It's as if all the young participants had wanted to make the same movie" (Ayala Blanco 1974, 2, 365).

This "same movie" the participants wished to make owes much to the enduring impact of the Tlatelolco massacre and the dilemma it represented for the participants in the student movement. One participant, Alfredo Gurrola, dismisses the minority of filmmakers whose work perpetuated nationalistic stereotypes and identifies the October 2 massacre as the competition's central issue:

> It had been less than two years since '68 . . . and all of us had a position regarding this. And when given a little camera, and the possibility to make and screen something, that was what motivated you. . . . The fact that they stirred up a competition with the theme of 'Our Mexico' [*sic*] meant that everyone, or at least 85 or 90 per cent of them, sometimes tangentially and sometimes directly, addressed this topic. There were others, sure, who filmed a landscape with a burro walking in front of the volcanoes, you know, right? (Vázquez Matecón 2012, 48)

Some of the motifs in Sergio García's *El fin* (1970), one of the Buñuel prize-winners, is paradigmatic in its representation of a peaceful hippie arcadia shattered by an armed soldier, a priest, a bureaucrat, and a conformist youth insistent that the bearded protagonist drink Coca-Cola rather than smoke marijuana. The competition screenings, held at the journalists' club in downtown Mexico City, received extensive coverage in the capital's mainstream press, and reporters and critics analyzed the films and assessed what they identified as an emergent, unprecedented new kind of independent cinema, dubbed by the daily *Excélsior* as "underground 8 mm cinema *a la Mexicana*" (García Michel 1973, 28). Following the first Luis Buñuel competition, the screen actors' union, student groups, cine clubs, museums, regional cultural and community centers, and many state universities organized Super 8 film events.

The second edition of the Luis Buñuel competition, with the theme of "The Principal Problem," exposed divisions. "What is undeniable about the competition," wrote one reporter,

> Is that it was influenced by the student movement of 1968. The demobilization created after October 2 meant that many activists abandoned political action and were absorbed, in one way or the other, by the '*onda*,' the 'counterculture,' etc., or simply remained isolated. No one had a clear idea what to do. The competition arose in the midst of this situation, managing to bring together new trends that sought to express themselves through film . . . for some it was a way of continuing the political struggle, or a recess while waiting for more favorable conditions, for others, it was a refuge, a defense against the situation which, in any case, they did not accept and did not understand, yet which caused them suffering. (Mendez 1999 [1972], 43)

As the Super 8 movement evolved, the participants revealed themselves to be less homogeneous, and disparate goals and strategies of the participants became apparent.

Some of the earlier uses of the 8 mm format—secret jailhouse tool for denouncing the conditions suffered by political prisoners, catalyst for a countercultural underground—reflect larger splits within the post-1968 Mexican left. In the aftermath of the October 2 massacre, some of those who had escaped the massacre kept up the general strike until December of that year. A small number of activists and artists went into exile, where, exposed to other countercultural expressions previously hidden behind the "cactus curtain" (the artist José Luis Cuevas's term for criticizing the isolation of Mexico's postwar cultural scene),[1] they gained new perspectives on the "global 1968" experience. The artist Felipe Ehrenberg, for example, describes an atmosphere "so repressive . . . that Martha [Hellión, his wife at the time] and I saw no other alternative than to say goodbye to our families" (Ehrenberg 2007, 162) and leave the country for an extended stay in England. There the two artists started a small press, Beau Geste, and published *Schmuck*, a periodical featuring the works of artists associated with the Fluxus movement. Ehrenberg also created art performances and completed an experimental film, *La Poubelle* (1970). Another small contingent chose armed struggle as an alternate strategy to change Mexican society, given the evident failure of peaceful protests. The Liga Comunista 23 de Septiembre (LC23S), the Partido de los Pobres, and other small guerrilla groups found inspiration in the Cuban experience and the writings of Régis Debray. The government used extrajudicial executions and torture in the so-called dirty war, their effort to eliminate these armed groups. Sergio García's *Ah, Verda'* (1973) makes playful reference to both the militant and countercultural options, narrating the adventures of a pair of hippies who plant explosives in symbolic urban locations—the monument to the Mexican Revolution, the ruling political party's headquarters—and lace the capital's water supply with LSD, provoking all the city's residents to set aside all their differences and join together in a peace and love trip, much to the amusement of the merry pranksters responsible. Some of the *superocheros* believed that community organizing, and alliances with workers, peasants, and others excluded sectors were the only viable, nonviolent path to social transformation. The Cooperativa de Cine Marginal (led by Gabriel Retes, Enrique Escalona, Carrasco Zanini, and Paco Ignacio Taibo II) made activist Super 8 documentaries about independent workers unions that sought to break free from government sponsorship and control. Their efforts to develop a community-based cinema practice, along the lines of Jorge Sanjinés and the Ukamau group in Bolivia (Sanjinés 1979), were dismissed by countercultural contemporaries as "a cinema of propaganda, lacking in cinematographic language" (García Michel 1973, 55).

More common than exile, political organizing or armed insurgency was the choice of a parallel, alternative society, the counterculture from which much of the *superocheros'* films emerge. The Mexican counterculture of the late 1960s and 1970, dubbed *la onda*, is distinctly a national expression of an international hippie phenomena. Mexico's rich indigenous cultures and progressive aspects of its post-revolutionary government had long made it an appealing destination for leftists, conscientious objectors, artists, blacklisted Hollywood filmmakers, Beats, and other dissidents, including Bruce and Jean Conner, Ron Rice, Timothy Leary, and William Burroughs. A 1957 article in *Life* magazine by New York banker and amateur mycologist R. Gordon Wasson, "Seeking the Magic Mushroom," did much to enhance Mexico's appeal, disseminating information about the teachings of María Sabina and the sacred mushrooms of Huatla de Jiménez, Oaxaca (Rothenberg 2003). Later, when the Mexican filmmaker

Nicolás Echevarría completed a documentary on this tradition, *María Sabina: mujer espíritu* (1979), it was a rare commercial success for ethnographic cinema (Rovirosa 1992, 34). Sabina, a Mazatec practitioner, was ostracized by her community because of her willingness to share these traditions with a New York banker and other outsiders, inarguably numerous, and rumored to include the likes of John Lennon, an undercover CIA agent, and several members of the Rolling Stones.

Researchers who published on Native American indigenous traditions of hallucinogenic plants further spread knowledge of these traditional practices to new audiences and enhanced the country's countercultural appeal (Schultes and Hofmann 1982; Benítez 1964; Benítez 1976; Myerhoff 1974; Furst 1972). Like Wasson's article, Carlos Castañeda's writings popularized these native traditions, ever more so as they evolved from pseudo-ethnography to the pure ethno-fictions. As a graduate student in anthropology at University of California, Los Angeles (UCLA), Castañeda published *The Teachings of Don Juan: A Yaqui Way of Knowledge* (1968) with a reputable academic press. This best seller among academic monographs purports to be the addled field notes of the author's tutelage under a Sonoran shaman between 1961 and 1965. Don Juan introduces his accolade to peyote, jimson weed, and Psilocybin mushrooms (which do not grow in the Sonoran desert), and imparts many wisdoms, most of them allegedly plagiarized (Fikes 1993; de Mille 1976; de Mille 1990). *A Separate Reality: Further Conversations with Don Juan* (1971) and *Journey to Ixtlan: The Lessons of Don Juan* (1972), now from a commercial publisher, followed this immensely successful fiction. Despite their dubious authenticity the books sold over ten million copies during the author's lifetime, and fostered countercultural tourism. Encapsulating a deep-seated yearning for an antimodernist, Native American hallucinogenic truth, Castañeda's fabrications struck a deep chord, as his accounts, like Wasson's, negotiated a cross-cultural divide and translated an intense subjective experience into a form that could be shared with others.

Filmmakers recorded similar trips, such as Bruce Conner's *Looking for Mushrooms* (1959–1967, 1996), a single frame record of his journey from San Francisco, California, to Huatla de Jiménez, where he hosted Timothy Leary. The film ends with a visually dense representation of the discovery of María Sabina's *niños santos* (as she called the hallucinogenic fungi). The news service Reuters reported that "hundreds of hippies are braving imprisonment and fines to penetrate [the] mushroom paradise in the State of

Oaxaca." One of these hippies, identified only as "David, from San Francisco," put the craving for mushroom this way: "The difference between LSD and the magic mushrooms is the difference between a stale hamburger and a T-bone steak" (Reuters 1970). Eventually she began to have doubts about these visitors, as she described to anthropologist Álvaro Estrada:

> For a time there came young people of one and the other sex, long-haired, with strange clothes. They wore shirts of many colors and used necklaces. A lot came. . . . These young people, blonde and dark-skinned, didn't respect our customs. Never, as far as I remember, were the *saint children* eaten with such a lack of respect. For me it is not fun to do vigils. Whoever does it simply to feel the effects can go crazy and stay that way temporarily. (Estrada 1981, 86)

Her openness however earned her the peculiar status of celebrity shaman: the Nobel laureate Camilo José Cela wrote an oratorio about her life, the Mexican rock band The Three Souls in My Mind composed a song about her,[2] Bob Dylan set a translation of her chants to music, and the experimental poet Jerome Rothenberg (2003, xvi) celebrated her as "a woman of language—what we would dare to translate, by a comparison to those most deeply into it among us, as 'poet.'"

One of the most viewed Mexican Super 8 films is a touchstone of the Mexican counterculture, Alfredo Gurrola's *Avándaro* (1971), a concert documentary of the festival of "rock y ruedas" ("rock and wheels," the "wheels" referring to a planned auto race that was canceled) or the "Mexican Woodstock" in Valle del Bravo, Estado de México. The festival was attacked from both the left and the right as an expression of cultural imperialism, social alienation, and moral decay. Gurrola's filmed record of the event, with its lingering images of the trash-strewn concert venue, is more ambivalent, reveling in the energy and crowds but also showing the menacing military presence, the recreational drug use, and the challenges of transporting between one hundred thousand and five hundred thousand music fans in and out of the provincial town. The mainstream broadcaster Telesistema Mexicana also recorded the musical performances, but these recordings were never exhibited. Soon afterward the government effectively banned live rock performances, fearful of what might happen if so many young people gathered together. The rock scene was forced underground into tenuous, transitory spaces, dubbed the *hoyos funquis* by countercultural author Parménides García Saldaña.

The *superochero* movement flourished at a moment when the nation's film industry, once the region's strongest, had declined further and further.

The downward spiral of Mexican commercial filmmaking, from the critical, artistic, and commercial successes of the "Golden Age" of the 1940s to its nadir in the late 1960s, can be attributed to numerous factors. The directors' union excluded new talents and protected an aging cohort increasingly out of touch with contemporary tastes. The government sought to revitalize the film industry in early 1970s through the Banco Cinemtatográfico, and newer directors (e.g., Jorge Fons, Jaime Humberto Hermosillo) addressed social issues previously absent from commercial cinema. But the commercial crisis produced openings for Super 8 filmmakers in the industry, and some *superocheros* moved on to commercial productions in 35 mm, like Gabriel Retes and Rafael Montero. After references to better-known films by 35 mm features by Alejandro Jodorowsky, Alfonso Arau, and screenplays adapted from his own fiction, the novelist and chronicler José Agustín (1996, 95) wrote:

> Where the counterculture most clearly expressed itself in cinema was in super 8, which enthused young people during the first half of the seventies because of its low cost and because it evaded censorship; in this way, by way of super 8, we saw a different Mexico, more truthfully, for better or worse. Sergio García, Héctor Abadie, Gabriel Retes, Alfredo Gurrola, and Rafael Montero made films that would be inexplicable without the counterculture of the sixties.

Disillusioned with the possibility of political action, and embittered by the massacre, many young people sought solidarity in an alternative, international counterculture, a recurring theme of the Super 8 movement.

But not all the Super 8 filmmakers shared these countercultural aspirations. Countless amateurs used the format to record domestic rituals and family events. Others had ambitions of making films appealing to wider audiences, but with values and sensibilities very different from those that dominated the competitions. Sergio Tinoco Solar stands out as a tireless and ambitious amateur whose small-gauge films—most of them features— are modeled on well-known commercial genres. Between the mid-1960s and the later 1980s, he made three in regular 8 mm, 46 in Super 8, one in 16 mm, and one on video, all in his hometown of Orizaba, Veracruz (Tinoco Solar 1988). He relied on relatives and friends for cast and crew for a Western; a science fiction feature about alien invaders; a drama of the Mexican Revolution; biographies of Jesus and Francisco Gabildo "Cri Cri" Soler, the composer of many beloved children's songs; a horror film; several musicals; literary and theatrical adaptations; and films for children. Always and decidedly amateur, yet mimicking the outdated formulae of the commercial cinema, Tinoco Solar replicated industrial conventions in Super 8 rather

Fig. 10.1. Poster for the "Primer Encuentro Internacional de Cine de Super 8." Courtesy of
Sergio García Michel.

Fig. 10.2. Poster for the 1978 Cinexpe Super 8 contest. Courtesy of Sergio García Michel.

than challenging them. The contradictory career of Sergio Tinoco Solar reflects the tensions between industrial and independent media, between commercial prototypes and precarious, improvised alternatives. These defined the fluid boundaries between amateur and professional media in Mexico at a time when both were in crisis.

The trajectory, preoccupations, and discontents to the Mexican Super 8 movement offer fascinating contrasts and parallels with contemporaneous Super 8, amateur, and radical filmmaking elsewhere in Latin America and the global south.

Flush with petro dollars and benefiting from a relatively open society and an active and vital small-gauge community, Venezuela was well-positioned to become a hub of global *superochero* activity. Indeed, the Caracas festival was dubbed the "Cannes of Super 8" (Neri and Márquez 2017 [1980], 105), yet the formalist, seemingly apolitical work that many of the locals made and screened there alienated their more politicized Mexican contemporaries. After the Cuban Revolution, the Mexican state maintained diplomatic relations with the Castro regime, despite pressure from the United States, which hoped to isolate or overthrow the Cuban state. For radical Mexican *superocheros*, inspired by the films of Santiago Álvarez, Julio García Espinosa, and Tomás Gutiérrez Alea, Havana was one of the most important hubs of radical cinema and a global tri-continental movement. While the Mexican filmmakers admired the work of their Cuban counterparts, upon traveling to the island the Mexicans discovered that their cinematic denunciations of the authoritarian tendencies of their government were not welcome in Cuba, where the Mexican state was widely perceived as a crucial ally. Curiously, the *superocheros* had little contact with contemporary independent filmmakers from their northern neighbors, though many members of the US avant-garde—Chick Strand, Bruce Baillie, Lenny Lipton, Ed Jones, and Willie Varela—filmed in Mexico during this period. Raúl López Herrera and Alfredo Nuñez (of the collective "No Grupo"), and the emigrant Manuel DeLanda are among the few who established significant contacts and exchanges with independent filmmakers in the United States, with the exception of those who moved there.

By the mid-1980s, the waning years of the national *superochero* movement, the most vibrant productions were made by those working in self-imposed exile. Long-time resident of Paris, Téo Hernández kept working in Super 8 until his premature death in 1992, thanks to a more supportive infrastructure (Nouguez and Nedjar 1999). Silvia Gruner created series of short, silent works that bring her body into dialogue with canonical references from art history, films created while she was studying at the Massachusetts College of Art and Design. Ricardo Nicolayevsky moved to New York City to study music and film and shot a remarkable series of short portraits of friends from the downtown post-punk scene there, as well as his peers from the Mexican underground. Not until digital technologies became available did he score and edit these *Retratos perdidos* (shot 1982–1984). In Mexico, the inaccessibility of film and processing made Super 8 increasingly less viable. Video wooed many of the independent makers away from the film emulsion to magnetic tape, which was supported by a series of video art biennales ("*Cronología parcial: imágen en movimiento*" 2015, 179–92). In 1989, a cultural center and microcinema devoted to Super 8—Sergio García's Foro Tlalpan—held a memorial service at which they buried a Super 8 camera behind the film format's last holdout. García himself went on to be a prolific videomaker, translating his countercultural vision of rock, political satire, and female rebellion into a new medium. For its duration, the *superochero* movement was a vital form of self-expression and communication for men and women coming of age in a nation in crisis and with no other access to filmmaking. As the anarchist poet Fernando Sampietro says sincerely to the camera in his untitled Super 8 short: "I want to be an actor, just as I had wanted to be a mathematician. But it's just an illusion. An illusion I'm making come true this very moment." For the duration of their collective effort, the *superocheros* embodied Sampietro's Quixotic impulse and showed that an alternative cinema, one reflective of their generation's preoccupations and isolated from commercial pressures, was not an illusion, but rather a reality.

Notes

1. Originally published in Mexico in *Novedades* (1958), this satire tells the story of a fictional artist named Juan, whose successful career hinges on his ignoring foreign influences and sticking closely to the formulas of the "Mexican school." José Luis Cuevas, "The Cactus Curtain," *Evergreen Review* 7 (Winter 1959): 111–20. The historian Claire F. Fox has recently suggested that this famous polemic of Cuevas's was in fact ghostwritten by the Cuban-American curator José R. Gómez Sicre. See Claire F. Fox, *Making Art Panamerican: Cultural Policy and the Cold War* (Minneapolis: University of Minnesota Press, 2013), 152–59.

2. Bob Dylan and Anne Waldman, *Fast Speaking Woman*, Rolling Thunder Revue (1975–76), based on Anne Waldman, *Fast Speaking Woman* (San Francisco: City Lights Books, 1975) and documented in the film *Renaldo and Clara* (Bob Dylan, 1978).

References

Acosta Urquidi, Magdalena. 2013. "Harry Wright y el Cinema Club de México." In *El cine en las regions de México*, edited by Lucila Hinojosa Córdova, Eduardo de la Vega Alfaro, and Tania Ruíz Ojeda, 205–49. Monterrey, NL: Universidad Autónoma de Nuevo León.

Agustín, José. 1996. *La contracultura en México: La historia y el significado de los rebeldes sin causa, los jipitecas, los punks y las bandas.* México, DF: Grijalbo.

Ayala Blanco, Jorge. 1974. *La búsqueda del cine mexicano.* México, DF: Universidad Nacional Autónoma de México.

Benítez, Fernando. 1964. *Los hongos alucinantes.* México, DF: Era.

———. 1976. *En la tierra mágica del peyote.* México, DF: Era.

Buil, José. 1997. *La línea paterna.* México, DF: El Milagro.

Castañeda, Carlos. 1968. *The Teachings of Don Juan: A Yaqui Way of Knowledge.* Berkeley: University of California Press.

———. 1971. *A Separate Reality: Further Conversations with Don Juan.* New York: Simon and Schuster.

———. 1972. *Journey to Ixtlan: The Lessons of Don Juan.* New York: Simon and Schuster.

Cela, Camilo José. 1967. *María Sabina.* Madrid: Ediciones de Son Armadans.

"Cronología parcial: imegen en movimiento." 2015. In *Sarah Minter: Ojo en rotación, imágenes en movimiento 1981–2015.* México, DF: Museo Universitario Arte Contemporáneo.

De Mille, Richard. 1976. *Castañeda's Journey: The Power and the Allegory.* Santa Barbara, CA: Capra.

———. 1990. *The Don Juan Papers: Further Castañeda Controversies.* Belmont, CA: Wadsworth.

Ehrenberg Felipe. 2007. "Cronologías." In *Manchuria: Visión Periférica.* México, DF: Diamantina.

Estrada, Álvaro. 1981. *María Sabina: Her Life and Chants.* Translated by Henry Munn. Santa Barbara, CA: Ross-Erikson.

Fikes, Jay Courtney. 1993. *Carlos Castañeda, Academic Opportunism and the Psychedelic Sixties.* Victoria, BC: Millenia Press.

Furst, Peter T. 1972. *Flesh of the Gods: The Ritual Use of Hallucinogens.* Prospect Heights, IL: Waveland Press.

García Michel, Sergio. 1973. *Hacia el 40. cine.* Zacatecas: Universidad Autónoma de Zacatecas.

"Manifesto: Eight Millimeters versus Eight Million." 1999 [1972]. *Wide Angle* 21, no. 3: 36–41.

Méndez, José Carlos. 1999 [1972]. "Toward a Political Cinema." *Wide Angle* 21, no. 3: 42–65.

Myerhoff, Barbara G. 1974. *Peyote Hunt: The Sacred Journey of the Huichol Indians.* Ithaca, NY: Cornell University Press.

Neri, Julio, and Mercedes Márquez. 2017 [1980]. "Fifth Caracas Super 8 Festival." In *Ism Ism Ism: Experimental Cinema in Latin America*, edited by Jesse Lerner and Luciano Piazza, 104–7. Oakland: University of California Press.

Reuters. 1970. "Hippies Flocking to Mexico for Mushroom 'Trips.'" *New York Times*, July 23, 1970. https://www.nytimes.com/1970/07/23/archives/hippies-flocking-to-mexico-for -mushroom-trips.html.

Rothenberg, Jerome, ed. 2003. *María Sabina, Selections.* Berkeley: University of California Press.

Noguez, Dominique, and Michel Nedjar. 1999. *Téo Hernández: Trois gouttes de mezcal dans une coupe de champagne.* Paris: Editions du Centre Pompidou.

Poniatowska, Elena. 1971. *La noche de Tlatelolco: Testimonios de historia oral*. México, DF: Era.

Rovirosa, José. 1992. *Miradas a la realidad: Entrevistas a documentalistas mexicanos*. México, DF: Centro Universitario de Estudios Cinematográficos/Universidad Nacional Autónoma de México.

Sanjinés, Jorge. 1979. *Teoría y práctica de un cine junto al pueblo*. México, DF: Siglo XXI.

Schultes, Richard Evans, and Albert Hofmann. 2015 [1982]. *Plantas de los Dioses: Orígenes del uso de los alucinógenos*. México, DF: Fondo de Cultura Económica.

Tinoco Solar, Sergio. 1988. *Cine experimental de Orizaba, su historia, su realidad, 1967–1988*. Orizaba: Sergio Tinoco Solar.

Vázquez Mantecón, Álvaro. 2012. *El cine super 8 en México: 1970–1989*. México, DF: Universidad Nacional Autónoma de México.

Waldman, Anne. 1975. *Fast Speaking Woman*. San Francisco: City Lights Books.

Wasson, R. Gordon. 1957. "Seeking the Magic Mushroom." *Life* 49, no. 19 (May 13): 100–120.

JESSE LERNER is a filmmaker, curator, and writer. He is author of *The Maya of Modernism*, *F Is for Phony*, *The Shock of Modernity*, *Ism Ism Ism*, and *The Catherwood Project*.

11

THE *VIDEOGIORNALE*

Social Movements and Amateur Media Technologies in Bologna between the Late 1980s and the Early 1990s

Diego Cavallotti

IN LATE 2014, A REPOSITORY OF AUDIOVISUAL MATERIALS from the late 1980s and early 1990s was discovered in Bologna by myself and the head curators of Home Movies-Italian National Amateur Film Archive, Paolo Simoni and Mirco Santi. This archive presents itself as the most complete audiovisual repository of Bologna's social movement scene of those decades and therefore offers new insights on its members and main events.[1] I took part not only in the recovery of these visual materials, but I also helped to gather them into a collection titled PVEH,[2] which is now housed in the Home Movies-Italian National Amateur Film Archive.

The PVEH collection includes almost four hundred audiovisual documents: one 16-mm film, U-Matic analog videos, VHS, S-VHS, VHS-C, Video8, and Hi8, plus many paper documents. The materials were deposited into the archive by Lino Greco, a former activist and film studies student at the University of Bologna (DAMS Program—Discipline Arte, Musica e Spettacolo; in English, Art, Music and Entertainment Studies school), who was keeping them in his house in Bologna.

During the recovery process, I suggested dividing the PVEH collection into various "thematic sections" and then organizing the sections chronologically. The first section includes videos shot in one of the main squatted buildings in Bologna, called Fabbrika, between the late 1980s and the

Fig. 11.1. Original box in which the videos were stocked. Photograph by author.

early 1990s, as well as videos shot during the student protests of 1990 (the so-called Panther movement). The latter group includes productions from the *Videogiornale* counter-informational video newsreel service, which will serve as this chapter's main case study, illuminating some of the core methodological questions and theoretical insights gained from the process of archiving this collection of visual materials. In the second section of the collection, there is a 16-mm film and several analog videos shot during protests against the war in Iraq (the First Gulf War) and protests against the ordered eviction of the Isola Nel Kantiere squatted building in the winter and spring of 1991. The third section comprises a group of videos from the Elicio Huerta "autonomous" audiovisual production school, which was founded by student veterans of the Panther protests in 1992 and 1993. Finally, for the fourth section I was able to collect videos from the LINK Project TV–Pratello TV local television project.[3] These preparatory and narrowcast materials were mainly used for a forty-eight-hour show that aired during a May 1992 block party in Bologna.[4]

Two different footage typologies compose each section. First, there is the camera footage of events occurring between 1989 and 1993 in Bologna within the context of the social movement scene. We can find here recordings of television on VHS (which were inserted in the edited versions of the *Videogiornale*) as well as VHS, Video8, and Hi8 raw footage of the 1990 university occupation; of several events and rallies that took place at Isola Nel Kantiere (a DJ pool party and a cyberpunk event called 3D INK, for instance); of the eviction of Isola Nel Kantiere; of interviews regarding the First Gulf War; and of the 1991–1992 house occupations. More specifically, the 1992 house occupation of the Pratello block represents the main set in which the LINK Project TV–Pratello TV experiment took place: indeed, part of the Pratello TV section of the PVEH collection is composed of the preparatory footage for the television airings in May 1992.

Second, there is the edited footage of these materials. The members of *Videogiornale* and the students of the Elicio Huerta School used the raw footage for such projects as the *Videogiornale* newsreels—the PVEH collection houses its 17 editions (January–March 1990) on VHS cassettes—and inquiries about Bologna's city life. Concerning the Pratello TV section, the collectives that joined the LINK Project TV–Pratello TV selected and copied the preparatory footage onto S-VHS cassettes, which were used for the narrowcasting of the Pratello TV programs.

Observing the composition of the whole collection forces us to acknowledge its complexity, which is primarily due to changes in technology and the proliferation of media formats in Italy in recent decades.[5] This complexity reveals a few key insights: It can be important for activists (such as those who filmed the materials in the PVEH collection) to quickly learn how to use newer equipment, as they often afford access to a broader demographic and make it easier to document events as they are occurring. It also shows us that activists often repurpose technologies (amateur home videomaking is a key example) for needs that differ from their original commercial uses.[6] Indeed, activist videomakers also often require quicker, more immediate exhibition and consumption for, among other reasons, the creation of cooperative networks and microcommunities (student protesters or the residents of the Pratello neighborhood, for example).[7]

Though technology plays a key role in the complexity of the collection, social and cultural issues factor in as well. In fact, the collected materials participate in a rather fluid dynamic between production and consumption. Their creators, who were at the time young students and community members, also identified with other groups (as we will later see with the LGBT community).[8] In other words, their activities did not appear in a social vacuum: they were intertwined with the history and sociopolitical environment of Bologna.

By the late 1960s, Bologna was the site for powerful protest movements. The protests of 1968 and, later on, 1977, made Bologna a veritable political laboratory for the experiments of the extra-parliamentary left. At the end of the 1980s—the *anni del riflusso* (the "years of reflux"), characterized by a retreat to the private sphere—these protest energies seemed to have run their course. Nonetheless, the end of the decade was a time of profound transformation for Bologna. The Italian Communist Party—which had governed the city since the end of World War II—was about to be dissolved. From its ashes would rise the Democratic Party of the Left, a group of democratic socialists[9] whose electoral platform seemed out of touch with the demands of Bologna's young students and punk groups. In other words, the audiovisual materials of the PVEH collection stemmed from a region-specific context in which deep political changes were happening. We can understand the specific features of the collection only if we take into account the singularity of Bologna's sociopolitical situation between the '80s and the '90s—it was one of the most prominent university towns in northern Italy, its municipality had been ruled by the Communist Party since the end of World War II, it was a destination for young students coming from all over Italy, and an open laboratory for social experiments (not by chance, was Bologna one of the outposts for the LGBT community in the early '80s).

Too proximate to be considered a part of history, yet already too distant to belong to the present, the audiovisual materials that constitute this collection inhabit an "intermediate space" as objects with an unsettled historical status. Their entrance into the archive therefore poses various methodological questions: What can we learn from the artifacts that archivists and historians attempt to piece together? To which analytical tools might they respond, even while their temporal proximity and ties to an informal institutional horizon make the recovery of related sources—as is the case with amateur cinema—impossible? How can we historicize these materials? This chapter addresses these questions through the concrete example of the PVEH collection, locating a particularly generative issue for such media products: how the activists of Bologna's social movement scene created their own media infrastructure. Because they mainly used consumer video technologies, the core issue at stake here is how they appropriated amateur media technologies of the late '80s and early '90s. Archiving the resulting media documents has yielded unique insights into the ephemeral social and technological formations that arose in this particular historical moment.

In order to understand these formations, we need to focus on how the activists combined the documentary objects that we have unearthed and collected (the 16 mm film, U-Matic analog videos, VHS, S-VHS, VHS-C, Video8, and Hi8 tapes) and their corresponding audiovisual equipment creating complex technical systems for filming, editing, and screening purposes. Understanding this process of appropriation and reuse of consumer video technologies within the context of a past social movement means shedding light on the technical practices of social organizations that don't exist anymore and were not based on official statutes and formalized protocols of behavior. So how can we track down how the process of adaptation and appropriation worked without the comfort of established historical sources? This is done here by addressing two specific historical source typologies in addition to the techno-material base of small-gauge film and analog video: local newspapers and oral histories/personal testimonies.[10] I will focus on the main issues concerning the process of adaptation and appropriation of consumer media technologies and the historical sources that the process entails, narrowing the scope of this chapter to the *Videogiornale* section of the PVEH collection.

The *Videogiornale*: A Case Study

Between 1989 and 1990, the Italian government discussed a proposed university reform of Socialist minister Antonio Ruberti. Ruberti's reform advocated more autonomy for each Italian university, and it foresaw the management of universities by private citizens or special interest groups. Interpreting these measures as a first attempt at the privatization of the public education system, the members of the Panther movement quickly succeeded in gaining the attention of major news outlets. This was a result of the ability of the activists to navigate a remarkably complex media landscape in which the television scene—above and beyond the overabundance of local and national newspapers—was approaching a duopoly dominated by RAI (the state-sponsored public service provider Radiotelevisione Italiana) and Fininvest (the mass of networks controlled by Silvio Berlusconi).[11] Because they were able to operate in this media environment, the members of the Panther movement were well positioned intellectually to reflect on the use of technology for communication. Not by chance, they relied heavily on fax technology. In addition, they were influenced by Okkupanet, the first Italian computer network to exploit university computing systems.[12]

Fig. 11.2. Small *Videogiornale* poster. Photograph by author.

Former activist Nando Simeone writes that Okkupanet was "initiated after about one month of university occupations. It involved all the major Italian universities, but particularly the science departments, and it may have been the first instance of computer use for political ends,"[13] at least in Italy.

At the University of Bologna, one of the primary means of communication was video. During student occupations, the militants of the Panther movement inaugurated a small, counterinformational video newsreel service called *Videogiornale*.[14]

This newsreel service had its offices in buildings occupied by students of the Bologna DAMS Program, and most of its contributors were DAMS film studies students.[15] The *Videogiornale* producers mobilized various consumer video technologies, including VHS recorders (for editing); VHS cassettes (for "screening"); and VHS, Video8, and—eventually—Hi8 cameras (for shooting footage).[16] The inauguration of the *Videogiornale* coincided with the first signs of commotion at the University of Bologna. Compared with other Italian universities, the Bologna protests were rather slow to develop—in Rome, for example, student occupations had begun on January 12, 1990, but Bologna remained silent until the Rector's office was finally occupied on January 22.[17] The following day, on January 23, an interdepartmental assembly was convened to recognize the de facto occupation of the humanities school building.

We can already observe in the first *Videogiornale* newsreel and in Panther activities at the University of Bologna a threefold stratification with significant archival and historical implications: First, we have the event, the interdepartmental assembly. Next, the footage of the event (shot with amateur consumer video technologies). And third, the editing of that footage into new audiovisual documents. First and foremost, we must describe the items entering the archive. The PVEH collection holds both original camera footage and edited videocassettes. The archived VHS tapes include both raw footage and the edited episodes of the *Videogiornale*, while the Video8 and Hi8 tapes are all raw footage. How can we connect these archival findings to the original context of production and consumption? In order to answer this question, we have to address a major point at stake here: VHS, Video8, and Hi8 cameras, cassettes, and recorders are all consumer video technologies, usually employed by amateur videomakers. How did *Videogiornale*'s crew adapt these technologies to its communication contexts? In other words, we have to understand not only how prominent formats such as the VHS standard worked back then, but also how VHS machines (camcorders, videorecorders, etc.) were connected to technical objects belonging to other standards (Video8 and Hi8) in order to create assemblages fitting the characteristics of a social movement—in our case, the 1990 student movement in Bologna.

These characteristics are informed by a close dialogue between the personal and the political, the singular and the plural, the individual and the community.[18] For instance, many members of *Videogiornale* were studying film history and media communication at the University of Bologna when the Panther movement took place. They transformed personal and intellectual interests and skills into something useful, documenting what was happening in the movement (and in the city of Bologna) through a video document. They acted as a media collective that helped other collectives— for instance, the LGBT group of the Panther (La Pantera Rosa, the Pink Panther)—to convey their messages. In doing so, they decided that their videos needed to be credited to the *Videogiornale* as a group and not to the individuals who shot or edited them.

In this working environment, the members of *Videogiornale* also made use of the technical media objects that were on hand accessible to a group of students that could not afford the best cameras, videorecorders, and editing stations available on the market. They appropriated consumer video technologies, decontextualizing them from their intended context of use—the family (for the home videomakers) or cineclubs that allowed the use of videotapes alongside small-gauge film. Drawing on this decontextualization, they managed to create a media network/assemblage that involved "elements that are stripped from former combinations, that enter into a new relation with one another, and that form a new general profile."[19] This definition of assemblage-dispositive by Francesco Casetti helps us to pinpoint the technical dynamics occurring in the *Videogiornale* editorial board: the activists used several consumer video technical objects—such as VHS, Video8, and Hi8 camcorders and tapes; VHS videorecorders; and televisions belonging to the university classrooms—out of their context or actually took them from the places where they were supposed to be used. Then, the members of the *Videogiornale* recombined these technical objects—for instance, they connected two videorecorders and built an ad-hoc editing station—in order to create the material base of a workflow: they filmed the main events concerning the university occupation in Bologna, edited the raw footage copying selected contents from the camera cassettes (VHS/Video8/Hi8 camera cassettes) onto VHS cassettes, and then screened the VHS cassettes in the occupied university classroom or during marching protests. Sometimes they inserted footage taken from television recordings (TV shows or films) into the edited VHS cassettes, mashing it up with raw camera footage. This is the reason why, in the *Videogiornale* section of the PVEH collection, we have raw footage of the events (on VHS, Video8, and Hi8 tapes); TV recordings (on VHS cassettes); and the edited versions of the video-newsreel (on VHS tapes).

A complex philological genealogy stems from this technological network. Let's take two archived VHS tapes as examples: the tape preserving the original camera footage for the January 23 student assembly (HMPVEH_BO_225, titled *Assemblea di lettere 23/1/90*) and the tape of the *Videogiornale*'s first episode (screened in late January 1990) that was compiled from that footage (HMPVEH_BO_25). What we notice between these two tapes is a genealogical relationship: *Assemblea di lettere 23/1/90* is the prelude to the first *Videogiornale* episode. In a separate paper document now housed in the PVEH collection, the *Videogiornale* contributors and editors made a list of "macro scenes" (complete with timestamp references) to be included in the edited episode.

But the process of reconstructing such a genealogy raises another question. We have to take into account the material conditions that enabled the creation of those archival finds.[20] What sort of modus operandi did the video journalists employ in their use of video technology? This question shifts our inquiry from the realm of objects to the realm of practices. In the process, it introduces a further methodological problem: namely that the traces produced by practices are ephemeral or even invisible. For this reason, we must rely heavily on the evidence of local news sources and personal testimony.

Local news sources took multiple approaches to the student protest movement, providing specific insights on the artistic and communicative efforts of the activists. We can trace in local news articles precise descriptions of *Videogiornale*'s assemblage-dispositives and more broadly an idea of the appearance—albeit superficial—of the 1980s and 1990s social movement scene in Bologna created by these outlets, intended for those who were not part of this scene. For our purposes, we have surveyed the local issues of the Italian Communist Party's daily *l'Unità* (in this period the Communist Party was installed as the leader of Bologna's local government), which in its coverage showed an interest in both explaining the motives and demands of student groups occupying the university and glossing over

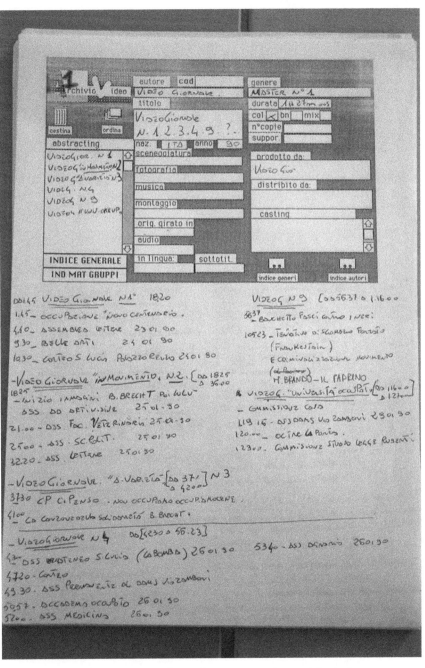

Fig. 11.3. List of "macro scenes" (complete with timestamp references) for the first *Videogiornale* issue. Photograph by author.

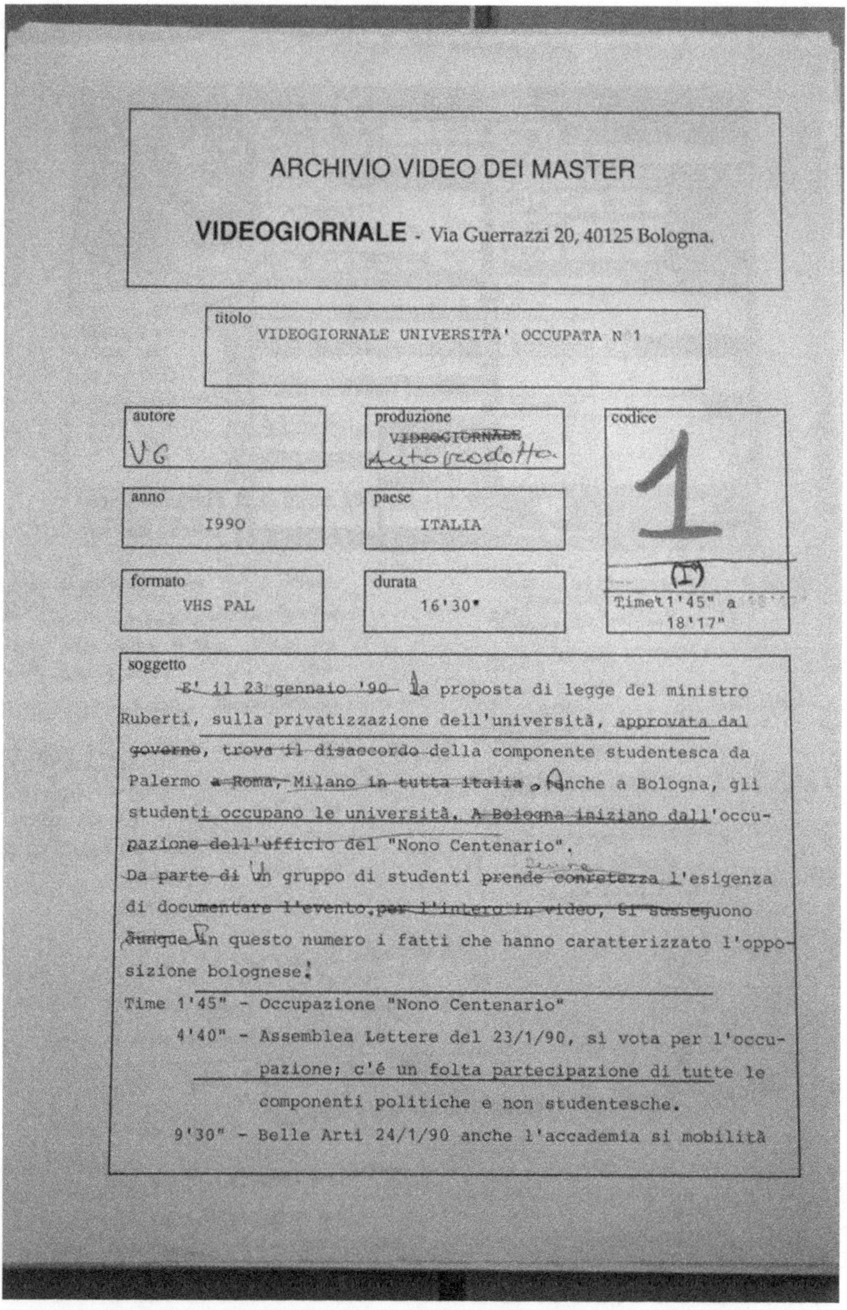

ARCHIVIO VIDEO DEI MASTER

VIDEOGIORNALE - Via Guerrazzi 20, 40125 Bologna.

titolo
VIDEOGIORNALE UNIVERSITA' OCCUPATA N 1

autore
VG

produzione
VIDEOGIORNALE
Autoprodotto

codice
1

anno
1990

paese
ITALIA

formato
VHS PAL

durata
16'30"

(I)
Time 1'45" a
18'17"

soggetto

E' il 23 gennaio '90 la proposta di legge del ministro
Ruberti, sulla privatizzazione dell'università, approvata dal
governo, trova il disaccordo della componente studentesca da
Palermo a Roma, Milano in tutta Italia, anche a Bologna, gli
studenti occupano le università. A Bologna iniziano dall'occupazione dell'ufficio del "Nono Centenario".
Da parte di un gruppo di studenti prende concretezza l'esigenza
di documentare l'evento, per l'intero in video; si susseguono
dunque in questo numero i fatti che hanno caratterizzato l'oppo-
sizione bolognese.
Time 1'45" - Occupazione "Nono Centenario"
       4'40" - Assemblea Lettere del 23/1/90, si vota per l'occu-
               pazione; c'é un folta partecipazione di tutte le
               componenti politiche e non studentesche.
       9'30" - Belle Arti 24/1/90 anche l'accademia si mobilità

Fig. 11.4. Synopsis of the first *Videogiornale* issue. Photograph by author.

some of the tensions internal to the Panther movement in Bologna. For *l'Unità* journalist Stefania Vicentini, whose job it was to cover the university commotion, this meant engaging the creative outlets that were in the student world, including—for example—the "DAMS newsreel service," better known as the *Videogiornale*.

In a 1990 article dedicated to the topic, Vicentini highlights the "tinkering spirit" of *Videogiornale*'s crew:

> In a purposefully "bohèmienne" locale there is a round table that hosts the *Videogiornale* contributors and editors. They gather there around 11 o'clock each evening to plan for the following day of university occupations. They assess the possibilities of various events, and they decide what should be filmed and who should film it. When multiple interesting initiatives overlap, the gathering almost always turns critical, seeing as the group has only three video cameras at its disposal. They "manually" edited their footage on two video recorders because they do not have a video processor for editing. Such technologies—the students explain—are much too costly, and even though everyone says the DAMS Program is well-funded, no money ever makes its way to the production equipment.[21]

Further on, Vicentini elaborates some key points:

> [The students prefer] direct recording techniques, with soft off-screen voice-overs that are careful not to interfere with the reality represented. Their video newsreel service also includes thematic segments—on the Ruberti reforms, on the students' demands—as well as specials on the protests in Palermo and Rome filmed by their own "on-the-scene reporters." "We work with humble means and the resulting quality of our productions is not so high," they shrug. "We try to improve it by inserting other film clips and footage chosen via the simple association of ideas." They may be modest, but they are certainly deliberate.[22]

In short, the *Videogiornale* was the work of young students with few resources who exploited amateur technologies, pushing them well beyond the bounds of their prescribed and "correct" uses. Former film studies student at the University of Bologna and *Videogiornale* contributor Lino Greco has confirmed these impressions in interviews—often with words more precise than Vicentini's—about the group's editing and mixing practices. Regarding the montage sessions, in fact, Greco affirmed that they used to work with "two VCRs and a tiny Sony monitor. During the last period of *Videogiornale* we tried to use more elaborated technologies, trying to practice with new sets. We managed to recover an editing station—which we seldom used because it didn't improve our videos sufficiently—and a 4-track

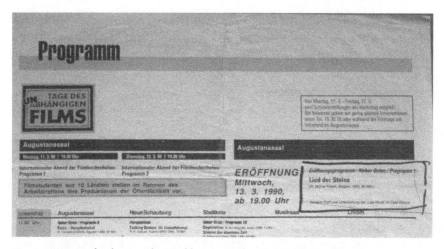

Fig. 11.5. Program for the Tage des Unabhaegigen Films Festival in Augsburg, Germany. Photograph by author.

audio-recorder. We mixed 'on camera,' using the 'insert' track. It was very homemade."[23]

Furthermore, in her article, Vicentini notes that the *Videogiornale* group made a spontaneous proposal to the city of Bologna, requesting that the big screen projector from the main football stadium be moved to Piazza Maggiore (the city's central square). This passing anecdote is of extreme interest to us because it confirms that the *Videogiornale* contributors and editors were open to many screening contexts, from outdoor sit-ins and occupied university classrooms to theatrical programs.

This should come as no surprise. The edited *Videogiornale* episodes were remarkably cohesive and coherent texts that could be projected in cinema theaters. To cite one instance, just three months into the student protests, the *Videogiornale* contributors were invited to exhibit their work at the *Tage des Unabhaegigen Films* Festival in Augsburg, Germany.

Organized by the city of Augsburg, the festival gave young video artists the opportunity to present their very first productions. The program included a selection of recent newsreels made by the *Videogiornale* group and an open discussion in which audience members were encouraged to engage with the material.[24]

This was a far cry from the situation in Bologna, where such effective organization was still hard to come by—as confirmed by Greco, on whose personal testimony we conspicuously relied in reconstructing the video newsreel's exhibition and consumption dynamics. He chaperoned us through the excavation site of the PVEH collection and provided us with relevant insights concerning the *Videogiornale*, newsreels of which were often screened in improvised conditions. Sometimes this referred to simple solutions like gathering around classroom televisions and video recorders to see what was happening with protesters in other university departments. Other times it meant relying on more complex solutions like the so-called audiovisual totem: a cart fitted with a television and a video recorder that rolled from classroom to classroom. Furthermore, thanks to the tactical use of access points to Bologna's electrical grid, the audiovisual totem allowed the students to continue screening their videos outside during moments of active protest such as sit-ins.[25]

Above all, the university screenings used consumer video technology to serve a fundamental purpose for the student protest movement. This technology helped them to strengthen their informal network[26] by working also as a video communication service that quickly became the vehicle for announcements on all the movement's daily activities. These improvised screenings were crucial to producing the multilayered collective subjectivity in which protesters could identify themselves not only as young students, but also as gays and lesbians, for instance. This was the case for the Pink Panther group, which became the reference point for LGBT protesters at the University of Bologna. In an archived VHS tape titled "Gay Pantera Rosa di Luciano Seminario Autogestito Gay/Lesbo" (HMPVEH_BO_252), the representatives of this gay-lesbian collective report to the other students on a variety of relevant protest meetings. In this tape, we find several rehearsals and takes of the same announcement/report, one of which was finally inserted in *Videogiornale*'s fifteenth episode. It was circulated in the halls of the humanities school, DAMS Program's facilities, the political science department, and elsewhere.

What momentum the Panther movement had gained it lost quickly. In March 1990, after the national assembly in Florence, internal disagreements brought the group to a slow crawl, then to a full stop.[27] With discussion of the Ruberti reforms fading from public attention, the Panther movement lost any claim to political relevance. Nevertheless, some aspects of the student protests continued and have relevance still today—namely, the use of amateur media for political ends. On the one hand, the relationship between the *Videogiornale* contributors, the technologies they employed, and the broader 1990 student movement seems to be characterized

Fig. 11.6. "Gay Pantera Rosa di Luciano Seminario Autogestito Gay/Lesbo" (HMPVEH_ BO_252). VHS Cassette. Photograph by author.

by economic scarcity and sociopolitical precariousness (after all, occupying a public university is an illegal act). However, on the other hand, there was a certain ingenuity to the ways in which these students adapted their chosen devices. In short, the video journalists learned to bend technology to their needs. They appropriated consumer video technologies for economic reasons, demonstrating a striking ability to accommodate technical objects to a variety of production and exhibition contexts such as homemade editing stations, theatrical projections, protest marches and sit-ins, and occupied classroom televisions. In this way, they were able to use media technologies in order to fulfill a crucial task: to take part in the construction of the movement's identity.

Conclusion

The description of these practices highlights how the contributors and editors of the *Videogiornale* worked. They appropriated amateur media technologies creating their own assemblage-dispositive. We can observe a basic heterogeneity generated by the turmoil of the historical moment (the student protests) and by economic imperatives (the video journalists improvised a series of super-low-budget technological solutions). In this so-cial environment, they borrowed video technologies intended for the con-sumer market and adapted them to the context of an occupied university's video newsreel service. This act of recombination was designed to allow for and facilitate the processes of shooting, editing, and exhibiting footage. Starting with VHS, Video8, and Hi8 video cameras and videocassettes, the students spliced in other devices (for example, two VHS video recorders for editing), creating an assembly line of technologies. This all led to the output of a final product—the VHS tape used to "transmit" their work within dif-ferent screening contexts: the movie theater (see, for instance, the Tage des Unabhaegigen Films Festival), the protest demonstration (the *audiovisual totem*), and the occupied classroom (the classroom TV and videorecorder). In this way, they formed a whole new media entity. This is not limited to the technical artefacts themselves; rather, it extends to include the constitution of new subjective and communitarian entities, implied but not determined by the act of recombination. In other words, the act of recombination in-volves more than just physical objects; it also involves the subjects that in-fluence that act (and are, in turn, influenced by that act). This underscores a final and fundamental point: the *Videogiornale* must be understood as a product whose very possibility lays in the interaction of technology and the sociopolitical dimensions of its production/use context, within a precise time span, and in a specific location.

In short, the dispositive-assemblage system of the *Videogiornale* teach-es us that when it comes to interacting with technologies of media there is no such thing as "a 'machine' that is pre-arranged once and for all, but rather [. . .] something that is repeatedly re-formed under the pressures of circumstance, and the elements of which are free to recombine. And we no longer have to deal with a 'machine' that captures whoever enters into its field of action, but rather with one that creates tension between its single components and their complex whole."[28]

If an assemblage-dispositive "is repeatedly re-formed under the pres-sures of circumstance," this means that it is articulated within the bounds of the specific historical events that surround it and against which it res-onates. In our case, these bounds were established by the context of the *Videogiornale*, which took shape specifically in Bologna, in the early months of 1990, and within the Panther movement (a student/social move-ment), and have been illuminated here by correlating the "technical base" of the assemblage-dispositive with local news sources and activist testimony.[29]

These sources are crucial to describe not only how the "machine" works but also how it resonates with the socio-political environment that surrounds it. In other words, the sources help the historian to find out how the assemblage-dispositive takes part in the production of the collective subjectivity of a social movement. Through these epistemological lenses, then, *Videogiornale* shaped a precise identity for Bologna's members of the Panther movement: they were media- and video-tinkerers, young students, radicals, and non-heteronormative, anxious to fight for the defense of common goods such as public education. A new generation of activists arising in a moment of profound change in Italian history.

Notes

1. For more on the radical political scene in Bologna, see Serafino D'Onofrio and Valerio Monteventi, *Berretta Rossa: Storie di Bologna attraverso i centri sociali* (Bologna: Pendragon, 2011), and Yannick Aiani, "Nel labirinto degli anni Ottanta: La riformulazione dell'azione collettiva e delle reti di cooperazione nei movimenti sociali a Bologna" (MA diss., University of Bologna, 2018). As regards the Italian "squatted buildings" movement, see Beppe De Sario, *Resistenze innaturali. Attivismo radicale nell'Italia degli anni '80* (Milan: Agenzia X, 2009).

2. The acronym *PVEH* refers to the different sections of this archive. More specifically, *P* stands for *Pantera* and *Pratello TV*, *V* for *Videogiornale*, *EH* for *Elicio Huerta's Audiovisual Production School*. I will describe the contents of each section further on.

3. "Pratello" refers to the via del Pratello, a street in Bologna that gives the Pratello neighborhood its name.

4. More precisely, Pratello TV started to air on May 27, three days before the block party, which lasted from May 30 to May 31, 1992. In many ways, the history of Pratello TV can be compared to that of "alternative television" in the United States. For more on alternative television see William Boddy, "Alternative Television in the United States," *Screen* 31, no. 1 (Spring 1990): 91–101; Deirdre Boyle, "From Portapak to Camcorder: A Brief History of Guerrilla Television," *Journal of Film and Video* 44, no. 1–2 (Spring-Summer 1992): 67–79; Deirdre Boyle, *Subject to Change: Guerrilla Television Revisited* (New York: Oxford University Press, 1997). In regard to Italy, we refer to a survey on several late 1990s/early 2000s street-TV projects: Franco Berardi, Marco Jacquemet, Giancarlo Vitali, *Telestreet. Macchina immaginativa non omologata* (Milan: Baldini-Castoldi-Dalai, 2003).

5. It is interesting to reflect on the relationship between video, technologies, and cultural forms. For more on this point see Jon Dovey, "Camcorder Cults," in *The Television Studies Reader*, ed. Robert C. Allen and Annette Hill (London: Routledge, 2004), 557–58.

6. That is, using technologies outside of their intended "space of communication." For more on this concept see Roger Odin, "The Home Movies and Space of Communication," in *Amateur Filmmaking: The Home Movie, the Archive, the Web*, ed. Laura Rascaroli, Gwenda Young, and Barry Monahan (New York: Bloomsbury, 2014), 15–21.

7. The PVEH collection is mainly composed by analog videos (there is only one 16-mm film). That is why, in the next pages, we will predominantly focus on analog video materials.

8. On "multiple identities" in a single social-movement/countercultural scene, see Donatella della Porta and Mario Diani, *Social Movements: An Introduction* (Malden: Blackwell Publishing, 2006), 98–100.

9. For more on this transformation see Piero Ignazi, *Dal PCI al PDS* (Bologna: Il Mulino, 1992), and Stephen Gundle and Simon Parker, *The New Italian Republic: From the Fall of the Berlin Wall to Berlusconi* (Abingdon: Taylor and Francis, 1996).

10. In regard to the notion of "domain of memory," we do not mean to bridge the gap between our theoretical/methodological set and the vast realm of *memory studies*. On the contrary, we aim to connect the "domain of memory" to the main issues concerning the "act of collecting memory." In other words, we aim to reflect on memory as an historical source. In this sense, our major reference is Pierre Sorlin and his essay "Le storie personali: Sfida alla tradizione storica," in *Che storia siamo noi?*, ed. Luisa Cigognetti, Lorenza Servetti, and Pierre Sorlin (Venice: Marsilio, 2008), 30–35.

11. For more on the history of the Italian media landscape see Irene Piazzoni, *Storia delle televisioni in Italia. Dagli esordi alle web tv* (Rome: Carocci, 2014), 181–85.

12. More specifically, Okkupanet took advantage of the computing system networks shared by the Italian hard sciences departments. Using these networks, researchers were able to share data and to experiment with ICT resources and technologies. See Nando Simeone, *Gli studenti della Pantera: Storia di un movimento rimosso* (Rome: Alegre, 2010), 73.

13. Ibid.

14. Almost in the same time period, similar efforts were performed behind the collapsing Iron Curtain with the so-called samizdat televisions. Regarding this topic, see Friederike Kind-Kovács and Jessie Labov, eds., *Samizdat, Tamizdat, and Beyond: Transnational Media During and After Socialism* (New York: Berghahn Books, 2013).

15. *Videogiornale*'s crew could count on many contributors. Among them, besides Lino Greco, we can recognize Luca Bic, Andrea Brugnoli, Daniele Calzetti, Andrea Cusatelli, Daniele Del Pozzo, Francesco Gallo, Daniele Gasparinetti, Claudio Lanteri, Roberto Marchionni, Clinio Occhi, Roberto Paganelli, Vincenza Perilli, Andreas Pichler, Silvia Storelli, Anna Visconti, Johanna von der Vring, Johannes Wilms, and Lulù Zuccatosta. Some of them are still to be identified and named; this will be the object of further research.

16. The PVEH collection holds seventeen episodes of the *Videogiornale*. The average episode length is about twenty minutes.

17. For more on the Rome occupations, see Simeone, *Gli studenti della Pantera*, 170.

18. Here, I refer to the notion of community in the broadest possible sense. In other words, it should be considered as stemming from the noun *community*, which is the general meaning used by Judi Hetrick in "Amateur Video Must Not Be Overlooked." In this case, the word "communitarian" refers to "what concerns a social collectivity" and it does not have any specific political connotation. See Judi Hetrick, "Amateur Video Must Not Be Overlooked," *The Moving Image* 6, no. 1 (Spring 2006): 72–77. The communitarian issue is also addressed by Deirdre Boyle and Ellie Rennie. See Boyle, "From Portapak to Camcorder," 72–74; Ellie Rennie, *Community Media: A Global Introduction* (Lanham: Rowman and Littlefield, 2006), 15–45.

19. Francesco Casetti, *The Lumière Galaxy: Seven Words for the Cinema to Come* (New York: Columbia University Press, 2015), 81.

20. For more on the material conditions of production see Tom Slootweg, "Imagining the User of Portapak: Countercultural Agency for Everyone!," in *Exposing the Film Apparatus: The Film Archive as a Research Laboratory*, ed. Giovanna Fossati and Annie van den Oever (Amsterdam: Amsterdam University Press, 2016), 183.

21. Stefania Vicentini, "Il 'Tg' del Dams su maxi-schermo?," *l'Unità*, January 31, 1990, 6.
22. Ibid.
23. Diego Cavallotti, "L'audiovisivo analogico della quotidianità: Discorsi, pratiche e testi del film e del video amatoriale tra gli anni Settanta e gli anni Novanta in Italia" (PhD diss., University of Udine, 2017), 398.
24. The PVEH archive holds a video documenting the group's participation in the festival. It is titled *Augsburg: Giovedì del DAMS, GI.5.4.89 dibattito con Agosti* (HMPVEH_BO_256).
25. For more on these screening solutions see Lino Greco's email to the author, July 11, 2017.
26. On the role of informal networks, see della Porta and Diani, *Social Movements*, 114–34.
27. For more on the national assembly see Simeone, *Gli studenti della Pantera*, 101–12.
28. Casetti, *The Lumière Galaxy: Seven Words for the Cinema to Come*, 81.
29. Instead of using the term *context*, we could refer to the notion of *ecology*. It would entail a shift of theoretical focus, from the assemblage-dispositive studies to the media ecology framework. See Michael Goddard, *Guerrilla Networks: An Anarchaeology of 1970s Radical Media Ecologies* (Amsterdam: Amsterdam University Press, 2018).

References

Aiani, Yannick. 2018. "Nel labirinto degli anni Ottanta: La riformulazione dell'azione collettiva e delle reti di cooperazione nei movimenti sociali a Bologna." MA diss., University of Bologna.
Berardi, Franco, Marco Jacquemet, and Giancarlo Vitali. 2003. *Telestreet. Macchina immaginativa non omologata*. Milan: Baldini-Castoldi-Dalai.
Boddy, William. 1990. "Alternative Television in the United States." *Screen* 31, no. 1 (Spring): 91–101.
Boyle, Deirdre. 1992. "From Portapak to Camcorder: A Brief History of Guerrilla Television." *Journal of Film and Video* 44, no. 1–2 (Spring-Summer): 67–79.
Boyle, Deirdre. 1997. *Subject to Change: Guerrilla Television Revisited*. New York: Oxford University Press.
Casetti, Francesco. 2015. *The Lumière Galaxy: Seven Words for the Cinema to Come*. New York: Columbia University Press.
Cavallotti, Diego. 2017. "L'audiovisivo analogico della quotidianità: Discorsi, pratiche e testi del film e del video amatoriale tra gli anni Settanta e gli anni Novanta in Italia." PhD diss., University of Udine.
De Sario, Beppe. 2009. *Resistenze innaturali. Attivismo radicale nell'Italia degli anni '80*. Milan: Agenzia X.
Della Porta, Donatella, and Mario Diani. 2006. *Social Movements: An Introduction*, Malden-Oxford-Carlton: Blackwell Publishing.
Dovey, Jon. 2004. "Camcorder Cults." In *The Television Studies Reader*, edited by Robert C. Allen and Annette Hill, 557–68. London: Routledge.
Goddard, Michael. 2018. *Guerrilla Networks: An Anarchaeology of 1970s Radical Media Ecologies*. Amsterdam: Amsterdam University Press.
Gundle, Stephen, and Simon Parker. 1996. *The New Italian Republic: From the Fall of the Berlin Wall to Berlusconi*. Abingdon: Taylor and Francis.

Hetrick, Judi. 2006. "Amateur Video Must Not Be Overlooked." *The Moving Image* 6, no. 1 (Spring): 66–81.

Ignazi, Piero. 1992. *Dal PCI al PDS*. Bologna: Il Mulino.

Kind-Kovács, Friederike, and Jessie Labov, eds. 2013. *Samizdat, Tamizdat, and Beyond: Transnational Media During and After Socialism*. New York: Berghahn Books.

Odin, Roger. 2014. "The Home Movies and Space of Communication." In *Amateur Filmmaking: The Home Movie, the Archive, the Web*, edited by Laura Rascaroli, Gwenda Young, and Barry Monahan, 15–25. New York: Bloomsbury.

Piazzoni, Irene. 2014. *Storia delle televisioni in Italia. Dagli esordi alle web tv*. Rome: Carocci.

Rennie, Ellie. 2006. *Community Media: A Global Introduction*. Lanham: Rowman and Littlefield.

Simeone, Nando. 2010. *Gli studenti della Pantera: Storia di un movimento rimosso*. Rome: Alegre.

Slootweg, Tom. 2016. "Imagining the User of Portapak: Countercultural Agency for Everyone!" In *Exposing the Film Apparatus: The Film Archive as a Research Laboratory*, edited by Giovanna Fossati and Annie van den Oever, 177–86. Amsterdam: Amsterdam University Press.

Sorlin, Pierre. 2008. "Le storie personali: Sfida alla tradizione storica." In *Che storia siamo noi?*, edited by Luisa Cigognetti, Lorenza Servetti and Pierre Sorlin, 21–36. Venice: Marsilio.

DIEGO CAVALLOTTI is Assistant Professor of Media Education at the University of Cagliari. He is author of *Cultura Video. Le riviste specializzate in Italia (1970–1995)* and *Labili tracce. Per una teoria della pratica videoamatoriale.*

12

"A VITAL HUMAN PLACE" FOR THE COUNTERCULTURE

Fifth Estate *and Amateur Film Culture in Detroit, 1965–1967*

Joseph DeLeon

FIFTY YEARS AFTER THE 1967 DETROIT REBELLION, MANY cultural events were held in 2017 to remember that turbulent summer.[1] One event was the "1967 Detroit: Home Movies" exhibition, sponsored by the Detroit Institute of Arts. The exhibition's curators asked former and current residents of the city to submit film reels of their home movies from the late 1960s to be screened publicly throughout 2017. One screening on June 1, 2017, illustrated the strikingly banal landscape of racial segregation in the city of Detroit in the months leading up to the rebellion. Each home movie in this screening showed a family enjoying the comforts of Detroit's middle-class enclaves and suburbs with children playing in front yards alongside new cars in the driveway. White children in the home movies played with other white children, and black children played with other black children.

The camera's gaze in these movies replicated the spatial division of blacks and whites in the de facto segregated city (Sugrue 1996). At the June 1 screening, only one film captured evidence of the rebellion, which occurred primarily in densely populated, majority-black inner-city neighborhoods. Shot by a bus driver after the fact, the film recorded footage of a crumbling neighborhood viewed from the driver's seat along his bus route. Appropriately, the single film during that day's screening from the "Motor

City" that traversed neighborhood borders was shot by the driver of an automobile from behind the wheel. As this single commemorative screening demonstrates, the domesticity embedded in the genre of amateur film and home movies captured the social geography of Detroit in 1967, recording the landscape of racial separation and imbalance of privilege that persist in the city to this day.

However, in 1960s Detroit, more than one amateur film culture existed. A platform for an alternative amateur film culture thrived through the efforts of the Detroit counterculture. The underground newspaper *Fifth Estate* organized in part this counterculture community, and its film culture existed at a purposeful remove from the amateur film practices that predominated in the city's suburbs. These two modes of amateur film culture make apparent the limitations and the possibilities of the amateur film movement and its engagement with politics and society. The suburban amateur film culture centered on home movies within the predominantly white, middle-class domestic sphere in the suburbs. The countercultural amateur film culture expanded the notion of the amateur to encompass wider realms of participatory culture and to foster the emergence of a countercultural public sphere precisely located in the economically and racially diverse neighborhoods of the Cass Corridor, Midtown, and on the Wayne State University campus.[2] This chapter argues for a shift from the former, more widely accepted, notion of amateur film as centered on the production of home movies in order to expand our understanding of amateur film culture to include practices such as activism, film criticism, and informal film exhibition within the 1960s US counterculture. I argue that this form of cultural production provides an important way to excavate the social and racial reality leading to the Detroit uprising while also offering a potentially emancipatory model for the role of film in social struggle.

Film and media studies has overlooked the Detroit counterculture's amateur film culture.[3] Amateur film history has traditionally centered on the lone domestic film-maker recording home movies far from the direct influence of official institutions of film production such as film schools and studios (Zimmerman 1995). In Detroit, the counterculture's commitment to amateurism extended beyond aesthetics. After World War II, discourse on amateur filmmaking within the US counterculture emphasized the social and artistic importance of film aesthetics. Filmmaker Jonas Mekas wrote in 1965 that underground films were "happy to call themselves home movies" (318). In his contemporary account of the counterculture, critic John Gruen

(1966, 112) similarly argued that the ad-hoc character of experimental films incorporated a home movie aesthetic through characteristics such as "a sense of intimacy and familial immediacy, the coziness of a primitive painting, a nostalgia for the hand-crafted, a lack of pretention, the transcendence of the creative urge over the confinements of a schooled technique."

Despite the valuing of a home movies aesthetic within mid-1960s underground film circles, such an aesthetic impulse was not the only aspect of amateur film culture carried over into the counterculture. Alongside an amateur aesthetic present in experimental film practice, Detroit's counterculture adopted aspects of amateur film culture with a different political orientation by building a community of film criticism, film production, and film screenings based on the New Left's political agenda of criticizing the Vietnam War, the House Un-American Activities Commission (HUAC), and local racism and police violence in Detroit.[4] Detroit's counterculture imbued amateur film practices with "participation" construed as a mode of political action.

By 1965, the activities of a few young Leftists helped bring Detroit into orbits of influence of the US counterculture. After he moved to Los Angeles with his mother, recent high school graduate and Detroit native Harvey Ovshinsky fell in with the local counterculture when he picked up a copy of the underground newspaper *LA Free Press* and became enchanted by the paper's coverage of antiwar politics and the local music scene. After briefly working for *LA Free Press*, Ovshinsky moved back to Detroit and started his own underground newspaper, *Fifth Estate*, in November of 1965.[5]

Meanwhile in Detroit, a group of artists, including poets John Sinclair and Robin Eichele as well as filmmakers Leni Sinclair and Emil Bacilla, had established in 1964 the Detroit Artists Workshop (DAW) with film allotted an important place. The DAW was an artist cooperative based in the arts communities at both Wayne State University (WSU) and the Red Door Gallery. As a "center of avant-garde film showings, exhibitions of paintings, and general 'hanging out'" (Eichele and Sinclair 1965, 23), the Red Door Gallery's closing in 1964 left a gap that the DAW sought to fill as a cooperative that could help artists in Detroit through collaboration. Just a few months before Ovshinsky began publishing *Fifth Estate*, the DAW sought "to draw upon the resources of every participating individual in order to perpetuate itself—and promote community thinking on an artistic and person level—through its own cohesive community nature" (Eichele and Sinclair 1965, 23). The DAW and *Fifth Estate* combined efforts to collaborate in late 1965, with Sinclair starting his weekly column "The Coat-Puller" in *Fifth Estate*'s second issue. Enthusiasts of the DAW film scene, described as "people who were studying film, people who were into film, and people who were looking to film," found a home alongside *Fifth Estate*.[6]

In 1966, *Fifth Estate* became one of the five founding newspapers of the Underground Press Syndicate (UPS), alongside *Berkeley Barb*, *East Village Other* from New York City, *LA Free Press*, and *The Paper* from East Lansing, Michigan. These underground newspapers imparted to readers "a sense of connection and belonging to the New Left," especially in communities in Midwestern cities like Detroit that are not usually included among coastal communities of art production and film exhibition (McMillian 2011, 7). While there were film columns in other underground papers, columns in the newspapers of the UPS typically focused on reviews of experimental and foreign films. For example, a 1967 *Berkeley Barb* issue contained a review of Yves Robert's film *La Guerre des Boutons* (1962) and discussed European art cinema (Lipton 6). Early in *Fifth Estate*'s existence, Ovshinsky recognized the role of film in the New Left community he sought to build through the paper, including "film workshops" alongside other social initiatives and art forms such as "a free university, good drama, crafts to make and to sell" ("Notes on Improving" n.d.). Such a focus on the practicalities of filmmaking offers a different image of film in the counterculture than other underground papers.

Once they began collaborating, *Fifth Estate* and the DAW were united in their opposition to the type of amateur film community already in the city, which was too invested in middle-class ideals to provide a suitable space for countercultural politics. One amateur film group was the Michigan Movie Makers Club, which met throughout the 1960s at a YMCA in downtown Detroit. Another group, the Michigan Council of Amateur Movie Clubs, held an annual film contest in Kalamazoo in southwestern Michigan starting in 1948. *Detroit Free Press* described the event as "limited to all 8-mm and 16-mm amateur movie makers in Michigan" ("Wilson Film Competition" 1949, 8). In 1962, the contest moved from Kalamazoo to suburban Detroit ("Cine Fans" 1962). By 1966, the group was holding the contest at the Northland Center, a suburban shopping mall built in 1954 in Southfield, a Detroit suburb ("Camera Clubs" 1966).

Supporting this suburban film culture through the 1960s was *Detroit Free Press* journalist Arthur Juntunen, who reviewed consumer camera technologies and gave tips on home movie production. Juntunen's articles

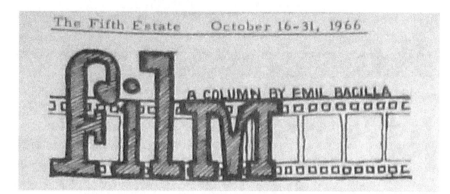

Fig. 12.1. Emil Bacilla, "Film," *Fifth Estate*, October 16–31, 1966, 5. Courtesy of *The Fifth Estate*.

covered how best to capture the Christmas holiday in a home movie (1963), how to choose a Super 8 projector for the home (1966), and how to "direct" a home movie (1968). As the topics of Juntunen's articles illustrate, the focus on amateur film clubs throughout the 1960s in Detroit developed out of a domestic idiom within the middle-class communities that hosted the amateur film groups and their movie contests. The city's suburban residents with enough expendable income to pursue filmmaking as a hobby were the target audience of this amateur film culture. The amateur film culture of Detroit's suburban sprawl became a target for the city's countercultural film community.

Fifth Estate and the DAW built an amateur film culture separate from that of the middle-class and far from the suburban complacency against which they fought. Within the first year of *Fifth Estate*'s existence, filmmaker Emil Bacilla started a film column in the paper.[7] His first column did not contain a review of a recent film release or a discussion of the aesthetics of avant-garde film, but with a polemic about the lack of a film scene in Detroit comparable to coastal US film cultures. Bacilla was influenced by West Coast film culture from the early 1960s, having lived in San Francisco in 1965 and having met filmmakers like Bruce Baillie. Bacilla (1966, 4) used *Fifth Estate* as a platform to declare in his first column: "Film, the liveliest art, is, for all intents and purposes dead. At least in Detroit." Echoing an impetus for the creation of other amateur film groups in the United States, Bacilla lamented the lack of a dedicated network for communication and collaboration that could inform filmmakers and film enthusiasts of each other's activities. As film scholar Melinda Stone (2003, 221) similarly writes of the San Diego Movie Club, self-made networks through amateur film groups gave budding filmmakers of all stripes a ready audience for their productions and provided their work with a legitimacy through shared screening spaces.

Bacilla's polemical tone in his first column reveals his fervent belief in what was needed to sustain a community of amateur filmmakers and film enthusiasts: participation through collaboration. Notably, Bacilla did not mention in his first column the activities of Detroit's suburban amateur film clubs, which were likely so far from the concerns of *Fifth Estate* and the DAW as to be unnoticeable. Bacilla (1966, 4) did note that the community forming around him gave him hope: "I . . . love Detroit. And I see things happening and struggling to make it a better place. This newspaper for example, and the ideals behind the Artists Workshop." Bacilla's statement here includes the DAW in a vision of how film can matter in the city, and in how film can play a role in further community adhesion. He committed to staying in Detroit to build the film community: "There must be other people who are interested in film somewhere around here. People who realize that film is an art form that requires a group of people working together" (Bacilla 1966, 4). Bacilla's conceptualization of what would sustain a film group in the counterculture echoes the strategies found in other amateur film groups in the United States in the mid-twentieth century, including: "to assist one another with their projects, improve their craft, and provide a regular audience for their productions" (Stone 2003, 220). Bacilla did acknowledge the activities of a local film group, Detroit's Midwest Film Society (MFS), but he criticized how the exodus of MFS members to film schools in Los Angeles and New York City threatened its existence. Here Bacilla indicates that an organized film community had to be based in Detroit to sustain an urban film culture.

Yet the *Fifth Estate* crowd was aware of the limits to creating a separate amateur film culture in Detroit. Getting a wider swath of Detroit's cultural scene to pay attention to the artists within the counterculture was challenging, in part because the *Fifth Estate* community chose not to maintain a high profile with lavish social events. As Sinclair summarized, "We're not artsy enough for them, don't put on big cultural parties and balls, don't charge $900 for paintings and hold cocktail open houses" (Askins 1969, 34). These factors led to a division in the amateur filmmaking communities. Separate from the suburban, bourgeois amateur film community was the young, urban one, which provided fewer barriers to access to encourage the participation of younger artists and activists from all class backgrounds. Through Bacilla's columns, *Fifth Estate* supported the need for a film community that could pool resources and provide a shared venue for participation in the rise of Detroit's arts community.

However, Bacilla's columns do at times provide similar tips as those written in the *Detroit Free Press* for the suburban film community. In other words, the film culture in Detroit adapted components from other amateur film groups as it also attempted to set itself apart from them within its own political context. By crafting their vision of amateur film culture to protect their political imperatives, Detroit's counterculture mounted a strategy of survival in a segmented city of enclaves. As Jeff A. Hale (2002, 129) writes: "The ideology of the Detroit hip community reflected a voluntary isolation from, and utter contempt for, the outside society." The adoption of strategies and screenings from amateur film culture within the counterculture demonstrates both the flexibility of the midwestern counterculture to adapt practices for their political purposes and the portability of aspects of amateur film culture throughout the 1960s.

Similar to the filmmaking tips offered by the official *Detroit Free Press* camera journalist, Arthur Juntunen, Bacilla also provided an overview of film advice for the amateur filmmaker. Bacilla sought to provide interested amateur filmmakers with budget-conscious information, such as how to cut costs in filmmaking, in addition to "general information on how to make films: how to get started, short-cuts, and things to help you once you get started" (1967a, 12). While Bacilla's columns do not last long in the scope of *Fifth Estate*'s history, his attempts to provide a platform for an amateur film culture to take shape through collaboration should be understood as a moment in which the counterculture modeled its actions implicitly upon the groups they set themselves against—namely, the local, middle-class amateur film culture. By providing similar advice and a parallel social function as that of Juntunen, we can see Bacilla's initiatives as similarly providing a shape for an amateur film culture, though arising out of the counterculture's political stance.

The amateur film culture idealized by Bacilla must have seemed to take shape with a subsequent move to the planned Plum Street neighborhood by *Fifth Estate* and the DAW, which promised to consolidate the concerns of the film community.[8] In a departure from Detroit's postwar urban renewal program, premised "on the destruction of some of the most densely populated black neighborhoods in the city," the city set out in 1966 to create a geographical home for the counterculture, one that could some day rival the Haight-Ashbury in San Francisco (Sugrue 1996, 49). The location for this softer municipal attempt at urban renewal was Plum Street.[9] Local news coverage framed the hippie district's opening in September of 1966 as bringing Detroit up to speed with other major cities: "New York has its Greenwich Village . . . and now Detroit has a beginning in Plum Street" (Holmes 1966, 3A). Plum Street's opening brought *Fifth Estate* and the DAW into close physical proximity. With closeness came further collaboration through film.

With an established film column and increased collaboration among countercultural groups in the Plum Street district, Bacilla's concerns then turned toward establishing an amateur film group reliant on participation in a countercultural community rather than on the atomized, consumerist experience of amateur filmmaking in Detroit's suburbs. By helping each other with projects, gathering resources to better their craft, and providing an audience for their productions, the nascent film group fostered through *Fifth Estate* operated like an amateur film group with the political orientation of the counterculture (Stone 2003, 220). Bacilla's idea of the film community in Detroit sought to include teaching others the practicalities of filmmaking in a culture of collaboration and community-building.

To this end, Bacilla acted to build the foundation for film activity guided through local institutions such as WSU. He remarked that the film courses at WSU could help both absolute beginners as well as "the most professional amature [*sic*]" to learn the in-depth subtleties of film-making (Bacilla 1967b, 16). Demonstrating the ideological split between the amateur film culture of the counterculture and the amateur film culture of Detroit's middle-class suburbs, Bacilla (1967b, 16) distinguishes WSU courses geared for the "amateur" from the adult education courses geared for "the home movie maker." This distinction is important, for the figure of the amateur for Bacilla is thus the young, countercultural amateur, not the older, suburban amateur who saw filmmaking as a domestic hobby. Bacilla's use of the term *amateur* here was an attempt to reclaim the term for the counterculture. To be an amateur to Bacilla meant to be in the vanguard of not just film as an art but as a political project in line with New Left activism.

Beyond Bacilla's columns, the film culture fostered by Detroit's countercultural community cultivated a social vision of film as a political art form through film screenings that critiqued a status quo of socially conservative norms. The Detroit community organized performative screenings

Fig. 12.2. Gary Grimshaw, a renowned graphic artist of psychedelic concert posters, was one of the two artists who created this "Phantasmagoria" advertisement in *Fifth Estate*'s August 30, 1966, issue. Courtesy of *The Fifth Estate*.

that satirized anti–New Left and anti-Communist propaganda and that served as a bridge between contemporary filmmaking and the wider concerns of the counterculture. One important screening that *Fifth Estate* held was the "Right-Wing Film Phantasmagoria" on September 10, 1966. The fundraiser screening, with proceeds going to *Fifth Estate* and the Detroit Committee to End War in Vietnam (DCEWV), included two right-wing films chosen for their hyperbolic and politically conservative perspectives for an audience made up of Detroit's counterculture. The public projection of the two films was intended to satirize and recontextualize the worldview on offer by both films.[10]

The films screened at the "Right-Wing Film Phantasmagoria" invited a disjunctive viewing experience and a satirical reading due to the gap between the films' ideological framing, the films' content, and the communal screening space itself. The participatory nature of the screening took shape through the recuperation of these films as humorous texts, sources of inspiration rather than dread. The first film to be screened, *While Brave Men Die* (dir. Fulton Lewis III, 1966), set out to depict the corruption within the peace movement. The CIA-produced film represents the peace movement as militantly radical in its intent. The film's voiceover says that the "so-called peace movement" is becoming more militant, equating the political leanings of radical Marxists and the "pacifists and liberals" that have come together for the anti–Vietnam War movement. *Operation Abolition* (dir. Fulton Lewis III, 1961) contains footage from a San Francisco protest of a Hearing of the Committee on Un-American Activities in 1960. Police attacked demonstrators with fire hoses after the latter were prevented from entering the hearing room. The HUAC used film footage of this event to make *Operation Abolition* and to present the HUAC as the victim of well-organized communist agents. By screening these two conservative films together, the Phantasmagoria fostered a mode of participation that encouraged a reading of such films with an arch sensibility through the context of an emergent idea of the "expansion" of film.

Film screenings such as the Phantasmagoria served two functions for Detroit's counterculture. In line with other amateur film groups, a group film screening secured a space for the display and discussion of filmmaking. The Phantasmagoria in particular tied the cooperative characteristics of the amateur countercultural film community to an emergent sense of the "expansion" of cinema. Film scholar Andrew Uroskie (2014, 13) argues that expanded cinema works in the 1960s provided a sense of "material, perceptual, affective, and institutional dislocation," which was ultimately a result of the remediation of cinema through the experience of new moving image media for the masses such as television. Often consisting of live performance, music, light shows, and projected films, expanded cinema challenged the unquestioned site of the exhibition of films as well as the context for the understanding of film as a medium (Joseph 2002). This introduction of a disjunction into the viewing experience aimed to introduce new perceptual experiences into the modern subject. *Fifth Estate*'s Phantasmagoria introduced a dislocation in understanding the political potential of films produced not only by their group but also by their ideological counterparts.

The ad-hoc techniques and textual properties of *While Brave Men Die* and *Operation Abolition* provided a disjuncture between the films' conservative content and the audience's Leftist orientation at the Phantasmagoria screening, revealing the texts to be unintentionally available for communal dissection and interpretation. The formal qualities of the films encouraged participation. One review of the Phantasmagoria called the films "an exercise in high cinema camp and low grade stupidity" ("High Camp" 1966, 1). A review in *Time* magazine of *Operation Abolition* underlined the technical failures that made it a source of mockery: "The movie is an abrupt, badly edited 45-minute short. Its eye-jolting camera work is murky, its soundtrack raucous and shrill" ("The Investigation" 1961). Media scholar Todd Gitlin (1987, 83) wrote that *Operation Abolition* provided an opportunity for activists to counter the film's intended anti-Communist message with a wry form of spectatorship: "*Operation Abolition* proved a camp favorite and an inspiration to campus activists more than a cautionary tale. . . . The lumbering Committee had made a recruiting film for a New Left that barely existed." Peter Werbe, *Fifth Estate*'s news editor at the time, wrote to *While Brave Men Die*'s director, Fulton Lewis III, that the film served as a far better recruitment tool for the New Left than for conservative causes: "Honestly, if the National Coordinating Committee to End the War in Vietnam were to make a film, I don't think it would be much different than the one you produced" (1966, 11). I argue that the "Right-Wing Film Phantasmagoria" film screening was similar to other communal screenings within US amateur film groups, but with an explicitly political purpose. The Phantasmagoria served a unifying function for Detroit's counterculture and budding amateur film community.

The Phantasmagoria built on preexisting notions of expanded cinema within Detroit as a participatory activity in the counterculture. As early as

1964, John Sinclair noted: "We are now in a period of expanded consciousness in all the arts" ("The Artists Workshop Society," 1). In *Fifth Estate*, an attention to an "expansion" in the arts emerged by 1966, primarily through advertisements and discussions of psychedelic light shows that accompanied local rock bands such as the MC5. One review of a light show and psychedelic concert in *Fifth Estate* remarked on the affordances of the concert space as a communal, mind-expanding endeavor: "A variety of unusual lighting effects synchronized with the penetrating rock sound are calculated to bring about a psychedelic experience in the minds of the participants, but like hypnosis, it required cooperation" (Grimshaw 1966a, 9). This experience both overwhelmed the senses and yet was rooted in the communal experience of cooperation.[11]

While not incorporating the psychedelic light shows found in other venues of the city, the Phantasmagoria included aspects of a performative orientation to film that paralleled the expansion of cinema. The Detroit counterculture harnessed an amateur film club model of communal screenings, but they also expanded the social role of film through the Phantasmagoria's performative, campy qualities, presaging the midnight movie circuit and other participatory film events of university film cultures.

Through the reconstitution of the Phantasmagoria's films as satirical, the youth counterculture in Detroit laughed at the disparity between the images and the narration. The screening thus mirrored the overall inclusive amateur orientation of *Fifth Estate*, aimed at expanding the audience's participation within film culture as a mode to foster adhesion into their community. The open-minded orientation around *Fifth Estate* encouraged broader participation in film practices that, in Los Angeles or New York City, were often prohibitive to members of the counterculture with less experience or professional training in film.

The Phantasmagoria appears in subsequent issues of *Fifth Estate* as a "proof-of-concept" for similar large-scale film screenings in Detroit. Ovshinsky remarked after this screening that *Fifth Estate* and the DAW intended to have more benefit screenings in the vein of the "Right-Wing Film Phantasmagoria." Ovshinsky wrote that the event spurred plans to build a combination café and movie house in the city. Echoing Bacilla's earlier polemic on film being dead in Detroit, the café and movie house were intended "to fill the coffeehouse gap. . . . There's so many gaps in this city and so many ideas, but getting the money is something else" (Ovshinsky 1966, 2). As so often occurred in the Detroit counterculture, this idealistic vision for reclaiming space for film outside of Detroit's suburbs met active resistance.

Despite the collective momentum of Bacilla's film column and performative screenings, the New Left political orientation of the DAW and *Fifth Estate* ultimately hindered the formation of a coalition beyond their countercultural sphere. In the next issue of *Fifth Estate* following the "Phantasmagoria," in October, 1966, John Sinclair reported that the MFS agreed to screen films with the DAW (2). Sinclair "immediately implemented" the idea (1966b, 2). At the first screening partnered with the MFS, Sinclair reported that flyers were handed out detailing the films to be shown at the workshop for the rest of the autumn season. For a moment, "everything was groovy" (2).

The city's class and racial politics quickly intervened. Sinclair reported that, after the first screening, one of the officers of the MFS received a threatening phone call from a member of a right-wing, white nationalist group in Detroit, called Breakthrough. The Breakthrough member warned the MFS not to associate with *Fifth Estate* or with the DAW. Sinclair (1966b, 2) wryly remarked that their "hangout for commies & junkies" was ultimately not suitable for "nice old movie-lovers." Breakthrough had previously targeted *Fifth Estate* by distributing leaflets in Detroit's west side that called the paper an "anti-Christian, anti-American hate sheet," largely due to *Fifth Estate*'s anti-Vietnam War stance ("Pro-War Group" 1966, 3). The further proposed screenings with MFS went "underground," according to Sinclair (1966b, 2). *Fifth Estate* contained no further mention of any screening partnered with MFS. Without a venue for community-oriented amateur film screenings, and with increased police scrutiny both before and after the 1967 rebellion, Detroit's counterculture moved away from constructing a Leftist film community of amateurs.

Conclusion

In 1960s Detroit, the counterculture community acted in a way that was different from both suburban amateur film groups and other counterculture film groups in that they affixed an activist orientation to components of amateur film culture, such as informal film criticism and participatory screenings. While the influence of experimental and avant-garde filmmaking is present within the group's activities, I maintain that their activities must also be seen as guided by strategies found within local and other amateur film groups throughout the United States. The 1960s underground press, in capturing a countercultural youth committed to theories of multimedia arts cooperatives and entranced with the expansion of cinema and other arts, documented their community through a program of visibility that included and privileged film.

The history of Leftist political uses of film in Detroit is an important addition to cinema history that makes the Midwest of the United States a vital site for excavating overlooked amateur film histories. These histories critique a suburban ideology in mid-century America, show a wider array of film practices and forms of collaboration of the American Leftist counterculture, and demonstrate that performative film screenings could be a political use of film within an amateur film group. As Detroit continues to look back in remembrance of its past, film and media scholars should not forget the use of film to connect countercultural amateurs looking to make Detroit "a vital human place" (Sinclair and Sinclair 1966, 2) during the 1960s.

Notes

1. During the early morning of July 23, 1967, Detroit police raided an unlicensed bar known as a *blind pig* on the city's Near West Side, a predominantly African American neighborhood. The raid soon sparked looting in protest of the city's long-standing institutional racism and entrenched segregation of African Americans. In response to cases of arson and the theft of firearms, Governor George Romney called in the Michigan State Police and the US National Guard. The rebellion went on to last five days, claiming forty-three lives. The uprising in Detroit against police brutality, racial profiling, and the lack of equal housing opportunities found similar articulations in other cities such as Newark (Fine 1995).

2. The "wider realms of participatory culture" encompass a countercultural critique of a generational complacency and a recognition of a necessary coalition between Leftist activist groups around the city. On the former point, *Fifth Estate* columnist John Sinclair's poetry on the passivity of TV spectatorship derides those "dying in their living room chairs" in "a house in a nice neighborhood / [with] a car & a TV set." For Sinclair, participatory engagement in the arts, including film, would disrupt this complacency (Sinclair 1966a). On the latter point, *Fifth Estate* regularly included columns about black activism and working-class issues, all grounded in the paper's vision to unite across coalitional lines of race and class. Discussing the electoral potential of black lawyer and activist Kenneth Cockrel and the advocacy of poverty-rights group West Central Organization, John and Leni Sinclair (1966, 2) wrote: "[We] are all going to have to start working with each other on all fronts, help each other out, and take advantage of what are our local possibilities are—like this newspaper, like the Artists' Workshop and the West Central Organization, . . . the Detroit Committee to End

War in Vietnam, . . . Kenneth Cockrel for state representative—all of these are manifestations of the same essential concerns, that Detroit be a vital human place for all of us."

3. In this chapter, I follow David E. James (2005, 138) regarding the instability of the definition of amateur film: "Always meaning several, often incompatible, things at the same time, and changing those meanings over the decades, the concept of amateur film has been endlessly reformulated and variously affiliated with or defined against adjacent terms, including personal film, home movies, the avant-garde or art film, the student film, the documentary, and even the industrial film itself."

4. The term *New Left* refers to the mid-1960s activist movements that emerged from the post–World War II civil rights movement and claimed expanded rights for an array of social groups. The New Left started from a labor rights platform in the earlier twentieth-century Marxist context of Leftist activism and then went on to critique social conservatism and cold war liberalism in the United States.

5. One cartoon slated for inclusion in the first issue depicted an American flag with bayonets for stripes. The cartoon offended the original printer, and *Fifth Estate* almost never got published. Ovshinsky received the help of an African American newspaper, *Star of the Black Madonna*, to print the first issue, revealing forms of collaboration not only within the largely white Detroit counterculture but also among broader racial and class coalitions in the city (Carson 2005, 128).

6. Robin Eichele (Detroit poet and filmmaker), in discussion with the author, July 26, 2017.

7. Later, in 1967, Bacilla also briefly wrote a film column for John Sinclair's own underground paper, *The Warren-Forest Sun* (also known as *The Sun*).

8. Prior to the Plum Street move, members of both groups lived and worked near each other by WSU, but the move to Plum Street is significant as an intended "hippie" district, influencing their vision of collaboration within the city (Carson 2005, 118).

9. The creation of Plum Street did entail evictions, which the following *Detroit Free Press* article glossed over in profiling the project: "Six months ago the block could look ahead to a few more years of crumbling before it was finally condemned and razed. The only people who might have missed it would have been the handful of poor families who lived there" (King 1966, 11A).

10. The politics of the Detroit film community can be read through Tepperman's (2014, 137) inclusion of "the *exhibition* of nonmainstream films" as a key component of post–World War II amateur film groups, with an additional shift toward political action.

11. Such a light show borrowed no doubt from the use of film projectors in Andy Warhol's Exploding Plastic Inevitable, which had performed in Michigan just a few months before the Phantasmagoria (Grimshaw 1966b).

References

"The Artists Workshop Society: A 'Manifesto.'" 1967 [1964]. *Collected Artists Worksheet—1965.* Detroit: Detroit Artists Workshop Press. Box 10, John and Leni Sinclair Papers, Bentley Historical Library, University of Michigan.
Askins, John. 1969. "Where Did John Sinclair Come From?" *Detroit Free Press*, December 14, 1969, 18–39, 61–63.

Bacilla, Emil. 1966. "Detroit Filmmaker Mourns Death of Local Flicks." *Fifth Estate*, September 15–30, 1966, 4.

———. 1967a. "Film," *The Sun*, no. 2 (Detroit, MI), April 1967, 12.

———. 1967b. "A Film Column Without a Clever Name." *The Sun*, no. 3 (Detroit, MI), April 1967, 16.

"Camera Clubs." 1966. *Detroit Free Press*, April 28, 1966, 14D.

Carson, David A. 2005. *Grit, Noise, and Revolution: The Birth of Detroit Rock 'n' Roll.* Ann Arbor: University of Michigan Press.

"Cine Fans to Meet." 1962. *Detroit Free Press*, October 4, 1962, 4E.

Eichele, Robin, and John Sinclair. 1965. "Getting Out from Under: Counter-Community." *New University Thought* 4 (2): 22–30.

Fine, Sidney. 1995. *Violence in the Model City: The Cavanagh Administration, Race Relations, and the Detroit Riot of 1967.* Ann Arbor: University of Michigan Press.

Gitlin, Todd. 1987. *The Sixties: Years of Hope, Days of Rage.* New York: Bantam.

Grimshaw, Gary. 1966a. "Detroit Freaks Out with First Participatory Zoo Dance." *Fifth Estate*, October 16–31, 1966, 9.

———. 1966b. "I'm Just Mod about Weddings." *Fifth Estate*, December 1–15, 1966, 5.

Gruen, John. 1966. *The New Bohemia: The Combine Generation.* New York: Shorecrest.

Hale, Jeff A. 2002. "The White Panthers' 'Total Assault on the Culture.'" In *Imagine Nation: The American Counterculture of the 1960s and '70s*, edited by Peter Braunstein and Michael William Doyle, 125–56. New York: Routledge.

"High Camp at Lower Deroy: The Film Phantasmagoria." 1966. *Fifth Estate*, September 15, 1966, 1.

Holmes, Susan. 1966. "Plum Street Officially Open." *Detroit Free Press*, September 25, 1966, 3A.

"The Investigation: Operation Abolition." 1961. *Time*, March 17, 1961, 17.

James, David E. 2005. *The Most Typical Avant-Garde: History and Geography of Minor Cinemas in Los Angeles.* Berkeley: University of California Press.

Joseph, Branden W. 2002. "'My Mind Split Open': Andy Warhol's Exploding Plastic Inevitable." *Grey Room* 8:81–107.

Juntunen, Arthur. 1963. "Start Yule Movie at Beginning." *Detroit Free Press*, December 12, 1963, 10C.

———. 1966. "Now You Can Have Super 8—And Keep Regular 8, Too." *Detroit Free Press*, August 18, 1966, 9D.

———. 1968. "A Word about Directing Your Home Movies." *Detroit Free Press*, September 26, 1968, 16C.

King, Wayne. 1966. "Arty Plum Street Plan Unfolds." *Detroit Free Press*, July 7, 1966, 11A.

Lipton, Lenny. 1967. "At the Flick." *Berkeley Barb*, November 17–23, 1967, 6.

McMillian, John. 2011. *Smoking Typewriters: The Sixties Underground Press and the Rise of Alternative Media in America.* Oxford: Oxford University Press.

Mekas, Jonas. 2000 [1965]. "Notes on Some New Movies and Happiness." In *Film Culture Reader*, edited by P. Adams Sitney, 103–7. New York: Cooper Square.

Ovshinsky, Harvey. 1966. "Detroit: A Progress Report." *Fifth Estate*, September 15–30, 1966, 2.

———. n.d. "Notes on Improving the *Fifth Estate* and Detroit in General." Box 1, Harvey Kurek Ovshinsky Papers, Bentley Historical Library, University of Michigan.

"Pro-War Group Tries to Smear Lafferty, Fifth Estate in 17th District." 1966. *Fifth Estate*, July 30, 1966, 3.

Sinclair, John. 1966a. "The Poem for Warner Stringfellow." Box 10, John and Leni Sinclair Papers, Bentley Historical Library, University of Michigan.

———. 1966b. "The Coat-Puller." *Fifth Estate*, October 1–15, 1966, 2.

Sinclair, John, and Magdalene Sinclair. 1966. "The Coatpuller." *Fifth Estate*, July 15, 1966, 2.

Stone, Melinda. 2003. "'If It Moves, We'll Shoot It': The San Diego Amateur Movie Club." *Film History* 15, no. 2: 220–37.

Sugrue, Thomas. 1966. *The Origins of the Urban Crisis: Race and Inequality in Postwar Detroit*. Princeton: Princeton University Press.

Tepperman, Charles. 2014. *Amateur Cinema: The Rise of North American Moviemaking, 1923–1960*. Berkeley: University of California Press.

Uroskie, Andrew. 2014. *Between the Black Box and the White Cube: Expanded Cinema and Postwar Art*. Chicago: University of Chicago Press.

Werbe, Peter. 1966. Letter to Fulton Lewis III. *Fifth Estate*, October 1–15, 1966, 11.

"Wilson Film Competition Is Opened." 1949. *Detroit Free Press*, December 29, 1949, 8.

Zimmerman, Patricia R. 1995. *Reel Families: A Social History of Amateur Film*. Bloomington: Indiana University Press.

JOSEPH DELEON is a PhD candidate in Film, Television, and Media at the University of Michigan, Ann Arbor.

13

INGVARS LEITIS'S SUBVERSIVE ETHNOGRAPHIC DOCUMENTARIES, 1975–1989

Cover Stories and National Representation in Soviet Latvia

Inese Strupule

A MATEUR FILMMAKING IN LATVIA DATES BACK TO THE country's first period of independence (1918–1940). There are a few preserved amateur films from this era, notably those made by freelance camera operator Pēteris Miezītis between 1925 and 1939, which are now held at the Latvian State Archive of Audio-visual Documents (Latvijas Valsts Kinofotofonodokumentu Arhīvs). During this period, there was a certain crossover between professional film industry and cine-amateurism in Latvia, the latter being largely practiced on the side by professionals working in the film industry. The amateur films that were created by Miezītis and others like him often concerned the filmmakers' families, friends, leisure activities, travel, as well as current events in the local area. This dynamic radically shifted after Latvia was annexed by the Soviet Union in 1940, when the distinction between the professional and amateur filmmaking spheres became more defined, and the bourgeois amateur filmmaker had to adapt to the social realities of a socialist state. As opposed to the Western camera enthusiast, Soviet amateurs were encouraged to join amateur filmmaking workshops, which were organized on a highly formalized basis and supported by the institutional networks of administered culture and professional unions (Vinogradova 2012, 211–25).

Anne White (1990, 35) observes that, in the Soviet Union, the year 1930 marked the beginning of the state-initiated mass construction of "clubs for the population," with the primary purpose being the socialization and politization of the masses through amateur artistic activities and propaganda work. However, the death of Joseph Stalin in 1953 inevitably lead to modification of the cultural policies in the Soviet Union. White describes how, during the period that is known as the Thaw of the late 1950s and early 1960s, there was a "blossoming of organized 'popular initiative[s]'" and of new forms of the so-called cultural enlightenment practices, aimed at "mobilizing the whole population by giving it the opportunity to participate in creative cultural activity, rather than being totally directed from above" (35). At the same time, the period of 1955–57 saw the transfer of the state clubs to trade unions "to encourage public responsibility and participation" (38). These factors stimulated the growth of the network of amateur creativity clubs at places of work, but also inadvertently led to the diminishing of the Party control and the possibility of exploring a larger world of ideological positions—albeit limited by the contours of state institutions—during the late Soviet era. Individual amateur filmmakers were encouraged to join clubs, as they were supported through the system of professional unions responsible for providing the material and technical base (Järvine 2005, 57–58). Most often, the clubs tended to be organized on the premises of factories, collective farms, research centers, or in the so-called Houses, or Palaces, of Culture, usually attached to such institutions.

As an unspoken condition of the state's endorsement of these clubs, amateur cinema was expected to transmit official ideological discourse. However, because amateur cinema, like other amateur arts, was primarily seen as a leisure activity rather than cultural production, no dedicated governmental entity or mechanism existed to control the output of amateur filmmaking clubs, as opposed to, say, the output of the professional film industry (Vinogradova 2012, 214). Thus, although overseen in its totality by the state, amateur filmmaking in the Soviet Union enjoyed a degree of creative and ideological latitude, which arose out of its institutionally looser constitution. In the case of the Soviet Union, amateur films that dared to address the taboo subjects of human rights violations and the curtailing of national freedom invariably emerged in particular within the so-called satellite states, where the regime never enjoyed the same degree of control.

This chapter examines the political use of amateur filmmaking in Soviet Latvia and aims to explore the ways in which, on occasion, amateur filmmakers articulated and promoted ideologies that were in conflict with those of the state. It will focus on a historian and amateur filmmaker, Ingvars Leitis, who made a series of documentary films on the subject of the communities of ethnic Latvians in Siberia between 1975 and 1989. These communities were formed in the mid-nineteenth century, when the Latvian-origin peasants of the Russian Empire went to Siberia in search of land. Over time, they were joined by a number of "undesirables" and convicts deported by the Tsarist authorities. As was the case with many other national minorities of the Soviet Union, the ethnic Latvians of Siberia suffered greatly during Stalin's purges of the 1930s; it was this aspect of their history that concerned Leitis the most. Between 1975 and 1989, Leitis made numerous trips to the Latvian villages of Siberia, where he filmed extensively and collected testimonies from the locals about their current life as well as the era of Stalin's purges. These materials were incorporated into several documentary films that explored the Soviet era crimes inflicted on these communities. In the milder political climate of *perestroika* (1985–1991), these films were archived by the Latvian Amateur Filmmakers' Society (Latvijas Kinoamatieru Biedrība, LKAB), and after the society's dissolution in 2008 were donated to the Latvian State Archive of Audio-visual Documents, and now are also available online on Leitis's YouTube channel.

This chapter explores the ways in which the concerns that defined the nature of dissent in Soviet Latvia—namely, human rights and national self-determination—were tackled in Leitis's films, and attempts to throw some light on the fraught relationship between nonprofessional individual filmmakers and the institutional structures constructed under state socialism. More broadly, through the prism of Leitis's life and work, this chapter also aims to trace the relationships between Latvian dissidents, cultural intelligentsia, amateur creative organizations, and the emerging political forces prior to and during the period of *perestroika* and the overall democratization that was encouraged under Mikhail Gorbachev. The analysis in this chapter will rely largely on Leitis's personal collection of films and other documents on the subject, his 2016 memoir, which documents his first trip to Siberia in great detail, as well as an interview with him conducted by the author in April 2017.

Contexts

Due to both its looser regulation and the provision of technical support to amateur filmmakers by the professional unions, amateur filmmaking culture in the Soviet Union encompassed a great deal of formal, thematic, and functional diversity. Prompted by the ill socioeconomic climate of the period now labeled as stagnation that began under the rule of Leonid Brezhnev (1964–1982), in the 1970s, many Soviet amateur filmmakers began to turn to social subjects in their films, often exposing and problematizing the shortcomings of the Soviet society and economy.[1] However, these social amateur films were conceived mostly within the spirit of *grazhdanstvennost'*, or civic-mindedness, and thus cannot be characterized as openly oppositional or "dissident." Susan Costanzo discusses this tendency in depth in relation to amateur theatre in the 1960s Soviet Union and defines *grazhdanstvennost'* as a civic spirit embedded in an artistic expression, committed to exposing social problems despite the risk of a backlash from the authorities. Despite the fact that the argument of *grazhdanstvennost'* was commonly used to defend controversial content, it was usually informed by "a genuine belief that loyal criticism would benefit Soviet art and society and would be tolerated as a logical extension of Nikita Khrushchev's 1956 denunciation of Stalinist excesses and subsequent de-Stalinization" (Costanzo 2008, 374, 380–81).

On the other hand, amateur film equipment was also at times used by Latvian dissidents with the clear political purpose of documenting the Soviet state's brutality. In the mid-1970s, for example, the Brūvers brothers, Pāvils and Olafs, together with Jānis Rožkalns, all renowned Latvian dissidents and the future members of the human rights group Helsinki-86, used amateur film as a tool against Soviet repression. On one occasion, they daringly shot footage of the KGB agents entering and leaving the KGB headquarters in Riga; later, they also managed to film the mistreatment of prisoners in one of Riga's prisons. The films were smuggled to the West and broadcast on television in 1975–76 in a number of countries (Misiunas and Taagepera 1993, 264). Despite the fact that Leitis also employed film as a tool in political activism, he did not view himself as part of the Latvian dissident community, saying he was never close with "the real dissent veterans, those Helsinkinians," and identifying more with the restrained opposition prevailing within the circles of Riga's cultural intelligentsia (Leitis 2017). Leitis admired what Rožkalns and the Brūvers accomplished (calling their films "the greatest achievement of Latvian cine-amateurism"), but he chose another oppositional path, undermining the Soviet regime from the inside by appropriating its cultural codes for his subversive ends (Ingvars Leitis, email to author, November 15, 2015).

Leitis began researching ethnic Latvian communities in Siberia in 1974 after an acquaintance told him an anecdote about a group of tourists who came across a Latvian village while on a trip to Sayan Mountains. Being a historian by education (Leitis graduated from the University of Latvia with a bachelor's degree in history in 1973), he began to look into the subject of Latvian migrants to Siberia. Leitis discovered a 1928 census that recorded approximately two hundred thousand Latvians living in Russia: "A huge number! A tenth of the [Latvian] nation," as he puts it (Leitis 2017). The existence of ethnic non-Russian communities in Russia was not a taboo topic in itself, and was in fact recorded officially, while various materials concerning the subject were archived in libraries available for academic research. For instance, in 1976, one of the leading Estonian historians of the time, Viktor Maamägi, published a monograph entitled *Estonskie poselentsy v SSSR, 1917–1945* (*Estonian Settlers in the USSR, 1917–1945*), which told the story of the successful and mutually fruitful integration of the ethnic Estonians of Russia into the Soviet collective farm system (Maamägi 1976). In his work, Maamägi carefully adhered to the official Soviet line on national minorities, which presented the point of view that the aspirations of the Baltic people and other non-Russian minorities of the Soviet Union were being realized in the emancipation of the working class engineered by the Soviet regime. Leitis, however, saw the potential of fostering national remobilization through exploring the seemingly neutral subject of the ethnic Latvian communities in Russia, especially bearing in mind that many issues faced by Siberian Latvians were pertinent for the Latvian Soviet Socialist Republic, too. Thus, the research and amateur films that resulted from Leitis's trips to Siberia can be viewed as an attempt to uncover the broader outline of the national history of Latvia in terms of an identity submerged by Soviet antinationalism and cultural colonization.

Leitis's project does indeed seem structured by elements that invite examination through the prism of postcolonial theoretical framework.[2] As Bill Ashcroft (2001, 45) has observed, the colonial subject's engagement in the dominant culture "becomes one in which consumption and production are deeply implicated, and the force of these processes may also lead to changes in that dominant culture itself." Ashcroft maintains that postcolonial resistance need not necessarily entail the utter refusal to engage with its forms and discourses, and that "the most effective form of resistance" has always been to gain control "over such things as language, writing and various kinds of cultural discourse," and to "make use of aspects of the colonizing culture so as to generate transformative cultural production" (45). This style of resistance is what Ashcroft calls "interpolation," and it involves interposing, intervening, and interjecting "a wide range of counter-discursive tactics into the dominant discourse without asserting . . . a separate oppositional purity" (47).

Ashcroft's ideas anticipate and resonate with Alexei Yurchak's social anthropology of Soviet system's decay. Yurchak (2005, 14) contends that, after the Stalinist era, the Soviet regime began to rely on an ossified system of representations, and "the form of ideological representations—documents, speeches, ritualized practices, slogans, posters, monuments, and urban visual propaganda—became increasingly normalized, ubiquitous, and predictable." Yurchak, borrowing a concept from Bakhtin, calls this phenomenon "authoritative discourse" (14). According to Bakhtin, such discourse has two properties. First, it is sharply defined with relation to other discourses around it, often by the recognizably special script in which it is coded. Second, its coexisting discourses refer to, and subsume themselves to it, without ever being able to change or penetrate it (14–15).

According to Yurchak (2005, 27), on the one hand, this situation limited the emergence of other forms of representation, lending an air of immutability to the Soviet regime; but on the other hand, the authoritative stance could be appropriated, which thus "enabled people to engage in new, unanticipated meanings, aspects of everyday life, interests, and activities, which . . . were not necessarily determined by the ideological constative meanings of authoritative discourse." Further, Yurchak draws on the Foucauldian thesis that the possibility of resistance to norms is embedded within the structure of power itself, as well as on Saba Mahmood's critique of the tendency to equate agency with resistance, and he develops these ideas further by arguing that agency can also be implied in acts that are "neither about change nor about continuity, but about introducing minute internal displacements and mutations into the discursive regime in which they are articulated"; such acts may seem inconsequential to both participants and observers, but with time lead to the regeneration of the system (27–28). In other words, the authoritative discursive conditions and gestures of the state could be appropriated in many different ways. Based on Ashcroft's and Yurchak's observations, in the course of this chapter I will attempt to demonstrate that Leitis's work can be interpreted as a process of developing strategies of (national) self-determination by using the Soviet regime's cultural capital and discursive tools, which prompted change within the system that provided them.

Riga—Vladivostok Cycling Tour

Based on the information Leitis was able to gather, he calculated that the scale of Stalin's purges of 1936–38 must have been enormous for the

Siberian Latvians. Despite Khrushchev's 1956 denunciation of Stalin and the subsequent process of de-Stalinization, the full extent of Stalin's crimes against Soviet people largely remained a secret and they were a highly sensitive topic. In spite of the widely publicized persecution of dissidents, in 1975, Leitis decided to organize an expedition in search of Latvian villages in Siberia with the purpose of learning about the life of the communities today and collecting evidence about the impact of the purges. Due to the state-imposed restrictions on interior travel such a journey would have to be justified, officially arranged, and supported by documentation. The regime was certainly not going to support a nationally minded investigation of Stalinist crimes. This is the reason Leitis conceived of a rather brilliant cover and decided to organize a cycling tourist trip to Siberia—as he puts it himself, "with a completely different purpose on paper, with Soviet slogans, dedicated to some anniversary or whatnot" (Leitis 2017). In other words, Leitis manipulated the state's authoritative discourse in order to carry out an investigation of the silenced parts of the history of the Siberian Latvian villages, a purpose which, if it had been avowed, would have certainly barred Leitis from making any such trip. By practicing this most effective form of resistance, to use Ashcroft's formulation, Leitis unleashed the transformative potential of his cultural production, which will be unpacked in the final part of this chapter.

This thirteen-thousand-kilometer trip required the sponsorship of various people and organizations; the degree of their awareness of Leitis's intentions and motivations varied. As Leitis's project had an ethnographic side to it, he used his academic contacts to provide further justification for his journey. As a result, a professor at the Latvian Academy of Sciences, Saulvedis Cimmermanis, agreed to support Leitis's project by providing him with ethnographic research materials in exchange for access to the invaluable ethnographic data that Leitis would collect (Leitis and Briedis 2016, 9). Leitis admits that his formal ethnographic research mainly involved the accumulation of descriptive detail of little interest and was at best an inconvenience for him. However, it was useful as a cover story in case of an encounter with the KGB (45). Here it is again evident that Leitis appealed to the discursive regime of an official science in order to be able to collect and disseminate information that was potentially disruptive to the state's dominant discourse.[3] Later, Leitis met professional photographer Uldis Briedis, who offered to join him on the trip. Briedis introduced Leitis to Gunārs Biezis, the editor-in-chief of *Zvaigzne*, a respectable Party-line

Fig. 13.1. Leitis and Briedis crossing the Urals, 1975. Photo by Uldis Briedis.

magazine with a large circulation published in Soviet Latvia. Biezis saw the appeal factor of the Riga–Vladivostok cycling tour and offered Leitis and Briedis the official support of *Zvaigzne* in exchange of them providing regular progress reports in the form of photographs and articles that would be published twice a month. In *Zvaigzne*, the tour was heralded, perfectly in line with the state's ritualized discourse, as a form of commemorating the thirtieth anniversary of the victory in the Great Patriotic War (9–11). Thus, the trip became a multilayered affair and was carried out from May to November 1975. Briedis photographed extensively, and Leitis came back with a collection of recorded audio footage. However, nothing was filmed that year.

Subsequent Trips and the First Film

Encouraged by the success of the first trip, Leitis decided to travel to Siberia again in 1976, this time to the village of Lejas Bulāna. At this point, he was trying to find a way of disseminating the gathered information in some forum in Latvia that would not alert the authorities. Just as Leitis used ethnographic research as a cover, so, too, did he deny any particular interest in amateur filmmaking and talks about it as merely a tool: "I took a camera in my hands for the first time in 1976 [because] I wanted to show what I was discovering in Siberia to people in Latvia. I was not interested in amateur filmmaking for any other reasons" (Ingvars Leitis, e-mail to author, November 15, 2015). Leitis's personal connections allowed him to obtain an 8-mm camera and film stock; thus Leitis managed to film salient aspects of his trip to Lejas Bulāna, which resulted in a thirty-minute film. The film also included some of Briedis's photographs from 1975 and audio recordings of interviews with locals from both trips. The recordings were both political (interviews containing testimonies about Stalin's purges) and folkloric (including segments of songs). Leitis provided the film's voiceover, which told the story (in accordance with his cover) of his research into Latvian villages in Siberia and hinted at the overall negative impact the Soviet regime had on Siberian Latvians. Leitis protected himself from the conflict with the law by playing by the rules of the official discourse: "The text [of my voiceover] was very aggressive and outspoken, but I adapted it to correspond to all the [legal] nuances. They could not pin [any accusation] on me. It could cause disfavor, but there was nothing criminal" (Leitis 2017).[4]

Later that year, Leitis started to show his film unofficially. Word traveled fast, and soon the film stirred the interest of Riga's creative intelligentsia. Seeking to avoid the attention that would have come from a showing in a public forum, Leitis screened the film in the private flats of sympathizers. As Leitis would later discover, one of these screenings was attended by an anonymous KGB informant who identified the attendees, reported on the overall atmosphere of the evening ("a spirit of nihilism and admiration for the West reigned there"), and reported on Leitis's film itself ("the film features many shots of dilapidated buildings, shows negative aspects of life; everything is presented in a tendentious way") (Informācija par Leiti Ingvaru no LPSR VDK informācijas analīzes daļas materiāliem). On the grounds of this report, Leitis was summoned by the KGB. Anticipating he would be asked to present his film for examination, Leitis re-edited the soundtrack to produce a different, self-censored one, without the aggressive voiceover. The result was, as Leitis puts it, "just pure ethnography" (Leitis and Briedis 2016, 307). Here Leitis again foregrounded the ethnographic quality of his project in order to disguise that he was essentially engaging in an act of criticizing the Soviet regime and exposing of its crimes. The musical folklore he had collected came in handy here: the new soundtrack consisted solely of songs, thus radically changing the meaning of the film. Nevertheless, the KGB officers retained this copy of the film, and Leitis never managed to recover it. However, this did not discourage Leitis from continuing to research and film.

In 1977, Leitis bought a 16-mm camera and traveled to Siberia in both 1977 and 1978, where he filmed extensively and recorded interviews with the locals, but also encountered more difficulties from the authorities. These trips were also officially presented as ethnographic fieldwork informally supported by the Academy of Sciences. This cover fitted well within the overall atmosphere of the "folklore wave" that started in the 1960s across the Soviet republics (Andreeva 2013, 215–16). Soviet folklore studies received a major boost from a significant number of expeditions to study folklore and the resulting publications of academic papers and collections of folk recordings (215–16). The Latvian Academy of Sciences, with its institutes for the study of history, folklore, material culture, language, and literature, became a perfect springboard for investigating nationally minded subjects of Latvian ethnic history and culture in a legitimate way. Nevertheless, Leitis's activities started to alarm the officials, and, during the 1978 trip, in Rižkovo, Leitis and his traveling companion Juris Riekstiņš were detained, searched, and extensively questioned about the purpose of their travel. Their passports were held by the local KGB, which prevented them from continuing the trip. Ultimately, no grounds for arrest were found, and Leitis and Riekstiņš were allowed to return to Riga. Upon his arrival home, Leitis received a serious warning from the Riga's KGB office against traveling to Siberia again; this temporarily put a stop to his activity, compelling him to keep a low profile for almost a decade. Later he wrote in his memoir, "I created a precedent within the Soviet penalty system: normally wrongdoers were sent to Siberia, I, on the contrary, was prohibited from crossing the Urals" (Leitis and Briedis 2016, 307).

Perestroika and the RRR Film Studio

The cultural and political climate changed drastically in Latvia and across the Soviet Union with Mikhail Gorbachev's ascendancy to power in 1985 and the official promulgation of *glasnost'* and *perestroika*. Having plenty of film footage and documentation he had collected over the years, Leitis felt that he could finally start editing and showing films about Latvians in Siberia openly without fear of official repression. In 1986, Leitis joined the amateur film studio of Riga Radio Factory (Rīgas radio rupnīca, RRR), which was founded in 1964 on the premises of the House of Culture attached to the factory. By the mid-1970s, the amateur filmmakers of the RRR, perhaps inspired by the folklore wave, had dedicated themselves to the exploration of the themes of Latvian ethnic history and culture and produced a wide array of amateur films on these topics. Save for their strong political dimension, Leitis's films fitted well into the studio's generic output. Nevertheless, Leitis's joining of the studio can be interpreted as just the kind of demi-oppositional move that meets the criterion of Ashcroft's interpolation. Even though, in 1986, the extent to which *glasnost'* would change the orienting points of state-supported cultural enlightenment was still unclear, Leitis jumped on the changes as early adopter, and saw that the structures of the amateur filmmaking network would allow him to not only use the studio's equipment, but also give him a platform for exhibiting his work, as amateur film studios' managers had to organize regular screenings to showcase the work of their authors.

In 1986, Leitis completed the film *Populārzinātniska lekcija par kādu vēstures tēmu* (*Popular Scientific Lecture on a Historical Subject*) using the photographs, film footage, and audio recordings from the 1975–78 trips to Siberia. This half-hour long film introduces the topic of the Latvian communities that Leitis visited, as well as briefly overviews testimonies to the violence visited on them by the Soviet state. The voiceover, which he had once expunged to keep it out of the hands of the KGB, was restored. The film begins with a brief introduction to the history of the main villages, with Leitis touching on the formative violence meted out by the Soviet system to them. He notes, as well, two contemporary phenomena: the decline in the population of Siberian Latvians and the sparse knowledge of the Latvian language, especially among the younger generation. Both factors have many causes, among which are the relocation or repatriation of Latvians in search of better lives. The fragmentation of communities as they mix with other ethnicities, the lack of a Latvian-language literature and press, and the absence of Latvian teachers have resulted in the fact that Latvian is spoken predominantly by the older generations.

Throughout *Populārzinātniska lekcija*, Leitis mixes the historical background with contemporary concerns about the educational problem in view

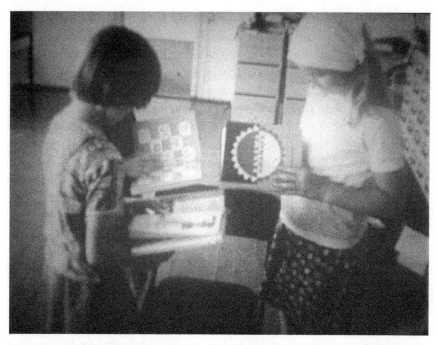

Fig. 13.2. The children of the village of Rižkovo are browsing through Latvian-language books brought by Leitis. Still from Populārzinātniska lekcija par kādu vēstures tēmu (1975–78).

of the kind of national culture renovation that would ameliorate the native language analphabetism in the Latvian villages. With this agenda, Leitis began to actively distribute and promote *Populārzinātniska lekcija* and his subsequent films, *Lejas Bulānas hronika* (*The Chronicles of Lejas Bulāna,* 1987) and *Ciemošanās Balajā* (*Visiting Balai,* 1987). He was helped by the fact that the RRR studio represented him to the community of amateur filmmakers; the films were entered into various amateur film festivals and film programs, with *Populārzinātniska lekcija* being awarded the best popular-scientific film at the twenty-ninth Republican Amateur Film Festival (April 8–11, 1987, in Riga). On the initiative of the RRR studio, Leitis's films were also shown in various cultural institutions across Latvia (A. Popova RRR Kultūras nama kinoamatieru studijas atskaites).

The authorial voice expressed through voiceover in *Populārzinātniska lekcija* is critical of the way active violence towards the Siberian Latvians has been succeeded by malign neglect of their national culture as an effect of the Russianization imposed by the Soviet regime. At the same time, Leitis's voiceover is almost a parody of the usual practice of relying on voiceover narration in the Soviet documentary and popular science filmmaking tradition, reminding the audience of the didactic manner in which the narrator in Mikhail Romm's classic Soviet documentary *Obyknovennyi fashizm* (*Everyday Fascism*, 1965) comments on the atrocities of the Nazi regime. This, combined with the tongue-in-cheek choice of title for the film, which does not convey much and replicates the language of a Soviet TV program, can be interpreted as appropriation and manipulation of the dominant discourse by Leitis, who, either deliberately or unwittingly, inhabited the Soviet cultural codes and interpolated them with subversive meanings.

Conclusion

Due to the limited and sporadic nature of exhibition in the sphere of amateur cinema, it is challenging to assess the sociopolitical and cultural impact of amateur films. Nevertheless, it is clear that Leitis's films left an imprint on the life of late-Soviet Latvian society. With the onset of *glasnost'*, the historic-ethnic themes that Leitis had been exploring in his work were truly picked up and developed both by professional filmmakers and often by fellow amateur filmmakers who encountered Leitis's films at screenings and festivals hosted by the amateur film networks.

Once Leitis was able to exhibit his films, they began to assume a presence beyond the sphere of filmmaking. The nationalistic dimension of Leitis's films, as well as their recording of testimonies to state-directed suppression of everyday Latvian life, found a sympathetic reception in the atmosphere generated by the national revival movement, the so-called Third Awakening, that started in 1986. This movement eventually led to the restoration of independence for Latvia in 1991. Leitis (Leitis and Briedis 2016, 307–8) recalls that his films were often shown at different events celebrating the Awakening throughout Latvia and set in motion many initiatives. After having raised awareness about the Siberian exile issue through his films, Leitis was invited to organize the Siberian Latvian Support Section by Arvīds Ulme, the director of the Club of Environmental Protection (Vides Aizsardzības Klubs, VAK). The Siberian Latvian Support Section was intended to bridge the cultural gap between Latvia and its Siberian exiles: its activists were behind the educational mission targeted at Siberian Latvians, as well as the repatriation support program (Bolševica 1989). This dynamic was very common in the era of *perestroika*. As White (1990, 36–37) observes, the appeal to reform through democratization, which sounded with increasing urgency in the socialist bloc countries from the mid-1980s onwards, was not only limited to reforms in the political sphere, but, as well, pushed for the development of civil society. This vision gave legitimacy to various nongovernmental organizations and cultural institutions as they pushed for reform.

Despite the particularities of Leitis's story, and his asserted disinterest in amateur filmmaking per se, the Leitis's case is still illustrative of certain patterns in the amateur filmmaking community in Soviet Latvia and other socialist states. For one thing, the improvisational organization of Leitis's project made him rely on formal and informal networks of people and organizations in order to bring it about. This was not unusual. Although the state provided a certain amount of training and equipment to amateur filmmaking organizations, often filmmakers found themselves having to use their connections and contacts to obtain materials or achieve results (Vinogradova 2016, 22–25). Apart from this, it was a common practice for amateurs to create a cover for their exploration of more controversial topics by sampling film that was made within the framework of accepted norms and forms of the official discourse and recontextualizing it to bring out more subversive or critical meanings. For instance, amateur filmmaker's Zigurds Vidiņš's documentary film *Pa mūsmājas logu (Through the Window of Our House*, 1984) is an insight into the history and the present day of a public park in Riga that, by overviewing the park's management issues in the spirit of *grazhdanstvennost'*, offers an implicit critique of the Soviet rule in Latvia (Strupule 2017, 69–71). Thus, despite the thematic controversy of some of the Soviet amateur films, including Leitis's documentaries, they were nevertheless largely dependent on the dominant discourse—as their production process depended on the state sponsorship—and did not constitute a self-contained oppositional purity.

It appears to be useful to step away from characterizing amateur films with critical elements as anti-Soviet and purely oppositional and their authors as intending to consciously subvert the established system and instead regard these critical elements as internal displacements and mutations in the discursive regime in which they are articulated, to use Yurchak's formulation. It is also important to bear in mind that even if Leitis's position was more politically conscious and perhaps more actively aimed at prompting actual change within the Soviet system, amateur filmmaking in Soviet Latvia, like many other forms of cultural production, was not necessarily informed by support or opposition towards the Soviet ideological system. However, it nevertheless became a platform for creating alternative political, social, and cultural meanings, such as the prospects for Latvian national identity development and national heritage preservation, thus introducing new and unanticipated meanings into the dominant culture. Thus, engaging with the forms and discourses of the dominant culture, and being able to circulate as part of a shared public discourse and to find resonance with audiences, often unleashed the transformative potential of many amateur films. What is interesting about Leitis's ethnographic documentaries is how they demonstrate the unexpected intervention of an independent historical investigation in a society in which the state supposedly organizes the cultural and historical education of its citizens. Leitis's amateur films intervened in the discourse of the cultural politics of Soviet Latvia at a crucial time, when the visible weakening of Soviet power intersected with the rising power of a national movement. This opens up space for debate on the role of amateur films in advancing our historical knowledge of the minoritized national arts and cultures.

Notes

1. This mirrored the tendencies in professional documentary cinema in Soviet Latvia and across the Soviet Union at that time. See Renāte Cāne, "Latvijas Dokumentālā Kino Komunikatīvo Funkciju Transformācija," PhD diss., Biznesa augstskola Turība, 2014, 120–28.

2. The potential of postcolonial studies applied to the relationship between the Baltic countries and the Soviet Union is explored in, for instance, Violeta Kelertas's edited volume, *Baltic Postcolonialism* (Amsterdam: Editions Rodopi, 2006).

3. In Soviet academia of the late socialist period, the discipline of anthropology was largely limited to the study of ethnicities and almost equated with ethnography. See Anatoly Khazanov, "The Ethnic Situation in the Soviet Union as Reflected in Soviet Anthropology," *Cahiers du Monde Russe et Soviétique* 31, no. 2/3 (1990): 213–15. Due to antinationalist stance of the official ideology, the concept of ethnicity remained ideologically and politically loaded, hence the scholars working in this field had to tread carefully up until the *perestroika* era. As a result, Soviet anthropological studies remained largely disconnected from modern Western developments in the field, and were marked by "backwardness" and "pseudohistoricism and adherence to rigid and scholastic schemata" (215).

4. Here Leitis in all probability refers to the Article 70 of the Criminal Code, "Anti-Soviet Agitation and Propaganda," which was a criminal offense in the Soviet Union and one of the main instruments for the prosecution of dissidents.

References

Andreeva, Evgeniia. 2013. "Fol'klornoe dvizhenie' kak kul'turnyi fenomen vtoroi poloviny XX v.", *Istoria i Sovremennost'* 2, no. 18: 215–31.

A. Popova RRR Kultūras nama kinoamatieru studijas atskaites, 1986–89, RKM-7239–41, Rīgas Kinomuzeja arhīvs, Riga, Latvia. [Work reports of the amateur film studio of the House of Culture of A. Popov's Riga Radio Factory, 1986–89, RKM-7239–41, Riga Film Museum's Archive, Riga, Latvia].

Ashcroft, Bill. 2001. *Post-Colonial Transformation*. London: Routledge.

Bolševica, Austra. 1989. "Krievijas Latviešu biedrība," interview by Ā. Bērziņš. *Dzimtenes Balss* 33, August 10, 1989, 5.

Cāne, Renāte. 2014. "Latvijas Dokumentālā Kino Komunikatīvo Funkciju Transformācija." PhD diss., Biznesa augstskola Turība.

Costanzo, Susan. 2008. "Amateur Theatres and Amateur Publics in the Russian Republic, 1958–71." *Slavonic and East European Review* 86, no. 2: 372–394. JSTOR.

Informācija par Leiti Ingvaru no LPSR VDK informācijas analīzes daļas materiāliem, 1976, DS-63007, Totalitārisma Seku Dokumentēšanas Centrs, Riga, Latvia. [Information about Ingvars Leitis from the analysis of the documents of the KGB of the Latvian SSR, 1976, DS-63007, The Centre for the Documentation of the Consequences of Totalitarianism, Riga, Latvia].

Järvine, Jaak. 2005. *Vzgliad v proshloe: Istoriia liubitel'skogo kino v byvshem SSSR i stranakh Baltii*. Põltsamaa: Vali Press.

Kelertas, Violeta, ed. 2006. *Baltic Postcolonialism*. Amsterdam: Editions Rodopi.

Khazanov, Anatoly. 1990. "The Ethnic Situation in the Soviet Union as Reflected in Soviet Anthropology." *Cahiers du Monde Russe et Soviétique* 31, no. 2/3: 213–21. JSTOR.

Leitis, Ingvars, and Uldis Briedis. 2016. *Latviešus Sibīrijā meklējot: Veloekspedīcija Rīga—Vladivostoka, 1975*. Riga: Mansards.

Leitis, Ingvars. 2017. Interview by Inese Strupule, April 19, 2017, Riga, Latvia.

Maamägi, Viktor. 1976. *Estonskie poselentsy v SSSR, 1917–1945*. Tallinn: Eesti Raamat.

Misiunas, Romuald J., and Rein Taagepera. 1993. *The Baltic States: Years of Dependence, 1940–1990*. London: Hurst.

Strupule, Inese. 2017. "Latvian Amateur Documentary Film, 1970s–1980s: Family, Community, Travel, and Politics in the Films of Uldis Lapiņš, Ingvars Leitis, and Zigurds Vidiņš." *Culture Crossroads* 10:63–76. http://www.culturecrossroads.lv/pdf/225/en.

Vinogradova, Maria. 2012. "Between the State and the Kino: Amateur Film Workshops in the Soviet Union." *Studies in European Cinema* 8 (3): 211–25. doi.10.1386/832111.

———. 2016. "Socialist Movie Making vs. Gosplan. Establishing an Infrastructure for the Soviet Amateur Cinema." *Iluminace* 28 (2): 9–27. http://www.iluminace.cz/index.php /en/article?id=199.

White, Anne. 1990. *De-Stalinization and the House of Culture: Declining State Control over Leisure in USSR, Poland, and Hungary, 1953–89*. London: Routledge.

Yurchak, Alexei. 2005. *Everything Was Forever Until It Was No More: The Last Soviet Generation*. Princeton: Princeton University Press.

INESE STRUPULE is a PhD candidate at the School of Slavonic and East European Studies, University College London.

PART IV

TRANSNATIONAL NETWORKS: AMATEUR CINEMA TRAVELS

14

WORLDLY MATTERS

Distributed Histories of Tunisian Amateur Cinema and the Screening of Nontheatrical Film

Samhita Sunya

IN 1964, THE ASSOCIATION DES JEUNES CINÉASTES TUNISIENS (Association of Young Tunisian Filmmakers, AJCT) paved the way for the establishment of the Festival International du Film Amateur de Kélibia (Kelibia International Festival of Amateur Film, FIFAK), a festival of amateur cinema held under the auspices of the Ministry of Culture. With the establishment of Journées Cinématographiques de Carthage (Carthage Film Festival, JCC) in 1966, the two ongoing festivals alternated for several years as biennial events held in Tunisia, each focused on the exhibition and promotion of amateur and professional films, respectively (Bourguiba 2013, 36).

In exploring the history of nontheatrical film culture in Tunisia, this chapter attends to the issue of *screening* in two senses—that of exhibition and distribution, and that of filtering and exclusion from histories of regional, national, and transnational cinemas. Noting that FIFAK, an ongoing festival dedicated to Tunisian and international amateur cinema, was the first Arab and African film festival, this chapter outlines the various global networks through which Tunisia remained a regional and international hub for nontheatrical film production and film culture. A look at FIFAK yields insights into practices of amateur cinema not only in terms of film production but also distribution and exhibition networks. In addition, the prominence of amateur festivals—as an interface between cinema, the specificity of its national contexts, and its regional and internationalist visions—speaks to the double marginalization of nonwestern practices in transnational accounts of amateur cinema and of amateur practices within accounts of national cinemas.

In the first section, I provide an overview of recent scholarly accounts of Tunisian cinema, noting that allegorical readings of specific post-1980s feature-film productions have dominated these accounts, in which historical and ongoing contributions of amateur cinema in Tunisia are only briefly glossed, if at all invoked. This is despite the latter's crucial role in the postindependence period in the production of films and in a thriving postindependence film *culture*, as the Tunisian amateur film movement emerged and grew in a vacuum of film schools and, eventually, a dearth of cinema halls.[1]

An understanding of distribution in a broader sense is crucial to addressing this gap and excavating a fuller account of Tunisian film culture in the period of the 1970s and 1980s, traceable in the coverage of Tunisian amateur cinema across a number of periodicals with widespread, international circulation. An analysis of the dissemination of this print record foregrounds the embeddedness of Tunisian film culture within multiple, overlapping networks structured by varied visions of amateur cinema. What emerges from this account is the historical centrality of amateur cinema, particularly through the institutions of AJCT (later known as FTCA) and FIFAK, in constituting not only a corpus of national films but also a much wider arena of (trans)national film culture.

National "Features" of Film Historiography

"Tunisia came to know the Cinema a few months after the first Cinema projection in Paris," writes Egyptian film critic-historian Samir Farid (1979, 50) in *Arab Cinema Guide*. The arrival of the Lumiére brothers, who shot a series of actualities in Tunis between December 1896 and January 1897, occurred on the heels of the 1881 French conquest of Tunisia (Aubert, Seguin, and Schmalstieg, 1996.). While several accounts of Tunisian cinema identify a national cinema that was properly inaugurated by Omar Khlifi's 1966 feature *Al Fajr* (*The Dawn*), others, such as that of critic Georges Sadoul (1959, 112), credit French filmmaker Jacques Baratier's 1958 *Goha* as "the first feature production from the young Tunisian cinema." Other films had been shot in Tunisia prior, such as French director Luitz-Morat's 1919 *Les Cinq*

Gentlemen Maudits (*The Five Accursed Gentleman*), not to mention Tunisian pioneer Albert Samama-Chikli's 1922 *Zohra* and 1924 *Ain Al-Ghazal* (*The Girl from Carthage*) (Berrah 1981, 140).

Multiple designations of firsts in histories of national cinemas belie the contested ideological foundations from which the very category of a national cinema emerges. Kmar Kchir-Bendana (2004, 36) takes the prescient approach of noting that in distinction from institutions of the state, ideologies of national identity are structured by representation and that Tunisian cinema becomes coherent not as "a political regime . . . a doctrine or a culture," but as the frame within which cinematic representations negotiate their relationship to ideologies of national identity. Sadoul's characterization of *Goha* as the first Tunisian feature, then, is one such position, which privileges the film's feature length and naturalizes the film's engagement with its eponymous folk character to its shooting on location in Tunisia—its French address and production contexts notwithstanding. Likewise, the anticolonial narrative and address of Khlifi's *Al-Fajr* inaugurates a position whereby, in Kchir-Bendana's (2004, 36) words, such films "define themselves as national because they are nationalist."

The complexities of cinematic negotiations with style and form, alongside nationhood, identity, and concomitant social histories in Tunisia and the Maghreb, respectively, constitute the foundations of recent English-language publications that include Robert Lang's (2014) *New Tunisian Cinema: Allegories of Resistance* and Suzanne Gauch's (2016) *Maghreb in Motion: North African Cinema in Nine Movements*. In both monographs, each chapter is dedicated to rich textual and contextual analyses of a specific film, of the "new" Tunisian and Maghrebi cinemas of the era between the mid-1980s and early 2000s, characterized by unprecedented formal and narrative choices that challenged heretofore conventional modes that had come to define their respective national cinemas, in departures from an earlier generation's espousal of a militant third cinema (Lang 2014; Gauch 2016). What remains out of view is the sustained impact of the amateur cinema movement in having nurtured many of the Tunisian filmmakers working in the post-1980s period.

The emphasis and methodological thrust of Gauch's and Lang's inquiries, among others, have been in readings of specific films that are taken not as representative but as representative of the heterogeneity and impossibility of any monolithic notion of Tunisian (or Maghrebi) cinema (Gana 2013). In the case of Tunisian cinema, this scholarship has noted the mid-1980s efflorescence of a "new" cinema, characterized by the variety of films and filmmakers that grappled with the increasingly authoritarian regime of Zine El Abidine Ben Ali, who had deposed erstwhile founding prime-minister-turned-president Habib Bourguiba. In her keen readings of films including Nacer Khemir's *Desert Trilogy* (1984–2005), Nadia El Fani's *Bedwin Hacker* (2003), and Nejib Belkhadi's *VHS Kahloucha* (2007), Gauch highlights their fulfillment, often through themes of romance, of Gayatri Chakraborty Spivak and other subaltern studies theorists' call to "learn from below—where 'below' signifies those residing in the interstices of class and citizenship, without political representation—through a process of what [Spivak] deems ethical singularity, or love" (Gauch 2016, 7). Spivak's identification of an "ethical singularity" emerges as a feminist insistence on modes of deeply personal relationality between the Self and the Other as a site of radical politics toward "an impossible social justice," outside of public debates and mass media (Devi 1994, 197).

In their introduction to *Mining the Home Movie*, Karen L. Ishizuka and Patricia R. Zimmerman (2007) characterize the endeavor of turning to amateur archives of home movies as a way of similarly learning from below. Ishizuka and Zimmerman invoke subaltern historian Ranajit Guha's remark that "the noise of history and its statist concerns have made historiography insensitive to the sighs and whispers of everyday life," as the political project of turning to amateur archives is one of examining histories, intimacies, and narratives of the everyday that are contained in amateur and private audiovisual collections and artifacts (7). It is also an attempt to overturn the pejorative sense of *amateur* (at least in English) toward the love that Spivak articulates as the political praxis of deeply personal modes of relationality. In the words of experimental filmmaker and thinker Stan Brakhage (2001, 144): "'Amateur' is a word which, in the Latin, meant 'lover'; but today it has become a term like 'Yankee' ('Amateur—Go Home'), hatched in criticism, by professionals who so little understand the value of the word or its meaning that they do honor it, and those of us who identify with it, most where they think to shame and disgrace in their usage of it."

Brakhage's lament, that amateur cinema has been dismissed by professional film critics, points to a parallel vacuum in transnational film historiography, by which the often-overlooked impact and importance of amateur cinema on film culture in Tunisia becomes a case in point. I emphasize both turns in film historiography—toward amateur archives and toward films that do not sit neatly in their national-cinema compartments—as endeavors

Third Cinema in
Tunisia → Ridha?

to account, in part, for the politics of films that do not take explicit or militant positions. In returning to earlier generations of amateur filmmakers in Tunisia that, in large part but by no means exclusively so, espoused the expediency of a militant, politically explicit third cinema, I turn from the politics of the production of individual films to those of the production of amateur infrastructures of film culture—from below, as it were.

In the case of Tunisia, it is the latter that threads together seemingly disparate strands of production, political sensibility, and circuits of identity. To put it another way, the trickling feature film output of this small country remains an inadequate barometer of the historical exuberance of Tunisia's film culture for decades. This is especially notable in light of the dearth of both film schools and cinema halls—a vacuum that was filled by the vibrancy of local chapters of cine clubs, which in turn nurtured the growth of local FTCA chapters. In accounting for this exuberance, the history of amateur cinema emerges from the margins as a juggernaut in endeavors to understand both histories of cinema in Tunisia and histories of amateur cinema in the world.

Decolonial Visions of Tunisian (Amateur) Film Cultures

A narrative of firsts that credits the 1964 establishment of FIFAK as the first Arab and African film festival and the 1966 completion of Omar Khlifi's 1966 film *Al Fajr* (*The Dawn*) as the first Tunisian film, offers an opportunity to reposition the role of amateur cinema in the postindependence project of building institutions of film culture.[2] Khlifi himself was an amateur filmmaker in the AJCT, later known as the FTCA, the role of which is emphasized in Maya Ben Ayed's (2017) illuminating account of animation in Tunisia. She writes that the history of animation in Tunisia began in 1965–1966 with an object animation film by Mongi Sancho, produced by FTCA—then known as the AJCT (241–42). The latter's role in establishing foundations for the robust film culture that flourished in the postindependence decades harnessed the energies of a prolific cine-club movement. This legacy outsized (and outlasted) that of state institutions—namely, the Society for the Production and Expansion of Cinema in Tunisia (SATPEC) in 1957, which in turn established the Gammarth production facility in 1967 (243). Noting that word of Sancho's animated films spread through Tunisian newspapers after they won awards at FIFAK, Ayed writes: "Many professional Tunisian filmmakers started their careers within [FTCA]. The FTCA and the Tunisian

Federation of Film-Clubs (FTCC) constituted something of a film school, where a younger generation learned to 'watch' and make films. Tunisia is, in fact, considered something of an exception in the Arab and African worlds in terms of the originality of its creation of cinephile associations" (244). Ayed's characterization of the historical importance of both FTCA and FIFAK points toward the synergistic relationships between amateur cinema and the emergence of professional filmmakers in Tunisia, stemming precisely from the "originality of its creation of cinephile associations."

The latter, as "something of an exception in the Arab and African worlds," indicates a history of film culture that is difficult to register, if not invisible, in textual readings of feature films that are limited in number (Ayed 2017, 244). Thus, one reconciles dismissive pronouncements such as the following by historian Kenneth Perkins (2014, 181–82): "The first Tunisian feature film since the 1930s, *al-Fajr* / *L'Aube*, directed by Omar Khlifi, a self-taught amateur filmmaker, appeared in 1966. . . . Other amateur filmmakers emerged in the late 1960s and 1970s, *but few made more than a single successful feature or had any significant impact on cinematic thinking in Tunisia*" (emphasis mine).

Patricia Caillé's analyses of contemporary contexts of FIFAK, in addition to writings and films by Hédi Khelil and Férid Boughedir, notably acknowledge amateur cinema's impact in Tunisia, in part as a response to postcolonial challenges of distribution (Caillé 2015; Boughedir 1993, 2016; Khelil 2007a; Caillé 2017; Khelil 2007b). Boughedir's 1987 documentary *Caméra Arabe* presents distribution as a central problem for filmmakers in Tunisia and other Arab countries due to monopolies by state companies and European distributors. In a 1972 essay, renowned film writer and founder of JCC Tahar Cheriaa (1972), too, held that filmmakers' responses to the problem of distribution would be the central determinant of liberation from both neocolonial and authoritarian apparatuses for African and Arab filmmakers.

The historical significance of Tunisian amateur cinema lay in its role as an interface via FIFAK and other festivals, between national, regional, and international networks that congealed in myriad visions of film culture. The latter term emphasizes the range of practices—the production of individual films being one among them—by which cinema is interwoven with the contexts through which it circulates. One institution of film culture, among other transnational networks in which FTCA participated, was Union Internationale du Cinéma d'Amateurs (International Union of

Amateur Cinema; UNICA). Established during the 1937 Paris world fair, UNICA, a federation of mostly European member organizations, committed itself to annual world congresses (De Jong 2015). The congresses emphasized exhibition over competition, and at the 1955 congress in France, the organization's criteria for amateur filmmaking was "any work created by an individual or group of individuals not working for profit or financial gain" (De Jong 2015). In 1959, UNICA came under the fold of UNESCO. By 1966, Tunisia became a member of UNICA and by 1970, hosted the "1st congress outside Europe" in Sousse (De Jong 2015).

By 1978 an entry on cinema in Tunisia, noting both JCC and FIFAK, appears in the annual *Variety* guide for the first time. Author Mohammed Rida optimistically asserts that "the past four years have witnessed the birth of the best phase of Tunisian cinema" (Cowie 1978, 315). It was not that the 1970 UNICA congress in Sousse alone prompted the entrance of Tunisian cinema into an anglophone arena of world cinema, but rather, that UNICA was one among other circuits that brought Tunisian cinema into wider orbits, as the exceptional energy of the movement precipitated Tunisia's visibility in regional and international networks through the 1970s and 1980s. The very structure of the *Variety* guide, at least through the 1970s, is symptomatic of the difficulty of accounting for this history. A section of it is devoted to nontheatrical film but only covers productions from North America and Europe; and entries that reduce other national cinemas to their feature-film output provide inadequate accounts of amateur and nontheatrical film.

In contrast to *Variety*'s first-time mention of Tunisian amateur cinema in 1978, coverage of FTCA and FIFAK appeared in several periodicals dedicated to Third-Worldist causes through the 1970s and 1980s. These included francophone periodicals *Afrique-Asie, Révolution Africaine, Jeune Afrique,* and *Afrique Nouvelle*; Hispanophone periodical *Estudios de Asia y Africa*; and anglophone periodical *Africa Now. Afrique-Asie*, for example, was founded in 1969 by Simon Malley, a journalist who worked for the National Liberation Front in Algeria and dedicated the periodical to third-world liberation struggles. According to Malley's obituary, "Tiers-mondisme [Third-worldism], critical of the continuing influence of colonialism, was by then [1969] briefly fashionable, and Malley became its best-known voice" (Brittain 2006).

Three things are notable across this coverage—first, the repeated pronouncement that FIFAK's importance as an amateur festival lay, among other things, in giving exposure to Palestine-related films; second, a

Un festival de jeune ci-néma populaire impor-tant : KELIBIA (Tunisie)

Le 8ème Festival International du Film Amateur aura lieu du 17 au 24 août 1975 à Kelibia. Il comprend les manifestations suivantes :

a) une compétition ouverte aux films d'amateurs sélectionnés à cet effet,

b) une présentation de films hors concours choisis en raison de leurs quali-tés ou de l'intérêt qu'ils peuvent susciter,

c) des colloques et des conférences-débats sur des sujets portant sur le ci-néma amateur.

La participation au Festival Interna-tional du Film Amateur est ouverte aux films sonores ou muets, de toutes origi-nes, de tous genres, de tous métrages, en noir et blanc ou en couleurs, en 8, super 8 ou 16 mm.

Tout cinéaste amateur désireux de par-ticiper au 8ème Festival International du Film Amateur doit adresser sa demande avant le 17 juin 1975 et faire parvenir son ou ses films, le 17 juillet 1975, délai de rigueur.

Est considéré cinéaste amateur, celui qui n'a jamais pratiqué d'activité rému-nératrice dans l'art et l'industrie cinéma-tographique.

Les demandes de renseignements, les correspondances et les envois de films doivent s'effectuer à l'adresse suivante :

**FESTIVAL INTERNATIONAL
DU FILM AMATEUR
B.P. 116 - TUNIS**

Fig. 14.1. A June 1975 edition of *Cinéma* (no. 199), published by the French Federation of Cine-Clubs, features a call for participation in the eighth edition of FIFAK.

pan-Africanist vision that characterized FTCA and FIFAK as exemplar and opportunity, respectively, for African filmmakers; and third, the sense of an amateur movement whose noncommercial nature was driven not so much by individual filmmakers' decisions to opt for "not working for profit or financial gain," but rather by conditions of absent infrastructures, neo-colonial distribution monopolies, and inadequate policies for competitive domestic production.

Ayed's aforementioned characterization of film culture in Tunisia as "something of an exception in Arab and African worlds" hints at two geographies—Arab and African—that, despite their necessarily fluid boundaries, have become more bifurcated, of which the increasing prominence of the acronym MENA (Middle East North Africa) is symptomatic.[3] As a category, MENA remains an object of academic studies, statist and NGO discussions of policy and humanitarian work—especially in the wake of the Arab Spring protests—and corporate divisions aimed at various markets. While studies of African cinema have remained enormously attentive to creative processes under postcolonial *economic* constraints of poor infrastructures, recent studies of Arab cinema have focused on creative processes under *political* constraints of failed states and authoritarian regimes (Harrow 2013; Shafik 2017). Furthermore, while certain African cinemas are often detailed as amateur and artisanal in their modes of production by necessity, they are more frequently framed by postcolonial studies, Global South studies, and/or third cinema studies, rather than of amateur cinema studies (Harrow 2013).

The 1970s–1980s print coverage of amateur cinema in Tunisia highlights such shifting constructions of various "worlds" in tandem with wider geopolitical shifts (e.g., the positioning of Tunisian cinema within accounts of Middle East/Arab/MENA studies versus African cinema).[4] While this earlier coverage characterized Tunisian amateur cinema as offering platforms for making and showing films that upheld the cause of Palestinian liberation, the latter was frequently invoked not only as an issue of the (pan) Arab world but as a node of tricontinental leftist solidarity. In addition, in the 1970s–1980s, the exceptional nature of film culture in Tunisia was repeatedly avowed as an exemplar for *African* filmmakers, specifically, who shared challenges of global economic disparities and the inefficacy of state policies in overcoming these gaps.

A 1970 article in *Jeune Afrique* is hardly alone in characterizing the exceptional nature of Tunisian amateur film (in finding no similar regional point of comparison), foregrounding the prominence of FTCA—composed of a number of clubs in various districts—as central to the infrastructures of Tunisian film culture (Hennebelle 1970). Its summary of cinema in Tunisia opens by detailing activities of FTCA, noting that the UNICA congress was held that year in Sousse—with FTCA being the only Arab or African member in the organization, and with Sousse the host of the first congress outside Europe. The latter section of the article also details the importance of JCC as a platform for the shared exhibition and distribution of African features among Tunisian audiences.

The article's account of a Tunisian film culture whose hallmark institution is identified as FTCA, is akin to both Ayed's account of animation in Tunisia and Hédi Khelil's *Abécédaire du Cinéma Tunisenne (Alphabet Book of Tunisian Cinema)*, a compendium accompanied by a plethora of archival images and DVD of *Panorama du Cinéma Tunisien, 1966–2006*, which together offer a multimedia history of Tunisian cinema (Khelil 2007a, 2007b). Khelil's hefty *Abécédaire* dedicates itself to FTCA, beginning, fittingly, with a detailed entry titled "A for Amateur"(2007a). While a study of the current structure and role of FTCA and FIFAK is beyond the scope of this chapter, endeavors like Khelil's compendium are a testament to the ongoing impact of FTCA's legacies on a contemporary generation of Tunisian filmmakers and film enthusiasts.[5] Among other initiatives to record and disseminate information about Tunisian cinema is *Cinéma Tunisien*, an online database of Tunisian filmmakers, films and festivals, archival documents, articles, and announcements. Launched by former FTCA member Mohamed Khiri, the database marks yet another instance of the ongoing contributions of FTCA members to a wider realm of film culture (i.e., beyond the organization and beyond institutions of amateur film, specifically) in Tunisia ("Cinéma Tunisien—La Référence Cinéma En Tunisie—Qui Sommes-Nous ?" 2020).

In this regard, the impact of amateur cinema in Tunisia is hardly debatable. The nature of the movement's output, activities, and political positions, however, were matters of vehement scrutiny by both outside critics and FTCA members. In a detailed report on FIFAK 1973 in *Révolution Africaine*, critic Abdelhakim Méziani (1973) decries the amateur cinema's ostensible preoccupation with sexuality that he alleges as tantamount to "intellectual masturbation." Opining that the highlight of FIFAK that year was its program on Palestinian cinema, he singles out a film titled *Réflexion* as redeeming an otherwise "disappointing encounter." *Réflexion*, Méziani notes, squarely addressed "the rights of man and the atrocities committed by imperialism, Zionism, and colonialism, saving amateur Tunisian cinema from inconsistency and, above all, from disengagement" (32).

The demand for widespread solidarity in support of the rights of the Palestinian people was circulated and upheld by several Third-Worldist periodicals in a statement titled "Manifesto for a Better Illustration of the Palestinian Cause in Cinema."[6] The initiative was led by *Afrique-Asie* and formally endorsed by several other periodicals, including *CinémAction* and *Les Deux Ecrans*, among others, such as Mexico City-based *Estudios de Asia y Africa* in 1982 (Quartucci 1982). The original call proposes a screenwriting competition for *fiction* films, whose winners would benefit from monetary and technical support. Intending to attract a variety of filmmakers, the manifesto suggests separate juries for Palestinian filmmakers, Arab filmmakers, and world filmmakers, in addition to emphasizing the importance of both commercial and noncommercial distribution.

Parts of the manifesto, reproduced in *Estudios*, include a call for depictions of the Palestinian struggle and people not through clichéd, propagandistic slogans but rather in multidimensional images to avoid extremes of either commercial escapism or didactic militancy, with the goal of appealing to wider audiences (Quartucci 1982, 292–94). The report in *Estudios* goes on to note, specifically, that "in response to the challenge of the Palestinian filmmakers, the 10th edition of FIFAK, organized by FTCA, took place last summer in Kélibia (Tunisia)" (293).

In this manner, both FIFAK and the activities of FTCA emerge as important nodes within a dialogic, transnational network of engagement with the question of (third) cinema's relationship to issues of social justice, form, and representation. On the one hand, one notes positions such Méziani's in 1973, deriding the tendencies toward "intellectual masturbation" on the part of Tunisian amateur filmmakers who did not engage pressing issues of "the rights of man" in a direct, head-on manner. On the other hand, the aforementioned manifesto as well as its 1982 invocation in *Estudios* reveals a discomfort with overtly militant, didactic films that are neither nuanced in their concerns nor pleasurable enough to productively garner the attention of large audiences. As the section in *Estudios* wryly ends: "While the events that we have just described take place, Latin America waits impatiently for *The Palestinian*, by Vanessa Redgrave, so far exhibited only in Venezuela, with full houses in the twenty special screenings to date" (Quartucci 1982, 294).

Specific points of self-reflection and debate over the goals of FTCA and FIFAK are candidly stated in a 1982 *Afrique-Asie* feature. The article leads with an overview of Tunisian amateur cinema, mentioning the uniqueness of FTCA as an organization that emerged, flourished, and contributed immensely to a thriving, postcolonial film culture that was built from scratch. Journalist Raphael Bassan's (1982) interview with former FTCA president Ridha Ben Halima and former committee member Fethi Kharrat follows, in which the two interviewees note that the lack of any national film industry was both a tremendous challenge and opportunity for innovation.

Having noted that "amateur or not: most of the cadres of the national cinema come out of FTCA," Bassan (1982) presses the interviewees to reflect on criticisms of the inevitable risks of pushing conformist, dogmatic visions of cinema, in light of the sprawling organization's de facto monopoly on Tunisian film production. Halima and Kharrat note that this was recognized as a problem soon after FTCA's establishment, which led to a drastic shift sparked by the influx of active student filmmakers in 1968 and culminated in "The Reform," a 1971 text aimed at codifying visions of FTCA and maintaining space for the ideal of a democratized, heterogeneous, and socially significant (amateur) film culture (Bassan 1982). The three tenets of FTCA, established by "The Reform," were (1) an organizational structure of collective, rather than hierarchical, administration, (2) a program of well-rounded, rigorous technical training, and (3) a commitment to a cinema of quality that would also be open and accessible to audiences (Bassan 1982). Regarding the second tenet, Halima and Kharrat note that FTCA initially held the assumption that fiction films required more training than documentary, and that mastery of the latter was necessary for progressing to the former, but that the organization let go of this assumption. In this manner, Halima and Kharrat explain, FTCA remains a work in progress, as an innovative institution that continues to reflect on its purpose and change accordingly.

As the overview and interview both assert the uniqueness of amateur cinema in Tunisia in contrast to film cultures of the neighboring countries of Egypt, Libya, and Algeria, they simultaneously stake the major successes of FTCA and FIFAK in having inspired and catalyzed similar movements and alliances with filmmakers in the above countries, among other African nations, particularly with the coming of Super 8 (Bassan 1982). As mentioned earlier, JCC founder Tahar Cheriaa (1972) detailed the structures of European distribution monopolies, the surmounting of which he identifies as the central obstacle for, and ultimate determinant of, the future of African filmmakers. Cheriaa concludes: "The only reasonable solutions that come to mind are . . . grouping and collective action on a regional plan, everywhere that a linguistic and cultural unity permits . . . Founding big distribution companies on a regional basis will permit a complete and positive change in the above-mentioned monopoly market and consequently, would lead the film distribution system in Africa to a direction progressively more compatible with African interests."

Irrespective of the scale of the interviewees' claim of FTCA's influence on other African filmmakers, the historical importance accorded to pursuits of transnational alliances dovetailed with calls for the strategic creation of wider distribution networks that could bypass the roadblocks of neocolonial distribution monopolies. The interviewees are unequivocal in identifying the 1965 launch of FIFAK's first international edition as FTCA's crowning achievement, accomplished with the additional support of UNICA on the heels of FIFAK's first edition as a national event under the auspices of the Ministry of Culture in 1964 (Bassan 1982). Yet, rather than identifying FTCA's involvement with UNICA as a primary end for its pursuit of transnational alliances, Halima and Kharrat are specific in noting FIFAK's aggregation of regional Arab-North African (Egypt, Libya, and Algeria), among other pan-African, collectives of filmmakers at the levels of production, exhibition, and distribution (Bassan 1982).

Citing festival director Radhi Trimeche, the headline of a 1985 report in *Africa Now* surmises, "Home Movies Could Mean 'Cultural Liberation': So Thinks the Director of this Year's Kelibia International Festival of Non-Professional Cinema—Sometimes Dubbed 'Bootlace Cinema'" (Martin 1985). This report, too, notes the potential afforded by Super 8 and amateur networks for African filmmakers who are plagued by poor production facilities and distribution monopolies. "It is surprising that there is not more Super 8 filmmaking [in Africa]," remarks the author, who continues, "Tunisia is a real exception with some 300 cine-club members" (Martin 1985). She further notes that while the festival sought alliances with African filmmakers and hosted meetings of the Association of Arabo-African Non-Professional Filmmakers, the representation of delegates and films from sub-Saharan Africa has remained thin. In Martin's report, too, the characterization of the exceptional nature of film culture in Tunisia persists, as well as the invocation of a pan-Africanist project of solidarity among filmmakers that remains yet incomplete.

The endeavors and challenges taken on by FTCA between the 1960s and 1980s, in tandem with the orientations of several periodicals and their respective publics, actively sought to forge new, strategic, collectives that were bound by multidimensional visions of decolonization—of reclaiming economic, political, and cultural power over images. That the latter was a question not only of production but also—and acutely so—of exhibition and distribution, emerges powerfully in a historical account of the transnational orientations of FTCA and FIFAK as institutions of Tunisian amateur cinema. In highlighting the history of amateur cinema in Tunisia as an innovative, energetic postcolonial movement that emerged in the absence of an already-extant film industry, I emphasize the central role—and ongoing legacies—of amateur cinema's contributions to (trans)national infrastructures of both film and film culture in Tunisia. What emerges is a particularly striking case in point of how major contributions and genealogies of amateur cinema can remain out of view in historiographies that, by default, grant primacy to auterist genealogies and/or feature-length films—even when these latter modes have been so deeply indebted to the former.

Notes

1. A 2014 Tunisia country report conducted by the European Union corroborates the widespread acknowledgment of very few cinema halls in Tunisia, noting "a dramatic fall in the number of cinema venues from 120 in 1956 to only 10 in 2013" (Helly 2014).

2. Regarding the first African film festivals, Lindiwie Dovey (2015, 94) notes that Journées Cinématographiques de Carthage (JCC) in Tunisia was "the first regularly held film festival established on the continent, founded in 1966." She offers a footnote that both acknowledges and waves aside FIFAK's prior establishment: "As Patricia Caillé notes . . . [FIFAK] has held 28 editions between 1964 and 2013, so is not as regularly held or as well known as JCC" (220n13). However, the notion that FIFAK was "not as regularly held" is misleading, as both JCC and FIFAK were alternating, biennale events for several years. While FIFAK may not be "as well known" on an international competitive festival circuit, I hope to show that it was of enormous significance within circuits of transnational amateur cinema and third cinema, among other networks.

3. Much of Roy Armes's work has been important in considering the overlapping geographies of African and Arab cinema; see, for example, Malkmus and Armes 1991.

4. Recent curatorial endeavors in the aftermath of the Arab Spring uprisings have sparked renewed, widespread interest in historical and contemporary Tunisian amateur films under the larger umbrella of Arab cinema and media art. Such exhibitions include the Goethe Institute's *Arab Shorts: Independent Short Films and Media Art*, which ran in 2009, 2010, and 2011. It circulated through Arab and German film festivals, in addition to taking online forms. It came together as a collective effort involving "the 21 Arab curators, the 118 filmmakers, the artistic director Marcel Shwierin, the representatives of Arab and German film festivals, and Stefanie Schulte Strathaus from the board of [distribution group] 'Arsenal'" (Hasenkamp, Ghada, and Klesse 2012, 7). One of the packages, curated by Walid Tayaa, was titled "Metaphor and Resistance in Tunisian Short Films," and the curator's statement begins, "Before the 14th of January revolution and for many years, the political regime in Tunisia fostered a poor concept of culture and art . . ." (143). MoMA, too, held a three-part exhibition in 2010 titled *Mapping Subjectivity: Experimentation in Arab Cinema from the 1960s to Now*, which later traveled to the Tate Modern. While curator Rasha Salti avowed that the research for the exhibition predated the Arab Spring uprisings, an interviewer prominently frames questions posed to Salti through the uprisings, in an article published with the tagline: "As

the political uprising in the Arab world continues, we talk to curator Rasha Salti about how it effects [*sic*] filmmakers and the role of video documentation during the protests" (Gray 2011).
  5. For more on the contemporary lives of FIFAK, see Caillé 2015.
  6. Printed in a 1981 issue of *Afrique-Asie*, the manifesto notes its signatories: "Appel signé notamment par *Afrique-Asie, CinémAction, Les Deux Ecrans*, etc." (i.e., "Call duly signed by *Afrique-Asie, CinémAction, Les Deux Ecrans*, etc.") (*Afrique-Asie* et al. 1981, 50). Similar manifestos regarding the cause of Palestine and filmmaking had been circulated since the 1970s, albeit without the mention of juries or FIFAK specifically. For more on this, see Dickinson 2018.

References

Afrique-Asie, CinémAction, Les Deux Ecrans, et al. 1981. "Manifeste Pour une Meilleure Illustration de la Cause Palestinienne au Cinéma." *Afrique-Asie*, no. 239 (May 11): 50.

Aubert, Michelle, Jean-Claude Seguin, and Manuel Schmalstieg. 1996. "Tunis–Villes–Catalogue Lumière." L'œuvre cinématographique des frères Lumière. Accessed July 10, 2017. https://catalogue-lumiere.com/ville/tunis/.

Aubert, Michelle, Jean-Claude Seguin, and Manuel Schmalstieg. 1996. *L'œuvre cinématographique des frères Lumière*. Paris: Diffision, CDE.

Ayed, Maya. 2017. "Cinema Against an Authoritarian Backdrop: A History of Tunisian Animation." In *Animation in the Middle East: Practice and Aesthetics from Baghdad to Casablanca*, translated by Cristina Johnston, 240–61. New York: I. B. Tauris.

Bassan, Raphael. 1982. "Les Amateurs Tunisiens: Une Expérience Pilote." *Afrique-Asie*, no. 272 (July): 46–47.

Berrah, Mouny. 1981. *Cinémas du Maghreb: Dossier*. Editions Papyrus.

Boughedir, Férid. 1993. *Caméra Arabe*. Paris: Médiathèque des Trois Mondes.

———. 2016. *Caméra d'Afrique 20 Ans de Cinéma Africain*. Paris: Institut Français, Département Cinéma [Éd., Distrib.].

Bourguiba, Sayda. 2013. "Finalités Culturelles et Esthétiques d'un Cinéma Arabo-Africain en Devenir: Les Journées Cinématographiques de Carthage (JCC)." Paris: Université Paris 1.

Brakhage, Stan. 2001. "In Defense of Amateur." In *Essential Brakhage: Selected Writings on Film-Making*, edited by Bruce R McPherson, 142–50. Kingston: McPherson.

Brittain, Victoria. 2006. "Simon Malley: Journalist with Rare Insight into Africa's Anti-Colonial Struggles." *The Guardian*. Accessed May 11, 2020. https://www.theguardian.com/media/2006/sep/27/guardianobituaries.pressandpublishing.

Caillé, Patricia. 2015. "Fifak 2013: Expressions Sexuées, Genrées et Générationnelles d'une Passion du Cinéma en Tunisie." *Diogène* 245 (1): 104–24.

———. 2017. "S'imaginer En Cinéma—Les Hésitations Genrées Des Cinéastes Amateurs En Tunisie." *Genre En Séries: Cinéma, Télévision, Médias* 5:290–316.

Cheriaa, Tahar. 1972. "Film Distribution in Tunisia." In *The Cinema in the Arab Countries*, edited by Georges Sadoul, 158–63. Beirut: Interarab Centre of Cinema & Television.

"Cinéma Tunisien—La Référence Cinéma En Tunisie—Qui Sommes-Nous?" 2020. Cinéma Tunisien. Accessed May 11, 2020. http://cinematunisien.com/qui-sommes-nous/.

Cowie, Peter, ed. 1978. *Variety International Film Guide*. Tantivy Press.

De Jong, Arie. 2015. "What Is UNICA?" Index of UNICA-Web Documents. 2015. http://www
.ariedejong.eu/unica-web/documents/whatisunica/whatisunica.pdf.

Devi, Mahasweta. 1994. *Imaginary Maps*. Translated by Gayatri Chakravorty Spivak. New
York: Routledge.

Dickinson, Kay. 2018. *Arab Film and Video Manifestos: Forty-Five Years of the Moving Image
Amid Revolution*. London: Palgrave.

Dovey, Lindiwe. 2015. *Curating Africa in the Age of Film Festivals*. New York: Palgrave
Macmillan.

Farid, Samir. 1979. *Arab Cinema Guide*. Cairo.

Gana, Nouri. 2013. "Visions of Dissent, Voices of Discontent: Postcolonial Tunisian Film and
Song." In *The Making of the Tunisian Revolution: Contexts, Architects, Prospects*, edited
by Nouri Gana, 181–203. Edinburgh: Edinburgh University Press.

Gauch, Suzanne. 2016. *Maghreb in Motion: North African Cinema in Nine Movements*.
Oxford: Oxford University Press.

Gray, Carmen. 2011. "Mapping Subjectivity: Arab Cinema at the Tate." Dazed, March 11, 2011.
http://www.dazeddigital.com/artsandculture/article/9926/1/mapping-subjectivity
-arab-cinema-at-the-tate.

Harrow, Kenneth W. 2013. *Trash: African Cinema from Below*. Bloomington: Indiana
University Press.

Hasenkamp, Günter, El-Sherbiny Ghada, and Antje Klesse, eds. 2012. "Arab Shorts:
Independent Short Films and Media Art." Geothe-Institut Kairo. Exhibition catalog.

Helly, Damien. 2014. "Tunisia Country Report." Preparatory Action: Culture in EU External
Relations. http://ec.europa.eu/assets/eac/culture/policy/international-cooperation
/documents/country-reports/tunisia_en.pdf.

Hennebelle, G. 1970. "Tunisie: L'heure Des Bilans." *Jeune Afrique* 504–521:54–56.

Ishizuka, Karen L., and Patricia Rodden Zimmermann. 2008. "Introduction: The Home
Movie Movement: Excavations, Artifacts, Minings." In *Mining the Home Movie:
Excavations in Histories and Memories*, edited by Karen L. Ishizuka and Patricia
Rodden Zimmermann, 1–28. Oakland: University of California Press.

Kchir-Bendana, Kmar. 2004. "Ideologies of the Nation in Tunisian Cinema." In *Nation,
Society and Culture in North Africa*, edited by James McDougall, 35–42. London:
Routledge.

Khelil, Hédi. 2007a. *Abécédaire du Cinéma Tunisien*. Tunis: SIMPACT.

———. 2007b. *Panorama du Cinéma Tunisien, 1966–2006*. Tunis: H. Khélil.

Lang, Robert. 2014. *New Tunisian Cinema: Allegories of Resistance*. New York: Columbia
University Press.

Malkmus, Lizbeth, and Roy Armes. 1991. *Arab and African Film Making*. London: Zed Books.

Martin, Angela. 1985. "Home Movies Could Mean 'Cultural Liberation': So Thinks the
Director of this Year's Kelibia International Festival of Non-Professional Cinema—
Sometimes Dubbed 'Bootlace Cinema.'" *Africa Now*, no. 54–56 (December): 60.

Méziani, Abdelhakim. 1973. "7éme Festival International de Kelibia: Une Rencontre
Décevante." *Révolution Africaine*, no. 496, 31–32.

Perkins, Kenneth. 2014. *A History of Modern Tunisia*. Cambridge: Cambridge University
Press.

Quartucci, Guillermo. 1982. "Seccion Cultural." *Estudios de Asia y Africa* 17, no. 2 (52):
292–99.

Sadoul, Georges. 1959. "Notes on a New Generation." *Monthly Film Bulletin* 28 (3/4): 111–17.
Shafik, Viola. 2017. *Arab Cinema: History and Cultural Identity: Updated with a New Postscript*. Rev. ed. Cairo: The American University in Cairo Press.

SAMHITA SUNYA is Assistant Professor of Cinema in the Department of Middle Eastern & South Asian Languages & Cultures at the University of Virginia.

15

EARLY INTERNATIONAL SUPER 8 FILM FESTIVALS

The Case of Caracas 1976–1980

Isabel Arredondo

Jim Piper (1974), a contributor to the US magazine *Super-8 Filmaker* [*sic*], surveyed the state of international amateur cinema and exclaimed: "Festivals are cropping up all over the country like dandelions in spring" (46). According to Bolivian filmmaker and film theorist Alfonso Gumucio Dagron (1981), by the late 1970s "there were as many Super 8 festivals as days in the year" (24).[1] This phenomenon took place concurrently with (and perhaps because of) the commercialization of Kodak's synchronized Super 8 cartridge in 1973, which eliminated the need for separate sound recording equipment (Newman 1975). According to Bruce Anderson (1977a), editor of *Super-8 Filmaker*: "The real strength of Super 8 is that it is easy and inexpensive enough for almost anyone to use" (3). Cheaper film stock and easy-to-use equipment put small-gauge cameras in the hands of a growing mass of consumers, some of whom used this technology not only to make home movies but to create films for international festivals.

This chapter examines one of the most active Super 8 festivals in the late 1970s and 1980s: the Festival Internacional del Nuevo Cine Super 8 (1976–1989) in Caracas. The festival's network expanded from predominantly North American participation to a wider global network of the International Federation of Super 8 Cinema.[2] This chapter shows how becoming a member of the Federation's open, decentralized network gave the Caracas festival an advantage in showcasing international films, while at the same

Fig. 15.1. Poster for the Super 8 film festival in Tehran. Scan by author.

time promoting local filmmakers. In paying attention to the movement of Super 8 festivals, an alternative geography of film culture emerges, with its centers located not in New York or Paris but in Tehran, Caracas, and Toronto instead. The chapter also examines the economic underpinnings of globalizing Super 8 networks.[3]

The International Federation of Super 8 Cinema

The sprouting of festivals was a global trend that coincided with the commercialization of several 8 mm cartridges from different brands, including Agfa, Kodak, and Fuji. To oversee the coordination of international festivals,

Super 8 filmmakers from multiple countries created a supranational organization, the International Federation of Super 8 Cinema.[4] The Federation was founded in Iran in 1975, moved its headquarters to Brussels in 1976, and finally settled in Montreal in 1980, where it remained until 1989. From 1985 on, the Federation was open to video works, and by 1989 most filmmakers used video and not Super 8.[5]

Exhibiting films that came from diverse geopolitical cinemas was of utmost importance to Federation members, as is shown by film-festival catalogs and Federation newsletters.[6] For example, in 1985, the Festival International du Film Super 8 in Brussels announced in its catalog that the Federation had members in fifty-two countries ("Assamblée," 11). Joining the Federation network or one of its festivals was easy. Filmmakers had only to submit a film to a festival in the Federation's circuit or request to be a representative. However, funding an international festival was more difficult. Groups in Caracas, Brussels, Toronto, Barcelona, Montreal, and Kelibia (Tunisia) were able to secure funding for an annual festival for at least six years. Other Federation groups in Tehran, Paris, Mexico City, San Juan (Puerto Rico), and São Paulo were not so successful in securing funding; as a result, their festivals were short lived or held sporadically.[7] The function of this network, which relied on the other festivals for the supply of films, was to expose noncommercial films to audiences in multiple countries. The Federation system, however, worked in a different way than other small-gauge organizations.

In the mid-1970s, organizations that attracted amateur filmmakers, such as Union Internationale du Cinéma (UNICA), had centralized networks. In contrast, the Federation is an early example of a decentralized small-gauge network. A "map" of the Federation at any given time during the 1970s and 1980s resembles the graphic that Alexander Galloway (Galloway 2010; Galloway and Thacker 2007), following Paul Baran et al. (1964), uses to illustrate decentralized networks. Galloway (2010) describes an archeology in which a network evolves from a centralized to a decentralized organization and, finally, becomes one that is distributed (289). In a decentralized network there is a core or "back-bone" of hubs, each with radiating peripheries (Galloway and Thacker 2007, 32). This core is not present in a distributed network, in which nodes (elements in a network) have approximately the same degree—that is, are equally important (31–32).

Decentralized nodes with their respective peripheries are connected to each other. In the 1970s, the Federation operated primarily in Iran

(Tehran), South America (Caracas), North America (Toronto), and Western Europe (Brussels and Barcelona). The Federation was an open network that was continually changing, albeit always with multiple connected centers. In the early 1980s, North African countries entered the network through Brussels via Kelibia, which had been the center of North African amateur filmmaking (though not specifically Super 8 works) since 1964. The Federation's connections to Asia and Australia, via Brussels, date from the mid-1980s.

Paying attention to networks, and not merely the screenings of films, helps to differentiate the structure among the various small-gauge organizations. UNICA's annual congress might resemble a Federation festival, in that both included films from many countries. However, these two organizations operated very different networks. In UNICA, an organization that had coordinated film clubs and organized international film contests since the 1930s, films were selected at the country level and then screened at a single annual congress. In the Federation, film festival directors traveled the network carrying films from festival to festival. At the same point in time that UNICA was centralized, the federation was decentralized.

Connecting filmmakers and exhibitors by coordinating festivals was the Federation's most important mission. Once a year, the Federation's board met to agree on the dates for each festival. Synchronizing the calendar was vital so that area representatives could move through the network, facilitating, in Tunisian festival organizer Ridha Ben Halima's words, the "jumping from festival to festival" (interview with author, March 23, 2016). For example, holding Kelibia a week after Montecatini (Italy) allowed audiences and film festival directors to attend Montecatini first and then travel by ferry to Tunis to attend the festival at Kelibia.[8] Dates of festivals often depended on the convenience of each local festival and even the availability of lodging. In the mid-1970s, the cycle of festivals typically started in Toronto in the spring, with the summer festivals in São Paulo and Caracas, and autumn festivals in Tehran and Brussels. Attending international film festivals gave directors an opportunity to exhibit their films, and, equally important, it allowed them to select entries for their next home festival.

The need for area representatives was peculiar to the technology of Super 8. The Super 8 cartridge contained reversal film—that is, film that when developed produces a positive rather than a negative.[9] Not having a negative made Super 8 films hard to replace; in fact, it was more expensive to make a copy of a Super 8 film than to shoot a new film. To lower the risk of losing films in the mail, the Federation entrusted area representatives with the transportation of films in their hand luggage. Julio Neri was, in addition to film festival director and juror, one such area representative (personal communication 2010, 2011). Not all areas of the world were equally represented. Some representatives covered large areas, such as South America and even the United States (Julio Neri) or North Africa and the Middle East (Ridha Ben Halima). Other representatives covered smaller areas, such as France (Yves Rollin) or Belgium (Marcel Croës and Robert Malengreau). In 1978, Neri brought the Venezuelan winners of his festival and films from Brazil, Mexico, Columbia, Peru, and Curaçao to Federation festivals.[10] Neri's visits to festivals were a way of circulating films around the network.

The Federation and UNICA's networks differed in style as well. UNICA was a centralized network governed by a board that determined how and where to organize its annual congress. The Federation was a decentralized network, and its most important role was facilitating connections that would maximize the movement of films through the network. In the Federation, each country maintained autonomy by organizing its own festivals. This chapter will now turn to the Festival Internacional del Nuevo Cine Super 8 (1976–1989) in Caracas, as it illuminates how the relationship between local and global cultures was articulated by festival organizers, filmmakers, and national authorities in the context of oil-boom economy and shifting geopolitical relations.

Venezuela, an Oil Economy

Since the 1950s, national and regional institutions in Venezuela have used art to create an image of Venezuela as a first-world country. Oil money created the conditions that led to the establishment of Super 8 festivals in Venezuela and Iran. In both countries, fossil fuel revenues gave purchase power to the middle class, who could afford to buy Super 8 equipment, and it also went toward the funding of local institutions that sponsored such festivals. In the case of Venezuela, the nationalization of the oil industry, which occurred in steps from 1972 to 1976, gave the country a profile somewhat different from that of other Latin American countries. The sharp rise in oil prices in the 1970s, as a result of the actions of the OPEC cartel (in which Venezuela was a significant player) brought in a flood of revenue to Venezuela. The price of a barrel of Venezuelan oil rose from $2.50 to $10.50

between 1972 and 1974, prompting the government under Carlos Andrés Pérez—elected in 1975—to embark on an ambitious government spending program connected to the ideal of "La Gran Venezuela" (Straka 2016). The Fundación para la Cultura y las Artes (FUNDARTE; http://www.fundarte.gob.ve/), was created in the mid-1970s to sponsor events like the renowned Caracas International Theater Festival. Besides bringing internationally famous theater groups to Caracas on a yearly basis, FUNDARTE subsidized independent, innovative, local theater groups, such as Tiempo Común. Super 8 film directors, like Diego Rísquez, and actors, like María Adelina Vera, Ivan Oropeza and Hugo Márquez, trained daily at Tiempo Común (Arredondo 2015). However, filmmakers had to finance their own films, often with the money earned from their jobs: Gianni Dal Maso and Marietta Pérez were photographers; Carlos Castillo and John Moore were designers; Ricardo Jabardo was a professor at the university; Diego Rísquez worked in advertising; and Julio Neri filmed weddings or other social events. Either way, municipal investment helped Super 8 filmmakers find their audiences, fed their work into the various Venezuelan art worlds, and garnered the support to create the first Super 8 film festival in 1976 (Crespo 1997).

The Caracas festival lasted from 1976 to 1989. In 1976 and 1977, when the festival was called Festival Internacional de Cine de Vanguardia, the primary network that supplied films to the festival came from the US magazine *Super-8 Filmaker*. Given the success of the first Caracas festival, its director, Julio Neri, was invited to Tehran's International Festival of Super 8 in October 1977, where Caracas officially joined the Federation. Soon after, Iran's central role in the Federation was affected by the Islamic Revolution. In 1978, Bassir Nassibi, director of the Tehran festival and president of the Federation, went first into hiding and then into exile (interview with the author, 2013, 2016). Venezuela moved to replace Iran as a pivotal member of the Federation, having the resources (a developed art world, knowledgeable audiences, institutions that were looking for international recognition, and a very active film festival director) to play this role. In the late 1970s and early 1980s, Caracas hosted the most important Super 8 festival, and, in 1979, Neri became the president of the Federation (Antillano 1978; "John Moore" 1978). As the following section illustrates, this growing network of small-gauge film cultures soon became internationalized, offering Venezuelan artists a chance to showcase their works throughout the world.

Caracas's Network Expansion

With the support of federal and municipal institutions, the Caracas festival broadened its network.[11] Initially, the Super 8 festival functioned within the network created by *Super-8 Filmaker*, primarily established in North America. Neri advertised the first Federation festival held in Caracas in two 1976 calendar sections of *Super-8 Filmaker* (see March 1976, 64; June 1976, 64); he received responses from around eight hundred people for the first festival and over two thousand for the second (Antillano 1977a, 10). The success can be partly explained by the scarcity of international Super 8 film festivals and by the generous prizes offered by the Caracas festival. Neri also used the calendar in *Super-8 Filmaker* for a second reason: to bring Venezuelan Super 8 films to other festivals. In March 1977, for example, he traveled with Venezuelan films to the II Toronto Super Eight Film Festival (April 1–3), where he gave a workshop on Latin American Super 8 ("Saturday, April," 1977, 4). As audiences in Caracas wanted to see films from other countries, Neri also brought back films from these same networks and became a de-facto country or area representative.

The Federation's area of operation was broader and more tightly woven than the *Super-8 Filmaker*'s network. At the Tehran festival in 1977, Neri established relationships with film festival directors Bassir Nassibi (Tehran), Enrique López Manzano (Barcelona), Chris Wordsworth (Great Britain), Rik Groenewegen (Netherlands), and Robert Malengreau and Marcel Croës (Brussels). Some of these festival directors invited him to attend their festivals. For example, during the same year, Neri went to Barcelona's Tercera Setmana del Film Super 8 (November 2–6, 1977) and to Belgium's festival at Louvain-La-Neuve, the 4é Festival National du Film Super 8 (November 11–13, 1977). As they moved through the Federation's network, area representatives had their expenses covered.[12] Film festival directors invited area representatives so that they could bring the films from their respective festivals. In 1977, for example, Rollin and López Manzano were invited as jury members to Belgium's third national festival ("Le Jury," 1977, 5). Federation film festival directors relied on each other to maintain the Federation's system.

Tracing Neri's travels to the different Federation-connected festivals illuminates the intense transnational efforts of the organization in the period right after its founding. A new touring year began in August 1978. After the third festival in Caracas took place, Neri embarked on a tour with the

Fig. 15.2. Poster for the 1st International Super 8 Film Festival at
Namur (Belgium). Scan by author.

Venezuelan winners. He also brought along films from other countries,
including Brazil, Mexico, Columbia, Peru, and Curacao. (Due to the political turmoil in Iran at that time, the Tehran festival was canceled.) Neri
returned to Belgium, this time to Namur (November 15–19), where he met
Rollin (vice president of the Federation), López Manzano, and many others.
The Federation's general meeting took place during the festival on November 18. As Nassibi, the Federation's president, was in hiding, the organization elected Neri as a new president for a three-year term. This decision

demonstrates how easily formal power could shift from the Middle East to South America or other regions, according to the contingencies of political unrest and emerging economies.

Neri's visit to Namur in 1978 also reveals that each festival within the Federation system was quite autonomous. This was recognized in the original version of the bylaws, which were written in Farsi at the first Iranian international festival in 1975 and ratified and translated into French at the second international festival in 1976. The rules did not specify how festivals were to be run, although they indicated that festivals could be national or international. Consequently, festivals chose the format that best suited their local needs. The organization only required that member festivals display the Federation's logo in their catalogs, press interviews, and posters—which they were happy to do, as the link to the Federation gave local festivals international status.

A comparison between Belgium and Caracas shows the differences between festival styles in this early period. The Belgian government pressed to decentralize cultural activities. Thus, in the mid-1970s the festival rotated between different host cities: Namur, Louvain-La-Neuve, and Brussels. By contrast, Venezuela's festival was firmly anchored in Caracas. A second difference was the structure of the festivals. In Caracas, there was only one festival, the international festival. In Belgium, the organizers split up the national filmmakers from the international filmmakers, which is why Namur simultaneously hosted the 5ᵉ Festival National du Film Super 8 and the 1ᵉʳ Festival International du Film Super 8. A third difference between these festivals concerned the events that complemented the screening of films. At Namur, the festival introduced a forum, which was presided over by Neri. The event was titled 1ᵉʳ Rencontre du Cinema Super 8 du Tiers-Monde (First Meeting of Super 8 Film from Third World Countries), with the aim of fostering dialogue among Third World filmmakers.[13] Caracas, however, opted for a more practical annex and invited professionals of the Super 8 world. Lenny Lipton and Mark Mikolas, authors of Super 8 manuals, lead workshops. The goal of some Super 8 filmmakers was to enter the commercial circle via the back door, by blowing up Super 8 to 35 mm. Neri's *Electofrenia* (1978), a film that won at Biarritz 35 mm festival, was considered a victory by the Caracas community and *Super-8 Filmaker* (Anderson 1979, 18–22). Thus, while Caracas and Brussels were linked together as Federation festivals, each had autonomy in regard to local agendas. In other words, the Federation was a decentralized network.

Fig. 15.3. Poster for the 6th International Super 8 Film Festival at Caracas. Scan by author.

Neri's travels, as reported in Venezuelan newspapers, demonstrate that Federation festivals also led to invitations from other festivals that were not part of the system. Local festivals in many countries could not find sponsors to permanently or semipermanently sustain their festivals.[14] In 1978, Neri visited the British Super 8 Film Festival in London, and then he went to Paris, La Rochelle, and Montpelier in France. Despite the fact that the United States did not have an international Super 8 festival, Neri attended other film festivals in New Jersey, New York, and Puerto Rico. New festivals were organized in 1979; for example, Neri attended the III Muestra de Cine Canario-Americano in Santa Cruz de Tenerife, Spain, where he was invited as a jury member. At this festival, Venezuelan films received numerous awards (Barlovento 1979). The Federation's network allowed Neri to access broader international networks in the Middle East and Europe.

The Super 8 Festival in Caracas

Participation in global networks, like film festivals, brought international films to cities around the world—including Caracas, a city that became heavily invested in Super 8 cinema.[15] For the first two festivals held in Caracas in 1976 and 1977, the majority of the entries came the United States. In 1976, for example, there were twenty-three entries from the United States, twelve from Venezuela, and ten from all the other countries combined. In 1977, the proportion of Venezuelan to United States films increased: twenty-one films came from the United States, eighteen from Venezuela, and twenty from all the remaining sixteen countries. Anderson (1977b), reviewing the Caracas festival for *Super-8 Filmaker*, observed that having films from these many countries made the festival a success: "While festival entries weren't always 'avant garde,' they were international" (46). Furthermore, as Caracas had become an international node, attending the festival was another way to connect to the worldwide filmmaking network. Anderson explained: "the Caracas festival and others like it give filmmakers from other cultures a chance to see what their fellow filmmakers are doing with Super-8" (48). Festival catalogs show that after Caracas joined the Federation, entries from Federation festivals increased and the proportion of US films decreased; by 1980, Belgium and Italy entered five films each, almost matching the six US entries. Entries from Venezuela increased as well, which probably indicates the success of the festival in encouraging endogenous filmmaking.

Caracas's established status in various international networks helped Super 8 gain the support of national and municipal institutions. Given the success of the Festival Internacional de Teatro de Caracas (Caracas International Theater Festival, 1971–present), Venezuelan institutions saw the Caracas Super 8 festival as another opportunity to transform the capital into a city of festivals (De Valck 2007, 70), what Stevens calls a "programmable" city.[16] In addition, as Venezuelan Super 8 filmmakers won important prizes abroad, officials associated with federal institutions were impressed. Film festival organizers Neri and Mercedes Márquez met annually with officials from the Ministry of Tourism, Cinemateca Nacional, and FUNDARTE to ask for funding. To demonstrate that the previous year's subsidy had resulted in high attendance at screenings and national interest in foreign visitors, the organizers carried a binder that displayed clippings from newspapers and magazine reviews.[17] In 1976 and 1977, national newspapers had published interviews with Bruce Anderson, *Village Voice* critic Gregory Battock, Super 8 guru Lenny Lipton, and sound specialist Mark Mikolas, which were then incorporated into the following year's festival catalog. Film critics and journalists in various Venezuelan publications, such as Pablo Antillano and Rodolfo Izaguirre, called attention to the success of Super 8 filmmakers at home and abroad, and encouraged government institutions concerned with cultural development to participate in the Super 8 festival.[18] Cinemateca Nacional de Venezuela made its auditorium available for the festival. A subsidy from the Ministry of Tourism and Information (in which Film, Radio and Television were housed) was used to buy a projector for the five-hundred-seat auditorium.[19]

The Caracas festival was not designed for mass audiences but rather young countercultural ones. A program of international films, a powerful projector, and a spacious auditorium attracted large crowds of people. Reporting on the 1977 festival, Anderson (1977b) wrote, "It was Bastille Day— Venezuelan style. Throngs of young film enthusiasts literally stormed the gates of the Cinemateca Nacional in Caracas . . . the [festival was] so popular in Venezuela that many who showed up at the theater never got a seat" (46). The Super 8 festival in Caracas energized a local network of knowledge-able audiences and created a forum for artistic discussion. In 1977, people in the audience openly rejected the film *Airs*, Stan Brakhage's entry for the festival. They booed throughout the twenty minutes of out-of-focus shots of clouds and sky. Restless, they made nasty comments during the projection. The audience's murmurs and complaints made their way into articles in the national press. Some film critics viewed the audience's reaction to *Airs* with dismay (Antillano 1977a, 1977b). However, media coverage of the festival polemics suggests that audience participation brought about concrete change at the most fundamental level. The community's rejection of *Airs* most probably explains why in 1978, the festival changed its name from Festival de Cine de Vanguardia to Festival Internacional del Nuevo Cine Super 8 (Antillano 1978, 22). The new name sheds its association with the New York underground movement and aligns the festival with the young audience. The Caracas festival opened a space for participatory criticism.

Federation festivals like Caracas served as clearinghouses for new ideas. A comparison between the prizes given at Caracas and Tehran demonstrates both an overall appreciation of Super 8 countercultural values and some specificity of local agendas. In some cases, audiences and the juries in Caracas and Tehran reacted similarly to films. For example, Carlos Castillo's *Hecho en Venezuela* (*Made in Venezuela*, 1977) won in the second years of both the Caracas and Tehran festivals.[20] Audiences in both oil-producing countries reacted against hyperconsumption. They applauded when "Venezuelan goods are placed on a chopping block and, one by one, are axed to pieces while the sound track does a soft-sell commercial for the Venezuelan economy" (Anderson 1977b, 47–48).

In other cases, local audiences' interests and tastes manifested in a heterogeneous reception across festivals. For instance, Ricardo Jabardo's *Más oveja serás tú* (*Don't Be a Follower*, 1977) passed unnoticed at Caracas but won major awards at Tehran.[21] Jabardo did not create *Más oveja* with an Iranian audience in mind, but his message applied to the situation in Iran. An animation with collages from television and newspapers, *Más oveja* encouraged audiences not to be mesmerized by consumer products and violent forms of religious control. In Tehran, this message could be read as a critique of the Shah's imposition of fast-pace modernization and as a rejection of the other option in the political spectrum: the clergy's attempt to restore traditional values (Sreberny-Mohammadi and Mohammadi 1994). At a time when the Shah's secret police, SAVAK, held a strong grip on the freedoms of Iranians, audiences at Teheran were pleased that *Más oveja* circumvented local censorship. In the interconnected world of Super 8, local agendas played a role in *Más oveja*'s prizes and in turn, the film's success had repercussion in Caracas. The Venezuelan press was delighted with Castillo's and Jabardo's prizes in Tehran (Tirado 1977), and the buzz led to more funding from the government for the third Festival Internacional del Nuevo Cine Super 8 (Meneses 1978).

At the Caracas festival, local audiences benefited from international programing, especially from underrepresented countries. Local filmmakers gained access to national and international public spaces. Federal institutions took note of the fact that Venezuelan artists were able to achieve international recognition and reacted with greater support. Finally, municipal institutions were able to brand Caracas as a cosmopolitan festival city.

Conclusion

If we focus our attention on the Super 8 festival movement, an alternative geography of film cultures emerges. Its centers are not located in New York or Paris, but in Tehran, Caracas, and Brussels. This chapter concludes that the type of network established by Federation members—chiefly the national representatives that together created an international organization—models a new sociality; that is, a new type of interaction among participant groups.

The interaction among Federation members demonstrates the great value of connectivity (Fischer 2013, 1–9) and connectedness (Dijck 2013). The Caracas festival relied on expanding its network to include films from abroad and to bring national productions to the Festival Internacional de Cine de Vanguardia. This chapter proposes that there is a strong correlation between connectedness and governance. The Federation network, and its peripheries, became decentralized to increase connectedness. By broadening its organization to include multiple nontraditional cites to host the festival, Caracas and Tehran, for example, were better able to respond to adverse, national conditions. Had Tehran been the only center in 1978, the Federation's network would have been seriously undermined. Because the Federation was decentralized, Caracas was able to take on the central role Tehran had played from 1975 to 1977.

In the interaction among Federation members, having a decentralized network had a profound effect. The Federation's bylaws did not regulate the functioning of local festivals to facilitate funding. Brussels and Caracas are examples that show that decisions made in regard to the organization of festivals on a local level required adapting funding strategies to various local agendas—as Neri and Malengreau, respectively, did for both festivals. In turn, securing funding facilitated connectedness—for example, having more funds for organization meant festival directors could invite more Federation members and filmmakers to their local festivals; thus, the increase in screenings upped the chances of a successful local event.

In the interactions among Federation members, openness and inclusiveness were significant. Unlike film clubs, which required certain membership, film festivals were public spaces. In addition, there were no restrictions on who could serve on the board. The Federation invited all who were interested to serve on the organization's board, which demonstrates the members' refusal to operate as gatekeepers. And, having few rules for inclusion facilitated the supply of films. Cooperation among festival officials from different countries was essential, which explains why the most important task at the Federation's annual meeting was setting the calendar. Only by coordinating an unregulated flow of films could the Federation, and its festivals, flourish.

Notes

1. This is my translation of "No sería exagerado afirmar que hay en el mundo tantos festivales de cine Super 8 como días en el año."

2. For festivals as networks see Elsaesser (2005), especially the chapter "Film Festival Networks."

3. Inspired by theorists such as Jameson 1998; Holt 2009; Wilson 1996; Giddens 1990; Inglis 2005; Castells 1996, 2010; and Borja, Castells, Belil, and Benner 1997, this chapter articulates the global into the local and vice versa.

4. The Federation's name originally was in French. Its translation into English appears as the "International Federation of Cinema Super 8" or the "International Federation of Super 8 Cinema."

5. When I asked questions about the Federation, the filmmakers' and film-festival directors' answers were scant and imprecise, to the point that I suspected that the organization did not exist. Sheila Hill, however, provided a photograph of one of the meetings. Later I found documents related to its creation in the Iranian magazine *Cinema ye Azad* and to the establishment of the Federation as an NGO (Cinémathèque Québécoise in Montreal). Any papers regarding Federation meetings in Brussels had been discarded before I began my research.

6. See https://super8festivals.org/ for the newsletter, posters, reviews and festival catalogs.

7. Álvaro Vázquez Mantecón (2012, 267–93) describes Federation festivals in Mexico. The festival in São Paulo lasted more than six years, but only as a national festival.

8. Ridha Ben Halim explained this strategy (interview with the author, March 23, 2016), and Romano Fatorossi, Montecatini's film-festival director, confirmed it (Fatorossi, interview with the author, June 6, 2017). A French filmmaker, Vicent Toledano, traveled by bike to Kelibia. Belgian filmmaker Manuel Gómez drove from Montecatini to Kelibia (Halima 2016).

9. Kodak created Super 8 using a similar principle to Polaroid photographs: once developed, the Super 8 film stock became the positive. Also available was 16 mm reversible film.

10. The winning films at the Caracas 1978 festival ("Chichu Olalde y Gianni Dal Maso" 1978, 3) were Chris Marker's *L'ambassade* (1973, France); Gianni Dal Maso y Chichu Olalde's *Legado de un aficionado* (Venezuela); Bernard Claydo's *Birthday Party* (Nigeria); John Moore's *Sensorial* (Venezuela); and René Metsch's *Portafolio* (Curaçao).

11. More research is necessary to establish the exact contributions of national and municipal institutions to the Super 8 festival. Film festival catalogs only give a list of the institutions sponsoring the festival. FUNDARTE, the Ministry of Information and Tourism, and Postal Services were the sponsors listed in 1978 (Antillano 1978, 7).

12. An invitation letter from Robert Malengreau, director of the Brussels film festival, to Howard Guttemplan, director of the Millenium gallery and film school in New York City, possibly from March 1997, specifies that lodging and food would be covered but not travel. Other festivals, such as Caracas, had more money and extended invitations that covered travel as well (Howard Guttenplan, interview with author, March 15, 2009 and April 30, 2013).

13. "1er Rencontre," 1978, 15. The list of the countries appears in an internal memo from the festival: "1er Rencontre du Cinema Super 8 du Tiers-Monde." *5e Festival Nationale du Film Super 8, Namur*. Internal memo, "Heure par heure." November 19, 1978.

14. For the factors in festivals' longevity see Stevens (2016).

15. For a larger study of interactions of cities and cinema, see Shiel and Fitzmaurice 2001.

16. According to Pazos (1988), the theater festival can be considered one of the first times the government subsidized culture, an event that, in my view, marks the beginning of making Caracas into a programmable city, a festival city.

17. In 2008, Márquez gave me the binder covering the period 1976 to 1982, the time in which she and Neri were the codirectors of the festival. The newspaper and magazine clippings in the binder have been fundamental to my evaluation of the impact of the festival including Antillano 1977b; Barlovento 1979; Meneses 1978.

18. See, for example, Izaguirre 1978, 1979, 1980a, 1980b, 1981 and Antillano 1977b.

19. Interviews with Germán Carreño, November 2016, and with Rodolfo Izaguirre, January 2010, both working in Cinemateca Nacional.

20. *Hecho en Venezuela* won the Jury's Special Prize at Tehran.

21. At Caracas, *Más oveja* won only an honorable mention at a local festival, the Concurso del Concejo Municipal de Caracas, and not the international Super 8 festival ("Cine Super-8 Venezolano" 1978). At Tehran, *Más oveja* won the festival's second prize, which, in reality, was the first prize, as this one had been declared void by the international jury. In addition, *Más oveja* also received awards of honor from the audience and students at the cinema and television school.

References

Anderson, Bruce. 1977a. "Publisher's Statement." *Super-8 Filmaker*, November 1977.

———. 1977b. "Caracas Festival: The Cannes of Super-8." *Super-8 Filmaker*, November 1977.

——— 1979. "Victory in Super-8: Smaller Format Makes Big Time." *Super-8 Filmaker*, November 1979.

Antillano, Pablo. 1977a. "¿Es nuevo el cine de Vanguardia?" *Buen vivir, Guía del entretenimiento*. September 2–10, 1977.

———. 1977b. "Memorias de un Festival de Super 8: Deshojando una Margarita." *Buen vivir, Guía del entretenimiento*. September 20–30, 1977.

———. 1978. "Cuando la Vanguardia Envejece." *Tercer Festival Internacional del Nuevo Cine Super-8*, Caracas. Caracas film festival catalog.

Arredondo, Isabel. 2015. "Entrevista con Iván Oropeza: Hugo Márquez y el teatro de calle en la Caracas de los años ochenta." *SituArte* 19 (July–December): 50–55.

"Assamblée Générale de la Fédération Internationale du Cinéma Super 8/Video." 1985. *7e Festival International et 12e Festival National du Film Super 8*. Brussels film festival catalog. https://super8festivals.org/

Baran, Paul, Sharla P. Boehm, and J. W. Smith. 1964. *On Distributed Communications*. Santa Monica, CA: Rand Corporation.

Barlovento, A. 1979. "En Sudamérica se sigue con enorme atención al movimiento documental canario." *El Día*, February 8, 1979.

Borja, Jordi, Manuel Castells, Mireia Belil, and Chris Benner. 1997. *Local and Global: The Management of Cities in the Information Age*. United Nations Centre for Human Settlements. London: Earthscan.

Castells, Manuel. 1996. *The Power of Identity*. Malden, MA: Wiley and Blackwell.

———. 2010. *The Rise of the Network Society*. Malden, MA: Blackwell.

"Chichu Olalde y Gianni Dal Maso Premiados en el III Festival Super 8." 1978. *Vamos al Cine*, no. 226: 3.

"Cine Super-8 Venezolano." *El Universal*, March 29, 1978.

Crespo, Milton. 1997. "El cine Super 8." In *Panorama histórico del cine en Venezuela, 1896–1993*, edited by José Miguel Acosta, 112. Caracas: Fundación Cinemateca Nacional.

Dijck, José van. 2013. *The Culture of Connectivity: A Critical History of Social Media*. Oxford: Oxford University Press.

8, Namur. Internal memo, "Heure par heure." November 19, 1978. https://super8festivals.org/

Elsaesser, Thomas. 2005. "Film Festival Networks: The New Topographies of Cinema in Europe." In *European Cinema: Face to Face with Hollywood*, 82–107. Amsterdam: Amsterdam University Press.

Fischer, Alex. 2013. *Sustainable Projections: Concepts in Film Festival Management*. St Andrews, Scotland: St Andrews Film Studies.

Galloway, Alexander R. 2010. "Networks." In *Critical Terms for Media Studies*, edited by W. J. T. Mitchell and Mark B. N. Hansen, 280–309. Chicago: University of Chicago Press.

Galloway, Alexander R., and Eugene Thacker. 2007. *The Exploit: A Theory of Networks*. Minneapolis: University of Minnesota Press.

Giddens, Anthony. 1990. *The Consequences of Modernity*. Stanford, CA: Stanford University Press.

Gumucio Dagron, Alfonso. 1981. *Super 8, teoría y práctica de un nuevo cine: Manual de apoyo técnico y práctico a la generación de talleres del Super 8*. Caracas: Wiphala.

Holt, Jennifer, and Alisa Perren. 2009. *Media Industries: History, Theory, and Method*. Chichester, UK: Wiley-Blackwell.

Inglis, David. 2005. *Culture and Everyday Life*. Abingdon, UK: Routledge University Press.

Izaguirre, Rodolfo. 1978. "Las Elecciones Presidenciales En Primer Plano." *El Nacional*, n.d.

———. 1979. "Festival De Super Ocho." *El Nacional*, n.d.

———. 1980a. "Electofrenia Gracia Y Patetismo De Unas Elecciones." *El Nacional*, n.d.

———. 1980b. "Cannes Del Super 8." *El Nacional*, n.d.

———. 1981. "Super Ocho a Las Ocho." *El Nacional*, n.d.

Jameson, Fredric, and Masao Miyoshi. 1998. *The Cultures of Globalization*. Durham, NC: Duke University Press.

"John Moore Premiado en el III Festival Super 8." *Vamos al Cine* 226 (1978): 4.

"Le Jury du Festival 77." 1977. *3e Festival National du Film Super 8, Liege*. Internal memo, 5.

Lipton, Lenny. 1975. *The Super 8 Book*. San Francisco: Straight Arrow Books.

———. 1978. *Independent Filmmaking*. New York: Simon and Schuster.

Mikolas, Mark, and Gunther Hoos. 1976. *Handbook of Super 8 Production*. New York: United Business Publications.

Meneses, Adriana. 1978. "Ives Rolling y Joseph Morder hablan de las ventajas del formato Super-8." *El Universal*, August 20, 1978.

Newman, Joyce. 1975. "Super-8: Past, Present and Future." *Super-8 Filmaker*, August 1975: 38–43.

"1er Rencontre du Cinema Super 8 du Tiers-Monde." 1978. *5e Festival National du Film Super.*

Pazos, Gloria. 1988. "Rajatabla, presencia y significación." *Latin American Theatre Review* 21 (2): 29–34.

Piper, Jim. "Running Your Own Film Festival." *Super-8 Filmaker*, August 1974.

Shiel, Mark, and Tony Fitzmaurice. 2001. *Cinema and the City: Film and Urban Societies in a Global Context*. Oxford: Blackwell.

Sreberny-Mohammadi, Annabelle, and Ali Mohammadi. 1994. *Small Media Big Revolution*. Minneapolis: University of Minnesota Press.

Stevens, Kirsten. 2016. *Australian Film Festivals: Audience, Place, and Exhibition Culture*. New York: Palgrave Macmillan.

Straka, Tomás. 2016. "Petróleo y Nación: El nacionalismo petrolero y la formación del Estado moderno en Venezuela (1936–1976)." In *La nación petrolera: Venezuela, 1914–2014*, 107–68. Caracas: Academia Nacional de la Historia, Universidad Metropolitana.

"Saturday, April 2, 1977." 1977. *2nd Toronto Super Eight Film Festival*, Toronto, Cananda. Programme, 2. https://super8festivals.org/.

Tirado, Ricardo. 1977. "Venezuela obtiene triunfos internacionales." *El cine*, December 11, 1977.

Valck, Marijke de. 2007. *Film Festivals: From European Geopolitics to Global Cinephilia*. Amsterdam: Amsterdam University Press.

Vázquez Mantecón, Álvaro. 2012. *El cine súper 8 en México 1970–1989*. México, DF: Filmoteca UNAM.

ISABEL ARREDONDO is Professor of Spanish at SUNY Plattsburgh. She is author of *Motherhood in Mexican Cinema, 1941–1991: The Transformation of Femininity on Screen.*

16

A GIFT TO MOTHER

"The Most Universally Appealing Kind of Film That Any Amateur Can Hope to Make"

Maria Vinogradova

ON JUNE 4, 1964, TONY ROSE, EDITOR OF the British magazine *Amateur Cine World*, opened the issue with a hymn to a single film, *A Gift to Mother* (dir. Movshin, 1963), which had just won a prize for overall excellence at the Vancouver International Amateur Film Festival. Made by a Leningrad-based photographer, David Movshin, the film became an international sensation in the world of amateur cinema. Rose (1964a, 753) praised its simplicity and universal appeal: "I rate it as the best bit of anti-Cold War propaganda ever to come out of Russia—particularly effective because it was not intended as propaganda or indeed as a festival prizewinner, but just a simple record of home life. The trouble with deliberate propaganda is that it always leaves us with the feeling that we are being 'got at'; the same objection tends to apply to amateur films that are made with the express intention of impressing competition judges." His excitement about Movshin's film is not merely admiration for a well-made amateur work. Rose calls it "the most universally appealing kind of film that any amateur can hope to make," one that "overthrows national barriers and makes the whole world kin" (753). In a letter to the editor in the previous issue of *Amateur Cine World*, reader A. W. Austin (1964, 717) asserted, "The Russian programme [of amateur films] convinced me that if Messrs. Khrushchev, Johnson, Chou en Lai, and Home, were all cine enthusiasts, the world would become a safer and happier place."

These responses reflect a search for identity and purpose for amateur cinema at the time when small-gauge equipment was becoming increasingly accessible and the cine club movement and festival scenes—local, regional, and international—were growing. One aspect of this search was related to the form and style of amateur films, where simplicity was particularly praised. Understood as a healthy balance among ambition, aesthetic sense, and available means, it appeared as the opposite of dilettantism, the notion that has traditionally shadowed amateurism. Another aspect engaged the question of purpose more directly. While many aspired to creating films with impact, it was clear to most they could not be evaluated according to prevalent aesthetic values. Instead, amateur films came to be valued for their communicative ability, how they enabled ordinary people to share experiences and worldviews and represent their communities. While most aspired to winning a prize, the ideology that permeated amateur film competitions was akin to the original Olympian ideal: participation matters more than accolades. International amateur film festivals were seen as breaking two boundaries. First, they publicly celebrated nonprofessional uses of a medium restricted by barriers of professionalism. Second, they shook the barriers of formal diplomatic structures and other state institutions that guarded communications with foreign countries. This barrier appeared almost impenetrable in the case of connections across the Iron Curtain. What the likes of Tony Rose and A. W. Austin were excited about in the case of Movshin's film was a newfound sense of purpose, the ability to connect with the Soviet Union and maintain peace in a world torn by political and ideological antagonism.

Focusing on the case of *A Gift to Mother* and its international circulation during the 1960s, this chapter draws attention to the role of amateur film exchanges as a channel of cultural diplomacy during the Cold War. These interactions spanned a broad range of frameworks, from small grassroots organizations to larger associations with varying degrees of involvement with state institutions, connecting amateur film communities as distinct as those of Western Europe, North America, and the USSR. The way in which the latter was shaped by its context of state socialism is another important focus of this chapter.

Soviet Amateurs Go International

Connections between Soviet film amateurs and their international counterparts began in 1957, the year often called the "second birth" of Soviet amateur filmmaking (Il´ichev and Nashchekin 1986, 15). Developing within state socialism, the practice of amateur filmmaking in the USSR differed remarkably from its Western counterparts. While the culture of amateur film clubs had developed in different parts of the world by the 1930s,[1] its Soviet version, arriving more than two decades later, was characterized by a degree of state support and connections with professional filmmakers unparalleled elsewhere. Efforts to build this support were led by film director Grigorii Roshal´, the most active advocate, frequently called "the father of Soviet amateur cinema."[2] This advocacy took a concrete shape through establishing a section for amateurs at the newly founded Union of Filmmakers. In the first few months of its operation, the section took steps to popularize amateur filmmaking, establish material infrastructure for its development, and spread awareness of it, so as to ensure cooperation of other organizations that could provide resources for film amateurs. Until the end of the 1950s, Soviet film amateurs either used discarded professional equipment or foreign 16 mm and 8 mm cameras bought at secondhand stores or on rare trips abroad. Domestically produced small-gauge cameras and projectors became available in the early 1960s.

The "second birth" of Soviet amateur filmmaking coincided with the Thaw, the decade of cultural revival, liberalization, and increased contacts with foreign countries that followed Khrushchev's denouncement of Stalin's dictatorial rule in 1956. It launched within one of the period's most symbolic events, the 6th World Festival of Students and Youth. The festival gathered in Moscow in July 1957 and became the first occasion in decades when Soviet people could meet their counterparts from all over the world (Gilburd 2012). The festival combined a three-day screening of amateur films with a conference that gathered representatives of international organizations. The Union of Filmmakers used the success of this event to make a case for further support of amateur filmmaking efforts. Cine amateurs shared in the festival's celebratory internationalist spirit, and transcripts of the conference discussions indicate appeals to amateur filmmakers of the world to unite and to create an international organization to strengthen connections.[3]

In the early 1960s, articles covering the practice and organization of Soviet amateur filmmaking began to appear in Western periodicals. Some in the French magazine targeted at amateurs, *Le cinéma pratique chez soi*, marveled at the resources made available by the state and workplace organizations to Soviet collectives developing at factories, schools, and universities. Its September–October 1962 issue translated an essay by Iakov Tolchan

(1962), vice president of the Union of Filmmakers amateur section, and a well-known documentary cinematographer whose career had begun in the 1920s with Dziga Vertov's *Kino-Pravda*. The essay was followed in the same issue by a review of Soviet 8 mm and 16 mm film cameras. A year later, in its July–August 1963 issue, Michel Dery interviewed Grigorii Roshal´, founder of the amateur film section, under the rubric "Eux et nous" ("them and us"). In Britain, *Amateur Cine World* published an English translation of Dery's interview (Dery 1963b).

A few months after this, Geoffrey Levy of London's amateur film group Grasshopper[4] visited Moscow, and in 1964 narrated this experience in *Amateur Cine World*'s two-part "An Amateur in Moscow" (1964a, 1964b). Pleased to find connections between amateur film cultures in countries on opposing sides of the Cold War, Levy still marveled at the support from the state and professional industry accorded to film amateurs in the USSR. He concluded by describing his conversation with Grigorii Roshal´: "Finally, Mr. Rochal had one more question to ask. 'Tell me,' he said, 'What salaries are paid to Secretaries, and other official clubs?' [sic] I realised then that we still had quite a lot to learn about one another" (Levy 1964a, 141).

Soviet connections with British amateur film circles were established with the help of Nina Hibbin, critic at the British *Daily Worker*. Having visited the Moscow International Film Festival several times, she was aware of the development of amateur filmmaking in the Soviet Union. She wrote to festival director Mikhail Romm in 1963, asking him to help the Grasshopper Group establish connections with Soviet amateurs.[5] It is unclear whether Hibbin assisted with organizing Levy's visit to Moscow. It appears from Levy's account that his encounter with Soviet amateurs was a matter of coincidence. On his way to Moscow he met Sergei Komarov, a renowned professor at the national film school, VGIK, who traveled on the same boat. Komarov extended an invitation to visit the Union of Filmmakers, as well as VGIK.

In early 1964, the Union of Filmmakers and the Grasshopper Group exchanged programs of amateur films that were shown in several cities across both countries. Both sides selected movies that had proved themselves well at national and international contests. The British program included such "hits" as *Victoria's Rocking Horse* and *Watch the Birdie* (dir. Gill 1964). On the Soviet side, six films out of eight in this ninety-minute program were about nature and travel. Another, *Liudiam bol´shogo serdtsa* (*To People of Generous Heart*, ca.1961), made by the prominent amateur film studio

Iunost' ("Youth"), tells of a skin donation drive organized to save the life of a local boy severely burned in a fire. The drive was organized by Rem Iustinov, the studio's director, who filmed people who responded to his call and saved the boy's life through a collective effort. According to Hibbin, the program enjoyed strong attendance and huge success among the British spectators. Natal´ia Venzher, the secretary of the International Section of the Union of Filmmakers, responded that the British program was equally successful in Moscow, Leningrad, Riga, Tashkent, and Tbilisi.[6] As Levy had reported at his presentation of British amateur films in Moscow, "The Russians all laughed in the right places, so I heaved a sigh of relief" (1964a, 141).

The Most Universally Appealing Film Any Amateur Should Hope to Make

International success of *A Gift to Mother* also occurred at the time of active development of the experimental film scene that defined itself in opposition to industrially produced theatrical cinema, in particular, in the United States. Film historian Jan-Christopher Horak (2002) has argued that there had been no principal difference between amateur and experimental filmmaking in the 1930s, when both formed what he called "the first American avant-garde." Toward the late 1950s, however, these two types of nonindustrial filmmaking were developing on increasingly diverging trajectories. In his 1966 article "What Is an Amateur Film?" Tony Rose addressed the common frustration among amateurs that many of their peers were employed in fields understood today as "creative industries." These included "technical employees of the film and industries, ranging from directors down to clapper boys," as well as professional writers "including journalists, authors and advertising copywriters, alongside any other professionals that could have unfair advantage as amateur filmmakers, including professional still photographers, commercial artists, art teachers, actors, cinema projectionists etc." Occupational skills gained through these professions, Rose speculated, were viewed as privileging participants in film contests. Rose pointed out that such a "list of banned occupations" had not yet been created, but he summarized the popular sensibilities that tended to separate the average amateur from more advanced peers (1966, 587). While voices within the amateur communities called for a more egalitarian film culture, the trend developing within avant-garde cinema after the 1950s, as Horak has observed, was toward a self-definition "exclusively in terms of personal expression." Ironically, Horak (2002, 19) argued, "their self-conscious declarations about their roles as film artists indicated a romanticized professionalization of the avant-garde project." For those who stood by filmmaking in the amateur mode, avant-garde, then, came to be perceived as another cohort of professionals to steer away from.

Conversely, Patricia Zimmermann (1995) observes the trend of appropriation of the home-movie style by the American film avant-garde since the 1950s. The home-movie style "does not conform to prescriptive formats: subjects interact with the camera as friends and openly pose, the camera firehoses, and scenes from daily life unroll unedited or in no particular narrative sequence" (146). Anthropologist Richard Chalfen (1987) earlier observed that in guidebooks for amateurs, "there are big differences between *filmmaking* and *moviemaking*, and the former, being vastly superior to the latter, should provide the proper model for all motion picturemaking" (68). Thus, avant-garde appropriation of the home-movie style, as described by Zimmermann, fully embraces *moviemaking*, adopting and legitimating it as a method of *filmmaking*. The latter remains within the boundaries of quality and cultural legitimacy that filmmaker and scholar Duncan Reekie (2007), in his study of underground filmmaking in the United Kingdom, described as an effect of the development of the art market and the ensuing commodification of artistic production. It is this commodification that many amateurs resented. Tony Rose (1966, 587), echoing Maya Deren's (1965) earlier definition, stated that "an amateur film is one made for love and not for profit." At the same time, other voices within the community stressed the impossibility of drawing a neat boundary between the amateur and professional. Thus, John Balmforth, in "The Case for the Amateur Pro," published in *Amateur Cine World* in April 1966, argued "the amateur film movement cannot achieve real stature or wide public acceptance until it has regular audiences through a *Little Cinema* circuit and until it has economic viability." A robust amateur film movement, according to Balmforth, necessitated "something approaching an amateur film *industry* to back it up" (1966, 526–27). Originally from Australia, he was a professional architect and advanced film amateur who occasionally created films for television on a freelance basis. A part of the reason he defended the "amateur pro" was the lack of time that made creating films in the purely amateur mode inaccessible to an average working person burdened with professional and family responsibilities. Interestingly, Balmforth employed the term *amateur film worker*, stressing labor, rather than leisure, as a defining component in amateur creativity.

The Soviet system of amateur studios after the late 1950s came close to the amateur film industry that Balmforth argued for, although in the USSR amateur films, as elsewhere, rarely reached audiences outside of amateur contests. Movshin's *A Gift to Mother* represented a borderline case that blended nonprofessional film work and drew on skills and resources generally unavailable to an average *moviemaker*, to use Chalfen's definition. Movshin's professional occupation, theater photographer, was on Rose's imaginary list of banned occupations. Additionally, a major role in the film was played by Vera Vel´iaminova, an acclaimed actress at Pushkin (now Aleksandrinskii) Theatre in Leningrad where Movshin was employed during the 1960s. Nor was this film "a simple record of home life," as Rose (1964a, 753) had put it but, rather, a skilled and candid imitation of it.

A *Gift to Mother* is a silent comedy telling a story of two boys baking a cake, in their mother's absence, to surprise her for International Women's Day, celebrated in the Soviet Union as an equivalent of Mother's Day. Their good intentions, together with a complete inability to demystify cake making, bring disastrous results, obvious in the expression of their little sister's face as she samples it, spits it out, and cries. Their mother, having returned home late at night, understands what has happened and secretly bakes a new cake, disguising it as her children's creation. The final scene shows the family at the table happily eating the cake, to the surprise of the boys and their sister at the miraculous transformation of their baking disaster.

In British amateur film circles, David Movshin was often called "the Frank Marshall of Moscow." Frank Marshall (1896–1979) was a successful and prolific Scottish film amateur known for his family films. As Ryan Shand (2015, 2) explains, family films became a distinct genre in Britain, "a category featuring family members, close friends, and/or pets, which tend to be shot either at the filmmaker's home, in his or her garden, or on vacation. . . . Marshall's family films, in particular, expand moments captured in private cine recordings into planned linear comic narratives." While Rose (1964b) initially understood that in *A Gift to Mother* Movshin used family members as actors, his interpretation of it as a family film caused a polemic in later issues of *Amateur Cine World*. As Ivan Watson (1966), its veteran contributor, expressed it, "I hope that nobody will say to me: 'This is the kind of family-film *anyone* could have made.' The answer is—"Yes, provided anyone could find two good-looking boys who are born actors, a little girl ditto, and a broad-beamed Mum who can portray mother-love without seeming mawkish."

Fig. 16.1. A frame from *A Gift to Mother*: the boys perplexed by baking. Courtesy of Chicago Film Archives (Nancy Watrous). Viewable online at www.chicagofilmarchives.org. Film Identifier: F.2005-01-0157.

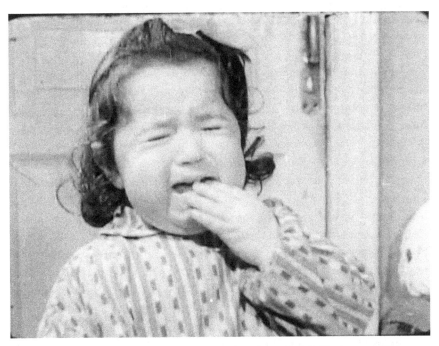

Fig. 16.2. A frame from *A Gift to Mother*: Testing the cake on the boys' little sister did not go well. Courtesy of Chicago Film Archives (Nancy Watrous).

Fig. 16.3. A frame from *A Gift to Mother*: Happy parents sampling the cake secretly remade by mother overnight. Mother played by Vera Vel´iaminova of Pushkin (now Aleksandrinskii) Theatre. Courtesy of Chicago Film Archives (Nancy Watrous).

In addition to being praised as a skillfully made film despite its seeming simplicity, *A Gift to Mother* appealed to its British audience by countering stereotypes about the stern attitudes of Russian people, showing a more humane face of the nation perceived as a Cold War threat. In the Soviet Union itself, embracing the family-film genre during the Thaw was a significant change. Thus, a 1927 circular letter in the archival collection of the Society of Friends of Soviet Cinema (Obshchestvo druzei sovetskogo kino—ODSK), the organization that took earlier efforts to develop amateur filmmaking between 1926 and 1932, called "filming one's immediate circle, relatives, piquant scenes and the like . . . [a] waste of film stock [that] should be completely excluded in our conditions."[7] By contrast, discussions within the Union of Filmmakers and its monthly journal *Iskusstvo kino* ("Film Art") in the late 1950s and 1960s abound with praise for films documenting family history. At a meeting of the Union of Filmmakers' amateur film section in December 1957, one amateur, Kurakin, among several examples that he used to argue for the benefits of using motion picture cameras in daily life, mentioned a personal story: "I have two daughters, and one of them is already fourteen. When I look at the screen, the daughter grows up in front of my eyes."[8] Explaining this rewarding personal experience, Kurakin alludes to this story's place within the broader national historiography. At the beginning of the 1964 documentary film *Ia—kinoliubitel'!* (*I Am a Film Amateur*) made at the professional Tsentrnauchfil'm studio, the voice-over states: "One's first baby steps are also one's first steps in amateur filmmaking." The film then presents a trajectory of development of these pursuits: having experimented with recording baby's first steps, our filmmaker soon finds himself filming his wife. This marks a transition to a new stage: while recording a newborn aims to create a visual account of its rapid growth as a "work in progress," turning to the wife represents a focus on an object that is more or less fully formed, and filming her is not to document her transformations but to appreciate her beauty. While switching from filming one's baby to filming one's wife represents, in this film, a shift of interest from creating a chronicle of events to embracing more aesthetic subjects, participation in a camera club would then mark a transition to a further stage: creating works that would appeal to an audience outside of the family. As the book also titled *I Am a Film Amateur* humorously put it, "A member of an amateur film club [is] an organized, purposeful film amateur, as opposed to a savage, unsociable one who wastes film stock for unknown reasons" (Guliakovskii et al. 1969, 179).

Enthusiasm about films on personal, family topics evolved against the backdrop of significant changes in lifestyle at the time. Khrushchev's promises of "good life" under socialism were connected with greater availability of consumer goods, while the housing program that his government developed at the same time enabled increasing numbers of Soviet families to move to separate apartments, further stimulating consumption and creating greater opportunities for pursuing hobbies, such as amateur filmmaking and other arts (Gorsuch 2011). As the Union of Filmmakers mobilized efforts to launch domestic production of small-gauge equipment, it was understood that amateur cameras and projectors would be developed along the lines of consumer goods, frequently on the margins of the military industrial complex and separately from professional equipment. Unlike in the earlier ODSK vision of the 1920s, filming one's immediate circle and relatives was no longer viewed as a "waste of film stock."

Within the Soviet mediascape of the Thaw period, increasing interest in amateur filmmaking accompanied interest in diverse uses of the short film: educational, popular science, industrial, advertising, as well as films for television. The 1960s were also a period of debate among Soviet archivists advocating the preservation of a greater range of audiovisual materials (Magidov 2005, 9),[9] and the latter should be understood within the broader interest in novel approaches to historiography that characterized the period.[10] Telecasts of amateur films became increasingly common in the 1960s. Central state television opened a department for amateur films in 1961. By 1965, the department reported it had produced 161 episodes dedicated to amateur cinema.[11] *Pravda* TV listings throughout the 1960s confirm that programs featuring amateur films were broadcast frequently, although rarely at a regular time. Local television stations cooperated with amateurs even more actively. Jaak Järvine (2005, 38), a veteran of the amateur film movement in Estonia, mentions that in the Ukrainian city of Donetsk the local station maintained connections with a network of amateur film reporters from nine cities. In 1965, Grigorii Roshal´ criticized the absence in Moscow of facilities for broadcasting films shot on 8 mm, which he called ridiculous, since such screenings were a norm in other cities, including Magadan, Riazan´, and Vladivostok.[12]

Within the range of subjects encouraged in amateur filmmaking, the family topic was recurrent not only in subject matter but also as metaphor. In 1965, Irina Malets, the editor of programs dedicated to amateur films on Soviet Union Central Television, summarized the results of the first years of organized efforts to develop amateur filmmaking:

> Twelve years ago [*sic*][13] the Union of Filmmakers gave birth to a new child, amateur cinema. Their films [at the time] were such that it was hard to tell a grandmother from a grandfather. Right now comes amateur cinema's age of adolescence with its searches, discoveries and whirlwinds, joys and sorrows. The child has grown up, it needs pocket money. The youth is going through such a difficult period, it needs parental attention, guidance and direction. Someone said here that VCSPS [All-Union Central Council of Trade Unions] is its father. The Union [of Filmmakers] is then its mother, she gave birth. But we can't say that her functions are fulfilled at this point. I know how much filmmakers need creative assistance.[14]

This metaphor outlines the situation around amateur cinema in quite a precise way. Indeed, significant institutional involvement underlays its revival. The process was initiated by the Union of Filmmakers, which orchestrated measures to create a production base and to popularize amateur films as well as the practice of filmmaking. The All-Union Central Council of Trade Unions (Vsesoiuznyi tsentral'nyi sovet professional'nykh soiuzov; VCSPS) joined in the efforts soon after that, committing material support to film, much as it supported other amateur arts, and in this sense, it played the role of a dependable father. The latter is exemplified in oral accounts of cine amateurs active during the Soviet period, as I learned when interviewing participants. According to Boris Sergeev, head of People's Film Studio Stroi-Fil´m in Leningrad, the famous professional actor-director Rolan Bykov was frequently sent to represent Soviet amateurs at international festivals but treated them with disrespect, "forgetting" to give them their prizes.[15] At the same time, a participant in the amateur studio of Moscow Institute of Steel and Alloys (Moskovskii institut stali i splavov) claimed that Bykov heavily borrowed ideas from the studio's 1963 experimental film *Romashka* (*Daisy*) for his *Aibolit-66* (1966, Mosfil'm).[16] Reflecting their growing dissatisfaction with the paternalizing attitude of professionals, during the Perestroika period amateurs sought independence from the Union of Filmmakers, creating the Society of Friends of Cinema (Obshchestvo druzei kino) in 1988. This organization, however, was short-lived and dissolved two years later.[17]

It is evident that Movshin created *A Gift to Mother* in an environment significantly different from that in which Frank Marshall worked. A member of the Leningrad Amateur Film Club, a studio that had a special status as coordinating center for other collectives, he had access to advanced equipment and professional consultations. His connections enabled him to cast a well-known theater actress in his film. Rather than using a fictional story with the goal of engaging his family members into filmmaking, he turned *A Gift to Mother* into an experiment that explored the limits of amateur creativity.

Making the Whole World Kin

Growing enthusiasm within international amateur film circles about the possibility of establishing connections across the divide of the Iron Curtain laid a path for the success of *A Gift to Mother* abroad. Roshal´'s correspondence with international organizations showed his genuine pleasure in such interactions, using the most polite language and a warm tone. This is especially true in his exchanges with Anthony Collins, director of the Vancouver International Film Amateur Film Festival for and founder of Canada's amateur film federation.[18] The two met at the 1963 Union Internationale du

Cinéma Congress in Denmark and corresponded for a year. Collins was likewise affectionate in his communication. Sharing a penchant for writing long letters (Collins even more so than Roshal´), they sent greetings to each other's wives, and Collins, evidently a new father, signed his letters as "Papa."[19] Roshal´ was not an easy correspondent: he wrote his letters in Russian, and it took weeks for Collins to find a translator. Roshal´ was spared this issue, since his union's administrative staff typed and translated letters. At one point Collins had to conduct an extensive search for a Cyrillic typewriter—which he was able to find at the University of British Columbia—to send a letter to Roshal´ in Russian, hoping to expedite communication over a pressing issue related to organization of the 1964 Vancouver festival.[20]

Roshal´ triumphantly returned home from Vancouver with the first prize for Movshin's *A Gift to Mother*, as well as prizes won by other amateur films at festivals in Vancouver and Montreal. He wrote his report to the Union of Filmmakers in a more pragmatic tone. While he praised the Vancouver festival for being generally "progressive," he mentioned that it still had not avoided certain decadent elements "common in foreign cinematography [such as] complex psychological opuses, 'stream of life,' [and] mystic revelations." At the same time, the success of Soviet amateur films, argued Roshal´, made evident that it was necessary to pay serious attention to international contacts Soviet amateur cinema brought.[21] Evaluated in the context of Roshal´'s other statements, this appears as a combination of effort to present the cause of amateur filmmaking in the light of Soviet ideological priorities, to colleagues and political authorities, while also reflecting his sincere belief in the necessity of disseminating Soviet values abroad. Roshal´ was keen to use amateur cinema for this kind of cultural diplomacy and, at the same time, to utilize the rewards of being loyal to the regime in order to further advocate for Soviet amateur cinema at home.

One unexpected difficulty that arose upon the festival's conclusion was the delivery of the cash prize of 250 Canadian dollars to Movshin. While rewarding amateurs with cash prizes was deemed unacceptable by the Union of Filmmakers (valuable prizes were offered in the form of film equipment rather than cash), owning foreign currency was outright illegal for Soviet citizens. This issue is not mentioned directly, but there is an obvious tension in correspondence as Natal´ia Venzher, the secretary of the international film section at the union suggested in her letter to Collins that he could, perhaps, transfer the money in the care of Grigorii Roshal´ through Vneshtorgbank, the state bank that handled international transactions.[22] The solution was found as Movshin, in a letter addressed to Collins ("written in perfect English," to Collins's surprise), requested a 16 mm camera in lieu of cash, which Collins communicated with relief to Venzher. Collins found a creative solution, buying a used Swiss Bolex H16 camera in good condition, since "evidently Grigori Rochal [sic] did not pass on to him the news that a new one could not be bought for much less than double the sum!"[23]

This correspondence provides the only clue to the personality of David Movshin, the man whose movie produced a small sensation in the international amateur film world. So popular was A Gift to Mother among amateur cine enthusiasts that a few clubs, such as the Metropolitan Motion Picture Club in New York, chose to make copies of it for their film libraries.[24] The Canadian amateur film association requested a copy for television.[25] Movshin's film continued to circulate for a few years, as indicated in an enthusiastic 1967 letter from Sidney Moritz, the director of Metropolitan Motion Picture Club. He reported that at his club's screening, the applause for A Gift to Mother "lasted for 26 ½ seconds, exceeding by 10 seconds an American prize winning movie, the runner-up to A Gift to Mother."[26] Such circulation of copies ensured an afterlife for this film, and the fact that the only known print of it survives at Chicago Film Archives illustrates the extent of its travels.[27] There is no evidence, however, that Movshin's film enjoyed an equal degree of success at home, as it is barely mentioned in Soviet publications of the time. Two decades later, in his book Kinoliubiteli—kto oni? (Film Amateurs—Who Are They?), Iakov Tolchan (1982, 18–19) praised the film as one of the successes of Soviet amateur filmmaking but referring, for the most part, to its enthusiastic reception abroad.

While participation in international festivals and competitions was the most visible part of connections between the Soviet amateur film movement and its counterparts in other countries, the cultural mission was likely accompanied by commercial interests of the Soviet industry that manufactured small-gauge film equipment. Exports began around the mid-1960s. Amateur Cine World frequently published advertising and reviews of the Soviet equipment, such as the Ambassador and Quartz "M" cameras, as well as the Luch-2 projector that had a reputation of "predictably, very solid in construction, reasonably compact and inexpensive" (Amateur Cine World 1965). This assessment stood in sharp contrast to the experience of Soviet amateurs who often complained about the low quality of domestically produced equipment. However, the Soviet industry maintained a special category of goods of "export quality" that were much more competitive. A representative of the military industry Kravtsova stated in 1965 that 60 percent of amateur film cameras in the department she supervised were sold for export to over twenty countries, including the United Kingdom, France, and Italy. Apparently these imports influenced the way Soviet manufacturers arranged their product lines, which resulted in proliferation of models that differed in only minor details. While Soviet consumers often found this confusing, trade official Latyshev argued at a 1967 meeting with the Union of Filmmakers: "Don't forget that we are connected with the external market and should be competitive there. Japan produces 108 types, West Germany 106, and Americans over a hundred. So, we can't limit the number of cameras."[28] Thus, although Soviet socialist economy, in theory, excluded competition in the domestic market, it still had to compete in international markets and, apparently, mimicked some capitalist marketing strategies. The international successes of the Soviet amateur film movement, such as *A Gift to Mother*, while showcasing the achievements of socialist lifestyle abroad, also arguably helped to promote export goods to the niche market that catered to nonprofessional film enthusiasts.

Conclusion

The case of *A Gift to Mother* illustrates the scope of the international amateur film movement's ambitions to find social and political relevance for its pursuits. While political activism in filmmaking is more often associated with radical political groups, such cases also demonstrate the ways in which moderate, nonpolitical hobbyists sought to engage with important subjects of the day as they explored the boundaries of nonprofessional, nonindustrial modes. In the Soviet case of state-sponsored amateur film clubs, rapid development of this culture in the 1960s, stimulated by efforts of film professionals, provides evidence of the evolution of the notions of production and consumption of cultural products in the political economy of state socialism, as well as the aesthetic implications of this evolution. Provided with the basic means for production of films, what Soviet amateurs ultimately produced in this system was a certain socialist lifestyle that symbolized the success of Soviet socialism in creating opportunities for personal development for every citizen. This cultural production extended toward promoting 8 mm and 16 mm film cameras and projectors of "export quality" on both sides of the Iron Curtain. A study of the socioeconomic history of Soviet amateur filmmaking thus reveals the functioning of a creative industry that combined social production at home with economic activities abroad. Regardless of the differences in national cultures, organized amateur filmmakers searched for forms and styles that engaged with the limitations imposed by the amateur mode of production and created an identity that would transform negative notions of dilettantism into a creative method.

Notes

1. See, for instance, the discussion of overseas connections of the British amateur film movement in the 1930s in Nicholson 2012, 38–39.

2. Valerii Volkov, former director of Leningrad Amateur Film Club, interview with the author, June 2009.

3. Transcript, international meeting of film amateurs at VI World Festival of Youth and Students in Moscow, RGALI (Russian State Archive for Literature and Art), Fonds 2936 (Union of Filmmakers), Op. 1, Ed. hr. 2297, July 30, 1957.

4. More on the Grasshopper Group in Chalke 2009.

5. Letter from Nina Hibbin to Mikhail Romm, December 14, 1963, RGALI, F. 2936 (Union of Filmmakers), Op. 3, Ed. hr. 74, pp. 10–11.

6. Letter from Natal′ia Venzher to Nina Hibbin (n. d.), RGALI, F. 2936, Op. 3, Ed. hr. 90, March 3–October 18, 1965, p. 2.

7. Circular information letter no. 2, RGALI, F. 2495 (ODSK—Society of Friends of Soviet Cinema), Op. 1, Ed. hr. 2, 1927, p. 1.

8. Transcript, joint session on technology between the Union of Filmmakers and Moscow film amateurs, RGALI, F. 2936, Op. 1, Ed. hr. 1031, December 23, 1957, pp. 25–27.

9. Suggestions to develop an archival policy for films created by amateurs did not materialize.

10. Roger Marwick (2011) speaks of "reinvigoration of historiography in the post-Stalin era" (50), the emergence of revisionism in Soviet historical science (49–72), and an "upsurge of popular interest [in history] after the Twentieth Congress [of the Communist Party]" (67).

11. Transcript, Union of Filmmakers discussing the state of amateur filmmaking in the USSR, RGALI, F. 2936 (Union of Filmmakers), Op. 1, Ed. hr. 337, November 17, 1965, p. 78.

12. RGALI, F. 2936, Op. 1, Ed. hr. 337, p. 11.

13. This is likely a transcription error, because Malets is obviously referring to 1957.

14. RGALI, F. 2936, Op. 1, Ed. hr. 337, p. 78. Translation by the author.

15. Boris Sergeev, interview with the author, October 18, 2012.

16. Ivan Orekhov, interview with the author, September 29, 2015.

17. Jaak Järvine, interview with the author, November 12, 2012.

18. Correspondence between September 30, 1963, and July 27, 1964. RGALI, F. 2936, Op. 1, Ed. hr. 2332.

19. Collins, letter to Roshal′, September 30, 1964, RGALI, F. 2936, Op. 1, Ed. hr. 2332, pp. 5–6.

20. Collins, letter to Roshal′, November 24, 1963, RGALI, F. 2936, Op. 1, Ed. hr. 2332, pp. 12–13.

21. Grigorii Roshal´, report of the trip to Vancouver International Amateur Film Festival, RGALI, F. 2936, Op. 1, Ed. hr. 2332, pp. 74–76.

22. Natal´ia Venzher, letter to Anthony Collins, July 4, 1964, RGALI, F. 2936, Op. 1, Ed. hr. 2332, p. 66.

23. Collins, letter to Venzher, July 16, 1964, RGALI, F. 2936, Op. 1, Ed. hr. 2332, p. 69.

24. Correspondence with Metropolitan Motion Picture Club (New York), RGALI, F. 2936, Op. 3, Ed. hr. 95, April 17–December 11, 1965.

25. Russian translation of an undated letter from Collins to Roshal´, RGALI, F. 2936, Op. 4, Ed. hr. 1431, October 4, 1966, pp. 1–2.

26. Sidney Moritz, letter to Union of Filmmakers, January 7, 1967, RGALI, F. 2936, Op. 4, Ed. hr. 1753.

27. Charles Tepperman brought this fact to my awareness in 2014 when we both screened amateur films at the Museum of Modern Art. I had been looking for a copy of this film for two years but could not find it in Russia.

28. Transcript, meeting of the amateur film section discussing equipment, RGALI, F. 2936, Op. 1, Ed. hr. 1232, April 12, 1967, p. 25.

References

Amateur Cine World. 1965. "Russian Luch-2 Projector." 1965. April 1, 1965, 436.

Austin, A. W. 1964. "The Frank Marshall of Moscow." *Amateur Cine World*, May 28, 1964, 717.

Balmforth, John. 1966. "The Case for the Amateur Pro." *Amateur Cine World*, April 21, 1966, 526–27.

Chalfen, Richard. 1987. *Snapshot Versions of Life*. Bowling Green, OH: Bowling Green State University Popular Press.

Chalke, Sheila. 2009. "Animated Explorations: The Grasshopper Group, 1953–1983." In *Movies on Home Ground: Explorations in Amateur Cinema*, edited by Ian Craven, 238–69. Newcastle upon Tyne: Cambridge Scholars.

Deren, Maya. 1965. "Amateur versus Professional." *Film Culture* 39 (Winter): 45–46.

Dery, Michel. 1963a. "Rencontre avec le metteur en scène russe Grigori L. Rochal, Président de la Section des Cinéastes Amateurs du S.R.K." *Le cinema pratique chez soi*, July–August 1963, 154–56.

———. 1963b. "A Free 35mm. Cine Camera and Ten Roubles a Year." *Amateur Cine World*, August 22, 1963, 308–9.

Gilburd, Eleonory. 2012. "The Revival of Soviet Internationalism in the Early to Mid 1950s." In *The Thaw: Soviet Society and Culture during the 1950s and 1960s*, edited by Eleonory Gilburd and Denis Kozlov, 362–401. Toronto: University of Toronto Press.

Gill, Alan. 1964. "Russian Amateur Film Show." *Amateur Cine World*, May 14, 1964, 673.

Gorsuch, Anne. 2011. *All This Is Your World: Soviet Tourism at Home and Abroad after Stalin*. New York: Oxford University Press.

Guliakovskii, E., Iu. Krauze, S. Medynskii, and Ia. Segel´. 1969. *Ia-kinoliubitel´*. Moscow: Molodaia Gvardiia.

Horak, Jan-Christopher. 2002. "The First American Film Avant-Garde, 1920–1959." In *Experimental Cinema: The Film Reader*, edited by Wheeler Winston Dixon and Gwendolyn Audrey Foster, 19–52. London: Routledge.

Il'ichev, Sergei, and Boris Nashchekin. 1986. *Kinoliubitel'stvo: Istoki i perspektivy*. Moscow: Iskusstvo.

Järvine, Jaak. 2005. *Vzgliad v proshloe: Kratkaia istoriia razvitiia kinoliubitel'stva v byvshem SSSR i v stranakh Baltii*. Tallinn: OÜ Vali Press.

Levy, Geoffrey. 1964a. "An Amateur in Moscow." *Amateur Cine World*, January 30, 1964, 141.

———. 1964b. "An Amateur in Moscow: Part 2." *Amateur Cine World*, February 6, 1964, 179.

Magidov, Vladimir. 2005. *Kinofotofonodokumenty v kontekste istoricheskogo znaniia*. Moscow: RGGU.

Marwick, Roger. 2011. *Rewriting History in Soviet Russia: The Politics of Revisionist Historiography 1956–1974*. New York: Palgrave Macmillan.

Nicholson, Heather Norris. 2012. *Amateur Film: Meaning and Practice, 1927–1977*. Manchester, UK: Manchester University Press.

Reekie, Duncan. 2007. *Subversion: The Definitive History of Underground Cinema*. London: Wallflower.

Rose, Tony. 1964a. "Meet Mr. Movshin." *Amateur Cine World*, June 4, 1964, 753.

———. 1964b. "The Two M's." *Amateur Cine World*, July 9, 1964, 41.

———. 1966. "What Is an Amateur Film?" *Amateur Cine World*, May 5, 1966, 587.

Shand, Ryan. 2015. "The 'Family Film' as Amateur Production Genre." *The Moving Image* 15, no. 2 (Fall): 1–27.

Tolchan, Iakov [transliterated Yakov Toltchan]. 1962. "L'essor de l'amateurisme en Union Soviétique." *Le cinema pratique chez soi*, September–October 1962, 205–207.

———. 1982. *Kinoliubiteli—kto oni?* Moscow: Sovetskaia Rossiia.

Watson, Ivan. 1966. "From Russia—With Laughter." *Amateur Cine World*, April 7, 1966, 455–56.

Zimmermann, Patricia R. 1995. *Reel Families: A Social History of Amateur Film*. Bloomington: Indiana University Press.

MARIA VINOGRADOVA is a film and media historian.

17

POSTCARDS FROM *YIDDISHLAND*

Amateur Filmmaking and Vernacular Yiddish Culture

Rachel Webb Jekanowski

THE FEW CANONICAL HISTORIES OF YIDDISH-LANGUAGE FILMMAKING—
Judith Goldberg's *Laughter through Tears: The Yiddish Cinema* (1983),
Eric Goldman's *Visions, Images, and Dreams: Yiddish Film Past and Present*
(1983), and J. Hoberman's *Bridge of Light: Yiddish Film between Two Worlds*
(1991)—have tended to focus on the emergence and abrupt termination of
commercial, studio-based Yiddish films.[1] Pictures like *East and West* (dirs.
Sidney M. Goldin and Ivan Abramson, 1923), *Jewish Luck* (dir. Alexander
Granovsky, 1925), *The Dybbuk* (dir. Michal Waszynski, 1937), *Green Fields*
(dirs. Edgar G. Ulmer and Jacob Ben-Ami, 1937), *Mamele* (dirs. Joseph Green
and Konrad Tom, 1938), and *A Letter to Mother* (dirs. Joseph Green and
Leon Trystand, 1939) were produced by Jews for Jewish audiences in urban
centers across Poland, Russia (and later, the Soviet Union), Austria, Germany, and the United States. Featuring Yiddish-language dialogue, musical numbers, and creative talent from Yiddish theater and literary circles,
these films conjure an imaginary world, where daily life is lived entirely,
effusively in Yiddish, by Jews and *goyim* (non-Jews) alike. According to
J. Hoberman (1991, 5–7), this minor cinema emerged between 1911 and the
early 1940s, coinciding with the emergence of cinema as a mass medium,
and peaked between 1935 and World War II, which Hoberman dubs the
"Golden Age" of Yiddish filmmaking. Although the exact numbers are elu-
sive, film scholars estimate that approximately 130 feature-length Yiddish

pictures were produced in Europe and the United States by commercial studios between 1910 and 1950 (Goldberg 1983, 11). As a form of popular cinema that appealed to predominately Jewish audiences through the use of a shared, vernacular spoken language, Yiddish-narrative films served to negotiate tensions around Ashkenazi Jewish migration and assimilation, changes to traditional *shtetl* (village) life wrought by modernity, Jewish national aspirations, religious practice, and secularism. In other words, Yiddish-language films constitute "not just a national cinema without a nation-state, but a national cinema that, with every presentation, created its own ephemeral nation-state" (Hoberman 1991, 5): a transnational *Yiddishland.*[2]

Emerging in parallel with this commercial filmmaking practice was a host of nonprofessional, nonstudio-based productions that have been largely overlooked in Yiddish cinema scholarship, which I will refer to here as amateur Yiddish films. Such amateur pictures (including travelogues, home movies, and short actuality pictures recording everyday street life) were shot by nonprofessional filmmakers for personal and noncommercial purposes, usually on small-gauge film stock, for limited exhibition within community and labor organizations, educational institutions, and family homes. They often recorded domestic scenes, captured historical events or family milestones like weddings or organized political marches, and documented middle-class lifestyles and leisure activities. Like the more well-known studio pictures, these interwar and pre-Holocaust amateur productions also responded to specific experiences of Eastern European and North American Jews, albeit in divergent ways.

As a marginal film practice within an already minor cinema, amateur Yiddish filmmaking raises provocative questions about vernacular cultural forms and the place of nonprofessional, noncommercial, and domestic filmmaking practices within national and linguistic cinemas. In this chapter, I examine a small archival collection of amateur Yiddish films held at the YIVO Institute for Jewish Research in New York City, a number of which were featured in a public exhibition, "16 mm Postcards: Home Movies of American Jewish Visitors to 1930s Poland," in 2010–2011, and eighty of which remain accessible online through the New York-based Center for Jewish History's digital collection.[3]

In the analysis that follows, the term *vernacular* will function along several registers. Within Yiddish studies, scholars including Jeffrey Shandler, Cecile Kuznitz, and Rebecca Margolis designate Yiddish as a Jewish vernacular language: a spoken language used for quotidian domestic, professional, and creative purposes, which helped bind together dispersed, transnational Jewish communities through shared cultural practices and communication.[4] Similarly, Yiddish culture (*Yiddishkeit*) has also been described as a vernacular form, in that it includes popular forms of expression and production that emerged "from the people" in dialogue with religious, educational, and cultural institutions. Following Miriam B. Hansen's (2009) theorization of vernacular modernism, I examine this collection of Yiddish amateur films as a form of vernacular Yiddishkeit, which document middle class American Jewish experiences and ambivalently mediate modernity's impacts on interwar Yiddish-speaking communities in Eastern Europe. Given the global decline of Yiddishkeit and Yiddish as a spoken vernacular language in the mid-twentieth century, Jeffrey Shandler (2006, 57) argues that Yiddish also acquired a "postvernacular" status over the last four decades, becoming invested with "new symbolic significance even as its primary semiotic value as a vernacular is in decline."

By tracing the negotiations between modernity, traditional Ashkenazi Jewish culture, and popular filmmaking practices that the creation of these amateur films represent, this chapter addresses two questions: How might amateur films mediate tensions between modernity and vernacular Yiddish cultures? Furthermore, how has the Center for Jewish History's digitized collection of amateur films been presented as examples of postvernacular Yiddish culture through their public exhibition? I argue that these films offer two related but distinct examples of how amateur cinema had been used to communicate American Jewish and Polish Jewish vernacular cultures, and what Laura Rascaroli, Gwenda Young, and Barry Monahan (2014, 3) term histories of everyday life "from below." I conclude this chapter by examining how this collection of films have been discursively positioned today as examples of postvernacular Yiddish culture through their preservation and public exhibition, both online and through the curated, site-specific exhibition "16 mm Postcards."[5] By revisiting these cinematic fragments of prewar Yiddishland, this chapter seeks to contribute to theorizations of the vernacular in amateur film studies and the roles of archival institutions in shaping postvernacular culture.

While most of the amateur Yiddish films in YIVO's film and video archive are silent (and thus do not feature any spoken Yiddish), their content offers strong parallels to the themes Hoberman (1991, 5) identifies in commercial silent and sound Yiddish filmmaking, namely: Eastern European Jewish immigrant experiences, negotiations of Jewish assimilation and cultural preservation, and tensions between "old world" traditions and modernity. These amateur texts therefore resonate as *yidish* in the duel meaning of the word: as encompassing the Jewish (yidish) people as well as the Yiddish language (5). A more sustained engagement with amateur and nonprofessional filmmaking as a distinct practice running parallel to commercial Yiddish film production, circulation, and exhibition histories can offer a valuable contribution to preexisting scholarly accounts of vernacular Jewish life onscreen, while teasing out some of the complexities around the vernacular, loss, and modernity within contemporary excavations of minor film cultures.

History from "Below" and the Promises of Modernity

The YIVO Institute for Jewish Research, located a block west of Union Square Park in Manhattan, houses one of the most prominent archival collections of Yiddish audiovisual materials in the world, including rare 16 mm and 8 mm amateur films (mostly home movies and travelogues), newsreels, and industrial films from the 1940s to the 1960s, many of which sought to promote Jewish international aid work for displaced Jewish communities (YIVO Institute for Jewish Research, 2020). Within YIVO's collection, the seventy-five "home movies" recorded by American Jews on their travels to Eastern Europe and Palestine during the 1920s and 1930s are among the most frequently accessed and consulted (YIVO Institute for Jewish Research, 2020). Shot by American Jews wealthy enough to travel abroad and purchase consumer technologies like handheld cameras, these silent films depict an array of domestic scenes, posed family portraits (often juxtaposed against monuments or iconic buildings), and street scenes within predominantly Jewish neighborhoods in Poland and Lithuania—including those in Krakow, Lodz, Warsaw, and Vilnius. Tourists and travelers also recorded footage in global cities like Berlin, New York City, and Paris, as well as picturesque views of the German and Polish countryside and Palestine under British Mandate. Joseph Waldman's (1936) amateur film, succinctly titled *A Trip to Poland and Palestine*, shot during his travels through Europe and Palestine in 1936, includes a fragmented array of images: planes departing from a modernist airport, a middle-class family waving and posing gleefully for the camera outside, a family visit to a planetarium, brief color footage of a garden, and a joyous wedding in a secular, well-to-do suburb of New York (fig. 17.1). For many contemporary

Fig. 17.1. An unidentified family, posing for Joseph Waldman's camera in *A Trip to Poland and Palestine*. Courtesy of the YIVO Institute for Jewish Research archives.

viewers, the scenes of shtetl life from Eastern European cities like Warsaw and Boryslaw will be particularly striking, offering a rare (if at points voyeuristic) glimpse of everyday life within Jewish communities prior to their annihilation under Nazism.[6]

It is from this collection that the twenty-six amateur films included in "16 mm Postcards" were drawn for public exhibition by Yeshiva University Museum in New York City, held from August 2010 to January 2011, in collaboration with YIVO and the Center for Jewish History. Following the exhibit, transfers of the films remain accessible to the public through the Center for Jewish History's digital collections and the YIVO Digital Archive on Jewish Life in Poland, digitized with the support of the Righteous Persons Foundation and the Steven Spielberg Foundation.[7] As products of the intersection of middle-class American culture, mass-produced consumer technologies, modern notions of travel as leisure, and the history of Eastern European Jewish immigration to the United States, these amateur films offer important historical glimpses into the lives of both the filmmakers and their subjects.

Amateur film scholarship repeatedly affirms associations between the nonprofessional production modes of amateur filmmaking and the ability of these films to accurately capture the historical experiences of everyday people. In their introduction to a special issue of *Film History* on amateur cinema, Melinda Stone and Dan Streible (2003, 123) link amateur filmmaking practice with expressions of folk culture, describing it as a "democratic folk art" rooted in a "love for the medium" and creative communities, independent of state institutions or industry. Home movies, travel films, and other nonprofessional film practices offer "valuable documents of people, places and eras" because of their seemingly intimate perspective into people's everyday lives "at a grassroots level" (123). Laura Rascaroli, Gwenda Young, and Barry Monahan (2014, 3) similarly associate amateur films with their value as historical documents, capturing potentially fleeting, intimate moments of ordinary life that might otherwise be overlooked or excluded from mainstream histories. As quotidian cultural documents, amateur films therefore offer both an affective experience of glimpsing past lives and a trove of historical detail from which researchers may excavate "historical accounts from below." For Patricia Zimmermann (1995, ix), home movies, as a prominent subsection of twentieth-century nonprofessional filmmaking, offer a particular lens into "the unstable intersection of family history, state iconography and consumer technology," as portable film technologies mediated representations and discourses about middle-class life and domestic space. While much of amateur filmmaking falls outside the conventional boundaries of nonfiction, it is the very nonprofessional qualities of such images—and their production within domestic, mundane, or marginal spaces—that hold such power over the real for contemporary viewers.

Although the films from YIVO's collection mostly conform to the aesthetics of the home movie and travelogue, these texts cannot be reduced to expressions of middle-class leisure, celebrations of the cinematic medium, or an uncomplicated Yiddish "folk" culture. The majority of these pictures were shot by well-to-do Jewish emigrés with the expectation that they would be shared with friends and family back in the United States, recording jubilant family reunions and international travels, as well as the worsening conditions of life for their friends, colleagues, and relations in Europe. In this sense, writes Roberta Newman (1993, 24) in an article about Jewish home movies during the interwar period, these films functioned as "artifacts of the Jewish communal ritual of returning home to Eastern Europe" during their moment of production and often continue to be understood within this context by contemporary viewers. Experiences of persecution and emigration shape these filmmaking practices as much as increased access to modern consumer technologies, popular trends in travel photography, and mass culture (24). The historical and archival value of YIVO's collection therefore rests not exclusively within the content or amateurish quality of the images themselves but the fraught contexts of their production during Adolf Hitler's rise to power. In documenting everyday street scenes and American Jewish experiences of comfortable travel alongside rising anti-Semitic persecution and the impacts of modernity on traditional shtetl life in Europe, these films hold juxtaposing histories of one of the twentieth-century's most notorious genocides from above *and* from below. In other words, amateur Yiddish films *do* capture intimate moments of people's lives but within the context of an extensively documented historical event. This problematizes film scholars' affiliation of amateur cinema with "histories from below," even as contemporary curatorial exhibitions of these films— such as the "16 mm Postcards" collection—claimed the archival value of these images in their documentation of vernacular life, as I argue in the next section of this chapter.

At the same time, American Jewish filmmakers' ability to afford these portable consumer technologies and leisure activities also speaks to their negotiations of modernity. Miriam Hansen (2009, 253), in her renowned study of mid-twentieth-century Hollywood cinema, argues that the "juncture of classical cinema and modernity reminds us . . . that the cinema was not only part and symptom of modernity's experience and perception of crisis and upheaval; it was also . . . the single most inclusive cultural horizon in which the traumatic effects of modernity were reflected, rejected or disavowed, transmuted or negotiated." For these travelers, amateur filmmaking offered a means of engaging with the promises as well as the "constitutive ambivalence" of modernity (255). As Hansen observes, the "spread of urban industrial technology, the large-scale disembedding of social (and gender) relations, and the shift to mass consumption entailed processes of real destruction and loss" (243). For interwar amateur Jewish filmmakers, this destruction and loss had particular, as well as more universal, resonances: the loss of traditional Yiddish cultural practices due to immigration, assimilation, and political persecution registered through an attention to documenting "old world" Jewish life as well as the prosperity of American experiences of modernity. In this sense, these amateur films echo Hansen's investment in the term *vernacular* over "the ideologically overdetermined term 'popular'" in her theorization of Hollywood cinema as an expression of modernism, given that these films similarly invoke a "dimension of the quotidian, of everyday usage" in their depictions of American and European Yiddish cultural experiences, along with a heavy dose of ambivalence (243).

Despite the specificity of these texts as products of American modernity, Eastern European immigration, and Yiddish culture, the identities of those passing or posing before the cameras—and the identities of many of the filmmakers themselves—remain largely unknown. Of the twenty-six films included in the "16 mm Postcards" exhibition, the provenance of twenty is recorded. (The creators of the others are unknown.) New York-based Jewish travel agent and journalist Gustave Eisner, for instance, produced a collection of 16 mm travel films between the 1920s and mid-1930s depicting cities as varied as Lodz, Warsaw, and Orzorków in Poland; Leningrad (today, St. Petersburg) and Moscow in Russia; and Berlin, Germany. Eisner immigrated to the United States in 1920 from Poland and maintained family, professional, and political ties to Jewish communities in Europe through his travel agency, which organized trips to his birth country and Palestine during the interwar period (Soyer 1993, 347). Five of Eisner's films were included in the original exhibit, most of which depict bustling urban street scenes, waving tourists, and views of the European countryside.

In contrast, Paysakh Zuckerman's half-hour documentary, depicting views of Kolbuszowa and other areas of Poland, is more in keeping with Charles Tepperman's (2015, 7–8) definition of amateur cinema as a noncommercial practice produced and circulated within nontheatrical networks. For Tepperman, the amateur participates in "a film culture outside the commercial mainstream" and exhibits relative skill and aesthetic investment in the craft (9). Commissioned in 1929 by the Kolbuszower Relief Association, an American *landsmanshaft* (a Jewish mutual aid society), *A Pictorial Review of Kolbishev* was exhibited the following year in New York at a charity fundraiser (Center for Jewish History 2010c). Ranging from busy market street scenes featuring Jewish schools and synagogues (fig. 17.2) to tightly framed portraits of smiling, well-to-do residents (fig. 17.3), the film unapologetically appeals to Jewish immigrants' feelings of pride and nostalgia for their Polish hometowns. Zuckerman does not demonstrate a profound investment in cinema's formal or aesthetic potential, however. Instead, the composition of the footage reflects the association's political commitment to Ashkenazi communities back home and early twentieth-century progressive beliefs in social uplift.

Fig. 17.2 and 17.3. Documenting Jewish Kolbuszowa across social class and religious practice in *A Pictorial Review of Kolbishev*. Courtesy of the YIVO Institute for Jewish Research archives.

The anonymity of many of the places, faces, and family relations across this corpus does little to detract from their visual power or from their positioning as visual evidence of another era. The significance of amateur films as historical traces of vernacular Jewish life and Yiddish world-building, particularly at the cultural level rather than the scale of the individual artist or skilled practitioner, assumes prominence in many of the contemporary discourses surrounding their public presentation and exhibition. Here, the consolidation of Yiddish memory and culture through cinema operates through people's belief in cinema's ability to register the everyday, combined with a working through of specific cultural concerns about assimilation, migration, racialized violence, secularism of modern life, and social mobility. In the exhibition's presentation of these artifacts, the nonprofessional aesthetics and production quality of these Yiddish films is leveraged as the means by which these films could accurately represent vanished Jewish life, in effect collapsing the amateur into the vernacular.

Postvernacular Film Archiving and Amateur Cinema as Vernacular Yiddish Culture

Negotiations of the vernacular, and vernacular cultural practices, are a key theme in contemporary studies of Yiddish language and culture. In her historical survey of the development of Yiddish studies as a discipline, Cecile E. Kuznitz (2002, 542) observes how late nineteenth- and early twentieth-century Jewish nationalists leveraged Yiddish as a vernacular language for European Jewish communities. In contrast to Zionists who "sought to revive Hebrew as a spoken tongue, most Diaspora Nationalists rallied around Yiddish as the vehicle of a modern, secular culture that could sustain Jewish life in the absence of a territorial base" (542). It was out of these debates around spoken language and their links to culture and national identity that Yiddish became associated with Jewish mass political movements in Europe and North America and notions of the *folk* or "common people" (542). As a *folksprackh*, the Yiddish term for a vernacular language (literally, "the people's language"), the use of Yiddish was often politically charged with nationalist overtones, particularly within countries with hostile anti-Semitic governments (Shandler 2006, 13). Ethnographic expeditions to Eastern European shtetls in the early twentieth century also invested the language with affective and ideological value, as folklorists and intellectuals sought to record traditional Jewish folk culture—from songs, to stories, and pictures—threatened by modernization and emigration.[8]

Following the steep decline of Yiddish culture and vernacular language worldwide between the 1930s and 1960s due to the Holocaust, Stalinist purges of Jewish intellectuals, and cultural assimilation in the Americas, this emphasis on vernacular manifestations of Yiddish language and culture shifted to a theorization of what Shandler terms the postvernacular.[9] According to Shandler (2006, 4), Yiddish acquired a symbolic and affective register outweighing its communicative value as a consequence of these historical events and shifting patterns of Yiddish language fluency. This rupture with prewar Yiddish and Yiddishkeit also reveals an important change in the formation and identities of the communities that develop around these cultural practices.[10] The concept of the postvernacular, Rebecca Margolis (2016, 4–5) asserts, offers a framework for "understanding post-Holocaust manifestations of Yiddish where a majority of both its producers and consumers employ fragments of the language to express aspects of their identity."

This transition from a vernacular cultural practice to a postvernacular one is significant because it has ramifications for the ways in which contemporary audiences and scholars affectively view, understand, and assess the historical importance of Yiddish-language films. Contemporary film audiences, for instance, might cultivate primarily affective or ideological relationships with the language on screen separate from Yiddish's instrumental value as a vehicle for everyday communication. Yiddish's postvernacular quality and the annihilation of the vibrant world of prewar Yiddish cultural production have had an impact on postwar scholarly and popular discourses surrounding commercial Yiddish filmmaking. Words evoking trauma, loss, memory, and the ephemeral, for instance, are frequently deployed in canonical histories. Judith Goldberg (1983, 24) prefaces her study of global Yiddish cinema by reminding her readers that Yiddish films were "dead" and nearly "forgotten" until recent years, making these texts into "records of a different time." Hoberman (1991, 11) similarly characterizes Yiddish cinema as "the representation of loss" of the old world, making these films "inherently unstable" cultural productions.

Such discourses of loss, in parallel with disciplinary engagements with the vernacular within Yiddish studies, seep into some of the curatorial decisions made by YIVO, the Yeshiva University Museum, and the Center for Jewish History in the presentation of "16 mm Postcards: Home Movies of

American Jewish Visitors to 1930s Poland." These amateur films, because of their nonprofessional nature and less polished formal qualities (including handheld shots, sparse edits that do not conform to commercial or art-house aesthetic standards, and directorial emphasis on recording real world events and excursions as they unfolded in front of the camera), offer the perception of an unfiltered glimpse into the past. In the introduction to the exhibition's website (the only element of the exhibit that remained publicly available after its conclusion), the films are couched in ethnographic terms of encounter and travel. These documentary records "invite" viewers to accompany the amateur filmmakers on their travels "to the sometimes familiar yet foreign landscape of vanished places in a vanished culture." As records of "journeys to the *Alte Heym,* the old homeland," the exhibition description continues, these films "offer a sensation of everyday life among Jews in 1930s Poland" (Center for Jewish History 2010a).

However, the snapshots of quotidian existence amassed in this collection offer a far from homogenous depiction of Jewish experience during this pivotal period. While many of the amateur films in "16 mm Postcards" foreground imagery of urban settings, several pictures seemingly celebrate the unexpected contrasts that arise within experiences of modernity, and between city and countryside, with a few quick edits. Gustav Eisner's seven-minute short, *Köln, Wiesbaden and Berlin* (recorded between 1929 and 1933), for instance, includes dreamy shots of the Rhine River Valley, complete with castle ruins, well-tended forests, and children playing atop wagons piled high with hay in pastoral fields. Rather than document the "everyday lives" of assimilated German Jews or the severe poverty in some Jewish neighborhoods as the exhibition's description suggests, Eisner focuses instead on a bucolic holiday, undertaken within several prominent areas of Germany. His leisurely views of the Rhine by boat, interspersed with images of the forest, abruptly cuts to a constellation of urban street scenes. Vertical pans of majestic stone façades are juxtaposed with blurry, handheld images of a city street taken by trolley car and a wide shot of the Brandenburg Gate (fig. 17.4). Through his brief montage, Eisner encapsulates experiences of modernity in two ways: through the bourgeois tourists he captures on their travels and through the pronounced contrast in transportation infrastructures, architecture, and technologies between rural Germany and modernist quarters of Berlin.

At the same time, as artifacts of twentieth-century modernity and Jewish history, the very title of the exhibition cements a pictorial and semiotic

Fig. 17.4. Brandenburg Gate, on the eve of World War II in *Köln, Wiesbaden and Berlin*. Courtesy of the YIVO Institute for Jewish Research archives.

link between amateur films and the postcard. As a mass-produced souvenir purchased during one's travels, the postcard can be used to send messages to loved ones and serve as a visual reminder of a trip. Displaying images of well-trodden destinations and monuments, and recorded by an unknown camera for popular consumption, the postcard communicates shared social understandings of a place's affective, historical, and cultural importance as well as highly personalized relationships to a location or journey. Postcards, like the 16-mm films in this exhibition, can only ever capture fragments of the *alte heym*, partial views of faraway landscapes and lives. In a sense, the comparison the exhibition erects between these two media forms subtly reinforces the romanticism of these "vanished places in a vanished culture" and the malleability of memory, rather than a claim to historical veracity. At the same time, the exhibition argues that the celluloid-based moving image offers a proximity to history that other technologies, like the still photograph, cannot. The technological limitations of "home moviemaking," according to the exhibit's webpage, actually facilitated the street views and exterior shots that today invest these images with their enormous historical value.

"Nearly all of the films in this exhibition were shot outdoors in daylight," according to the exhibit's historical overview, because indoor lighting was, at that point, "insufficient" to properly expose the celluloid film (Center for Jewish History 2010b). The exhibition's articulation of the amateur moving image as a serendipitous window onto a vanished past—a postcard-in-motion—makes the mediated nature of these depictions of Yiddishland more apparent, rather than less.

The postvernacular context of the exhibition serves to further inscribe these amateur films as textual evidence of interwar European, specifically Polish, vernacular Jewish culture. A resurgence of interest in Yiddish films along with other forms of Yiddishkeit since the 1970s, concurrent with the previously examined discourses of cultural loss, has prompted a deep commitment to chronicling and preserving such vernacular cultural productions. Moving-image archives with a focus on Yiddish-language and Jewish films have emerged in a number of countries, including the National Center for Jewish Film, founded in 1976 at Brandeis University in the United States (which has restored thirty-eight Yiddish feature films since its establishment) and Steven Spielberg's Jewish Film Archive, housed by Hebrew University in Israel since 1987.[11] The introduction of digital technologies has arguably facilitated this archival impulse, resulting in a proliferation of educational resources and other texts online. The digitization of YIVO's amateur film collection for public access online confirms this trend. Postvernacular archival practices such as these become what Shandler (2006, 130) describes as "exercises in cultural salvage." Like performing *klezmer* music, preserving Yiddish films becomes a symbolic attempt to "reconstitute Jewish culture destroyed in the Holocaust, to 'bring back,' to 'resurrect' to 'heal.'"

Furthermore, the transnational nature of these amateur films' production by American Jews in Poland, Germany, and other parts of Central and Eastern Europe—and their contemporary digital exhibition for audiences within and beyond the United States—positions this collection within debates around Yiddish cinema as a deterritorialized yet nationally coded film practice. As Liz Czach (2014, 30) observes, models of national cinema rarely include nonprofessional forms of filmmaking. Amateur cinema, which for Czach includes "a broad swath of filmic material including most forms of nonprofessional films made on nonstandard gauges" like 16 mm and 8 mm, offers a wealth of insight into a national community's values, composition, national narratives, and cultural practices. This array of practices, she contends, ought to be included within studies of national cinemas. Some texts, she admits, are easier to recuperate than others how-ever: films that demonstrate aesthetic significance or "the serious amateur's polished professionalism . . . will more readily be integrated into a national cinema narrative" (31).

Jerry White (2004, 225) also argues for a more diverse reading of cin-ematic practices to incorporate both commercial and noncommercial filmmaking into scholarly understandings of national cinema, including feature-length narrative, documentary, avant-garde, and political cinemas. Although he does not specifically refer to amateur filmmaking in his reas-sessment of the national cinema model, considering nonprofessional films would contribute to the diversity of film practices for which White argues, highlighting how small or stateless cinemas can similarly function along national lines. Reclamation of small-gauge and amateur Yiddish films into scholarly accounts of Yiddish-language cinema would certainly expand the "horizons" of this filmmaking tradition, to use Czach's (2014, 36) turn of phrase. However, her assertion that "identifiably authored amateur films of aesthetic significance" are easier to recuperate within the preexisting national cinema model does not necessarily hold true in respect to ama-teur Yiddish films (36). Whereas the "historical value" of an amateur film is often "contingent on [its] proper contextualization including indications of author, time, and places depicted" (36), the trauma and cultural destruc-tion of the Holocaust has prompted a reevaluation of the significance of *all* moving images depicting prewar Jewish communities and Yiddishkeit. As a result, the documentary value of these texts, as well as the affective nature of viewing these images in light of the structuring absence of the Holocaust, imbues these amateur films with the weight of this historical trauma, which in turn shapes their archival value.

Conclusion

While amateur films seemingly offer rare glimpses into vernacular cultural practices, the institutional collection and exhibition of these cultural ar-tifacts as representations of social "histories from below" require further critical examination. This is particularly the case for communities facing intergenerational trauma, loss of language, and what Marianne Hirsch (n.d.) calls "postmemory" in the wake of attempted genocide: affective, and heavily mediated, stories and experiences transmitted from one generation to the next that seem to "constitute memories in their own right." Like the preservation of Irish Gaelic in the Republic of Ireland and efforts by the Mohawks of Kahnawà:ke to revive Kanien'kéha (Mohawk) suppressed by Canada's residential school system, the resurgence of Yiddish among non-native speakers paradoxically challenges and reaffirms associations between language, cultural survival, and historical trauma. The Center for Jewish History's curated exhibition of twenty-six amateur Yiddish films in "16 mm Postcards," and their subsequent exhibition online, sought to position these films as evidence of pre-Holocaust vernacular Eastern European Jewish culture. However, in doing so, the exhibition predominately framed these materials through postwar historical memory, thereby relegating Yiddish to a lost past rather than a living cultural practice.

Following Hansen's theorization of vernacular modernism, this chapter has sought to unpack some of the productive yet unresolvable tensions around vernacular and mass cultures through this particular collection of Yiddish travelogues and home movies. Such efforts to preserve Yiddish cinema—along with folk songs, dances, and literary texts—position these cultural productions as historical evidence of prewar Jewish culture for contemporary audiences. It is precisely this negotiation of the vernacular *within* a postvernacular moment that motivates so many recent archival initiatives to preserve, catalog, and share the vibrant textures of Yiddishkeit. By offering a path into Yiddishland, an ephemeral country held together by its shared *mamaloshen* (mother tongue), these amateur films contribute to our understanding of postvernacular Yiddish preservation practices, while also raising new questions about the boundaries of a "national" cinema.

Notes

1. The Yiddish language emerged in Eastern Europe, derived from a dialect of German and written in the Hebrew alphabet, incorporating words assimilated from other neighboring languages. It developed as a secular language of daily life and commerce for Ashkenazi Jewish communities in Eastern Europe. Both the Yiddish language and *Yiddishkeit* spread throughout the rest of the Jewish Diaspora, including North and South America, the Middle East, and parts of Asia and southern Africa with waves of Jewish immigration. At its peak around 1938, there were approximately eleven million Yiddish speakers primarily located in Eastern Europe and North America (Shandler 2006, 1).

2. Jerry White (2004, 225) also cites Yiddish cinema as an example of a cinematic practice that coalesced historically around "a sense of non-geographically contiguous national belonging."

3. A full list of film titles featured in the "16 mm Postcards" exhibition is available online through the Center for Jewish History's digital collection, see: https://www.cjh.org /16mmpostcards/Original_Films.php.

4. See Cecile Kuznitz, "Yiddish Studies"; Jeffrey Shandler, *Adventures in Yiddishland*; and Rebecca Margolis, "New Yiddish Film and the Transvernacular."

5. Although the physical exhibition closed in 2011, a digital version of "16 mm Postcards" remained accessible on the Center for Jewish History's website for several years afterwards. At the time of this publishing, the exhibition's website (https://www.cjh.org /16mmpostcards/) still hosts a description of the exhibition but not the films themselves.

6. Glenn Kurtz (2014) makes a similar argument about the unexpectedly historical significance of a 1938 home movie shot by his grandfather, David Kurtz, on a summer vacation in Europe with his wife Liza. Glenn Kurtz observes that the home movie, which includes three minutes of footage from a predominately Jewish town in Poland, functions as "a memorial to [the town's] lost Jewish community and to the entire annihilated culture of Eastern European Judaism" (5).

7. See the YIVO Digital Archive on Jewish Life in Poland for a full listing of the digitized amateur films. http://polishjews.yivoarchives.org/videos.

8. For two studies of such ethnographic movements, and their links to concomitant Yiddish cultural production, see Gottesman 2003 and Rosenberg 2011.

9. On the eve of World War II, around eleven million people spoke Yiddish globally, but by the turn of the twenty-first century, the number of estimated speakers fell below one million (Shandler 2006, 1).

10. A notable exception are Hasidic Jewish communities in Paris, Buenos Aires, Jerusalem, Montreal, and New York who continue to speak Yiddish as a daily language.

11. See the National Center for Jewish Film. "About NCJF." http://www.jewishfilm.org /about.htm; and Steven Spielberg Jewish Film Archive. "About the Archive." http://www .spielbergfilmarchive.org.il/about.htm.

References

Center for Jewish History. 2010a. "16 mm Postcards: Home Movies of American Jewish Visitors to 1930s Poland." https://www.cjh.org/16mmpostcards/Original_Films.php.
———. 2010b. "The Historical Context." https://www.cjh.org/16mmpostcards/Context.php.
———. 2010c. "Panorama." https://www.cjh.org/16mmpostcards/Panorama.php.
Czach, Liz. 2014. "Home Movies and Amateur Film as National Cinema." In *Amateur Filmmaking: The Home Movie, the Archive, the Web*, edited by Laura Rascaroli, Gwenda Young, and Barry Monahan, 27–37. New York: Bloomsbury Academic.
Eisner, Gustave, dir. 1929–1933. "Köln, Wiesbaden and Berlin." 7 mins (1 reel), 16 mm. The Archives of the YIVO Institute for Jewish Research, call no. YIVO VM 26.
Goldberg, Judith N. 1983. *Laughter through Tears: The Yiddish Cinema*. Rutherford, NJ: Fairleigh Dickinson University Press.
Goldin, Sidney M., and Ivan Abramson, dirs. 1923. *Ost und West* (*East and West*). Austria. 85 mins, DVD. Restored and distributed by the National Center for Jewish Film.
Goldman, Eric A. 1983. *Visions, Images, and Dreams: Yiddish Film Past and Present*. Ann Arbor: University of Michigan Research Press.

Gottesman, Itzik Nakhmen. 2003. *Defining the Yiddish Nation: The Jewish Folklorists of Poland*. Detroit: Wayne State University Press.

Granovsky, Alexander, dir. 1925. *Menakhem Mendl (Jewish Luck)*. Soviet Union. 100 mins, DVD. Restored and distributed by the National Center for Jewish Film.

Green, Joseph, and Konrad Tom, dirs. 1938. *Mamele*. Poland. 97 mins, DVD. Restored and distributed by the National Center for Jewish Film.

Green, Joseph, and Leon Trystand, dirs. 1939. *A Brivele der Mamen (A Letter to Mother)*. Poland. 106 mins, DVD. Restored and distributed by the National Center for Jewish Film.

Hansen, Miriam Bratu. 2009. "The Mass Production of the Senses: Classical Cinema as Vernacular Modernism." In *Disciplining Modernism*, edited by Pamela L. Caughie, 242–58. Basingstoke: Palgrave Macmillan.

Hirsch, Marianne. n.d. "Postmemory." Accessed May 8, 2020. https://www.postmemory.net/.

Hoberman, J. 1991. *Bridge of Light: Yiddish Film between Two Worlds*. Philadelphia: Temple University Press.

Kurtz, Glenn. 2014. *Three Minutes in Poland: Discovering a Lost World in a 1938 Family Film*. New York: Farrar, Straus and Giroux.

Kuznitz, Cecile E. 2002. "Yiddish Studies." In *The Oxford Handbook of Jewish Studies*, edited by Martin Goodman, Jeremy Cohen, and David Sorkin, 541–71. Oxford: Oxford University Press.

Margolis, Rebecca. 2016. "New Yiddish Film and the Transvernacular." *In geveb: A Journal of Yiddish Studies*, December 2016, 1–30. http://ingeveb.org/articles/new-yiddish-film-and-the-transvernacular.

National Center for Jewish Film. n.d. "About NCJF." Accessed March 8, 2020. http://www.jewishfilm.org/about.htm.

National Center for Jewish Film. n.d. "Pre WWII Polish-Jewish Travelogues." Accessed March 8, 2020. http://www.jewishfilm.org/Catalogue/poland.htm.

Newman, Roberta. 1993. "Home Movies and the *Alte Heym* (Old Home): American Jewish Travel Films in Eastern Europe in the 1920s and 1930s." *Jewish Folklore and Ethnology Review* 15, no. 1: 22–28.

Rascaroli, Laura, Gwenda Young, and Barry Monahan. 2014. "Introduction. Amateur Filmmaking: New Developments and Directions." In *Amateur Filmmaking: The Home Movie, the Archive, the Web*, edited by Laura Rascaroli, Gwenda Young, and Barry Monahan, 1–12. New York: Bloomsbury Academic.

Rosenberg, Joel. 2011. "The Soul of Catastrophe: The 1937 Film of S. An-sky's *The Dybbuk*." *Jewish Social Studies* 17, no. 2 (Winter): 1–27.

Shandler, Jeffrey. 2006. *Adventures in Yiddishland: Postvernacular Language and Culture*. Berkeley: University of California Press.

Soyer, Daniel. 1993. "The Travel Agent as Broker between Old World and New: The Case of Gustave Eisner." In *YIVO Annual*. Vol. 21, *Going Home*, edited by Jack Kugelmass, 345–68. Evanston, IL: Northwestern University Press and the YIVO Institute.

Stone, Melinda, and Dan Streible. 2003. "Introduction: Small-Gauge and Amateur Film." *Film History* 15:123–25.

Tepperman, Charles. 2015. *Amateur Cinema: The Rise of North American Moviemaking, 1923–1960*. Oakland: University of California Press.

Ulmer, Edgar G., and Jacob Ben-Ami. 1937. *Grine Felder (Green Fields)*. United States. 97 mins, DVD. Restored and distributed by the National Center for Jewish Film.

Waldman, Joseph, dir. 1936. *A Trip to Poland and Palestine.* 14 mins (1 reel), 16 mm. The Archives of the YIVO Institute for Jewish Research, call no. YIVO VM beta07-00_01_14.

Waszynski, Michal, dir. 1937. *Der Dibuk (The Dybbuk).* Poland. 123 mins, DVD. Restored and distributed by the National Center for Jewish Film.

White, Jerry. 2004. "National Belonging: Renewing the Concept of National Cinema for a Global Culture." *New Review of Film and Television Studies* 2, no. 2 (November): 211–32.

YIVO Digital Archive on Jewish Life in Poland. 2014. "Videos." Accessed July 4, 2020. http://polishjews.yivoarchives.org/videos.

YIVO Institute for Jewish Research. 2020. "Film and Video Archive." Accessed July 4, 2020. https://www.yivo.org/film.

Zimmermann, Patricia R. 1995. *Reel Families: A Social History of Amateur Film.* Bloomington: Indiana University Press.

Zuckerman, Paysakh, dir. 1929. "A Pictorial Review of Kolbishev." 35 mins (1 reel), 16 mm. The Archives of the YIVO Institute for Jewish Research, call no. YIVO VM 13.

RACHEL WEBB JEKANOWSKI is Banting Fellow at Memorial University of Newfoundland's Department of English, in affiliation with the Nexus Centre for Humanities and Social Sciences Research.

INDEX

CPSIA information can be obtained
at www.ICGtesting.com
Printed in the USA
LVHW092229110121
676256LV00005B/101